riginal · Danbi Original · Danbi Original · Danbi Original · Danbi Original · Danbi Original · I

CHOCOLAT

vol.4

JiSang Shin·Geo

ice Kunion

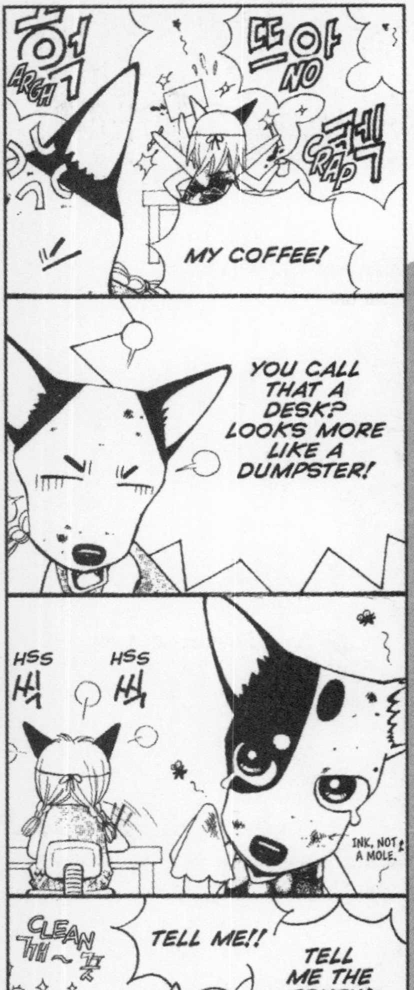
ARGH
NO
CRAP
MY COFFEE!
YOU CALL THAT A DESK? LOOKS MORE LIKE A DUMPSTER!
HSS
HSS
INK, NOT A MOLE.
CLEAN
TELL ME!!
TELL ME THE TRUTH!
YOU DON'T WORK, YOU JUST CLEAN YOUR DESK ALL THE TIME, RIGHT?
NOPE, POOPYHEAD WORKS FASTER THAN LIL'CHEAPSKATE.

WORDS FROM THE CREATORS

I watched this TV show where a boy told a girl that he liked her. He was handsome, tall, stylish and outgoing but she refused to go out with him. I thought that maybe she didn't like his voice…? But then one of the friends came to the camera and said that the girl's best friend had a crush on the boy, and that's why she is not going out with him. The girl tried to stop her friend from saying anymore and got all teary-eyed. Oh, the beautiful drama of teenagers…I'm so lucky I'm drawing <Chocolat> for them, sharing their world.

Ji-Sang Shin & Geo

The Animal Family of
Ji-Sang Shin and GEO

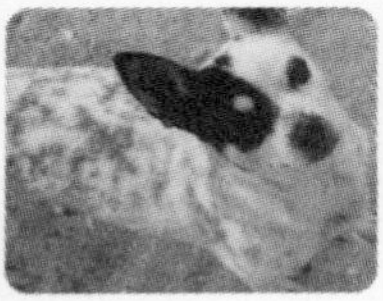

Jjae-Jjae
Age : 10 years old
He is the oldest of our family and can read our minds just by taking a glimpse at us.

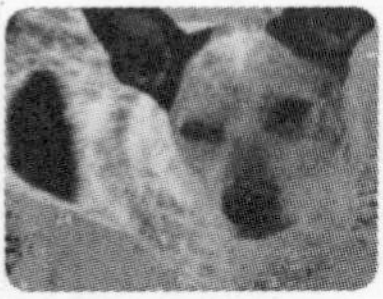

Ah-Dda
Age : 7 years old, son of Jjae-Jjae
He might not look it, but he is a genius!! ^o^

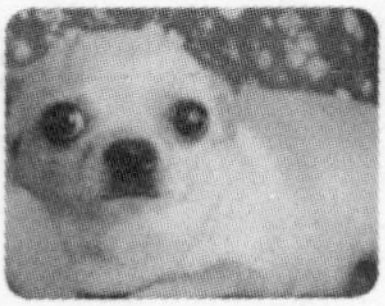

Mi-Mi
Age : 8 years old
Despite her age, she still considers herself to be the princess of the family.

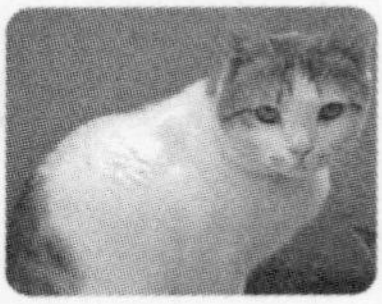

Ho-Bbang
Age : 3 years old
He used to be a poor street cat, but has become a high class cat. Charm point··· his checks are so red it looks like he's blushing.

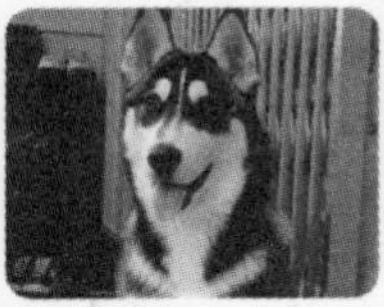

Tae-So
Age : 8 months old
He is the bad boy of the family, currently living in exile in the front yard.

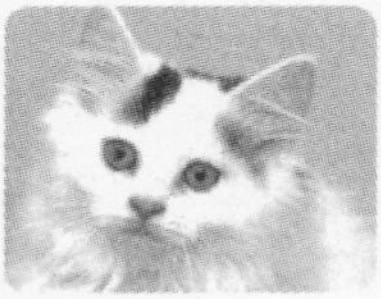

Dal-Ee
Age : 4 months old
She is the youngest of our family.
She might look like a princess, but she is actually a total tomboy.

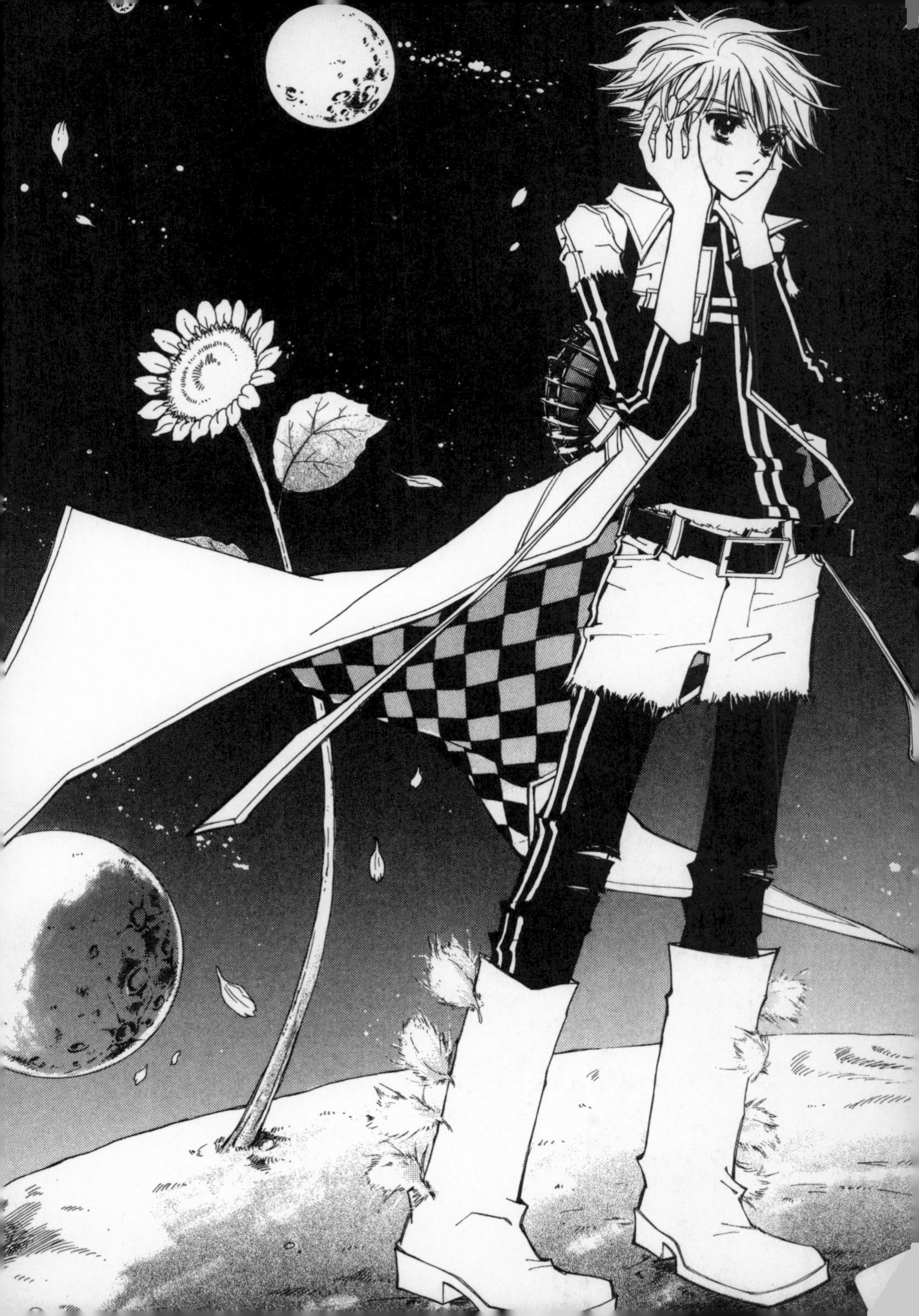

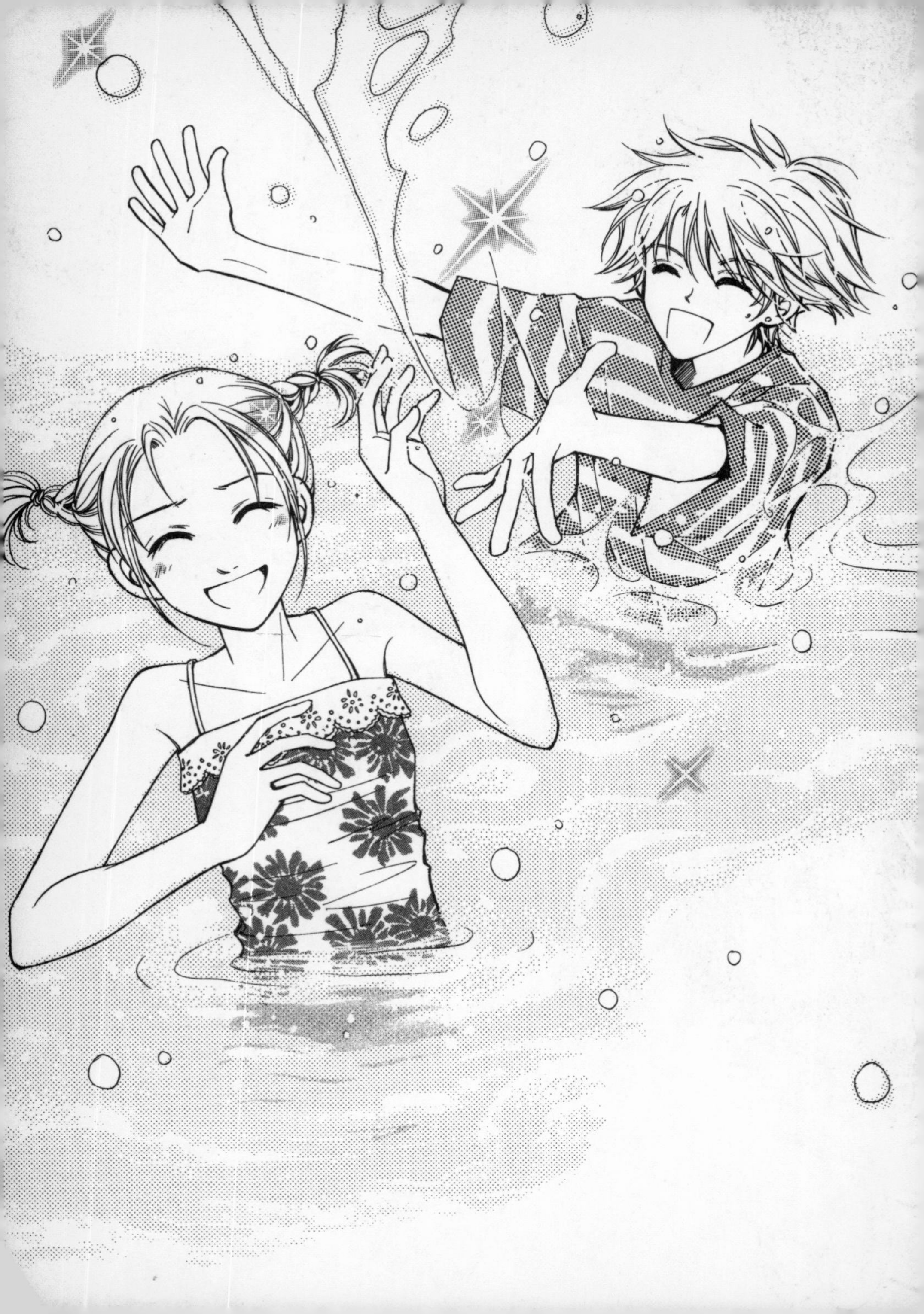

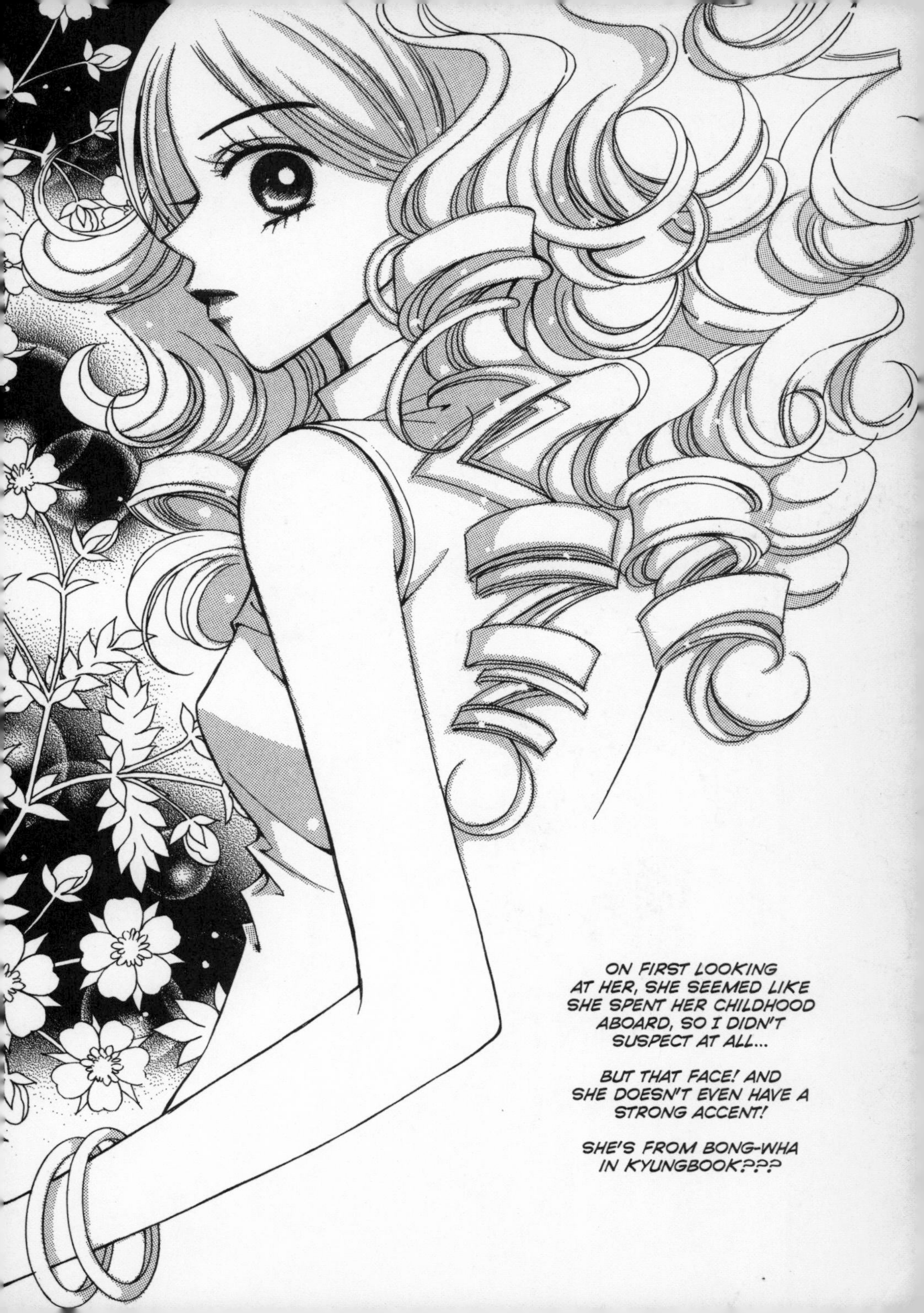
ON FIRST LOOKING AT HER, SHE SEEMED LIKE SHE SPENT HER CHILDHOOD ABOARD, SO I DIDN'T SUSPECT AT ALL...
BUT THAT FACE! AND SHE DOESN'T EVEN HAVE A STRONG ACCENT!
SHE'S FROM BONG-WHA IN KYUNGBOOK???

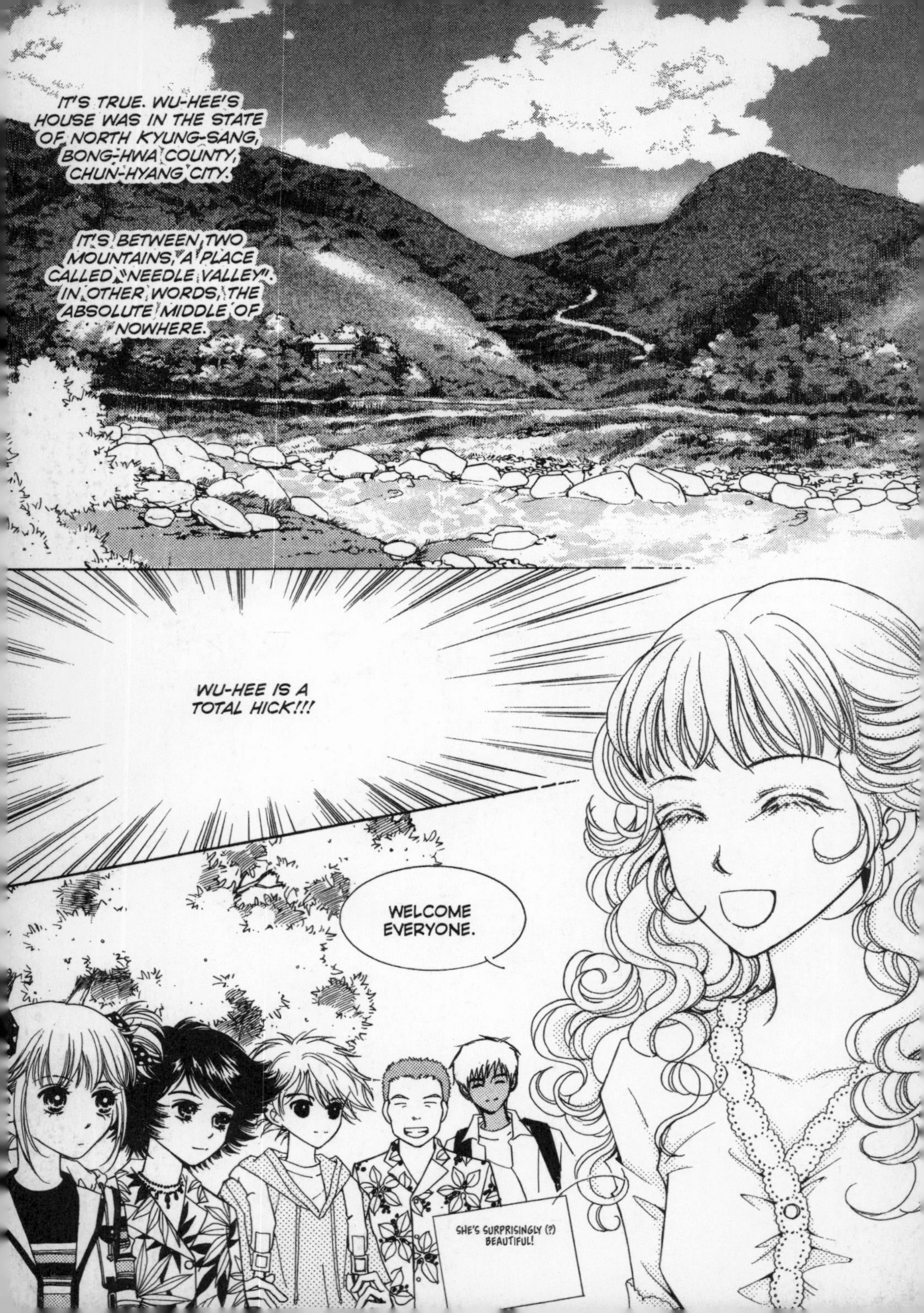
IT'S TRUE. WU-HEE'S HOUSE WAS IN THE STATE OF NORTH KYUNG-SANG, BONG-HWA COUNTY, CHUN-HYANG CITY.
IT'S BETWEEN TWO MOUNTAINS, A PLACE CALLED "NEEDLE VALLEY". IN OTHER WORDS, THE ABSOLUTE MIDDLE OF NOWHERE.
WU-HEE IS A TOTAL HICK!!!
WELCOME EVERYONE.
SHE'S SURPRISINGLY (?) BEAUTIFUL!

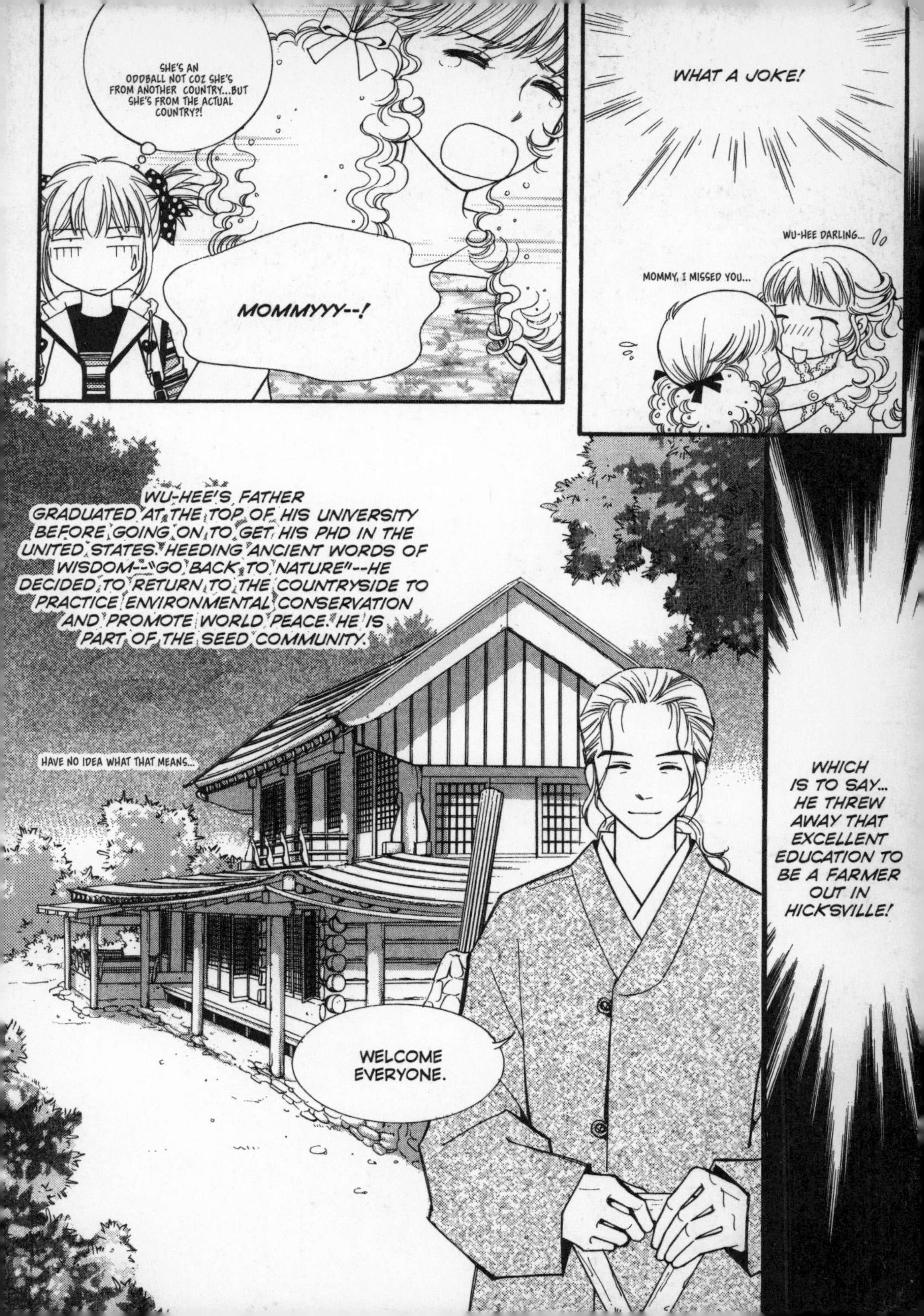
SHE'S AN ODDBALL NOT COZ SHE'S FROM ANOTHER COUNTRY...BUT SHE'S FROM THE ACTUAL COUNTRY?!
MOMMYYY--!
WHAT A JOKE!
WU-HEE DARLING...
MOMMY, I MISSED YOU...
WU-HEE'S FATHER GRADUATED AT THE TOP OF HIS UNIVERSITY BEFORE GOING ON TO GET HIS PHD IN THE UNITED STATES. HEEDING ANCIENT WORDS OF WISDOM--"GO BACK TO NATURE"--HE DECIDED TO RETURN TO THE COUNTRYSIDE TO PRACTICE ENVIRONMENTAL CONSERVATION AND PROMOTE WORLD PEACE. HE IS PART OF THE SEED COMMUNITY.
HAVE NO IDEA WHAT THAT MEANS...
WELCOME EVERYONE.
WHICH IS TO SAY... HE THREW AWAY THAT EXCELLENT EDUCATION TO BE A FARMER OUT IN HICKSVILLE!

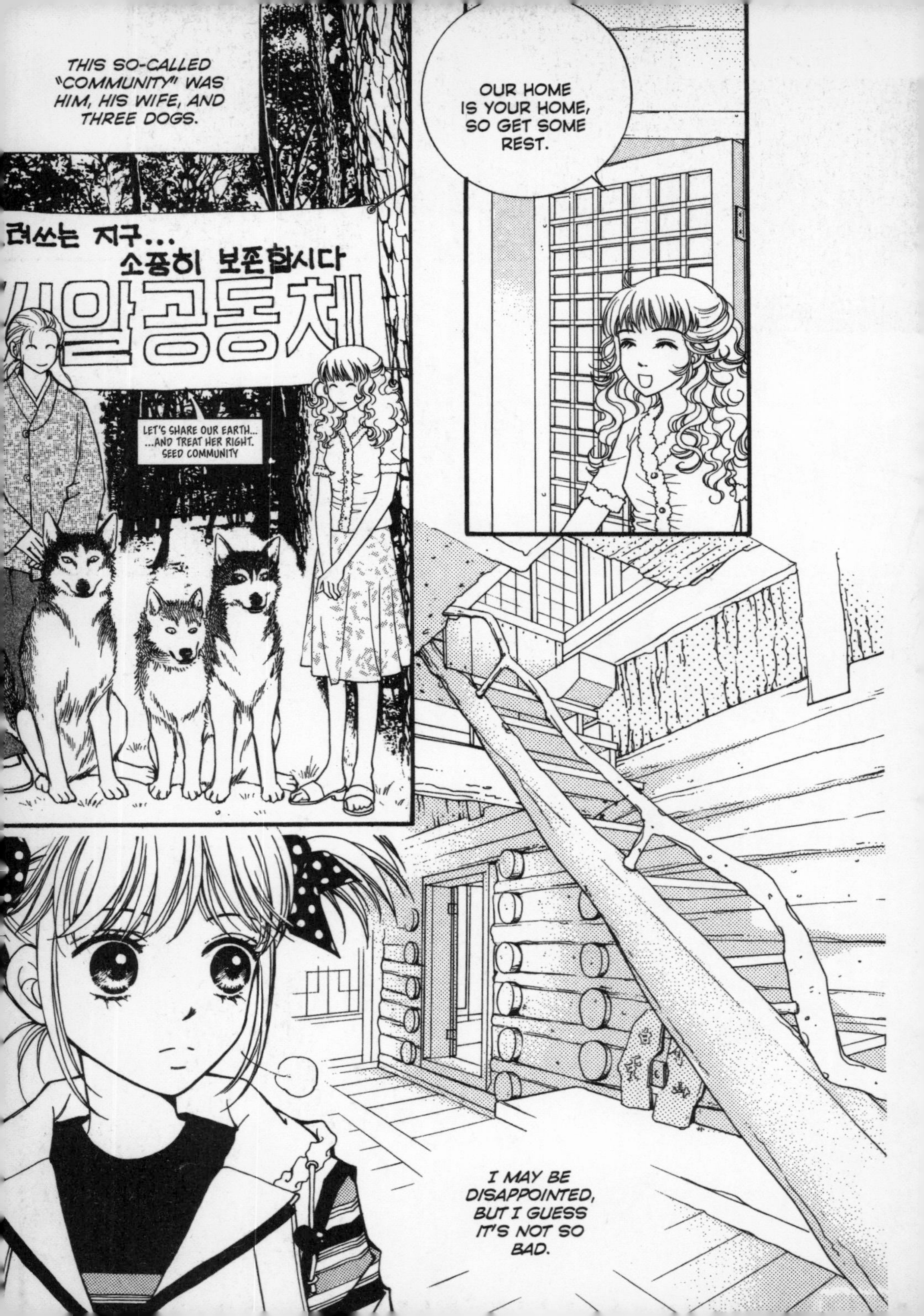

THIS SO-CALLED "COMMUNITY" WAS HIM, HIS WIFE, AND THREE DOGS.
려쓰는 지구...
소중히 보존합시다
LET'S SHARE OUR EARTH... ...AND TREAT HER RIGHT. SEED COMMUNITY
OUR HOME IS YOUR HOME, SO GET SOME REST.
I MAY BE DISAPPOINTED, BUT I GUESS IT'S NOT SO BAD.

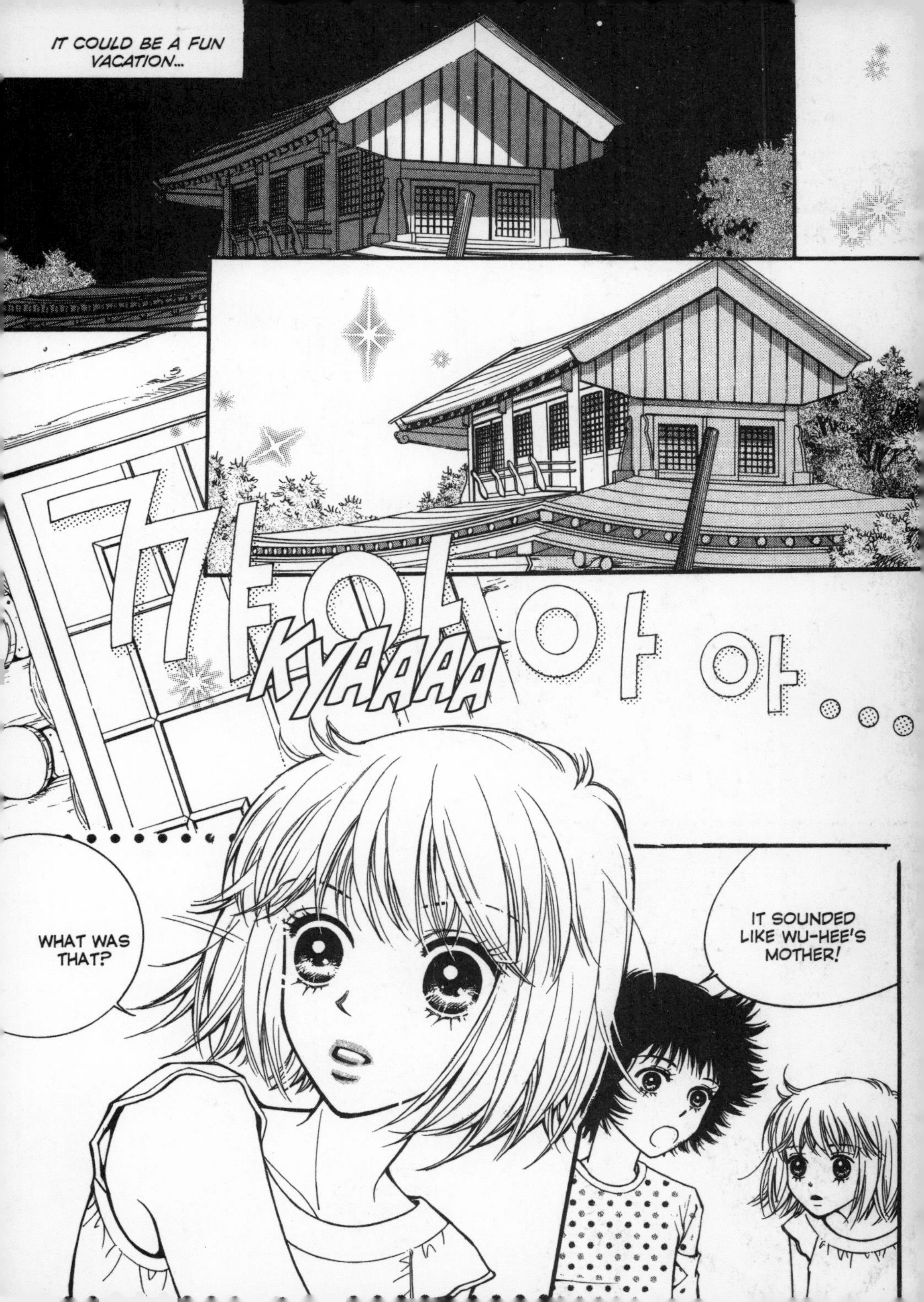
IT COULD BE A FUN VACATION...
꺄아아아...
KYAAAA
WHAT WAS THAT?
IT SOUNDED LIKE WU-HEE'S MOTHER!

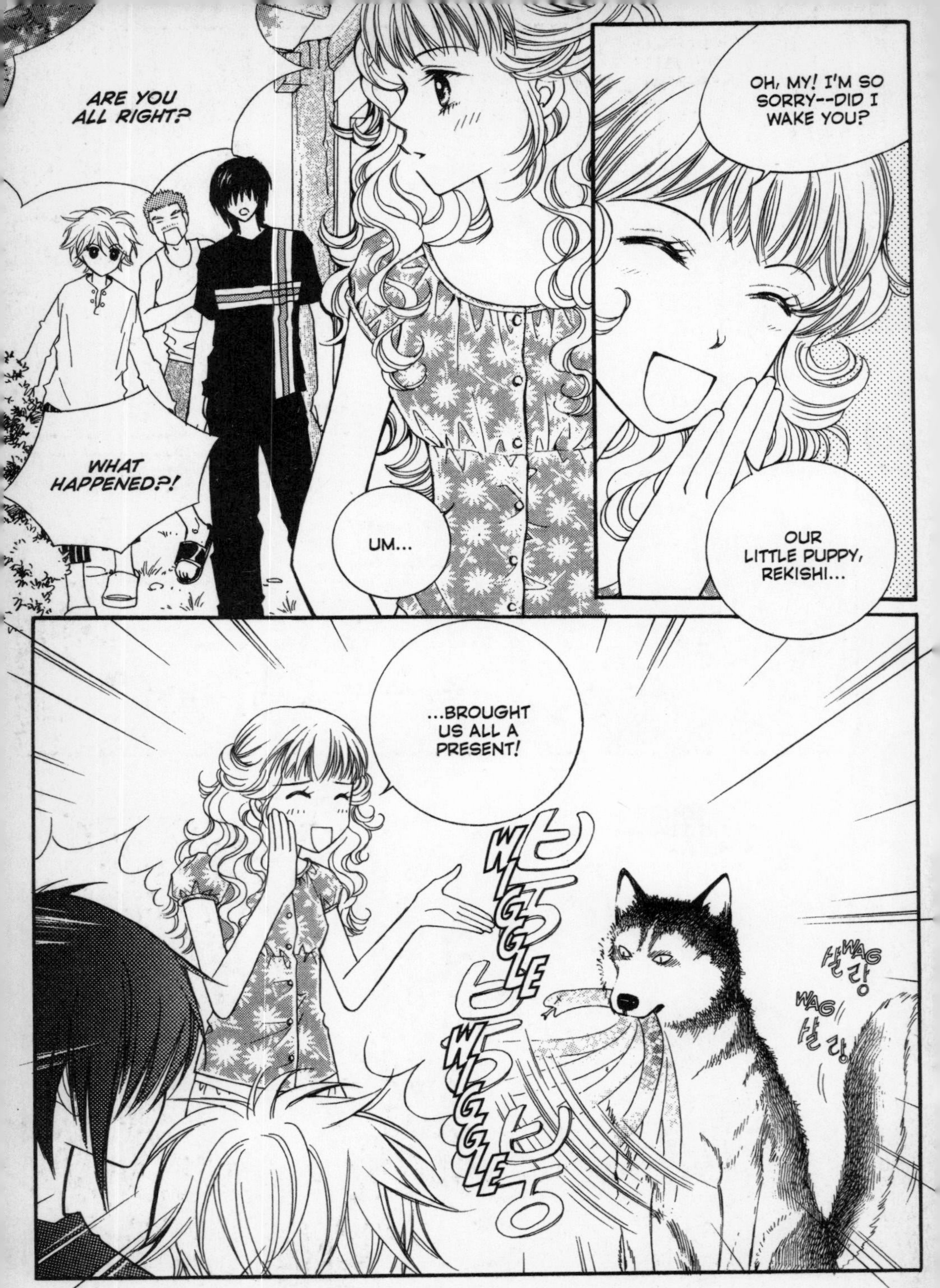
ARE YOU ALL RIGHT?
WHAT HAPPENED?!
UM...
OH, MY! I'M SO SORRY--DID I WAKE YOU?
OUR LITTLE PUPPY, REKISHI...
...BROUGHT US ALL A PRESENT!
WIGGLE
WIGGLE
WAG
WAG

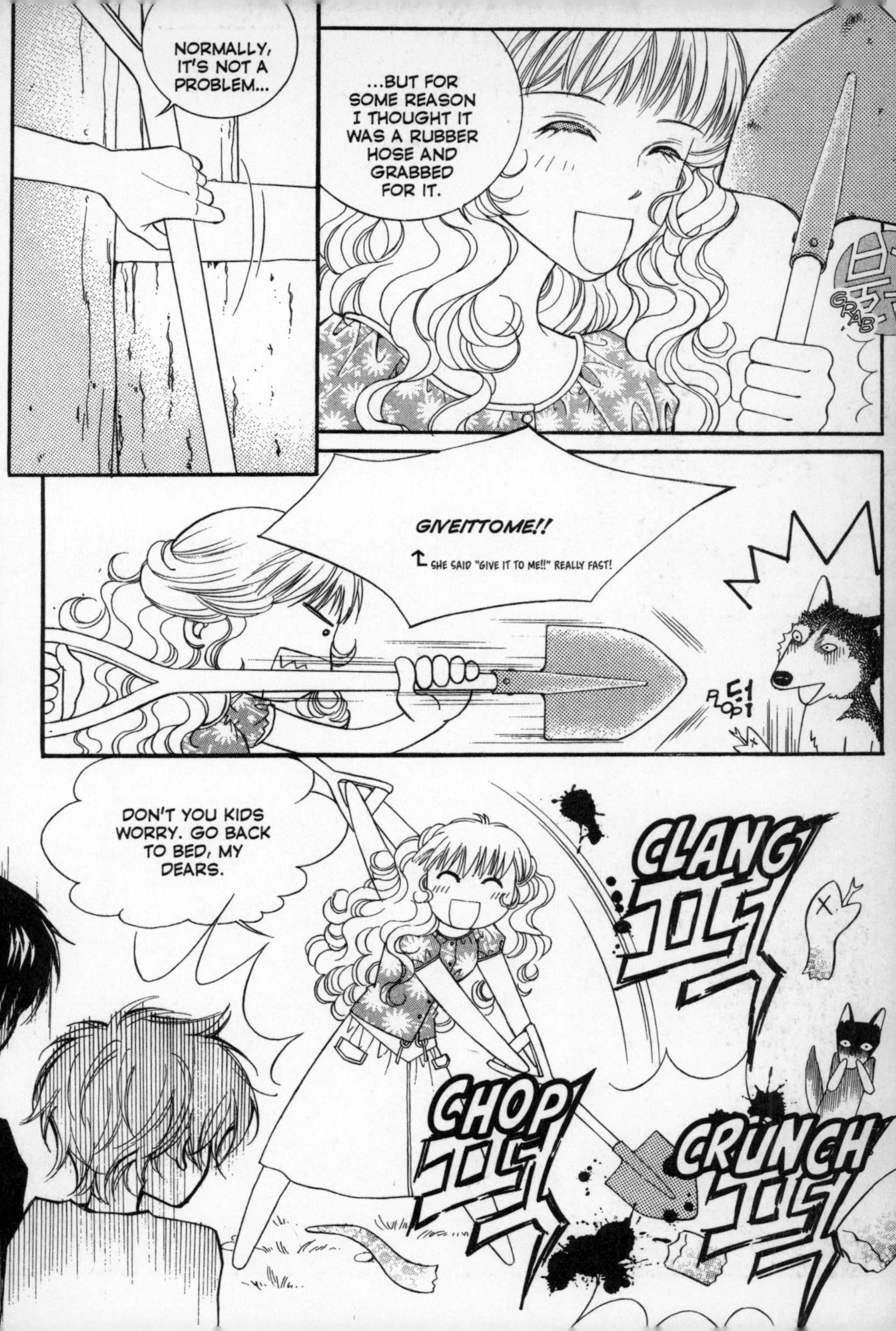
NORMALLY, IT'S NOT A PROBLEM...
...BUT FOR SOME REASON I THOUGHT IT WAS A RUBBER HOSE AND GRABBED FOR IT.
GRAB
GIVEITTOME!!
SHE SAID "GIVE IT TO ME!!" REALLY FAST!
FLOP
DON'T YOU KIDS WORRY. GO BACK TO BED, MY DEARS.
CLANG
CHOP
CRUNCH

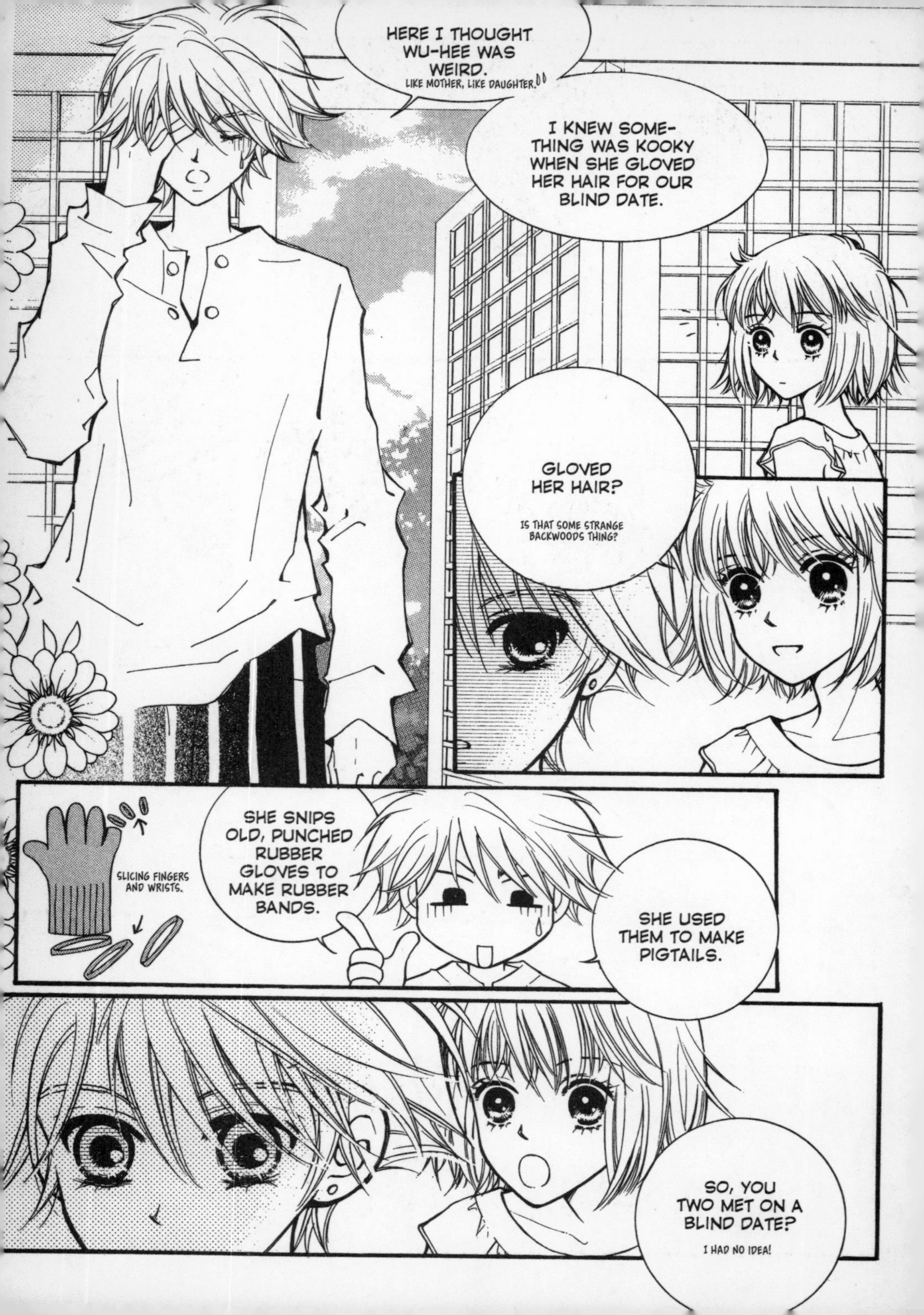
HERE I THOUGHT WU-HEE WAS WEIRD.
LIKE MOTHER, LIKE DAUGHTER.
I KNEW SOME-THING WAS KOOKY WHEN SHE GLOVED HER HAIR FOR OUR BLIND DATE.
GLOVED HER HAIR?
IS THAT SOME STRANGE BACKWOODS THING?
SLICING FINGERS AND WRISTS.
SHE SNIPS OLD, PUNCHED RUBBER GLOVES TO MAKE RUBBER BANDS.
SHE USED THEM TO MAKE PIGTAILS.
SO, YOU TWO MET ON A BLIND DATE?
I HAD NO IDEA!

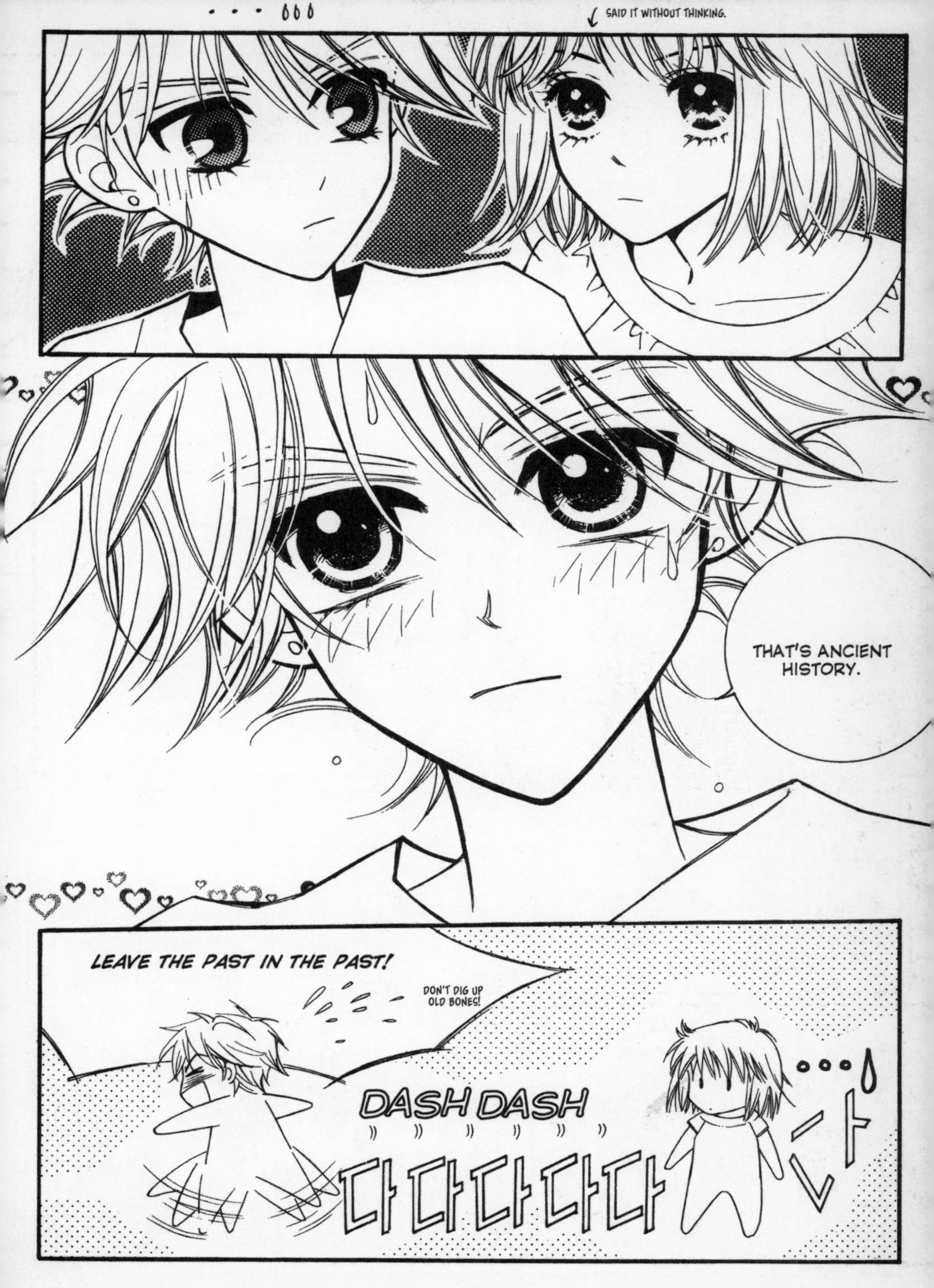
SAID IT WITHOUT THINKING.
THAT'S ANCIENT HISTORY.
LEAVE THE PAST IN THE PAST!
DON'T DIG UP OLD BONES!
DASH DASH
다다다다다다

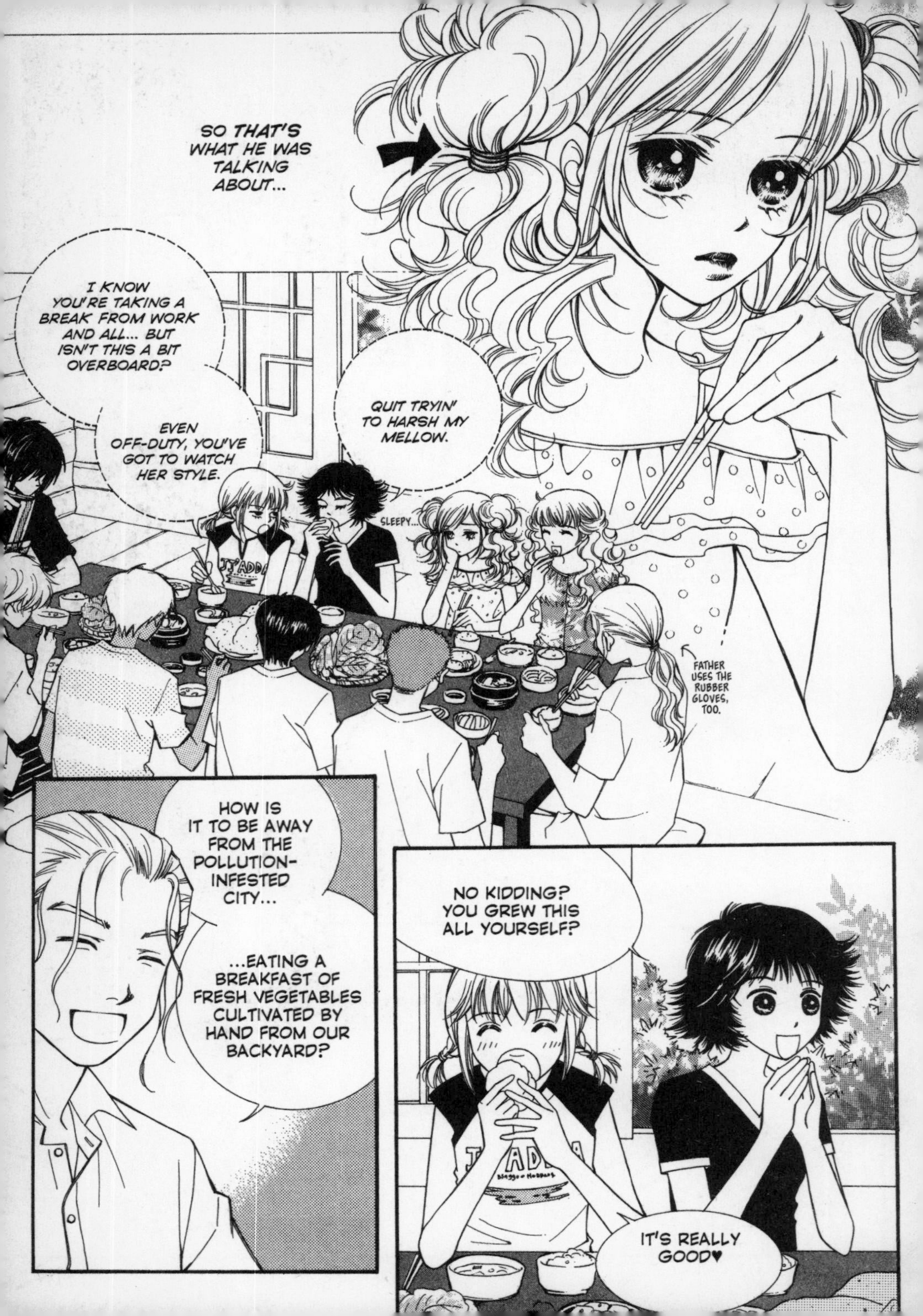
SO THAT'S WHAT HE WAS TALKING ABOUT...
I KNOW YOU'RE TAKING A BREAK FROM WORK AND ALL... BUT ISN'T THIS A BIT OVERBOARD?
EVEN OFF-DUTY, YOU'VE GOT TO WATCH HER STYLE.
QUIT TRYIN' TO HARSH MY MELLOW.
SLEEPY...
FATHER USES THE RUBBER GLOVES, TOO.
HOW IS IT TO BE AWAY FROM THE POLLUTION-INFESTED CITY...
...EATING A BREAKFAST OF FRESH VEGETABLES CULTIVATED BY HAND FROM OUR BACKYARD?
NO KIDDING? YOU GREW THIS ALL YOURSELF?
IT'S REALLY GOOD♥

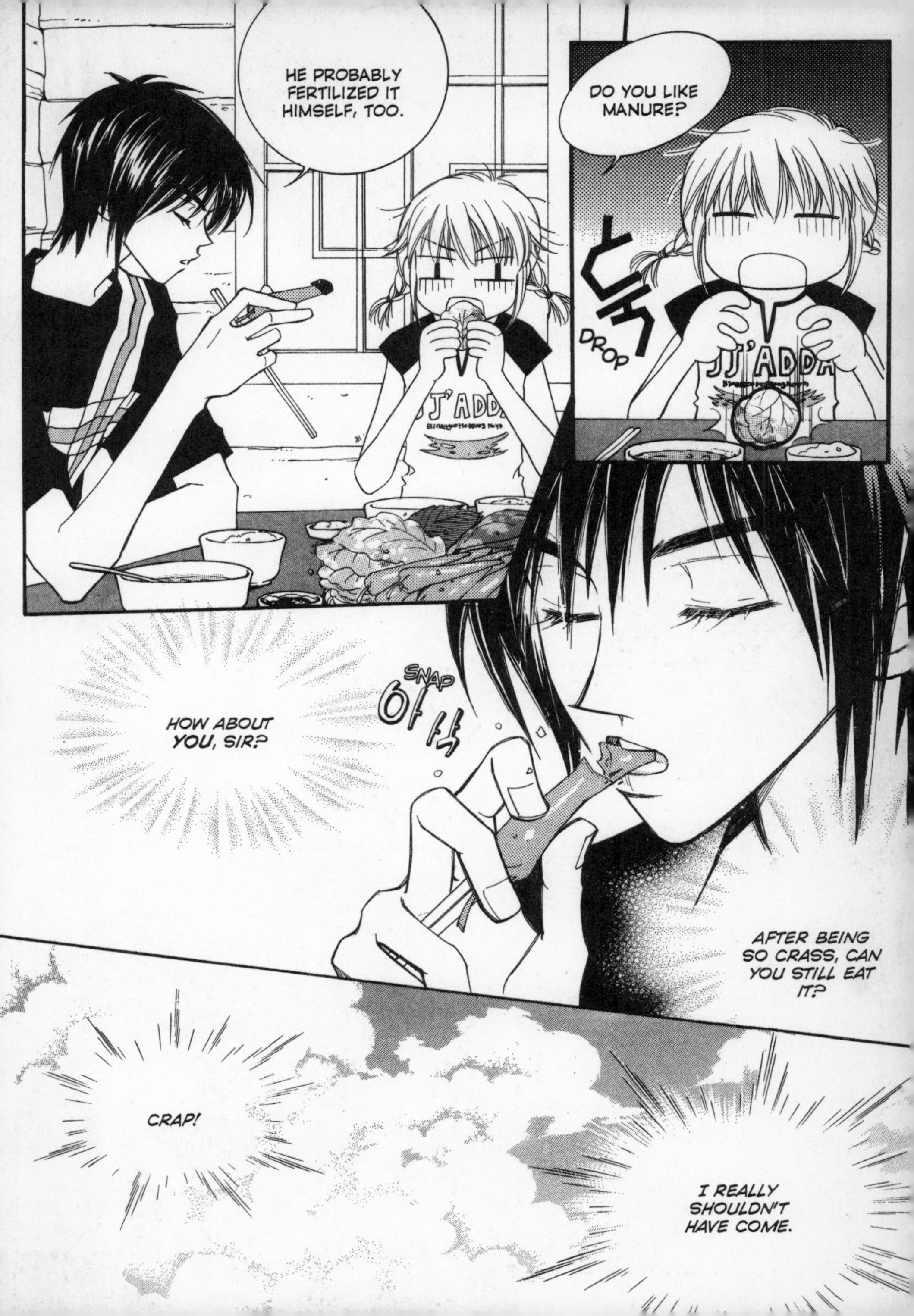
HE PROBABLY FERTILIZED IT HIMSELF, TOO.
DO YOU LIKE MANURE?
DROP
HOW ABOUT YOU, SIR?
SNAP
아삭
AFTER BEING SO CRASS, CAN YOU STILL EAT IT?
CRAP!
I REALLY SHOULDN'T HAVE COME.

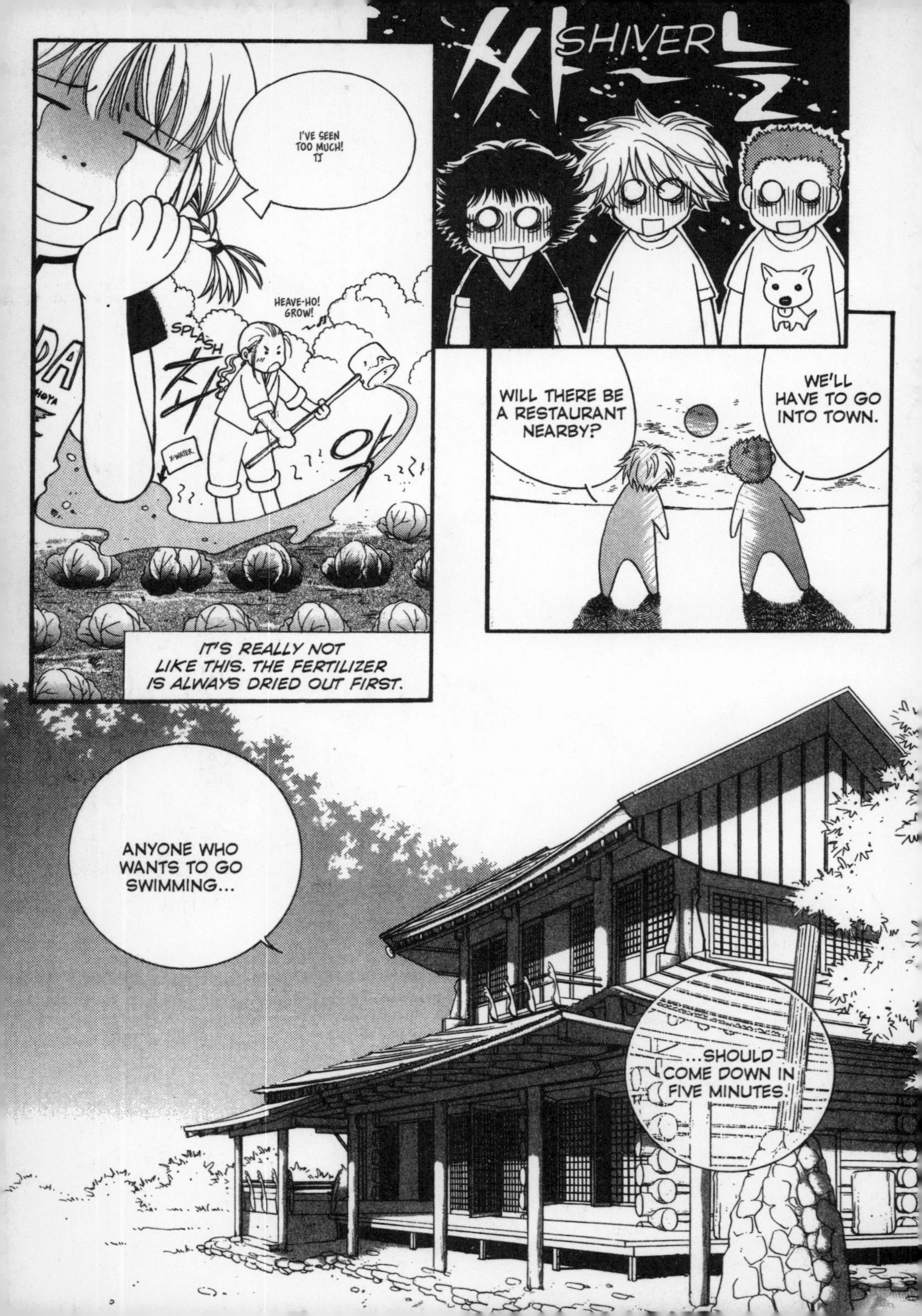
I'VE SEEN TOO MUCH! TJ
HEAVE-HO! GROW!
SPLASH
DA
X-WATER.
IT'S REALLY NOT LIKE THIS. THE FERTILIZER IS ALWAYS DRIED OUT FIRST.
SHIVER
WILL THERE BE A RESTAURANT NEARBY?
WE'LL HAVE TO GO INTO TOWN.
ANYONE WHO WANTS TO GO SWIMMING...
...SHOULD COME DOWN IN FIVE MINUTES.

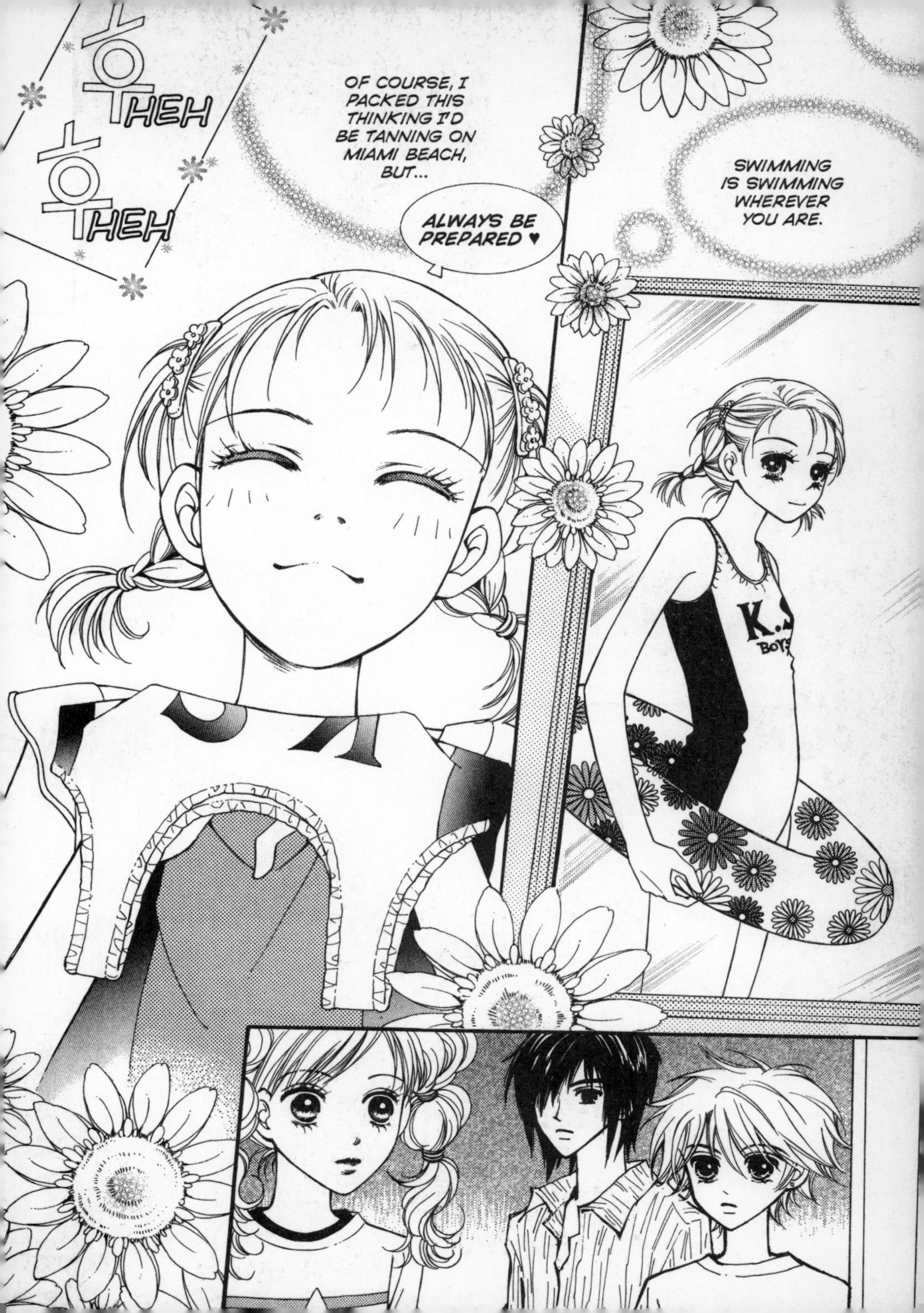
HEH HEH
HEH HEH
OF COURSE, I PACKED THIS THINKING I'D BE TANNING ON MIAMI BEACH, BUT...
ALWAYS BE PREPARED ♥
SWIMMING IS SWIMMING WHEREVER YOU ARE.

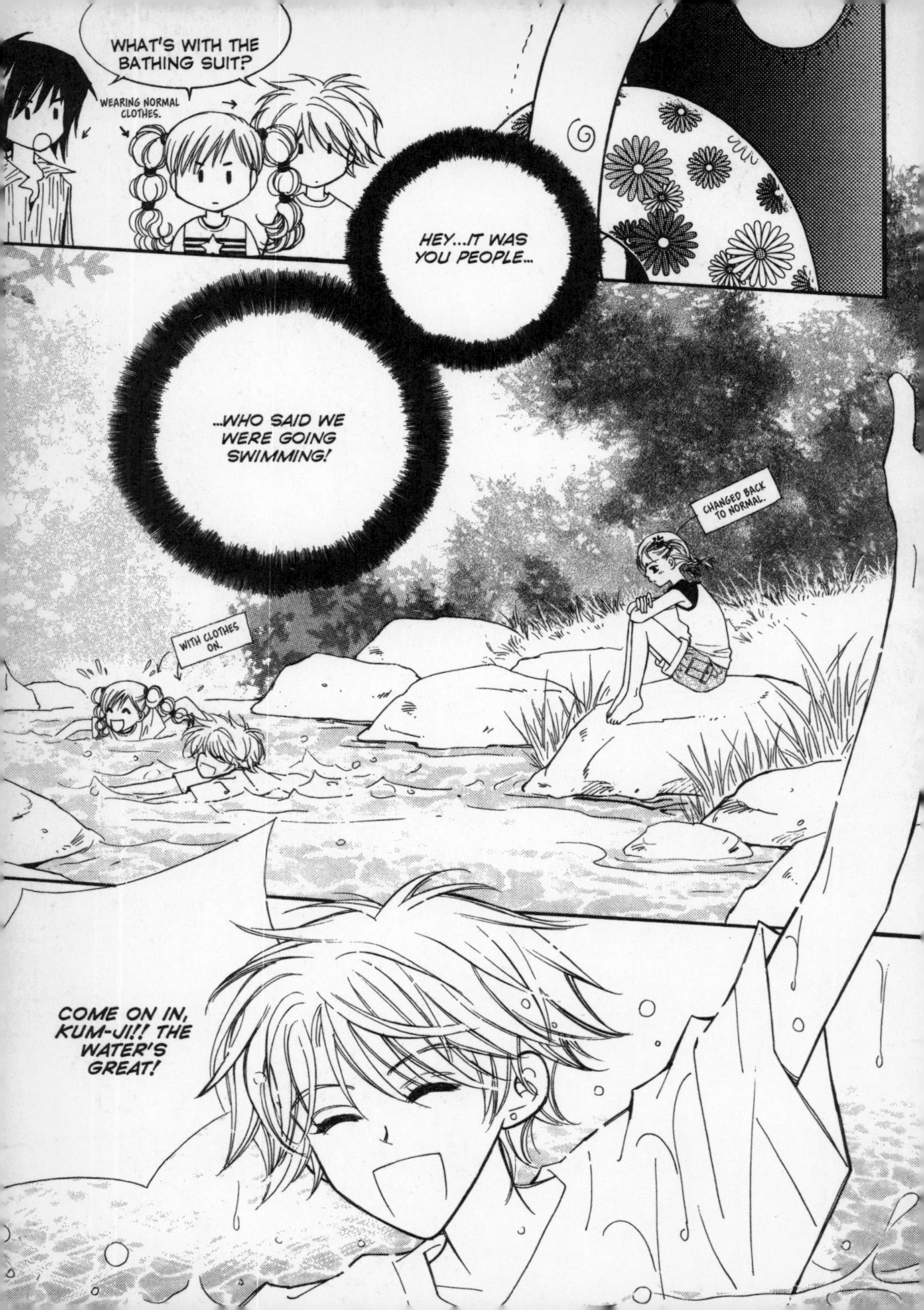
WHAT'S WITH THE BATHING SUIT?
WEARING NORMAL CLOTHES.
HEY...IT WAS YOU PEOPLE...
...WHO SAID WE WERE GOING SWIMMING!
CHANGED BACK TO NORMAL.
WITH CLOTHES ON.
COME ON IN, KUM-JI!! THE WATER'S GREAT!

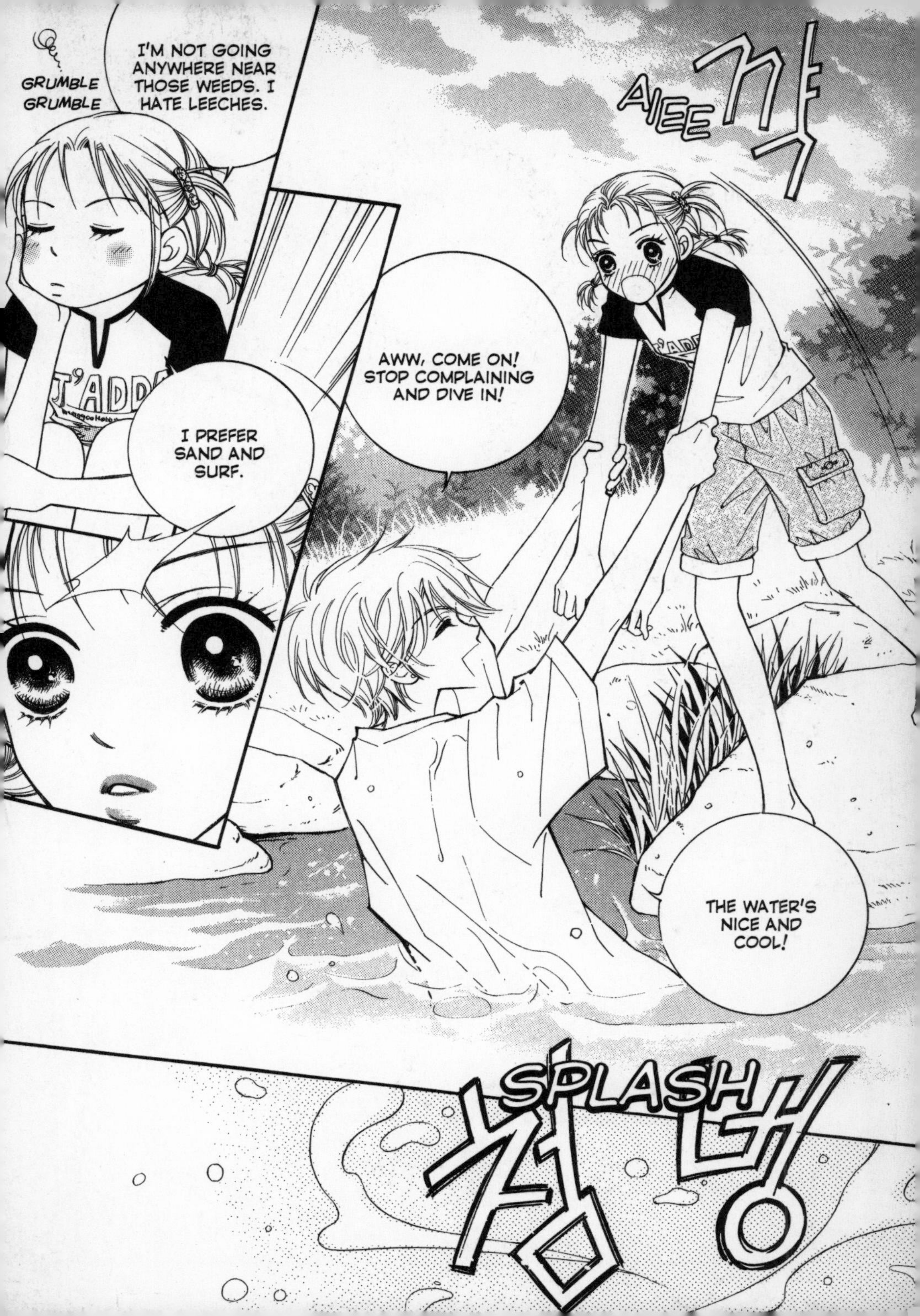
GRUMBLE GRUMBLE
I'M NOT GOING ANYWHERE NEAR THOSE WEEDS. I HATE LEECHES.
I PREFER SAND AND SURF.
AIEEE 꺄
AWW, COME ON! STOP COMPLAINING AND DIVE IN!
THE WATER'S NICE AND COOL!
SPLASH 첨벙

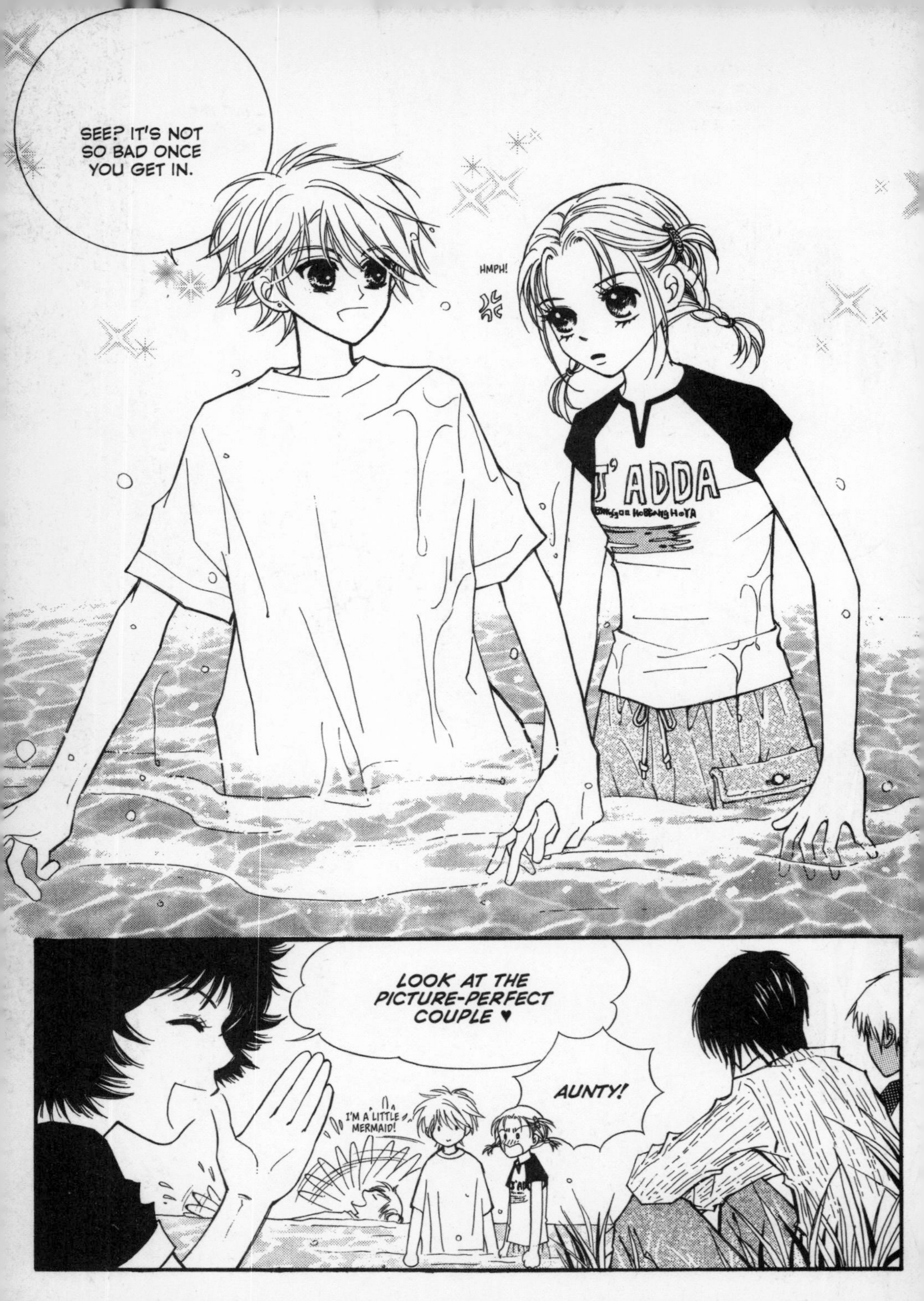
SEE? IT'S NOT SO BAD ONCE YOU GET IN.
HMPH!
J'ADDA
LOOK AT THE PICTURE-PERFECT COUPLE ♥
I'M A LITTLE MERMAID!
AUNTY!

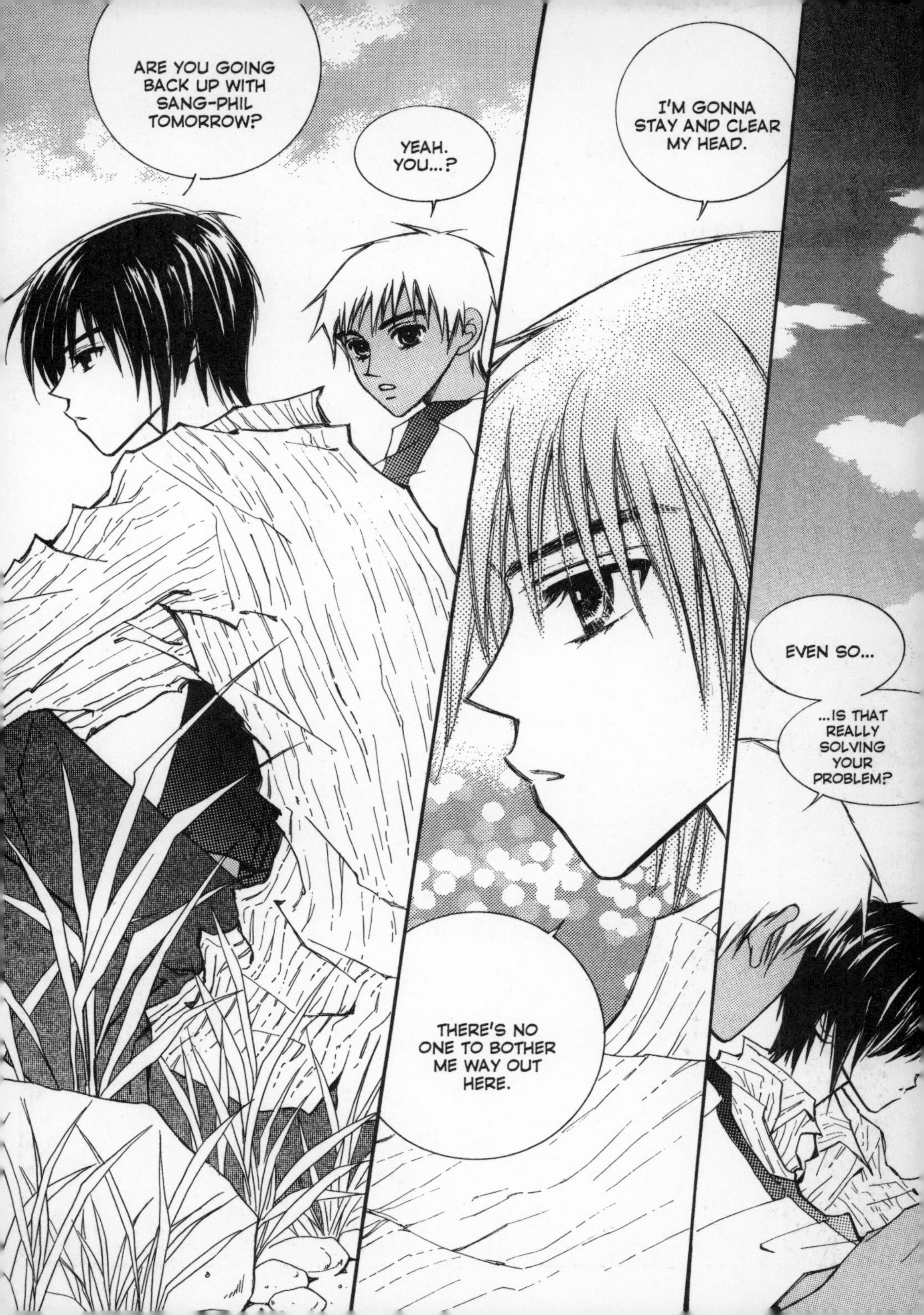
ARE YOU GOING BACK UP WITH SANG-PHIL TOMORROW?
YEAH. YOU...?
I'M GONNA STAY AND CLEAR MY HEAD.
THERE'S NO ONE TO BOTHER ME WAY OUT HERE.
EVEN SO...
...IS THAT REALLY SOLVING YOUR PROBLEM?

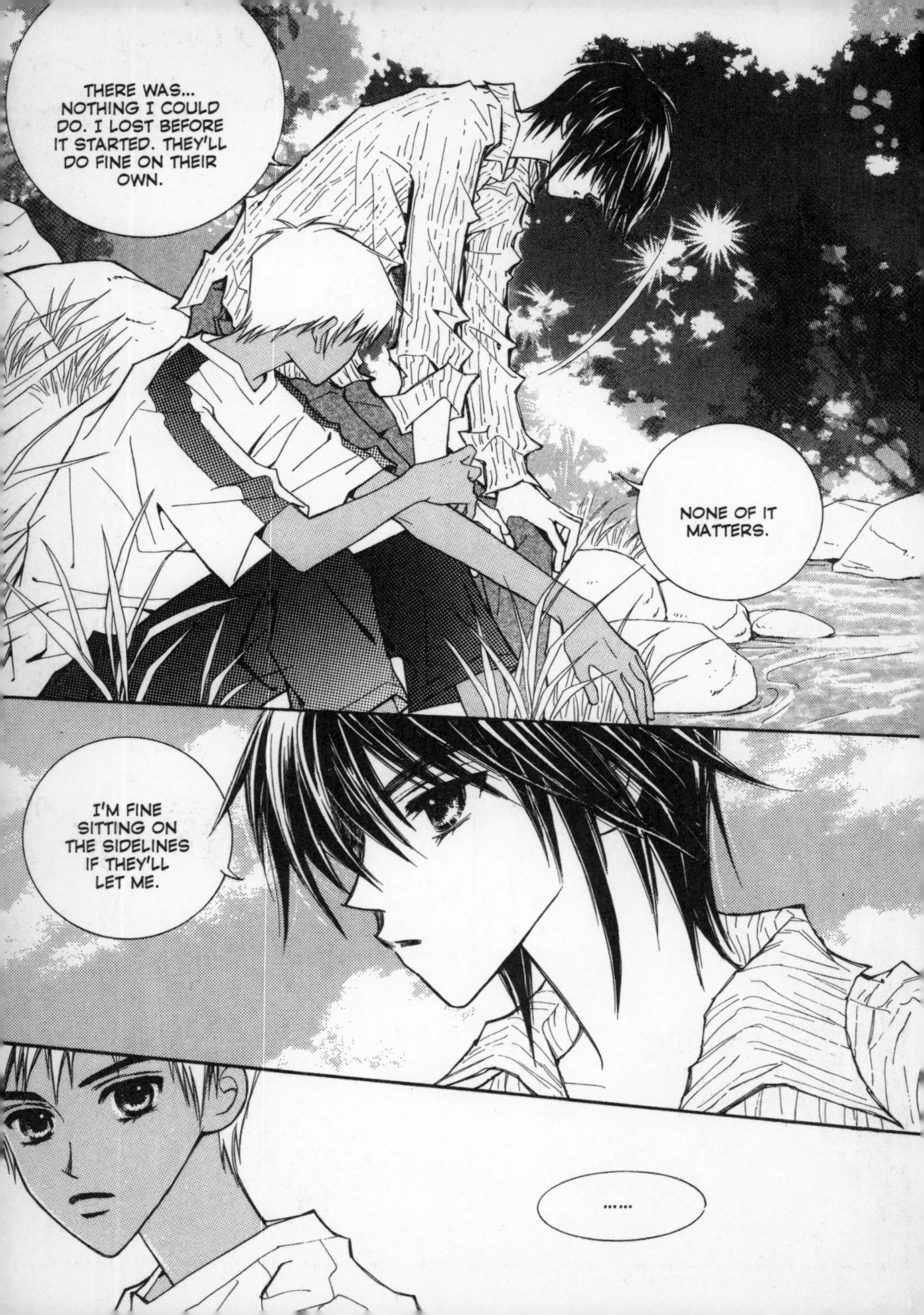
THERE WAS... NOTHING I COULD DO. I LOST BEFORE IT STARTED. THEY'LL DO FINE ON THEIR OWN.
NONE OF IT MATTERS.
I'M FINE SITTING ON THE SIDELINES IF THEY'LL LET ME.
......

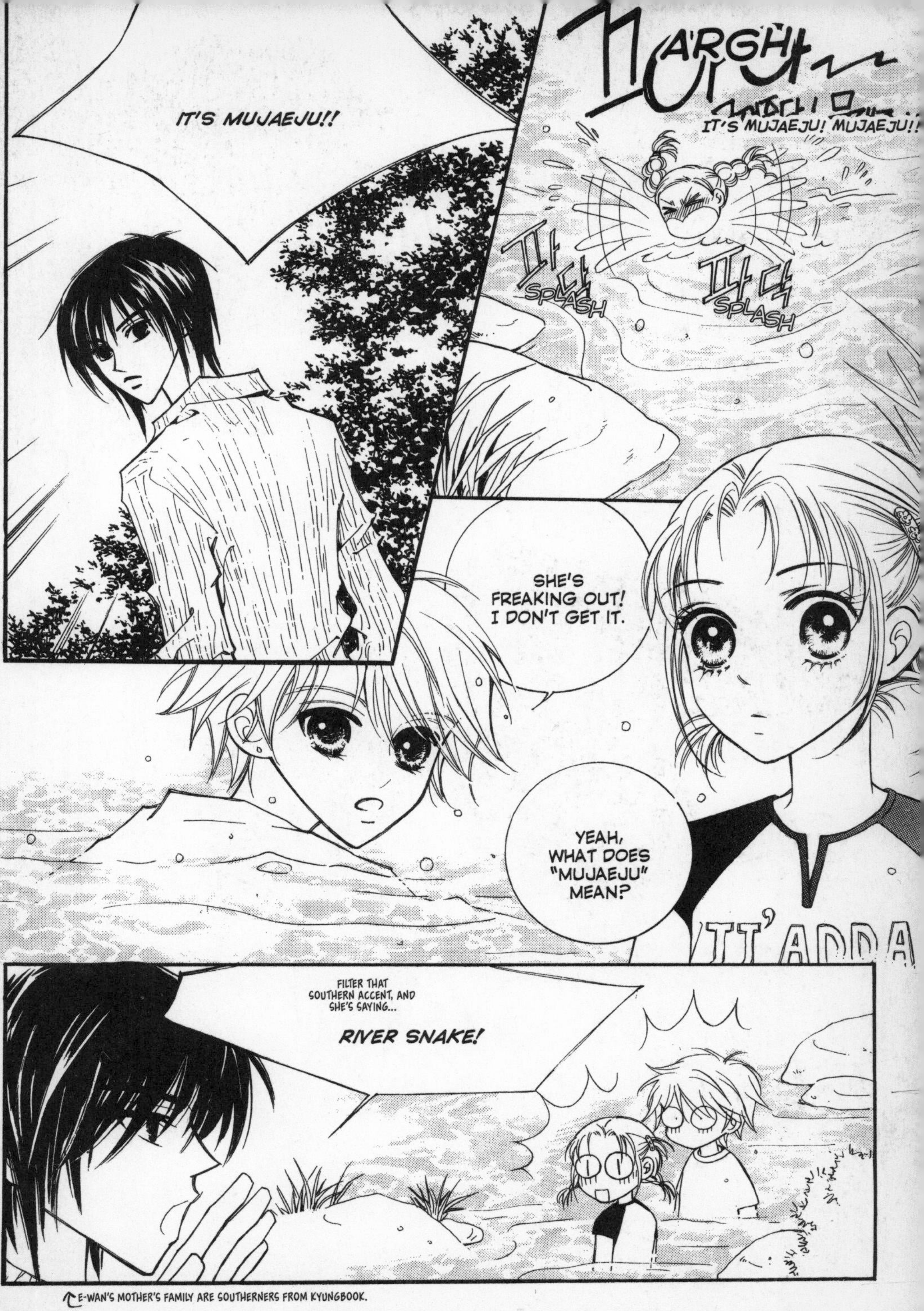
IT'S MUJAEJU!!
ARGH
IT'S MUJAEJU! MUJAEJU!!
SPLASH
SPLASH
SHE'S FREAKING OUT! I DON'T GET IT.
YEAH, WHAT DOES "MUJAEJU" MEAN?
FILTER THAT SOUTHERN ACCENT, AND SHE'S SAYING...
RIVER SNAKE!

E-WAN'S MOTHER'S FAMILY ARE SOUTHERNERS FROM KYUNGBOOK.

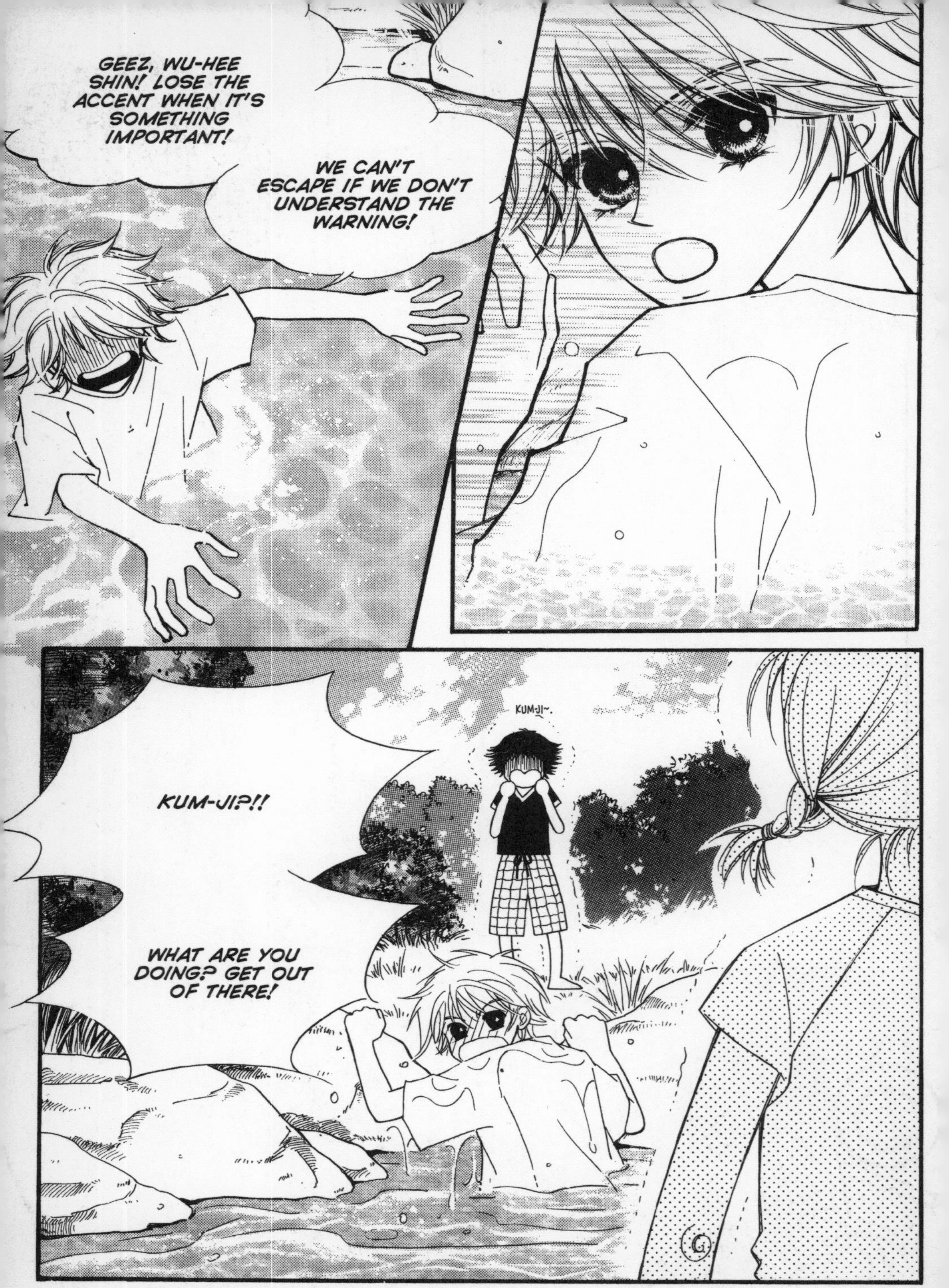
GEEZ, WU-HEE SHIN! LOSE THE ACCENT WHEN IT'S SOMETHING IMPORTANT!
WE CAN'T ESCAPE IF WE DON'T UNDERSTAND THE WARNING!
KUM-JI?!!
WHAT ARE YOU DOING? GET OUT OF THERE!
KUM-JI~.

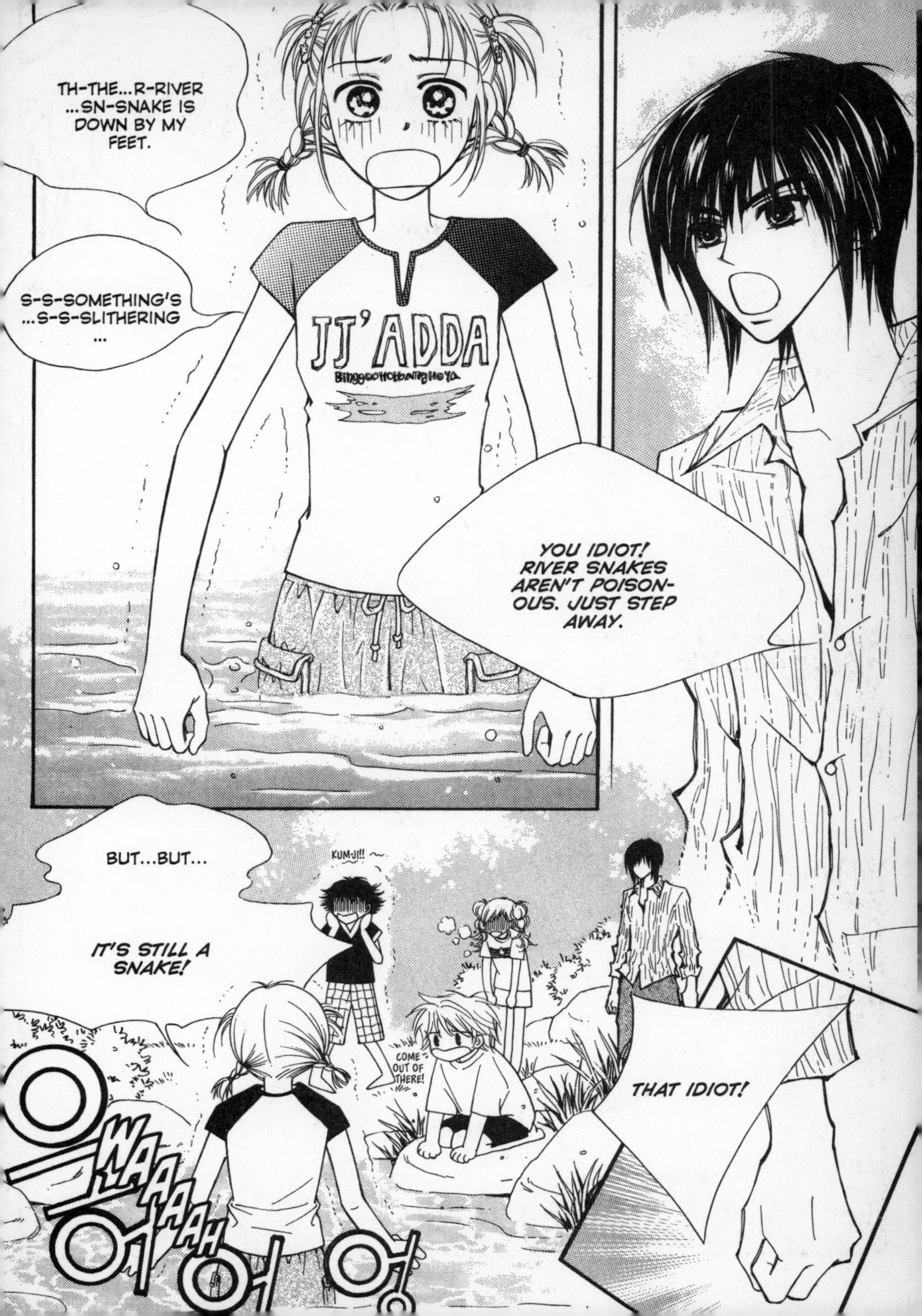
TH-THE...R-RIVER ...SN-SNAKE IS DOWN BY MY FEET.
S-S-SOMETHING'S ...S-S-SLITHERING ...
JJ'ADDA
YOU IDIOT! RIVER SNAKES AREN'T POISON-OUS. JUST STEP AWAY.
BUT...BUT...
IT'S STILL A SNAKE!
KUM-JI!! ~
COME OUT OF THERE!
WAAAAH
THAT IDIOT!

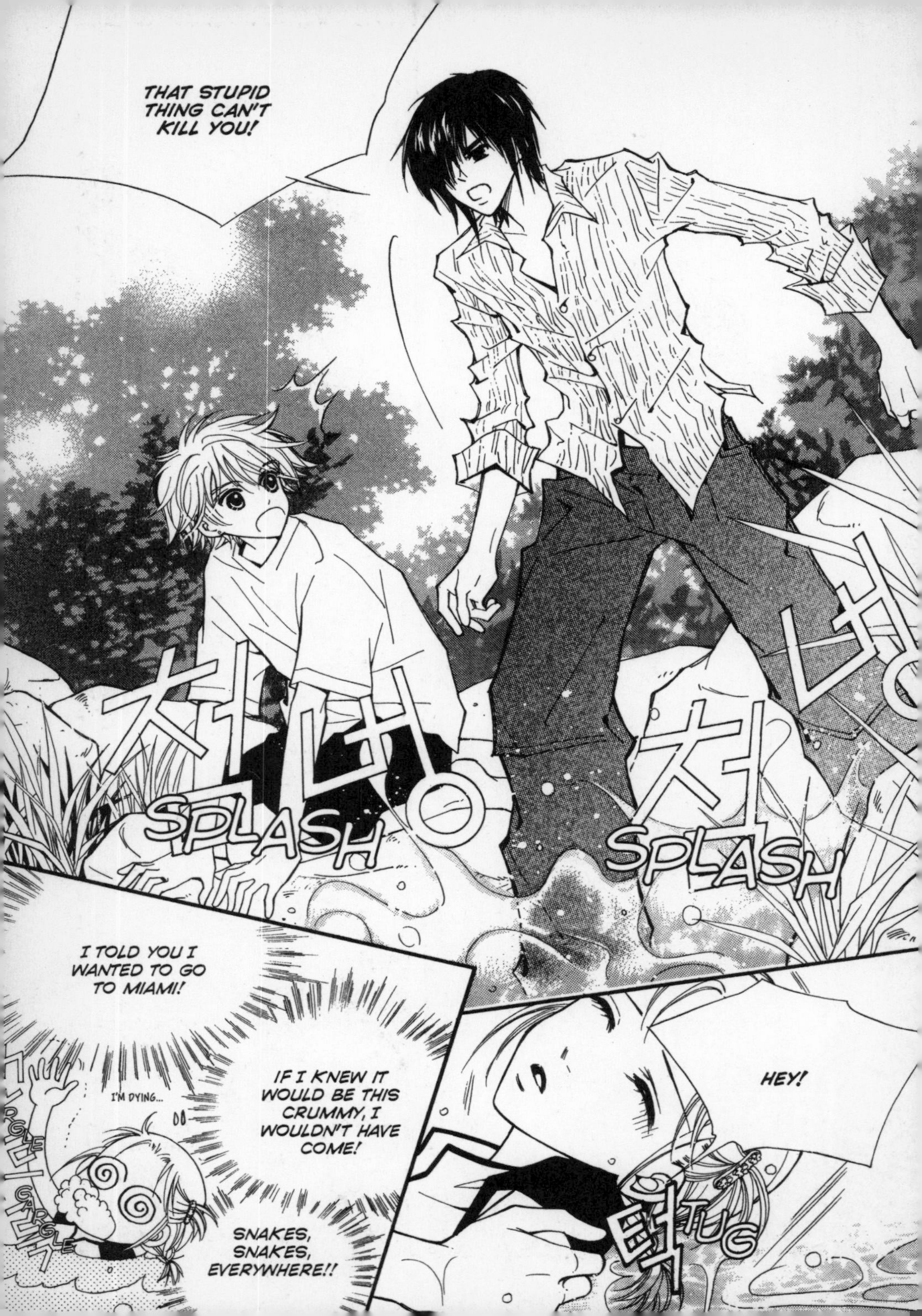
THAT STUPID THING CAN'T KILL YOU!
SPLASH
SPLASH
I TOLD YOU I WANTED TO GO TO MIAMI!
I'M DYING...
IF I KNEW IT WOULD BE THIS CRUMMY, I WOULDN'T HAVE COME!
GARGLE
GARGLE
SNAKES, SNAKES, EVERYWHERE!!
HEY!
TUG

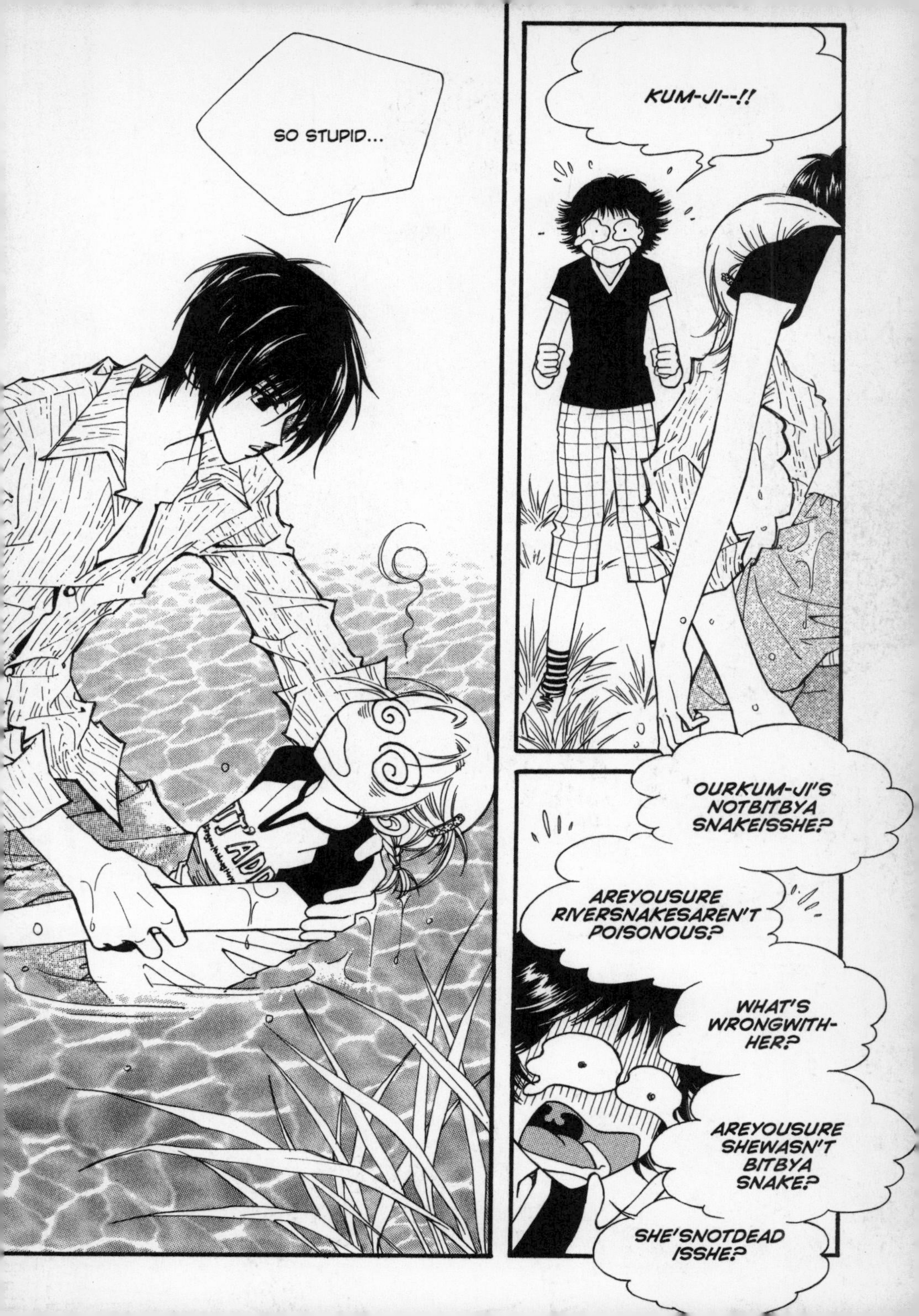
SO STUPID...
KUM-JI--!!
OURKUM-JI'S NOTBITBYA SNAKEISSHE?
AREYOUSURE RIVERSNAKESAREN'T POISONOUS?
WHAT'S WRONGWITH-HER?
AREYOUSURE SHEWASN'T BITBYA SNAKE?
SHE'SNOTDEAD ISSHE?

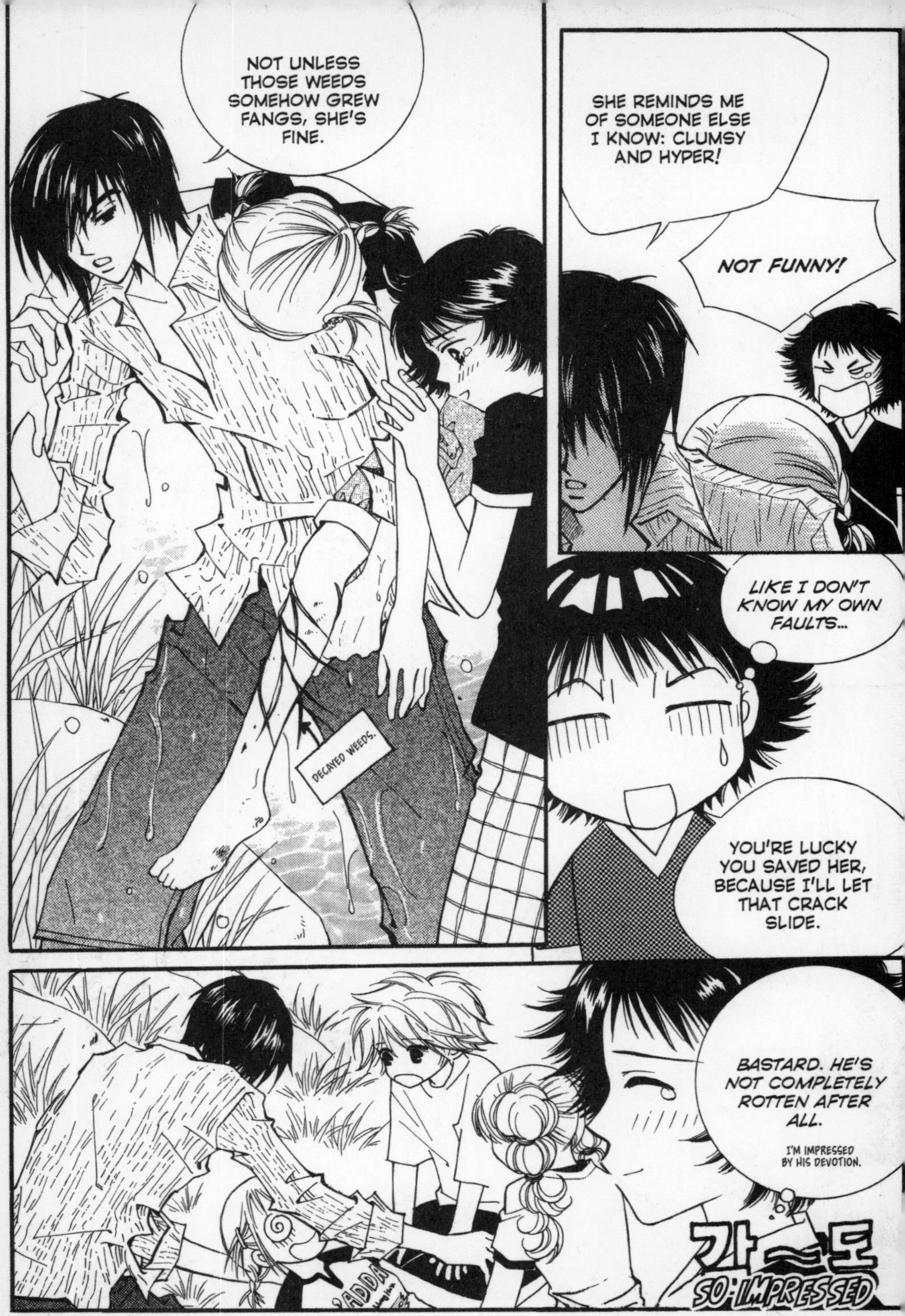
NOT UNLESS THOSE WEEDS SOMEHOW GREW FANGS, SHE'S FINE.
DECAYED WEEDS.
SHE REMINDS ME OF SOMEONE ELSE I KNOW: CLUMSY AND HYPER!
NOT FUNNY!
LIKE I DON'T KNOW MY OWN FAULTS...
YOU'RE LUCKY YOU SAVED HER, BECAUSE I'LL LET THAT CRACK SLIDE.
BASTARD. HE'S NOT COMPLETELY ROTTEN AFTER ALL.
I'M IMPRESSED BY HIS DEVOTION.
가~도
SO: IMPRESSED

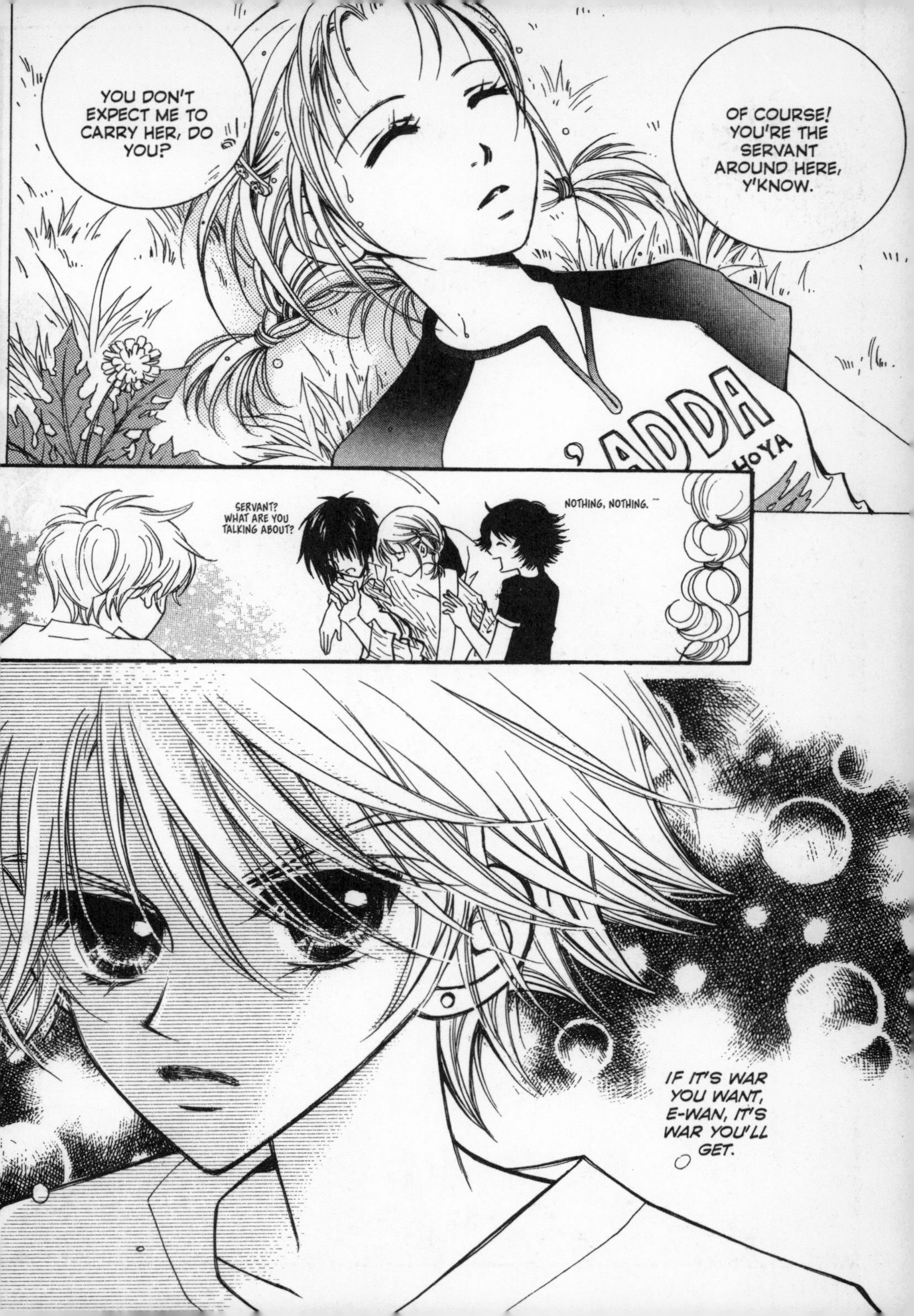
YOU DON'T EXPECT ME TO CARRY HER, DO YOU?
OF COURSE! YOU'RE THE SERVANT AROUND HERE, Y'KNOW.
ADDA HOYA
SERVANT? WHAT ARE YOU TALKING ABOUT?
NOTHING, NOTHING. ^^
IF IT'S WAR YOU WANT, E-WAN, IT'S WAR YOU'LL GET.

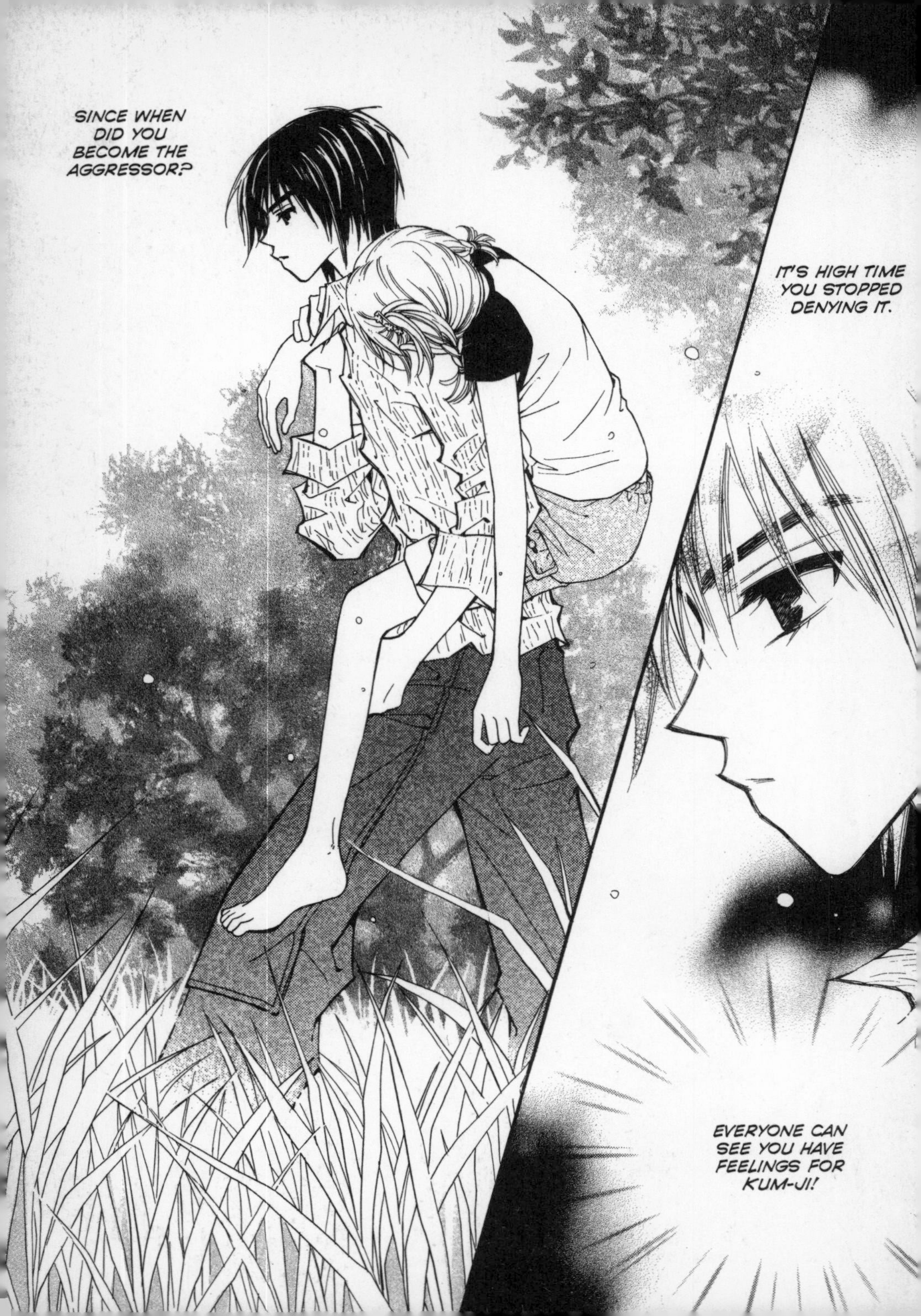
SINCE WHEN DID YOU BECOME THE AGGRESSOR?
IT'S HIGH TIME YOU STOPPED DENYING IT.
EVERYONE CAN SEE YOU HAVE FEELINGS FOR KUM-JI!

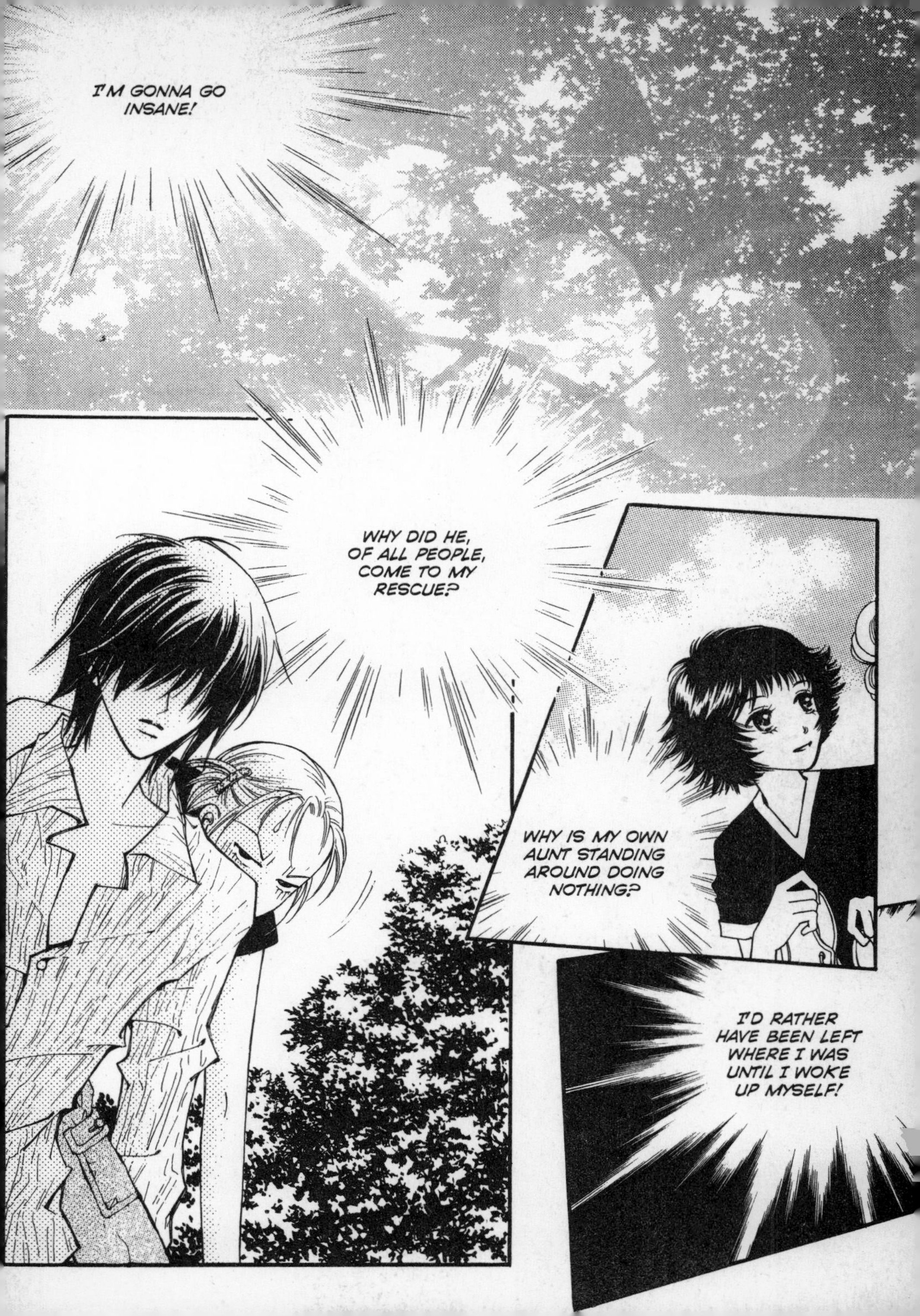
I'M GONNA GO INSANE!
WHY DID HE, OF ALL PEOPLE, COME TO MY RESCUE?
WHY IS MY OWN AUNT STANDING AROUND DOING NOTHING?
I'D RATHER HAVE BEEN LEFT WHERE I WAS UNTIL I WOKE UP MYSELF!

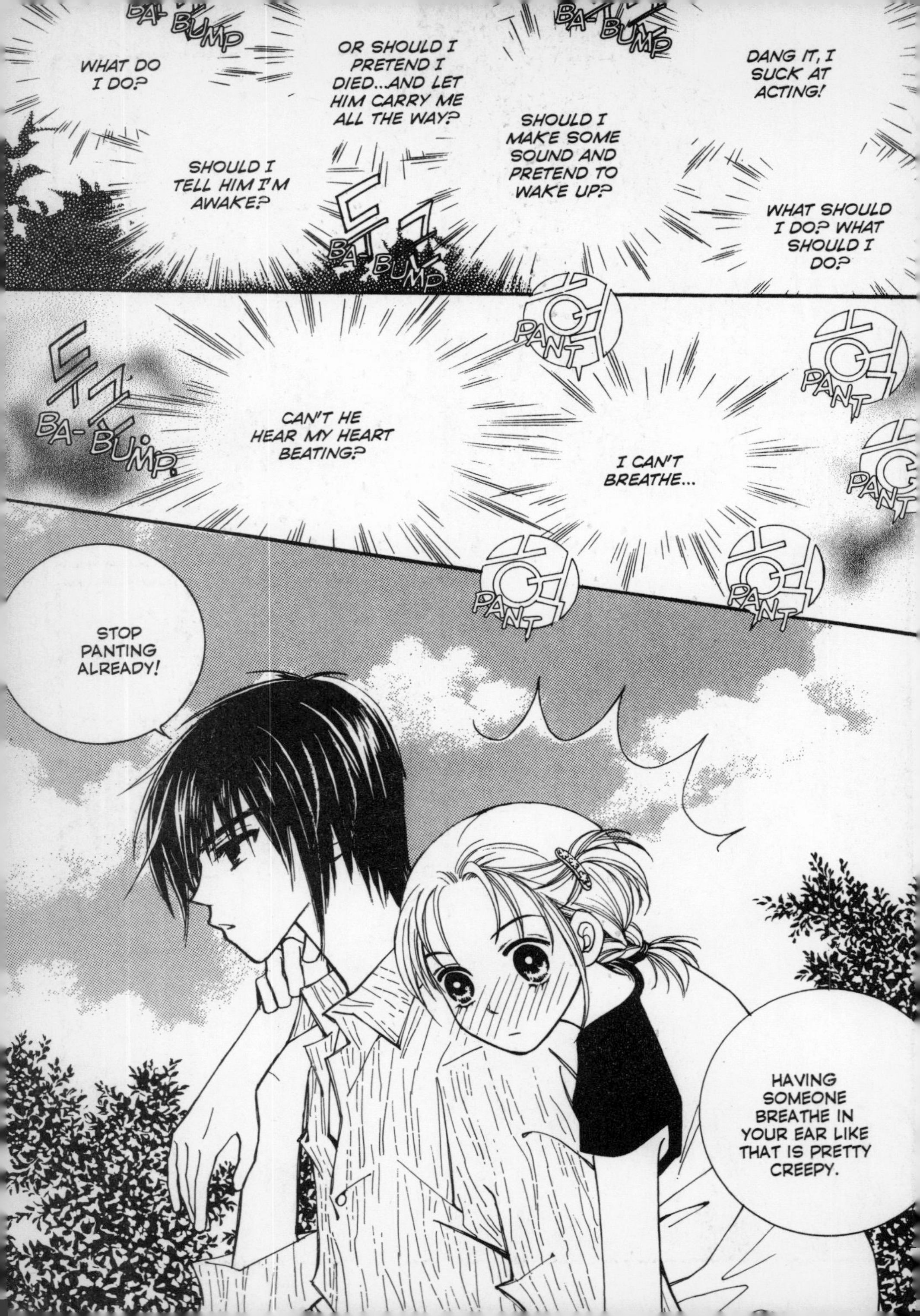
BA-BUMP
WHAT DO I DO?
OR SHOULD I PRETEND I DIED...AND LET HIM CARRY ME ALL THE WAY?
BA-BUMP
DANG IT, I SUCK AT ACTING!
SHOULD I TELL HIM I'M AWAKE?
BA-BUMP
SHOULD I MAKE SOME SOUND AND PRETEND TO WAKE UP?
WHAT SHOULD I DO? WHAT SHOULD I DO?
PANT
PANT
BA-BUMP
CAN'T HE HEAR MY HEART BEATING?
I CAN'T BREATHE...
PANT
PANT
PANT
STOP PANTING ALREADY!
HAVING SOMEONE BREATHE IN YOUR EAR LIKE THAT IS PRETTY CREEPY.

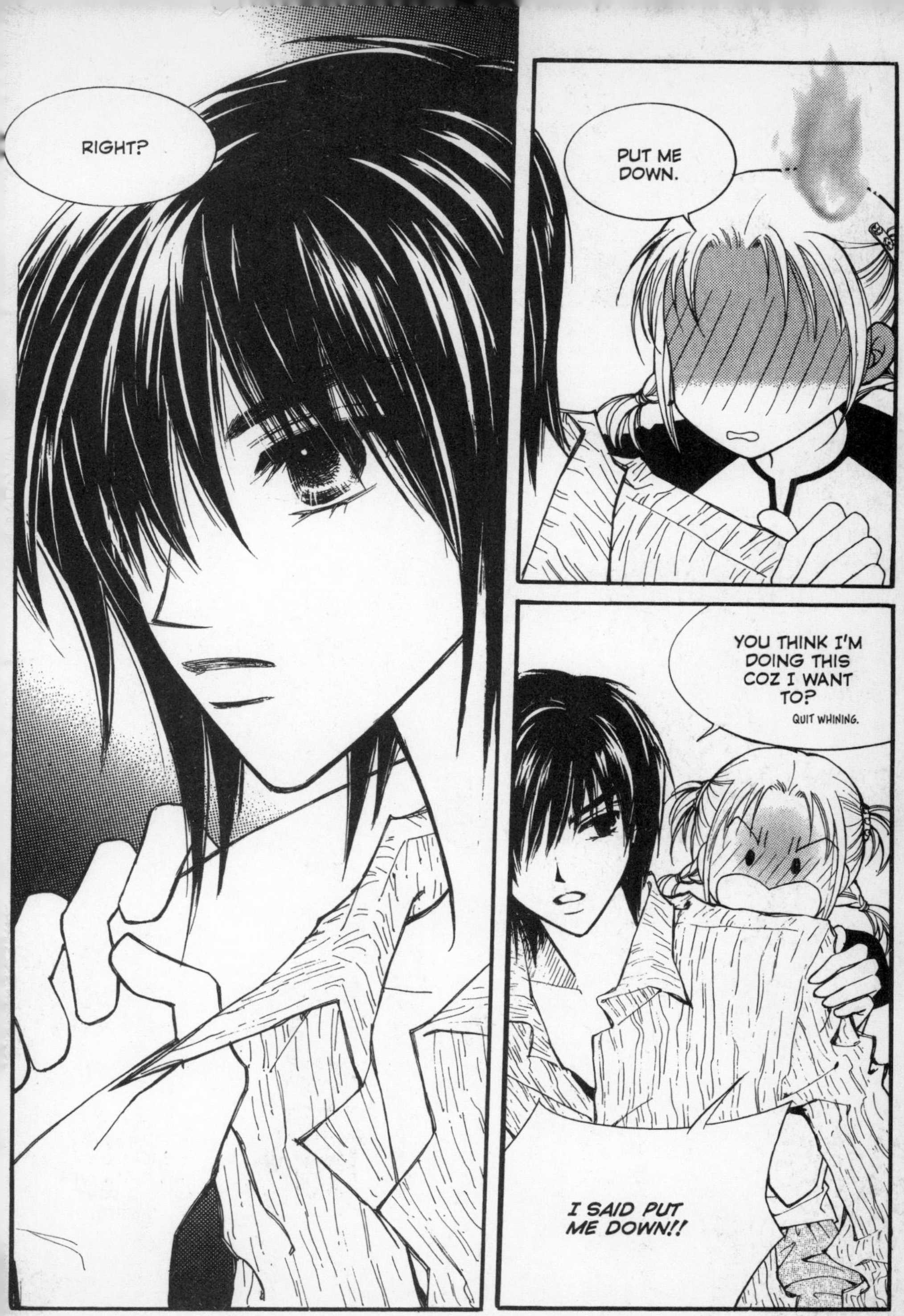
RIGHT?
PUT ME DOWN.
YOU THINK I'M DOING THIS COZ I WANT TO?
QUIT WHINING.
I SAID PUT ME DOWN!!

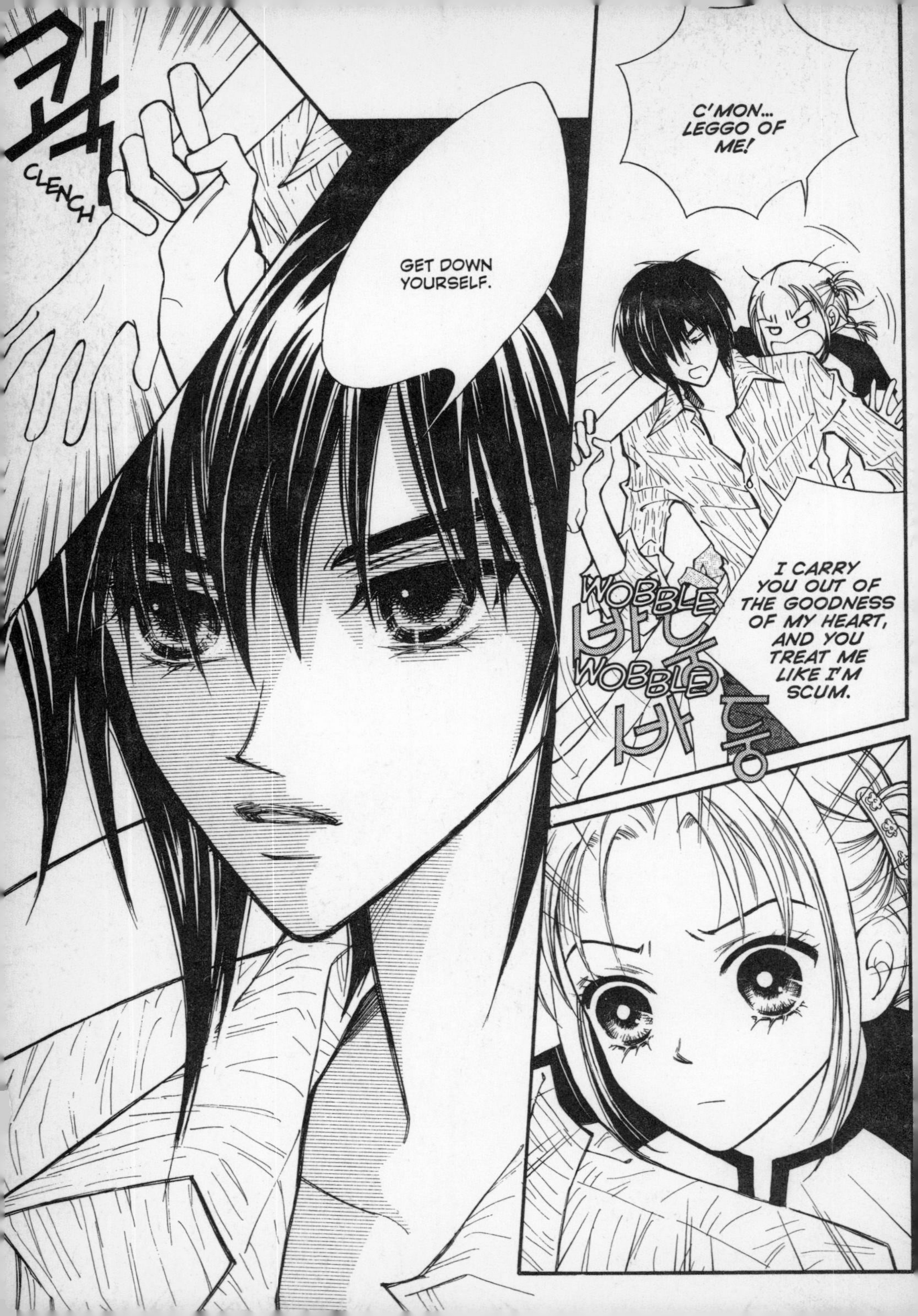
콱
CLENCH
GET DOWN YOURSELF.
C'MON... LEGGO OF ME!
WOBBLE WOBBLE
I CARRY YOU OUT OF THE GOODNESS OF MY HEART, AND YOU TREAT ME LIKE I'M SCUM.

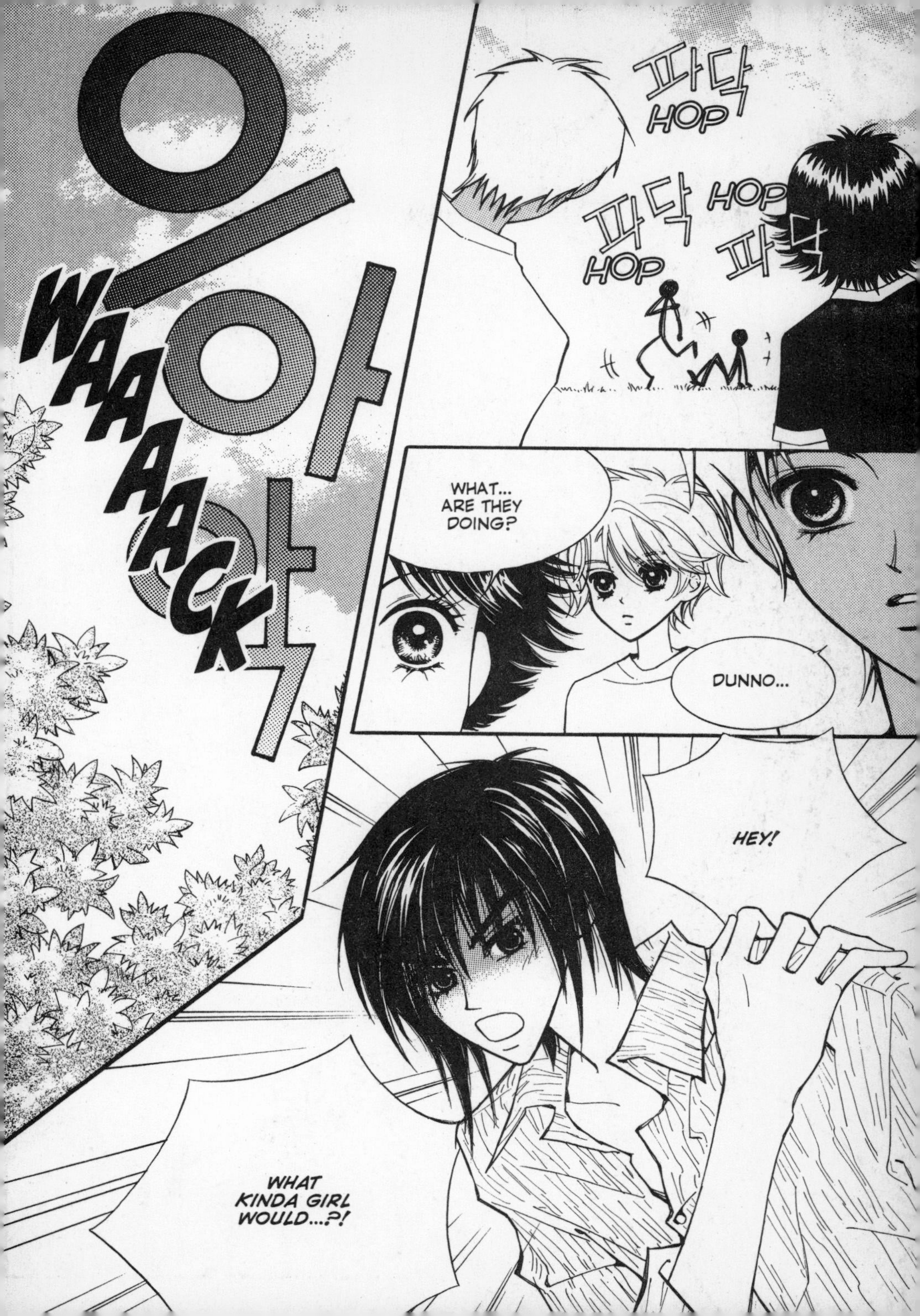
으아악
WAAAAACK
파닥
HOP
파닥 HOP
HOP
파닥
WHAT... ARE THEY DOING?
DUNNO...
HEY!
WHAT KINDA GIRL WOULD...?!

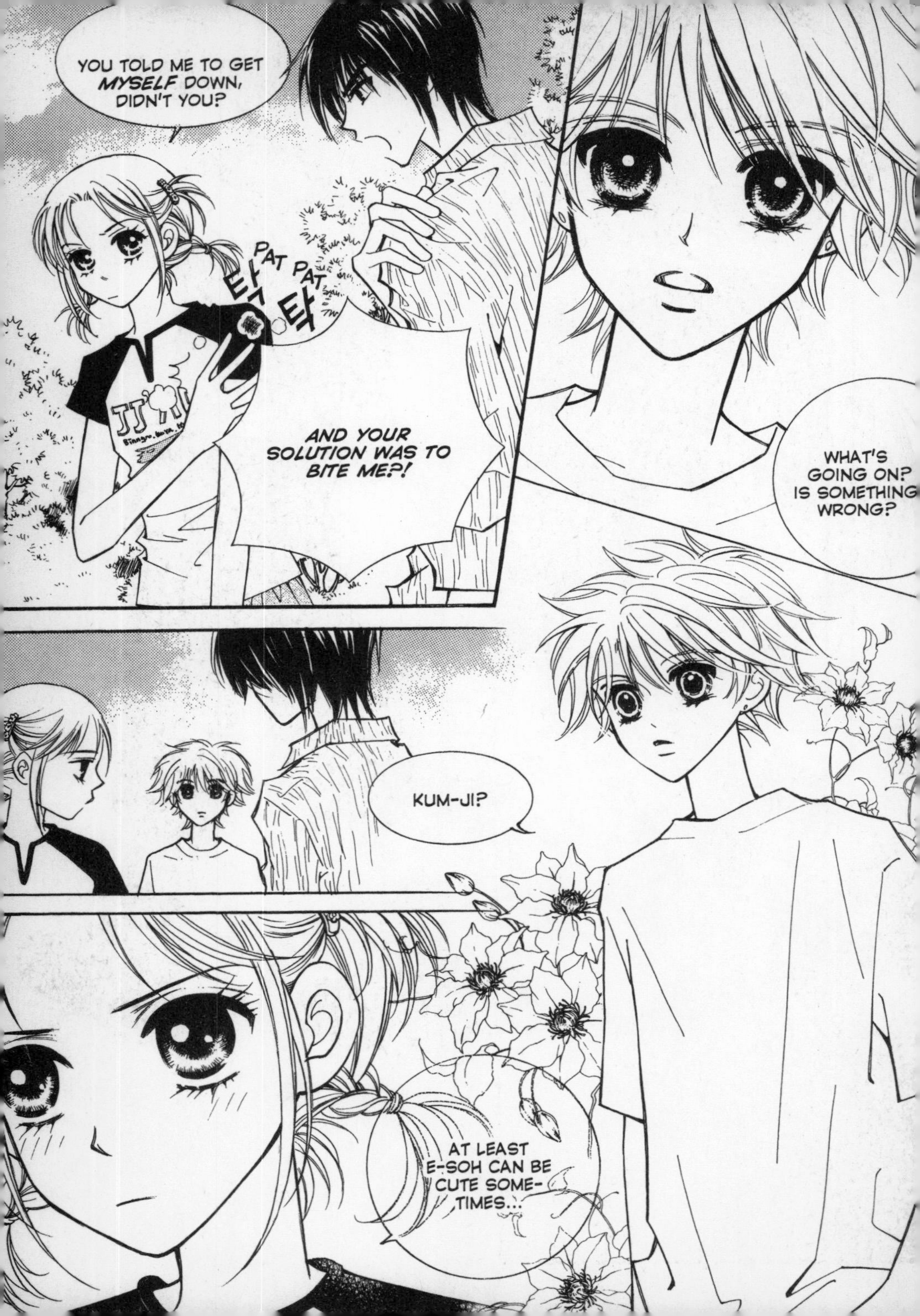
YOU TOLD ME TO GET *MYSELF* DOWN, DIDN'T YOU?
PAT PAT
탁 탁
AND YOUR SOLUTION WAS TO BITE ME?!
WHAT'S GOING ON? IS SOMETHING WRONG?
KUM-JI?
AT LEAST E-SOH CAN BE CUTE SOME-TIMES...

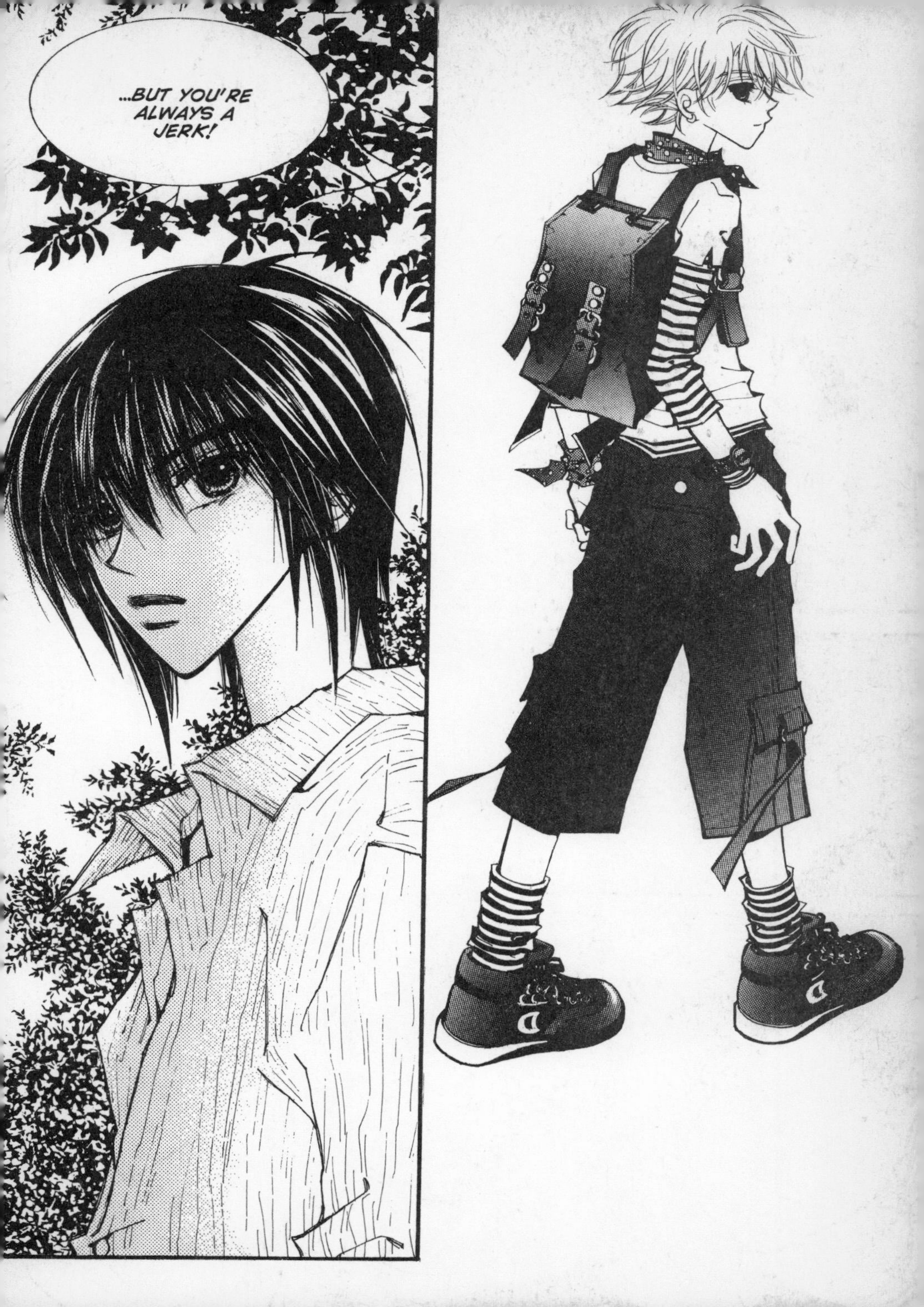
...BUT YOU'RE ALWAYS A JERK!

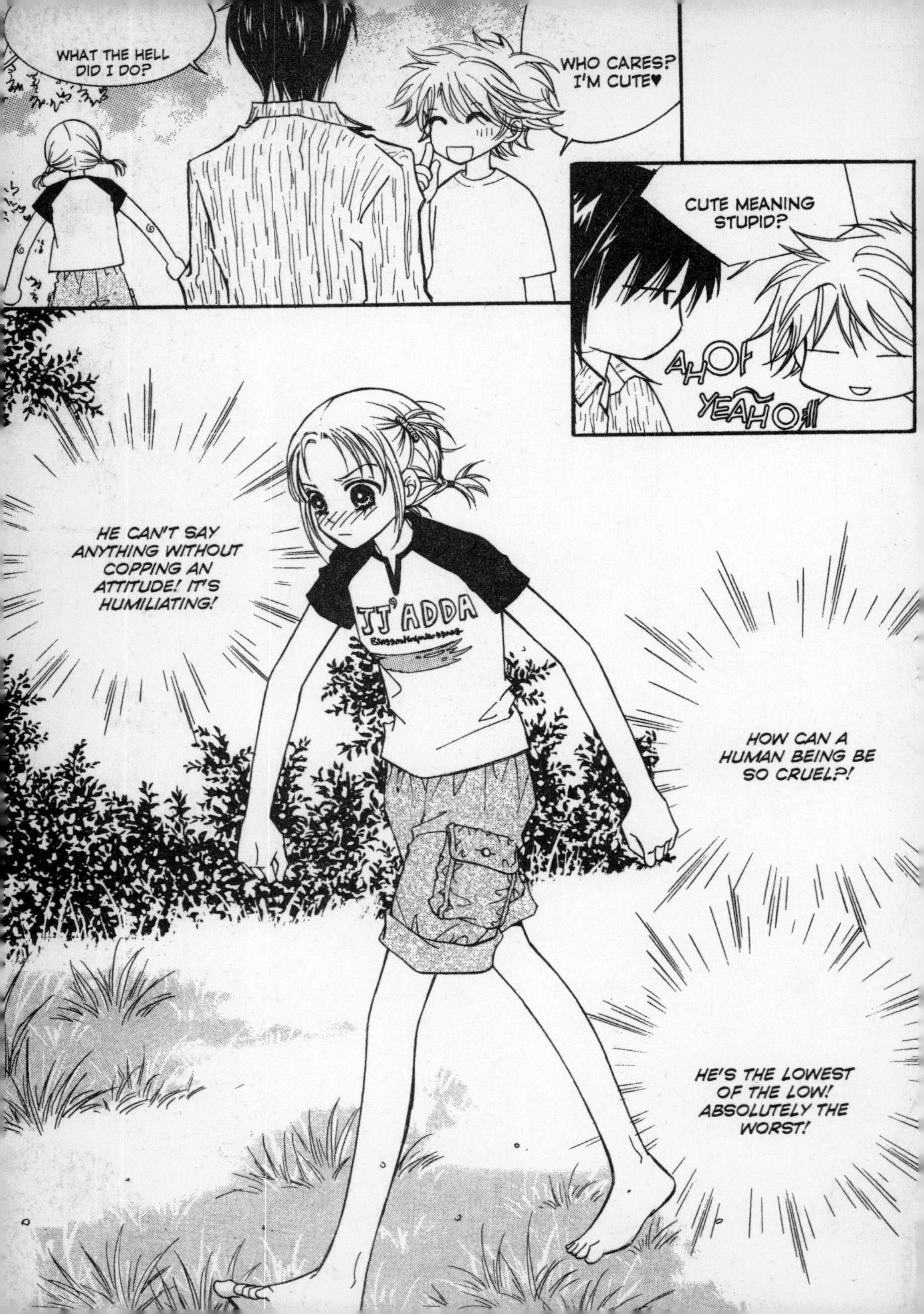
WHAT THE HELL DID I DO?
WHO CARES? I'M CUTE♥
CUTE MEANING STUPID?
AHO
YEAHO
JJ'ADDA
HE CAN'T SAY ANYTHING WITHOUT COPPING AN ATTITUDE! IT'S HUMILIATING!
HOW CAN A HUMAN BEING BE SO CRUEL?!
HE'S THE LOWEST OF THE LOW! ABSOLUTELY THE WORST!

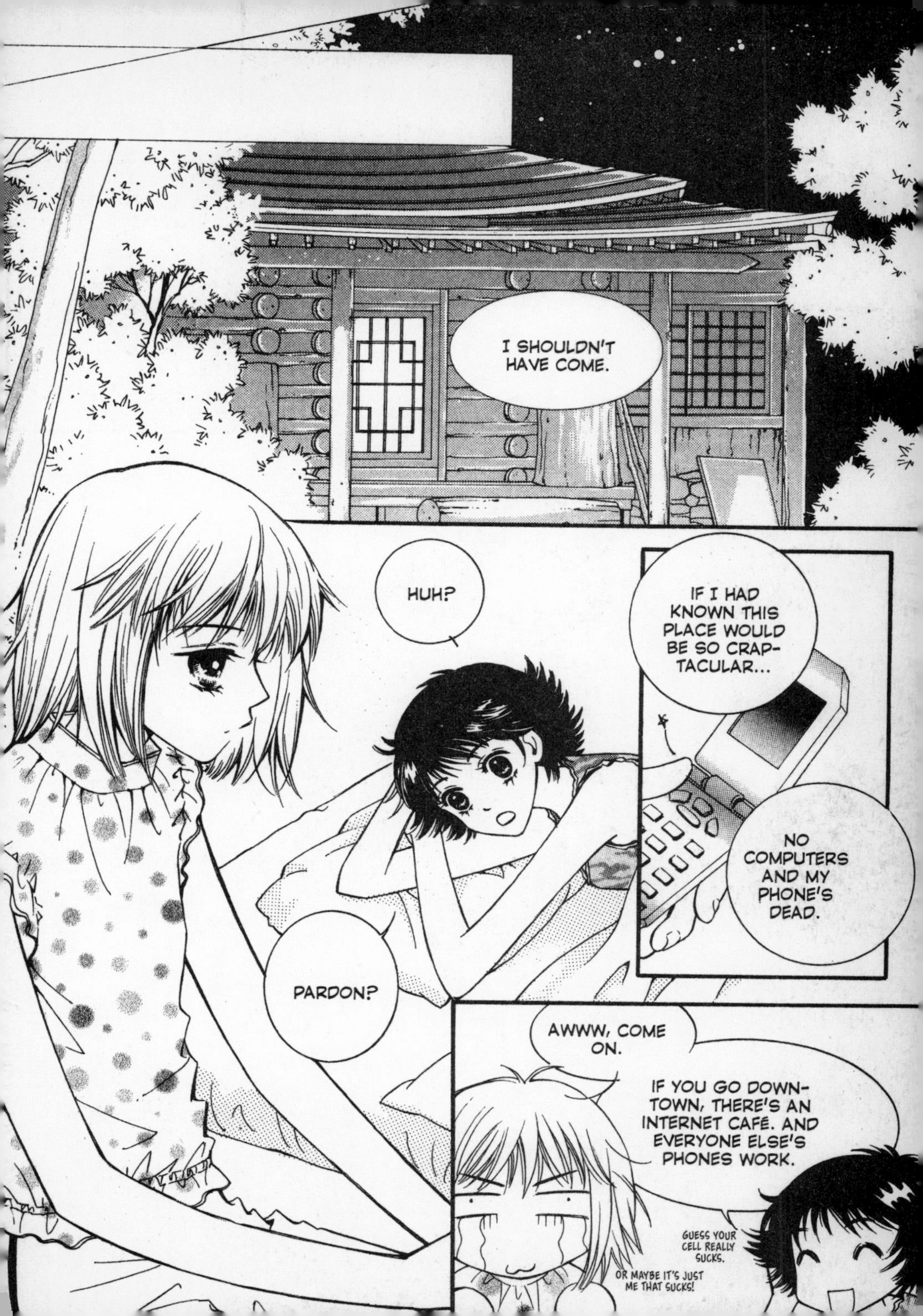
I SHOULDN'T HAVE COME.
HUH?
IF I HAD KNOWN THIS PLACE WOULD BE SO CRAP-TACULAR...
NO COMPUTERS AND MY PHONE'S DEAD.
PARDON?
AWWW, COME ON.
IF YOU GO DOWN-TOWN, THERE'S AN INTERNET CAFÉ. AND EVERYONE ELSE'S PHONES WORK.
GUESS YOUR CELL REALLY SUCKS.
OR MAYBE IT'S JUST ME THAT SUCKS!

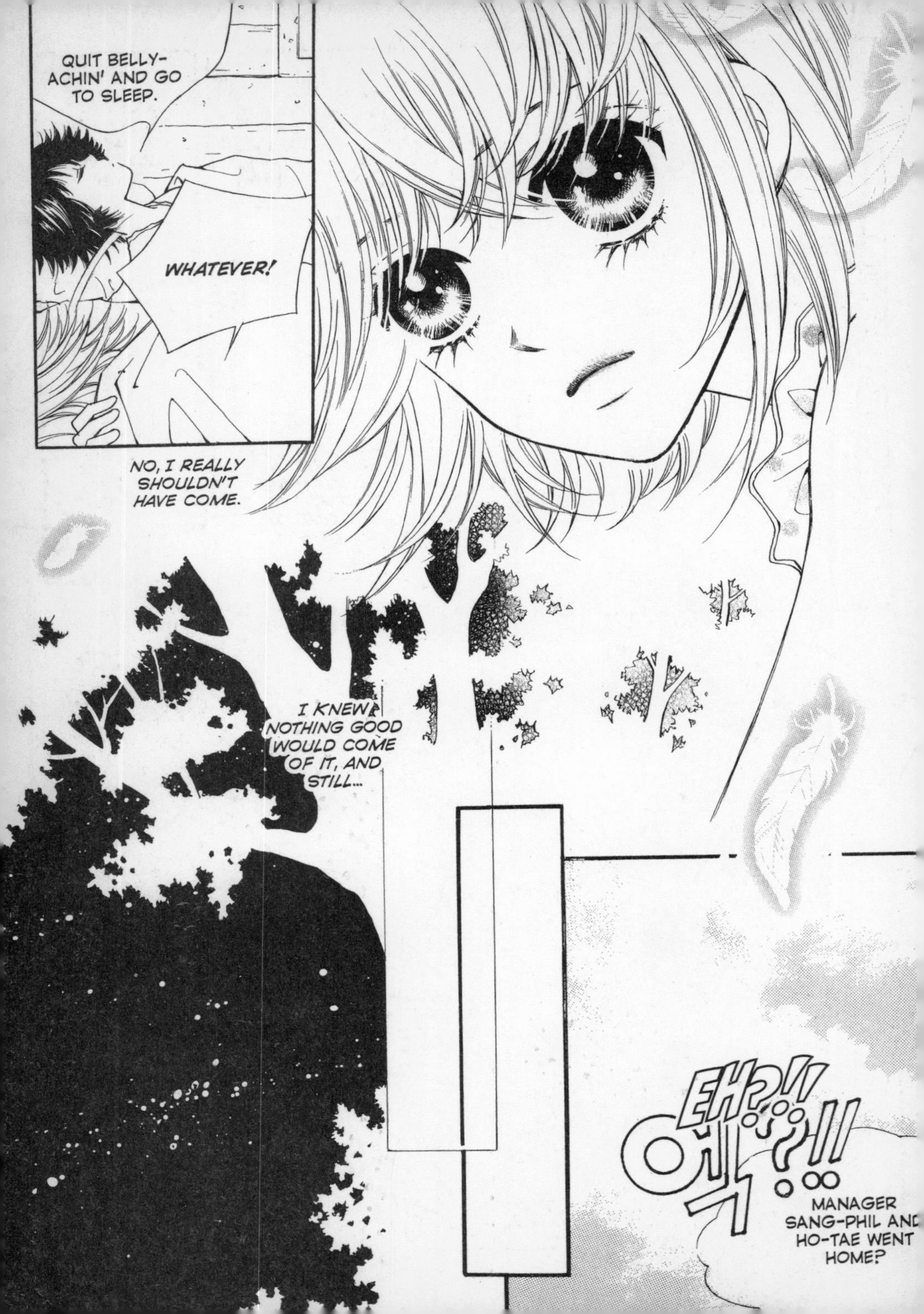
QUIT BELLY-ACHIN' AND GO TO SLEEP.
WHATEVER!
NO, I REALLY SHOULDN'T HAVE COME.
I KNEW NOTHING GOOD WOULD COME OF IT, AND STILL...
EH?!!
MANAGER SANG-PHIL AND HO-TAE WENT HOME?

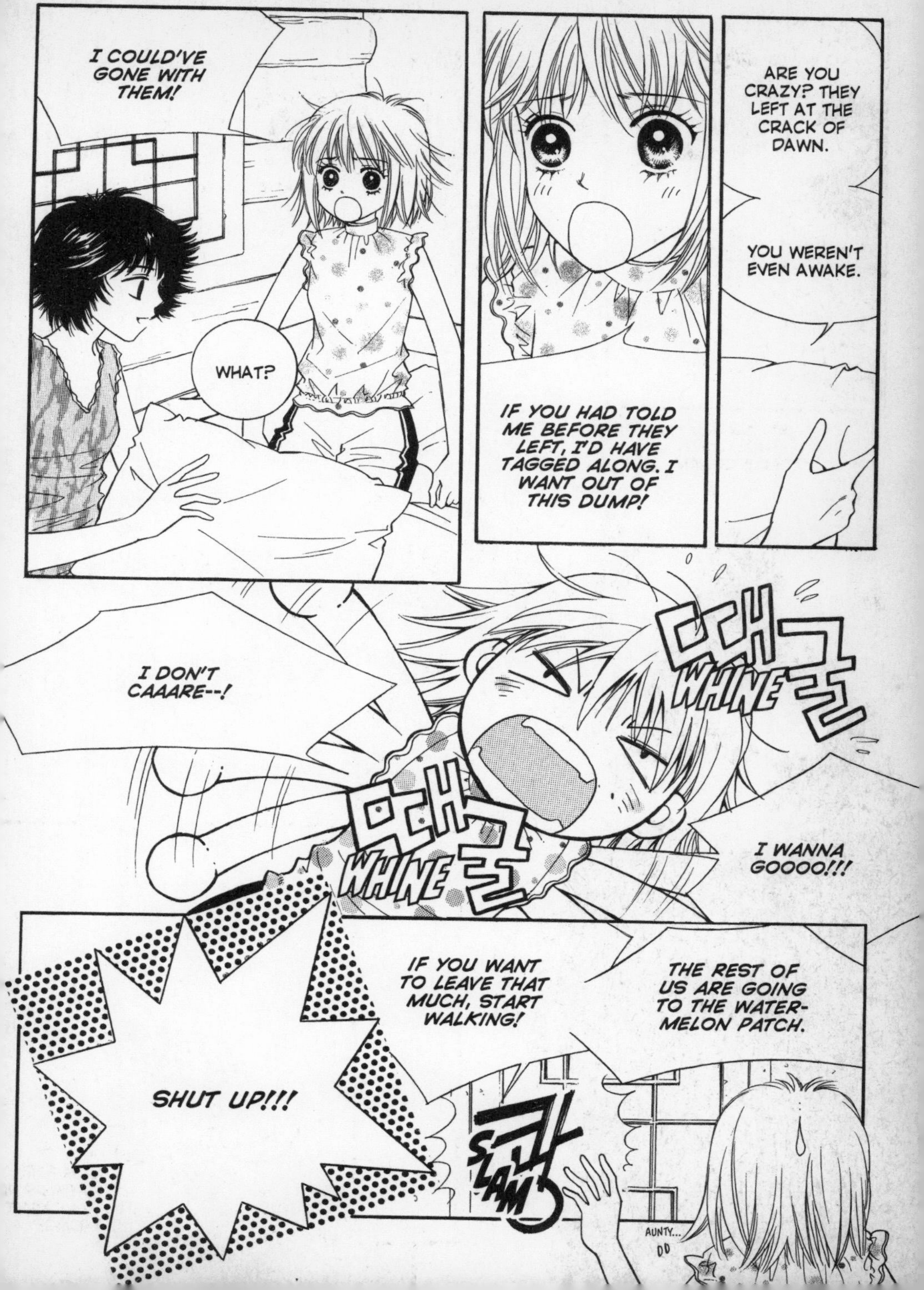
I COULD'VE GONE WITH THEM!
WHAT?
IF YOU HAD TOLD ME BEFORE THEY LEFT, I'D HAVE TAGGED ALONG. I WANT OUT OF THIS DUMP!
ARE YOU CRAZY? THEY LEFT AT THE CRACK OF DAWN.
YOU WEREN'T EVEN AWAKE.
I DON'T CAAARE--!
WHINE
WHINE
I WANNA GOOOO!!!
SHUT UP!!!
IF YOU WANT TO LEAVE THAT MUCH, START WALKING!
THE REST OF US ARE GOING TO THE WATER-MELON PATCH.
SLAM
AUNTY...

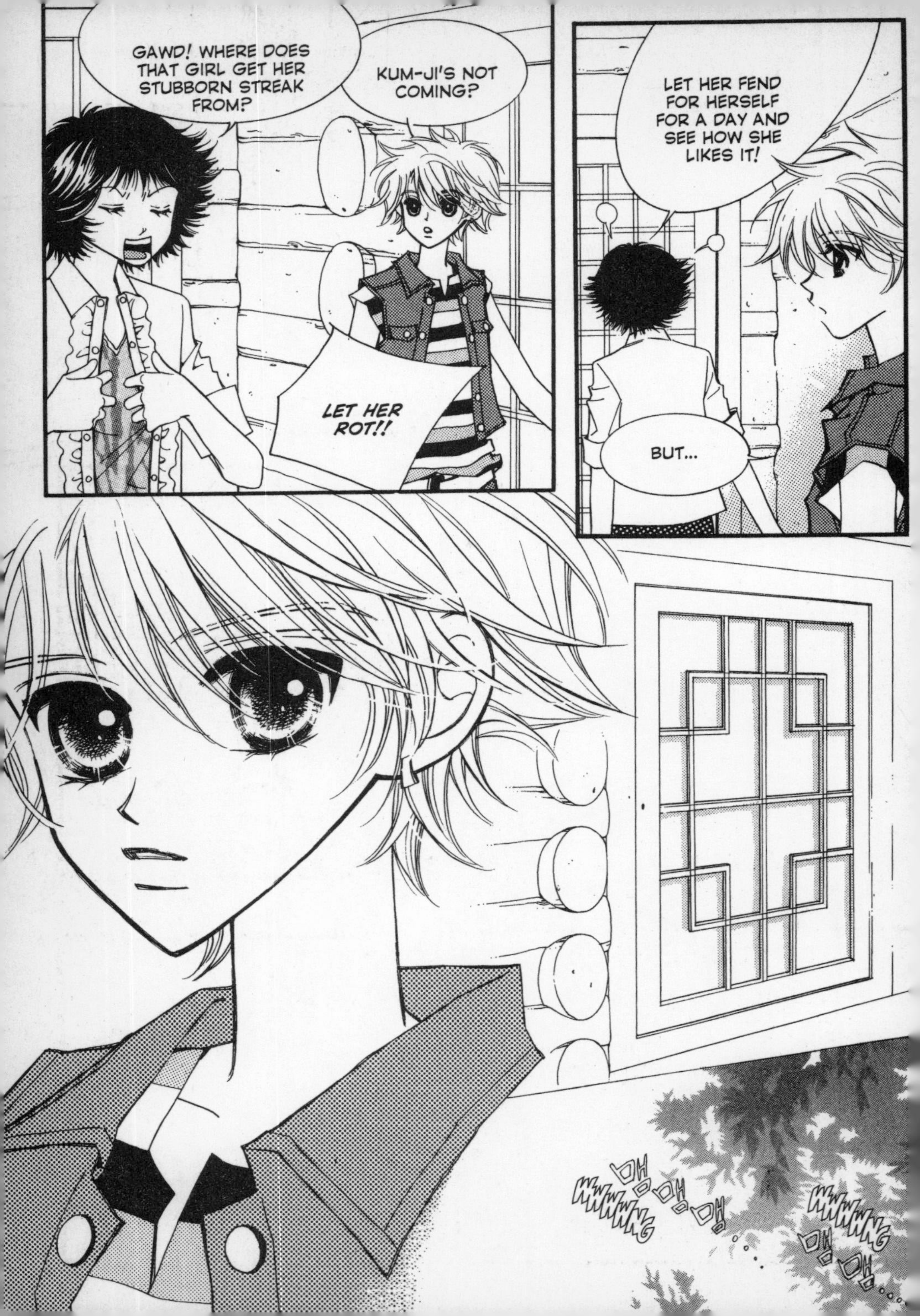
GAWD! WHERE DOES THAT GIRL GET HER STUBBORN STREAK FROM?
KUM-JI'S NOT COMING?
LET HER ROT!!
LET HER FEND FOR HERSELF FOR A DAY AND SEE HOW SHE LIKES IT!
BUT...
WWWWWNG
OHoOHoOHo...
WWWWWNG
OHoOHo...

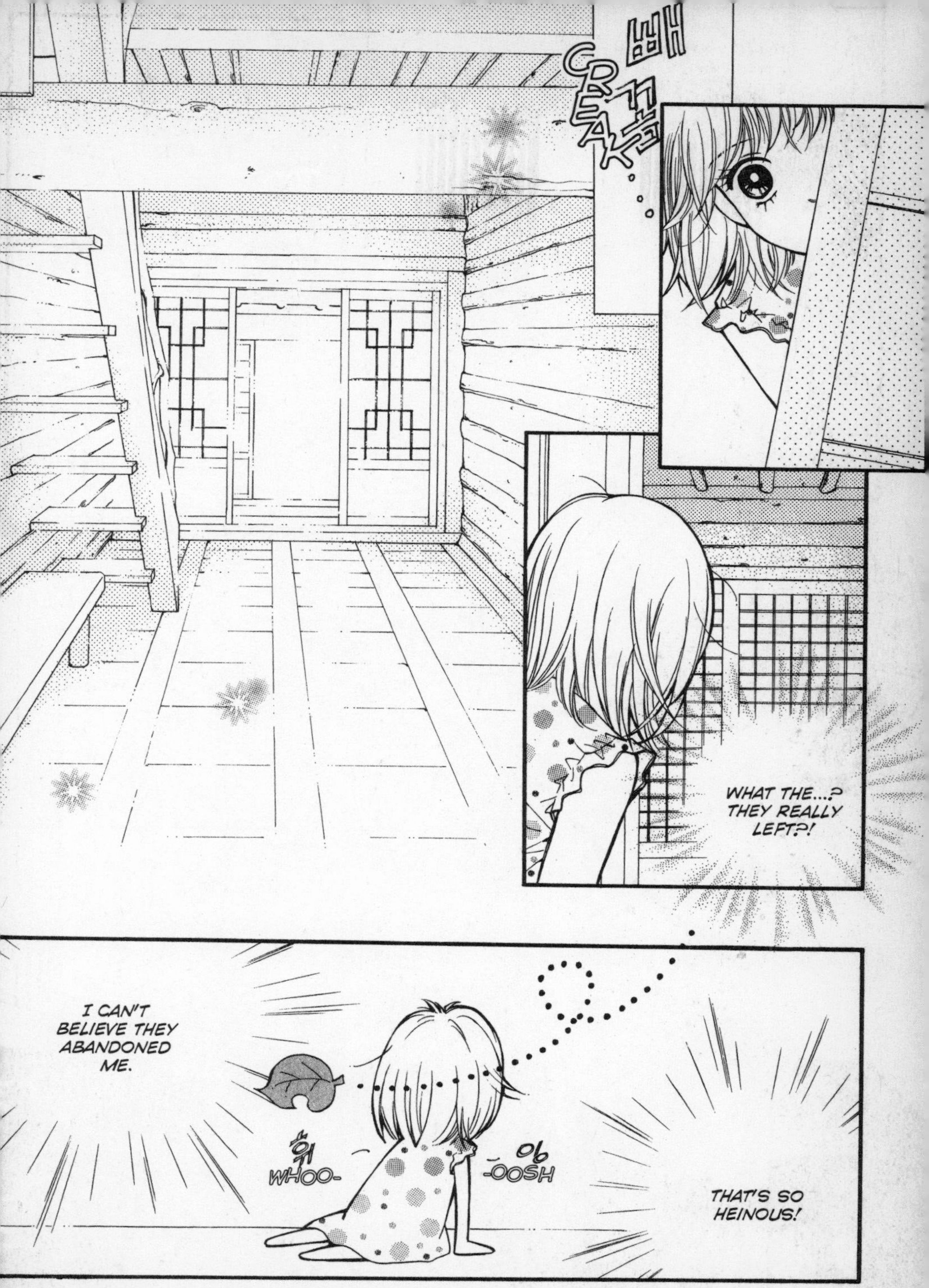
CREAK
WHAT THE...? THEY REALLY LEFT?!
I CAN'T BELIEVE THEY ABANDONED ME.
WHOO-
-OOSH
THAT'S SO HEINOUS!

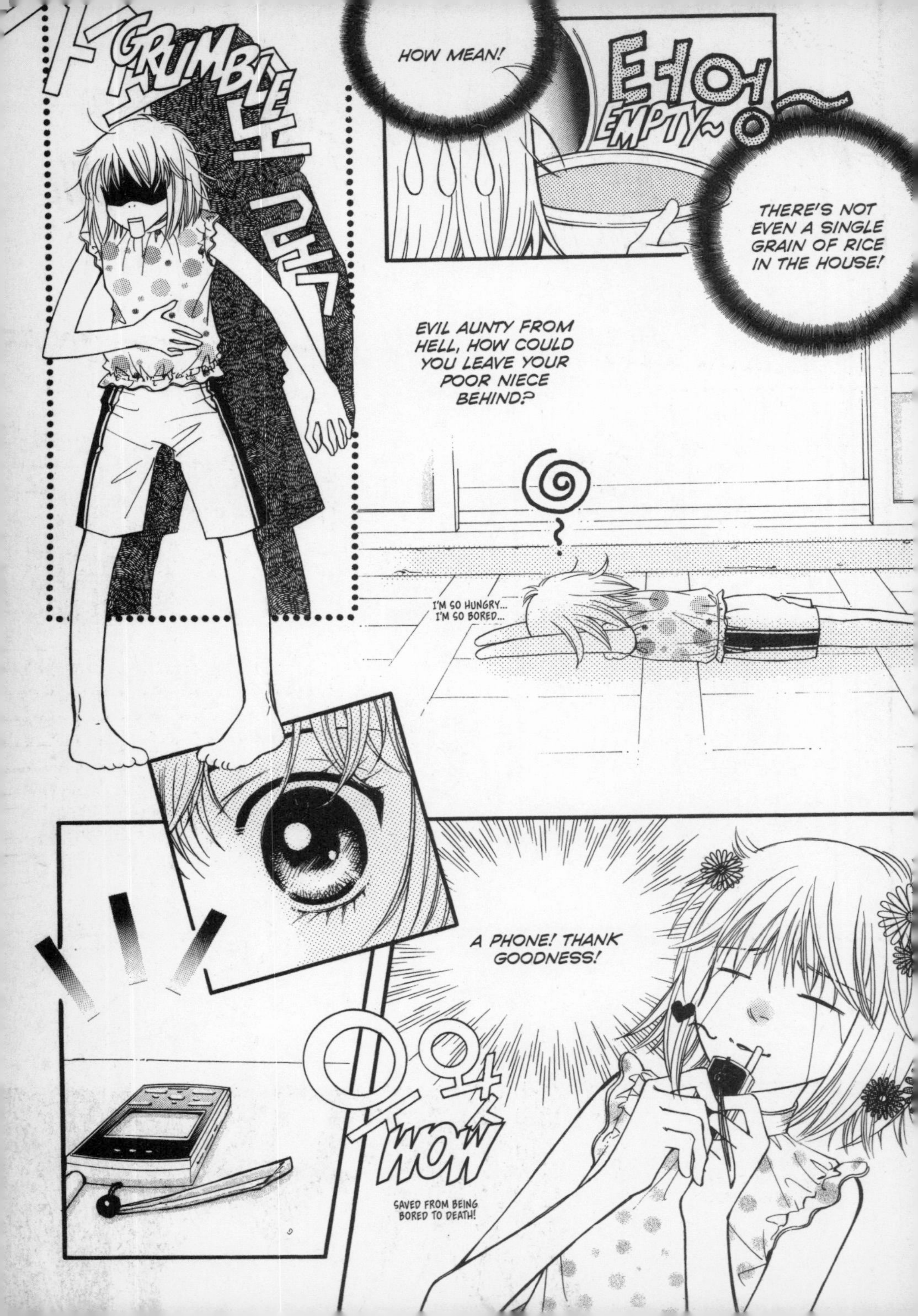
GRUMBLE
HOW MEAN!
EMPTY~
THERE'S NOT EVEN A SINGLE GRAIN OF RICE IN THE HOUSE!
EVIL AUNTY FROM HELL, HOW COULD YOU LEAVE YOUR POOR NIECE BEHIND?
I'M SO HUNGRY... I'M SO BORED...
A PHONE! THANK GOODNESS!
WOW
SAVED FROM BEING BORED TO DEATH!

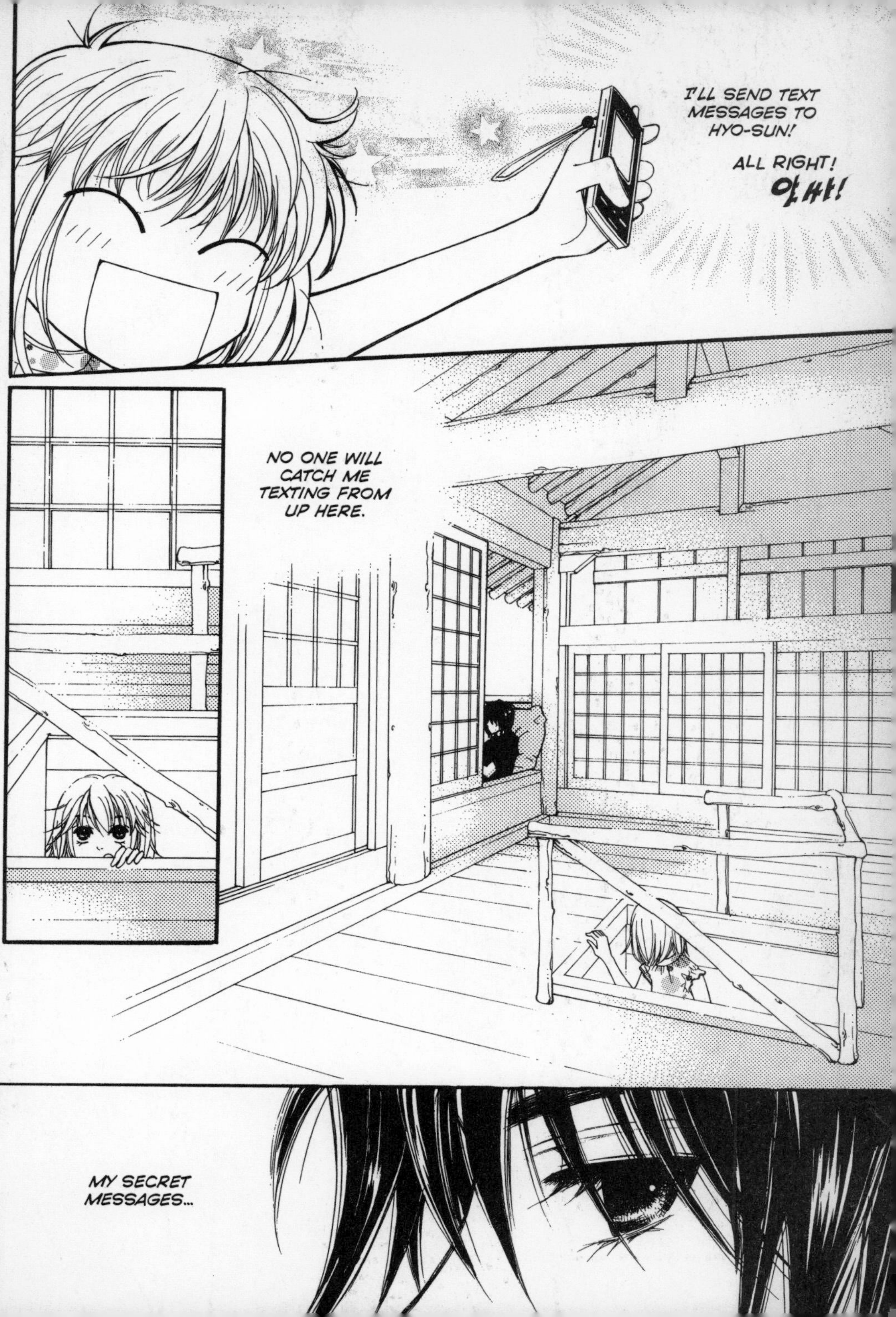
I'LL SEND TEXT MESSAGES TO HYO-SUN!
ALL RIGHT!
앗싸!
NO ONE WILL CATCH ME TEXTING FROM UP HERE.
MY SECRET MESSAGES...

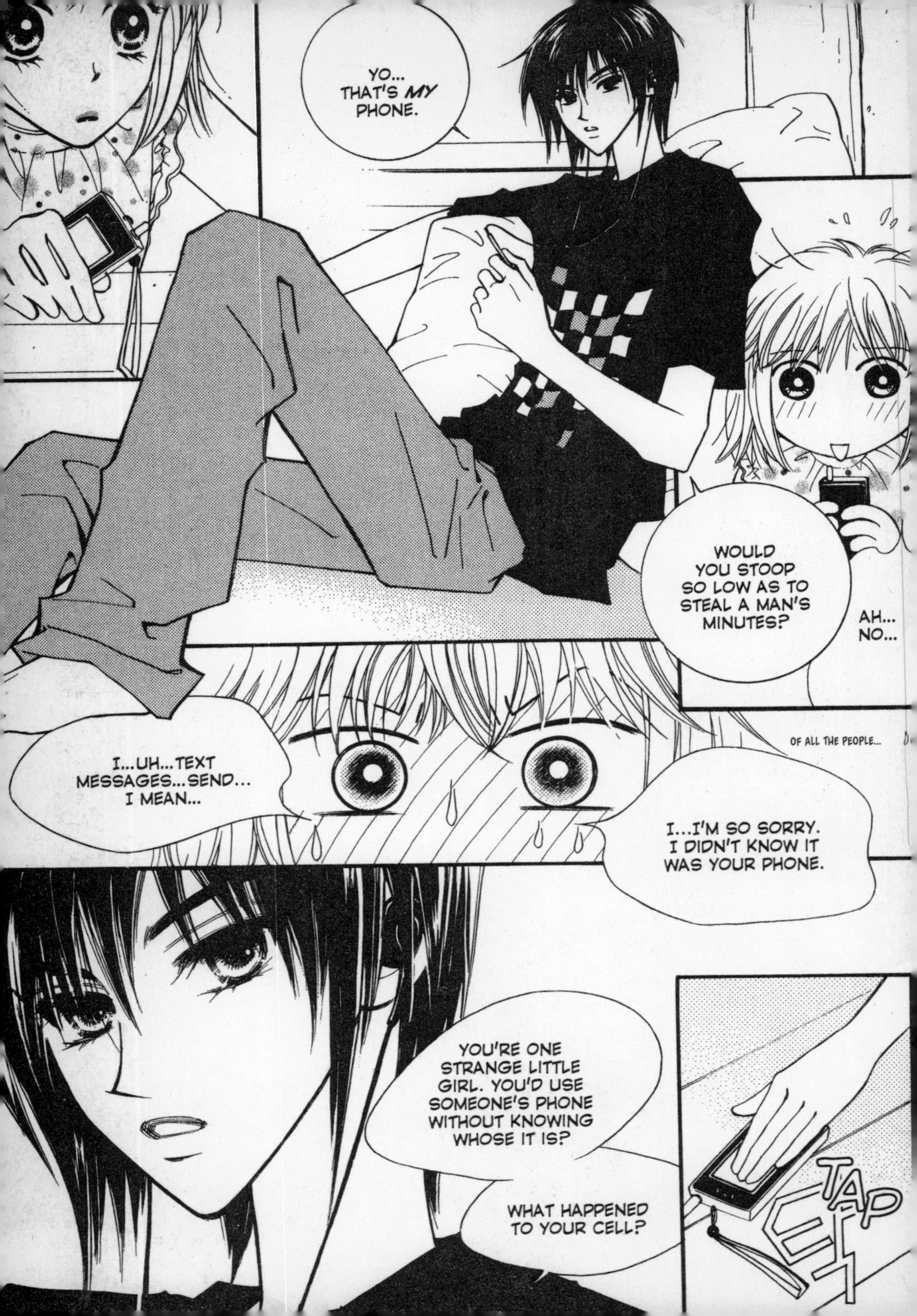

YO... THAT'S *MY* PHONE.
WOULD YOU STOOP SO LOW AS TO STEAL A MAN'S MINUTES?
AH... NO...
I...UH...TEXT MESSAGES...SEND... I MEAN...
OF ALL THE PEOPLE...
I...I'M SO SORRY. I DIDN'T KNOW IT WAS YOUR PHONE.
YOU'RE ONE STRANGE LITTLE GIRL. YOU'D USE SOMEONE'S PHONE WITHOUT KNOWING WHOSE IT IS?
WHAT HAPPENED TO YOUR CELL?
TAP

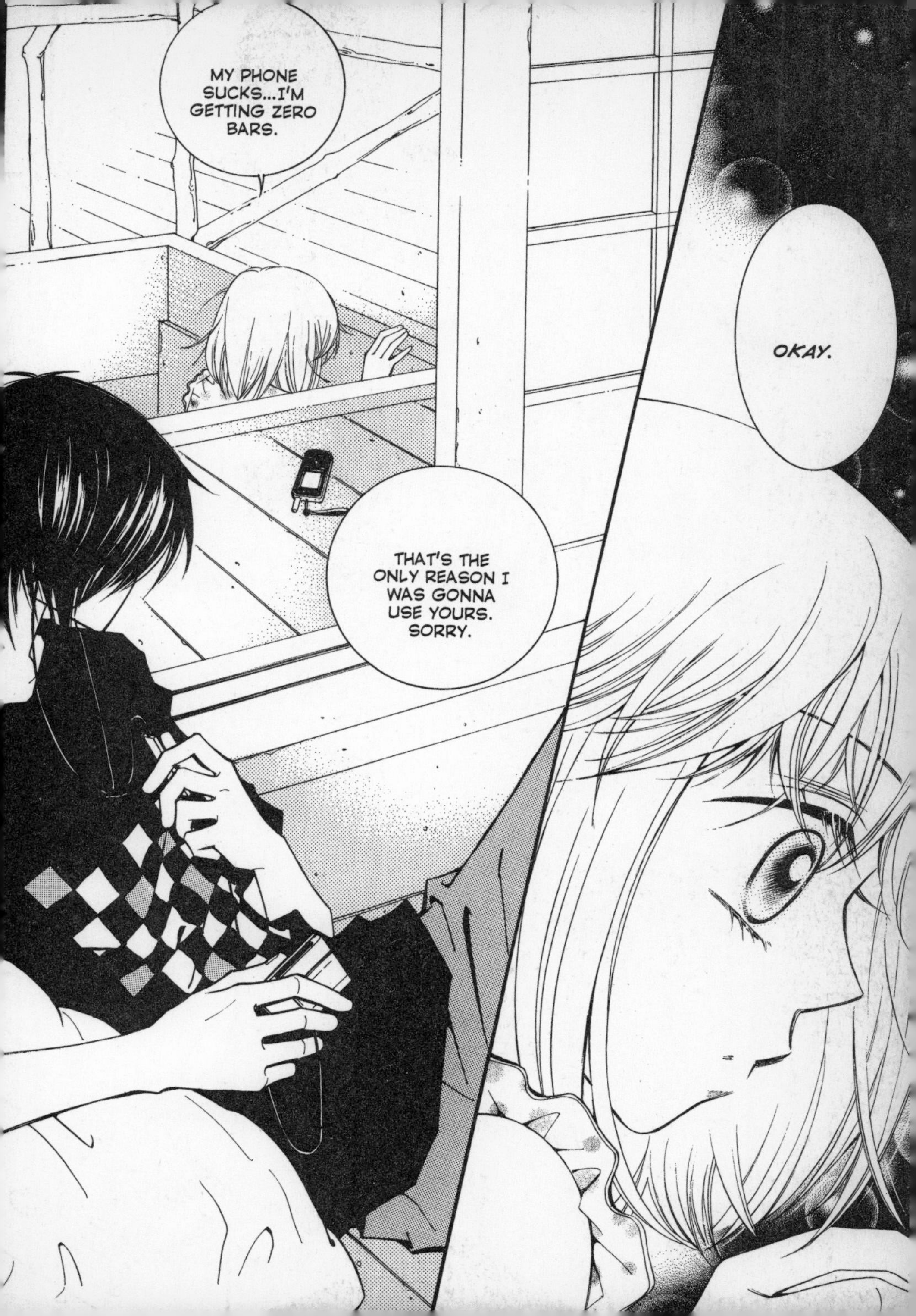
MY PHONE SUCKS...I'M GETTING ZERO BARS.
THAT'S THE ONLY REASON I WAS GONNA USE YOURS. SORRY.
OKAY.

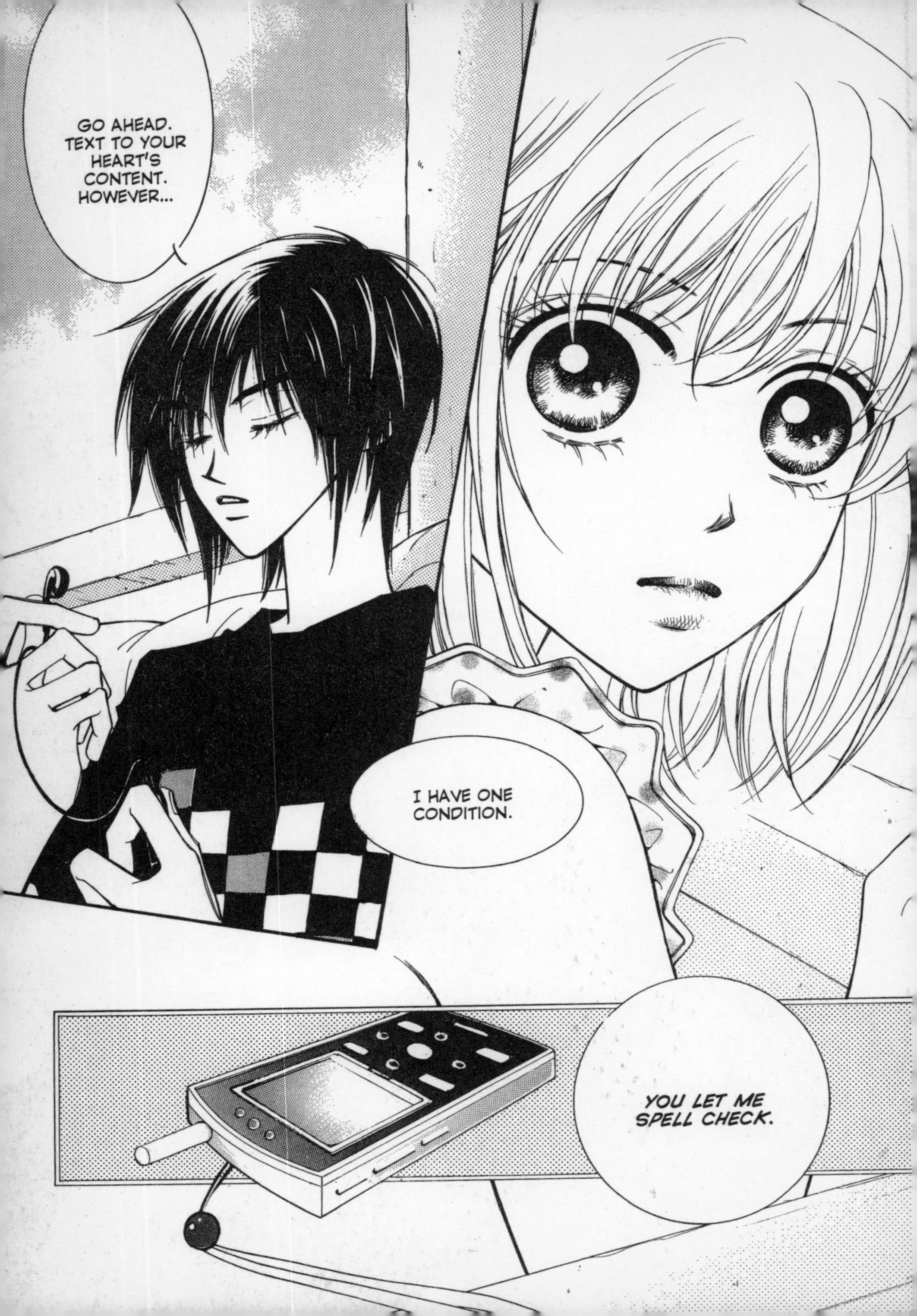
GO AHEAD. TEXT TO YOUR HEART'S CONTENT. HOWEVER...
I HAVE ONE CONDITION.
YOU LET ME SPELL CHECK.

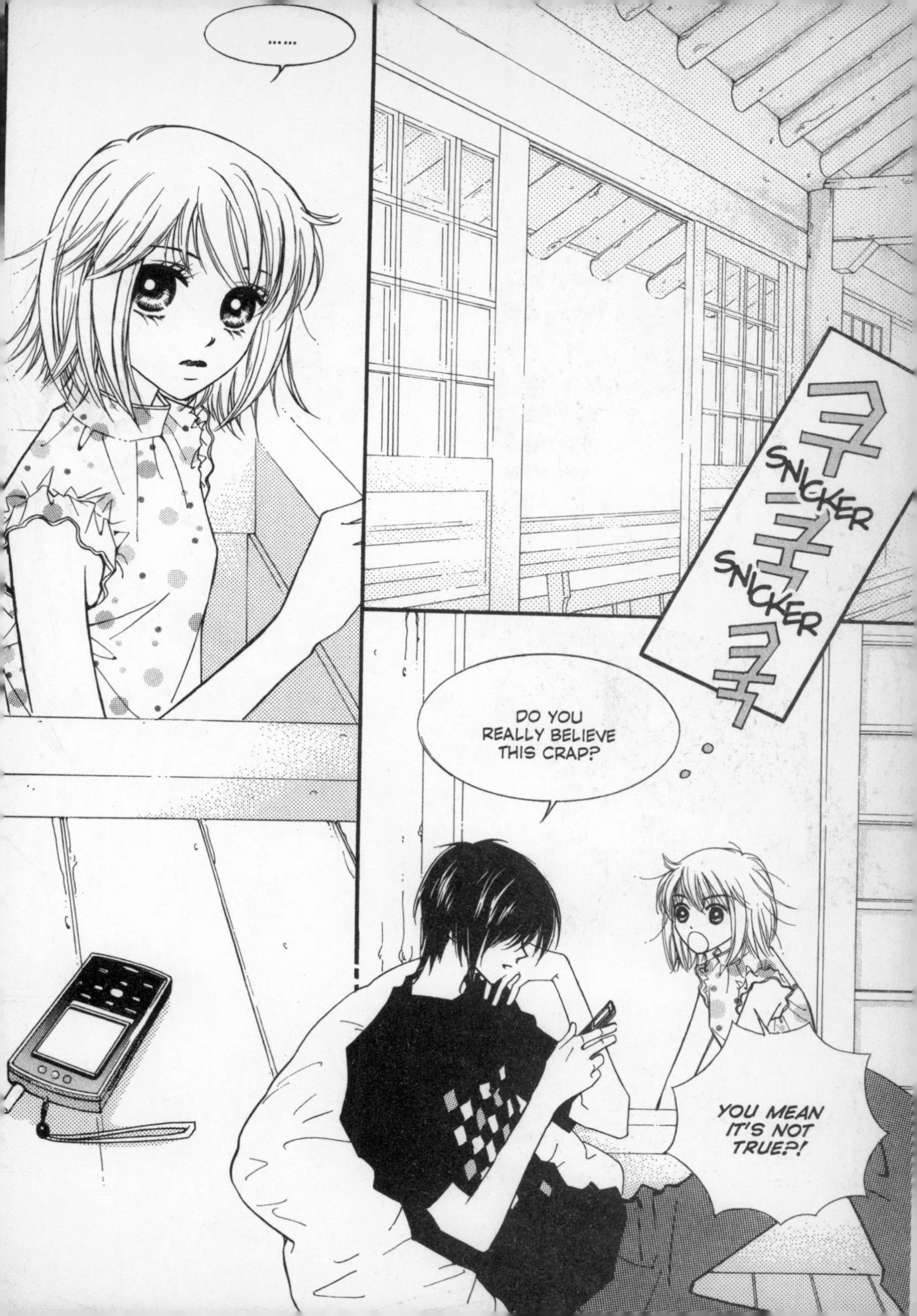

......
ㅋㅋㅋ
SNICKER SNICKER
DO YOU REALLY BELIEVE THIS CRAP?
YOU MEAN IT'S NOT TRUE?!

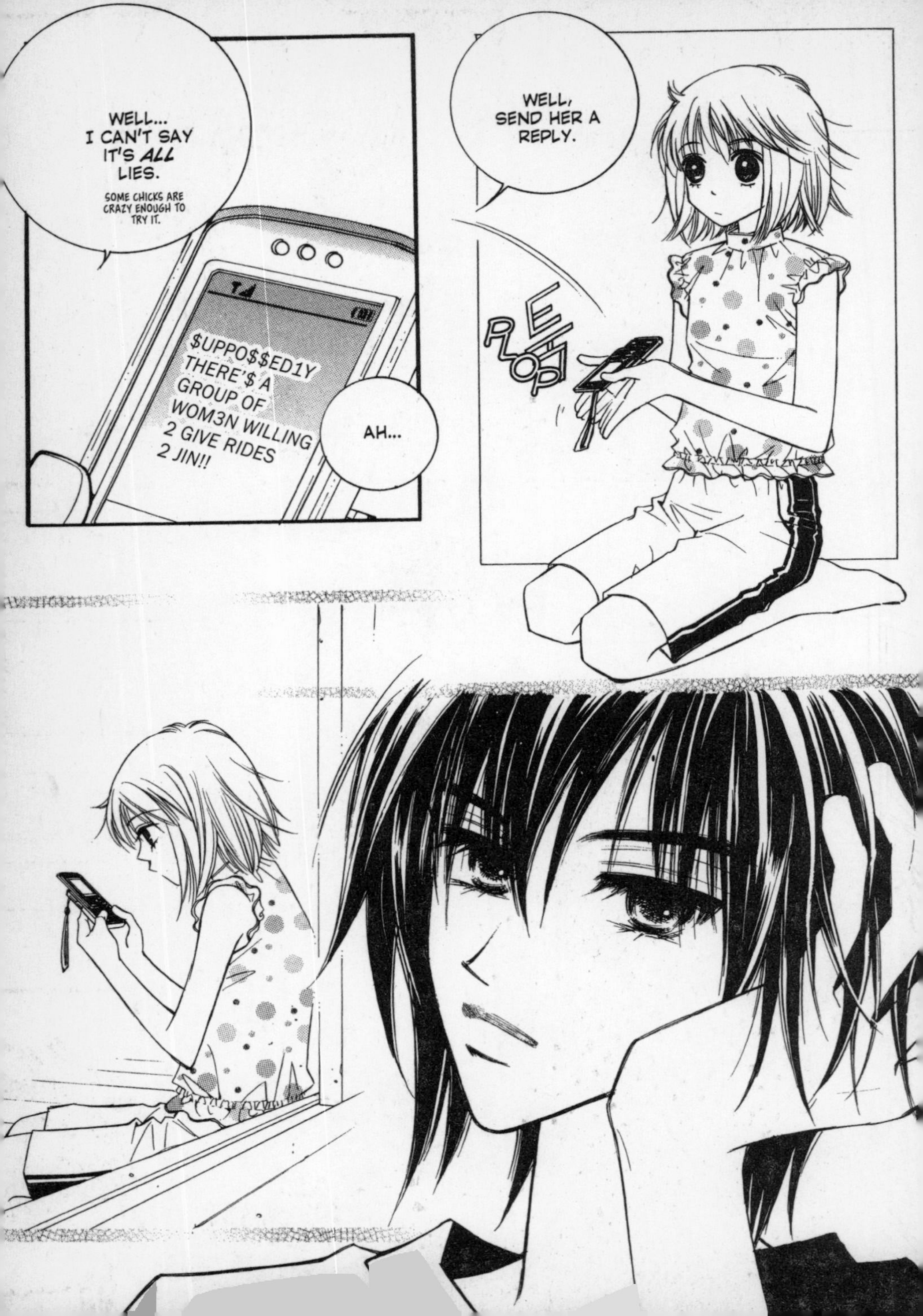
WELL... I CAN'T SAY IT'S ALL LIES.
SOME CHICKS ARE CRAZY ENOUGH TO TRY IT.
$UPPO$$ED1Y THERE'$ A GROUP OF WOM3N WILLING 2 GIVE RIDES 2 JIN!!
AH...
WELL, SEND HER A REPLY.
FLOP

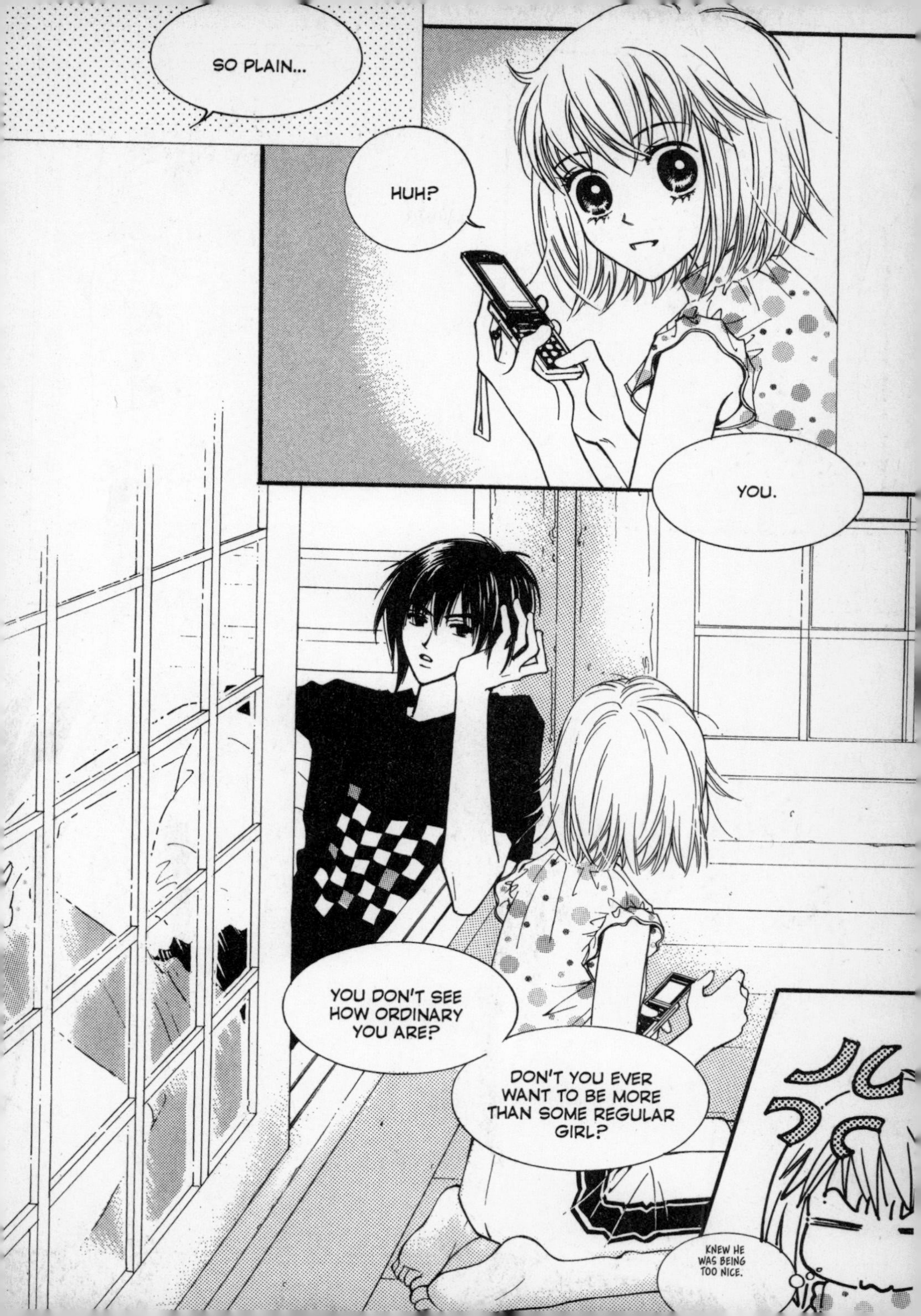
SO PLAIN...
HUH?
YOU.
YOU DON'T SEE HOW ORDINARY YOU ARE?
DON'T YOU EVER WANT TO BE MORE THAN SOME REGULAR GIRL?
KNEW HE WAS BEING TOO NICE.

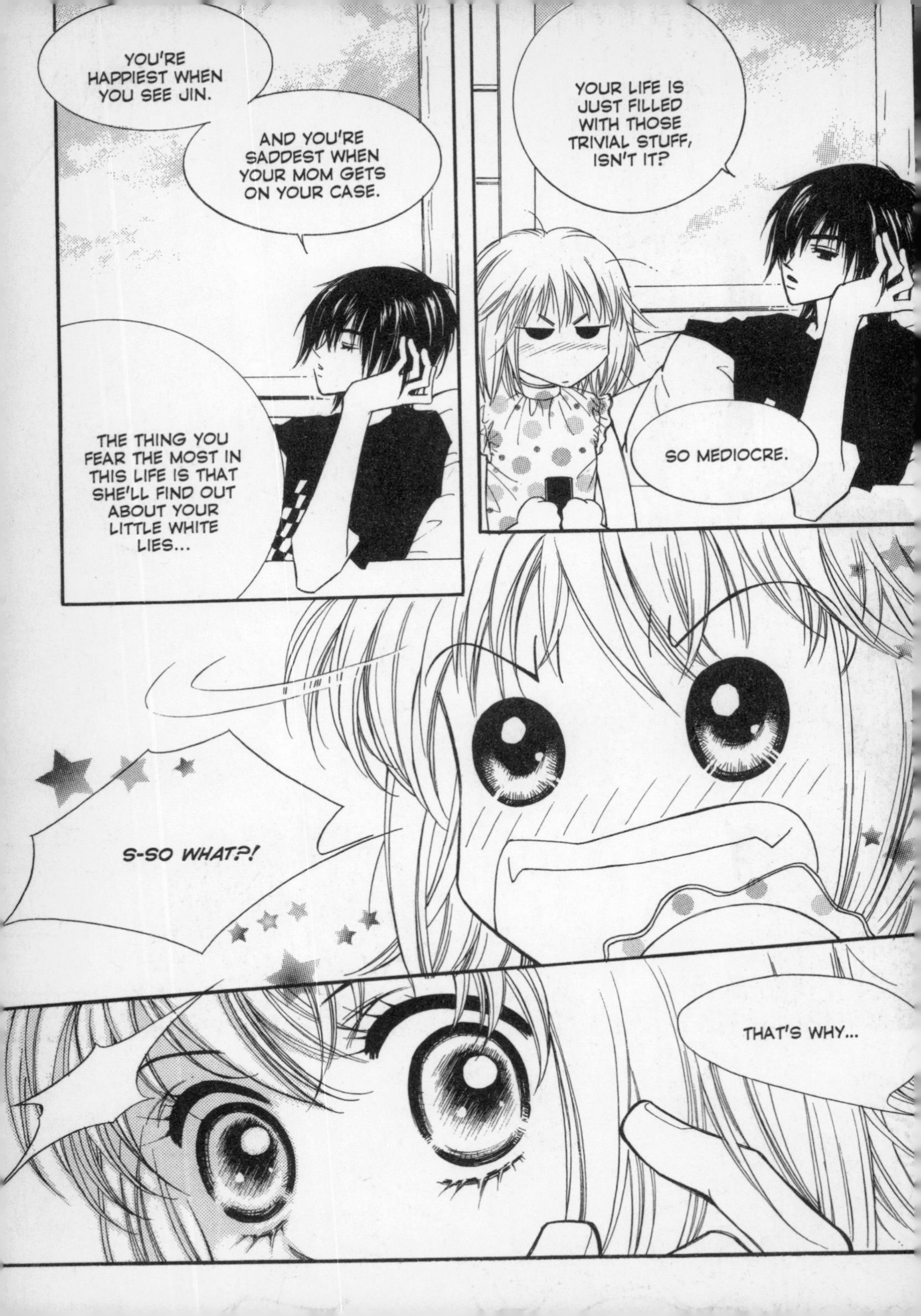
YOU'RE HAPPIEST WHEN YOU SEE JIN.
AND YOU'RE SADDEST WHEN YOUR MOM GETS ON YOUR CASE.
THE THING YOU FEAR THE MOST IN THIS LIFE IS THAT SHE'LL FIND OUT ABOUT YOUR LITTLE WHITE LIES...
YOUR LIFE IS JUST FILLED WITH THOSE TRIVIAL STUFF, ISN'T IT?
SO MEDIOCRE.
S-SO WHAT?!
THAT'S WHY...

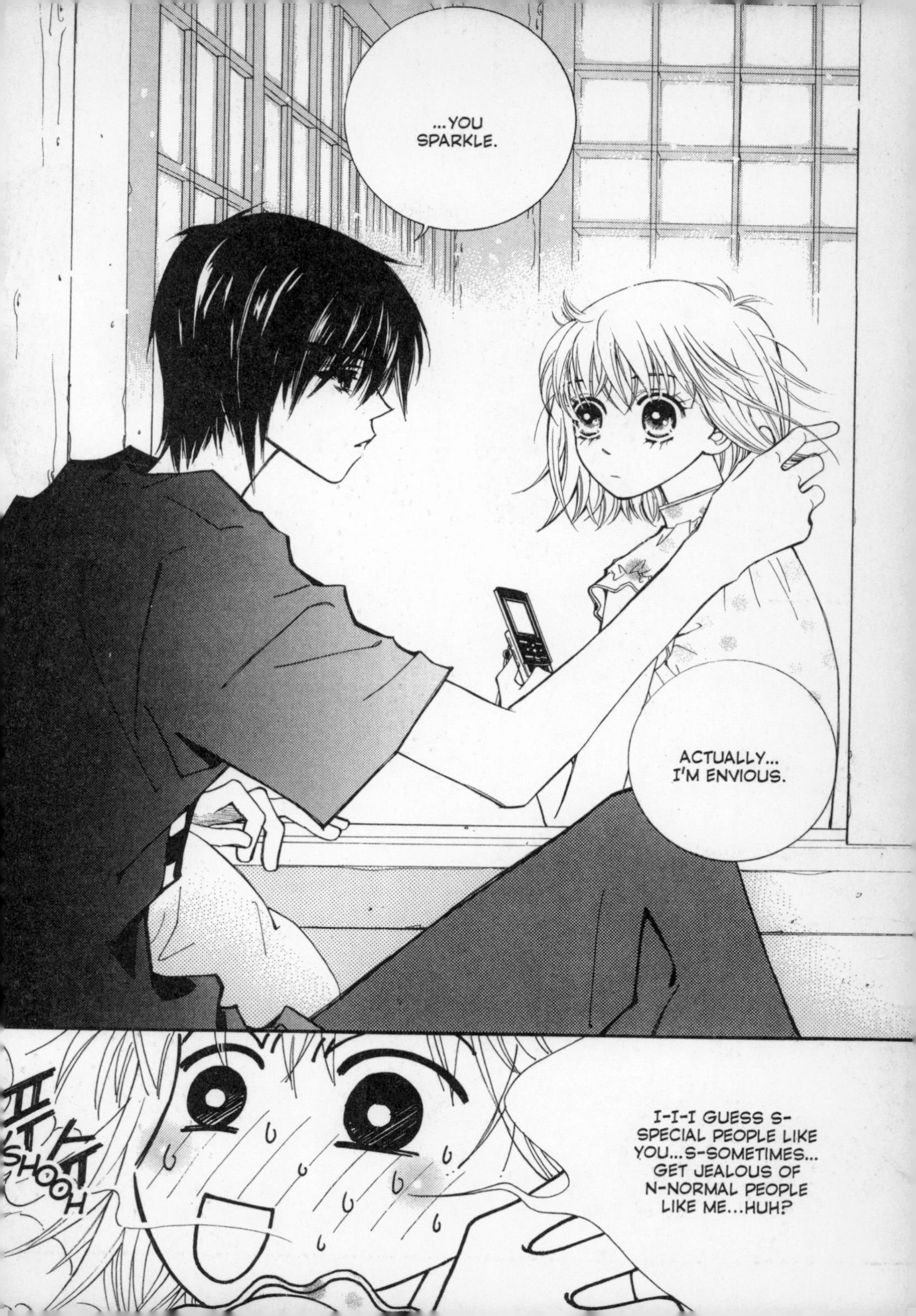
...YOU SPARKLE.
ACTUALLY... I'M ENVIOUS.
SHOOH
I-I-I GUESS S-SPECIAL PEOPLE LIKE YOU...S-SOMETIMES... GET JEALOUS OF N-NORMAL PEOPLE LIKE ME...HUH?

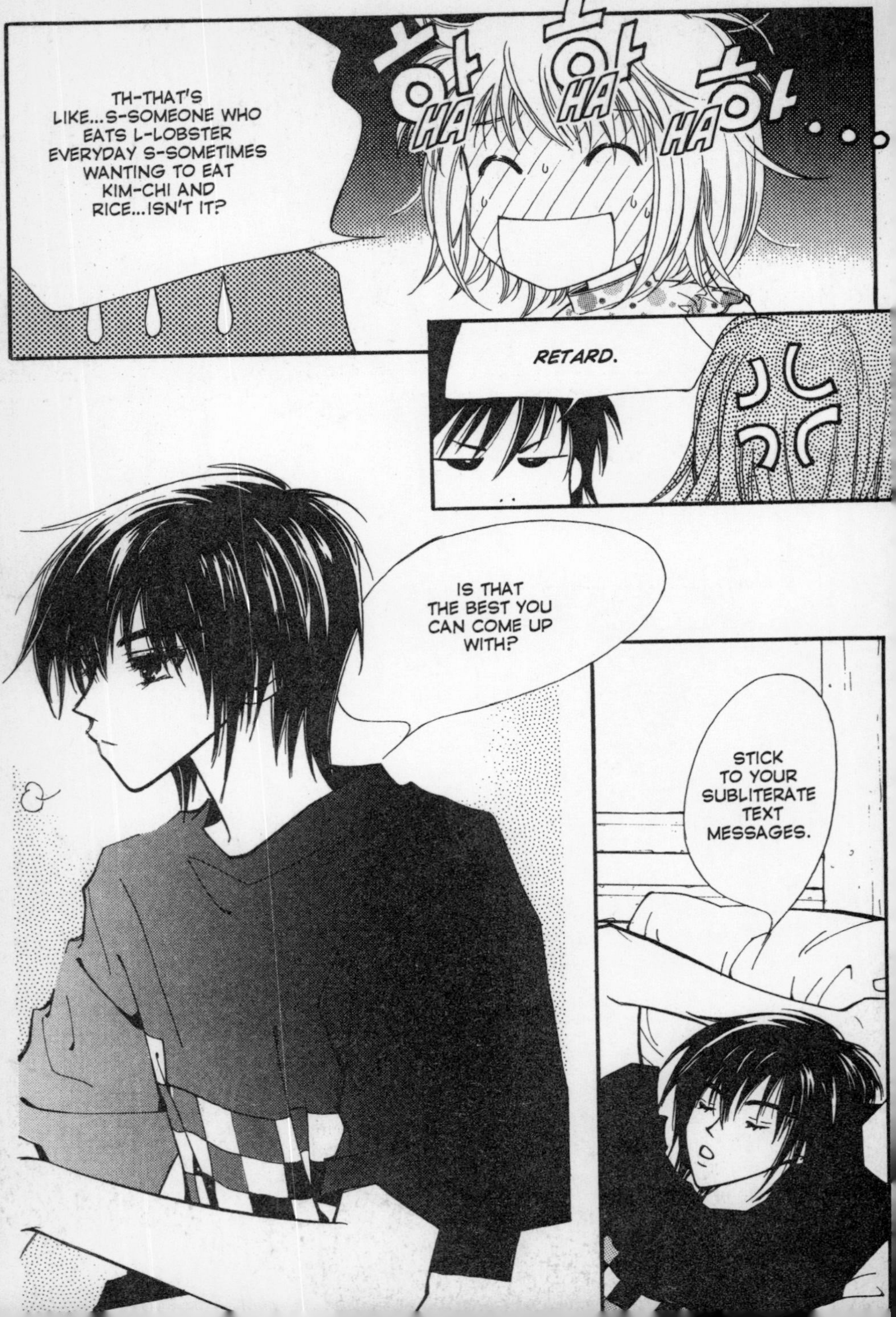

TH-THAT'S LIKE...S-SOMEONE WHO EATS L-LOBSTER EVERYDAY S-SOMETIMES WANTING TO EAT KIM-CHI AND RICE...ISN'T IT?
하 HA
하 HA
하 HA...
RETARD.
IS THAT THE BEST YOU CAN COME UP WITH?
STICK TO YOUR SUBLITERATE TEXT MESSAGES.

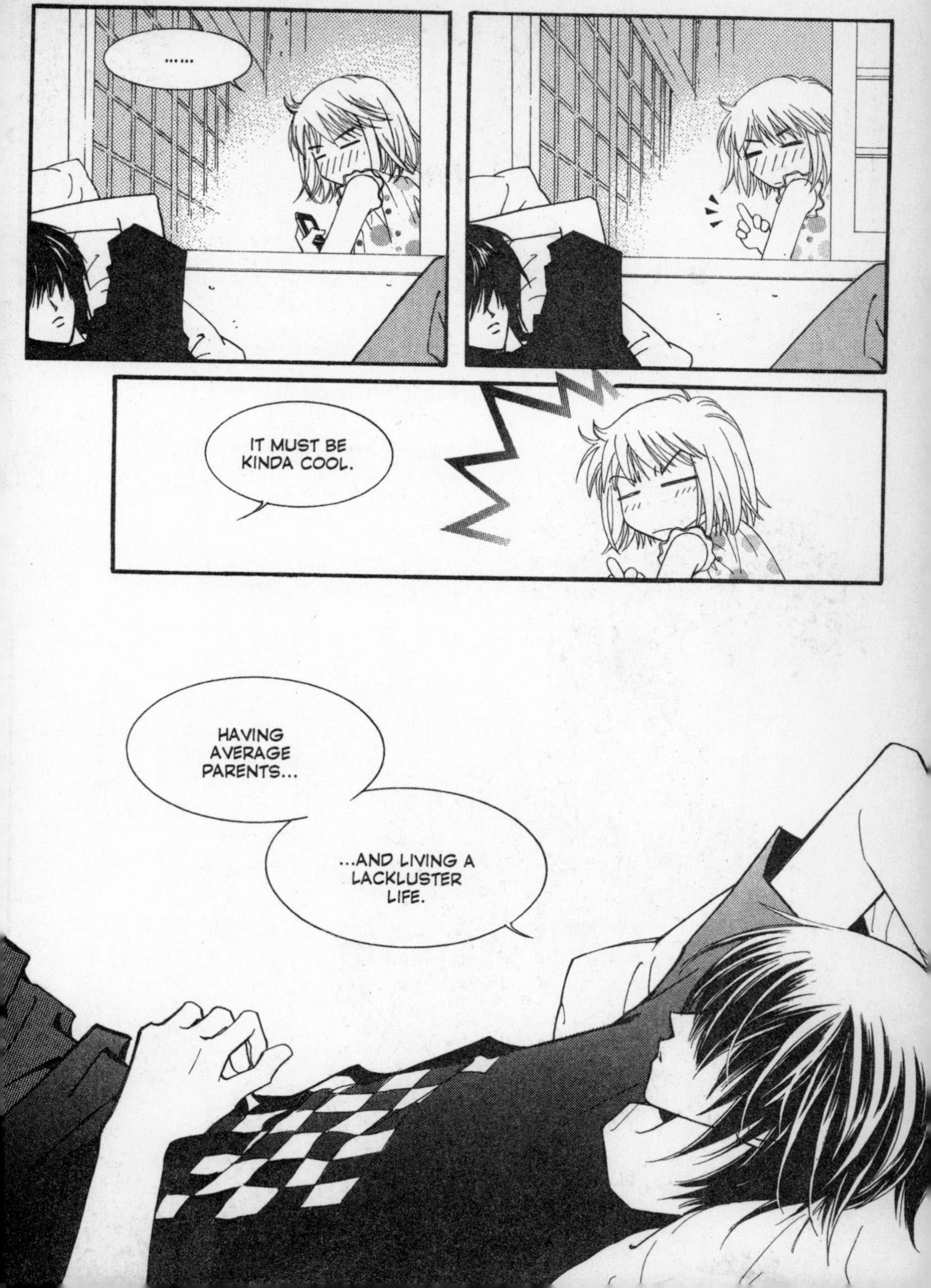
……
IT MUST BE KINDA COOL.
HAVING AVERAGE PARENTS...
...AND LIVING A LACKLUSTER LIFE.

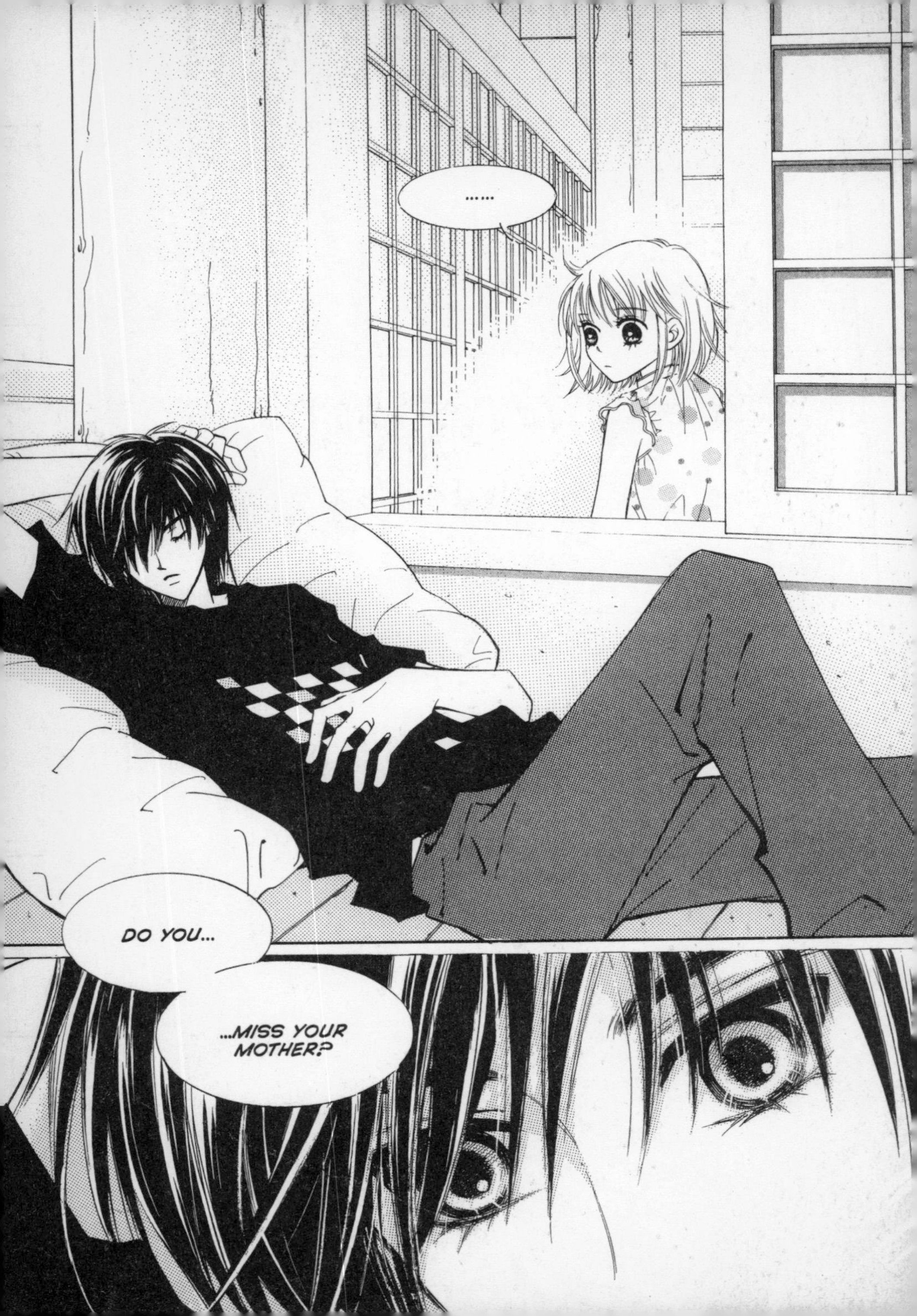
……
DO YOU...
...MISS YOUR MOTHER?

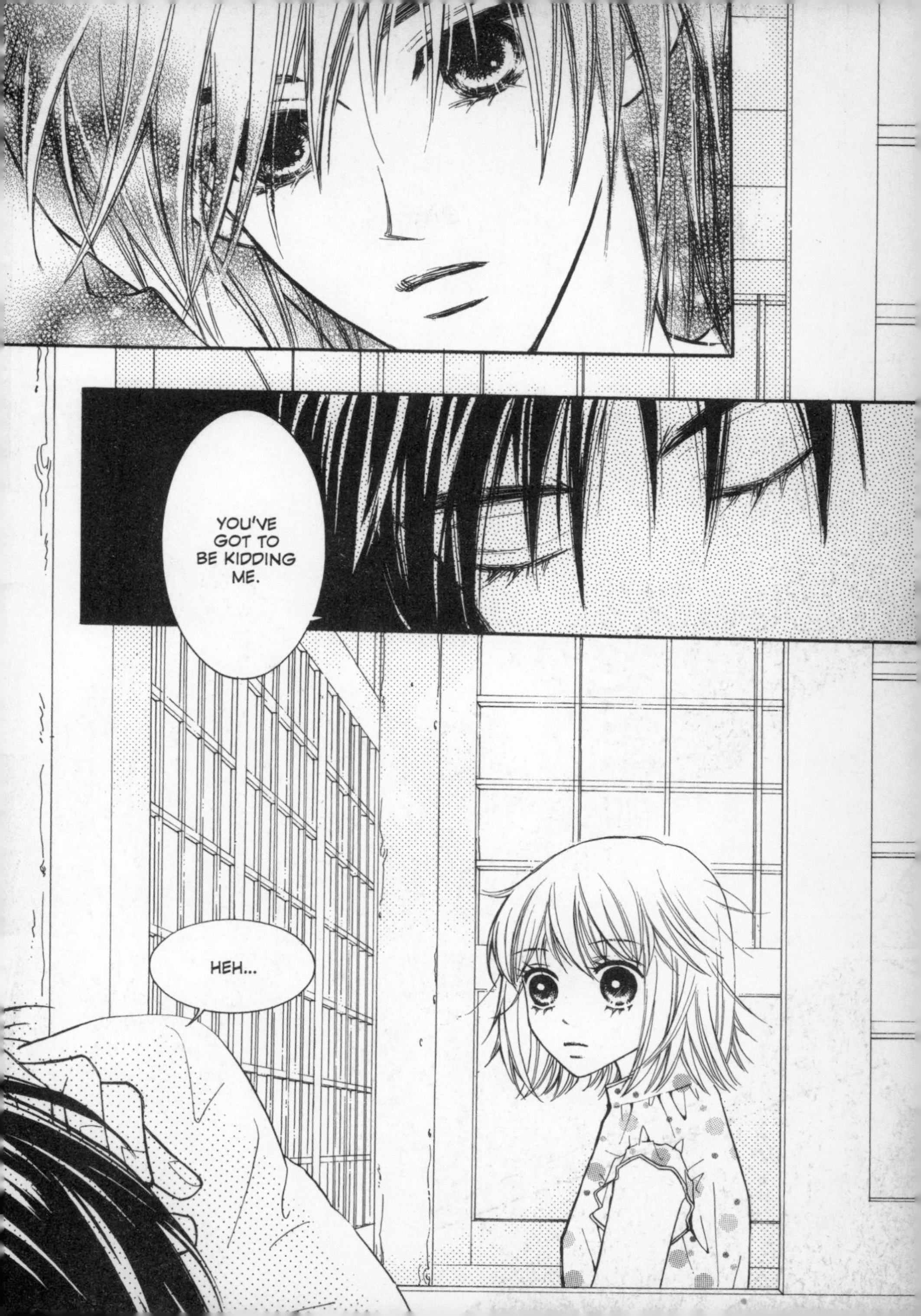
YOU'VE GOT TO BE KIDDING ME.
HEH...

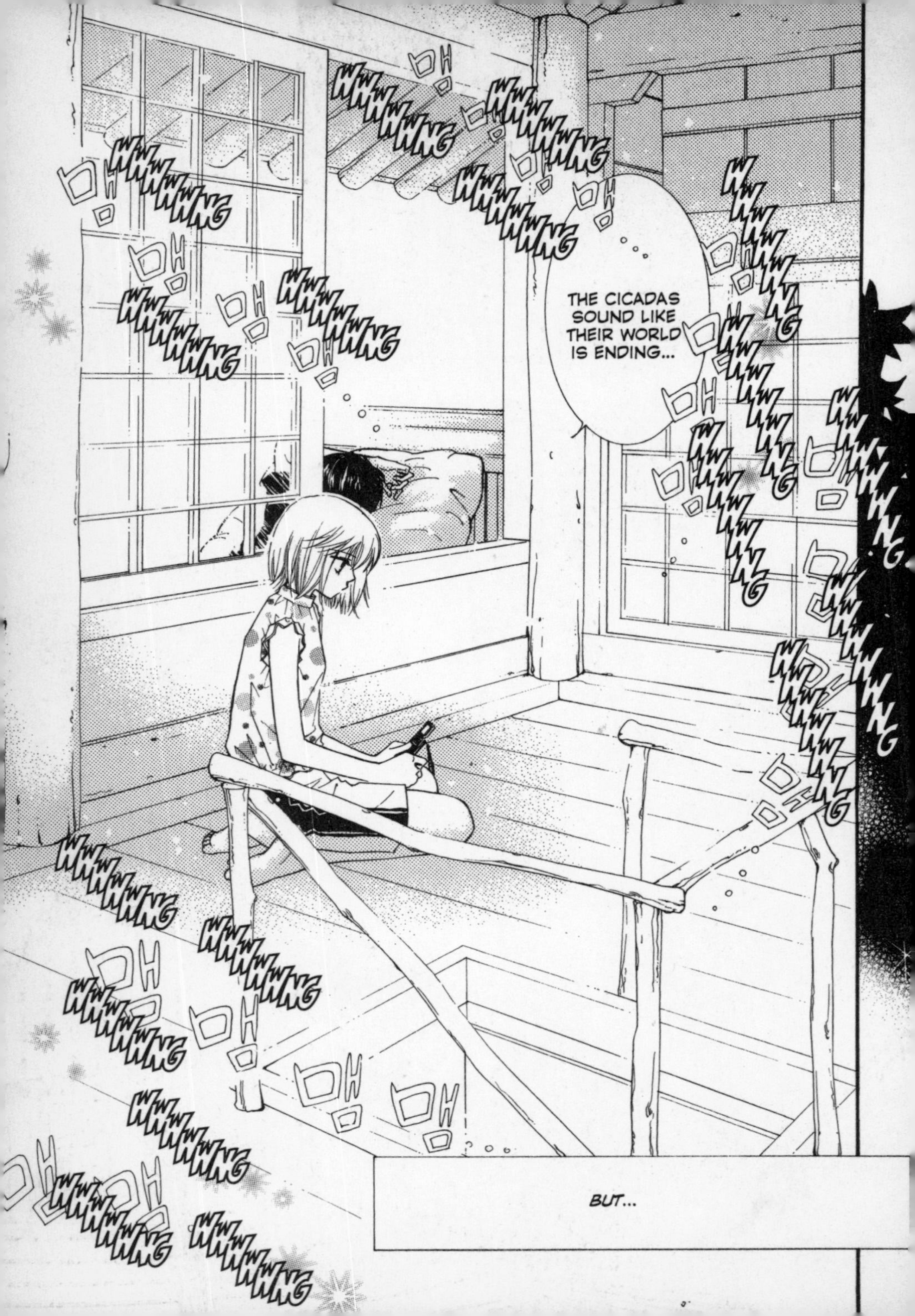
THE CICADAS SOUND LIKE THEIR WORLD IS ENDING...
BUT...

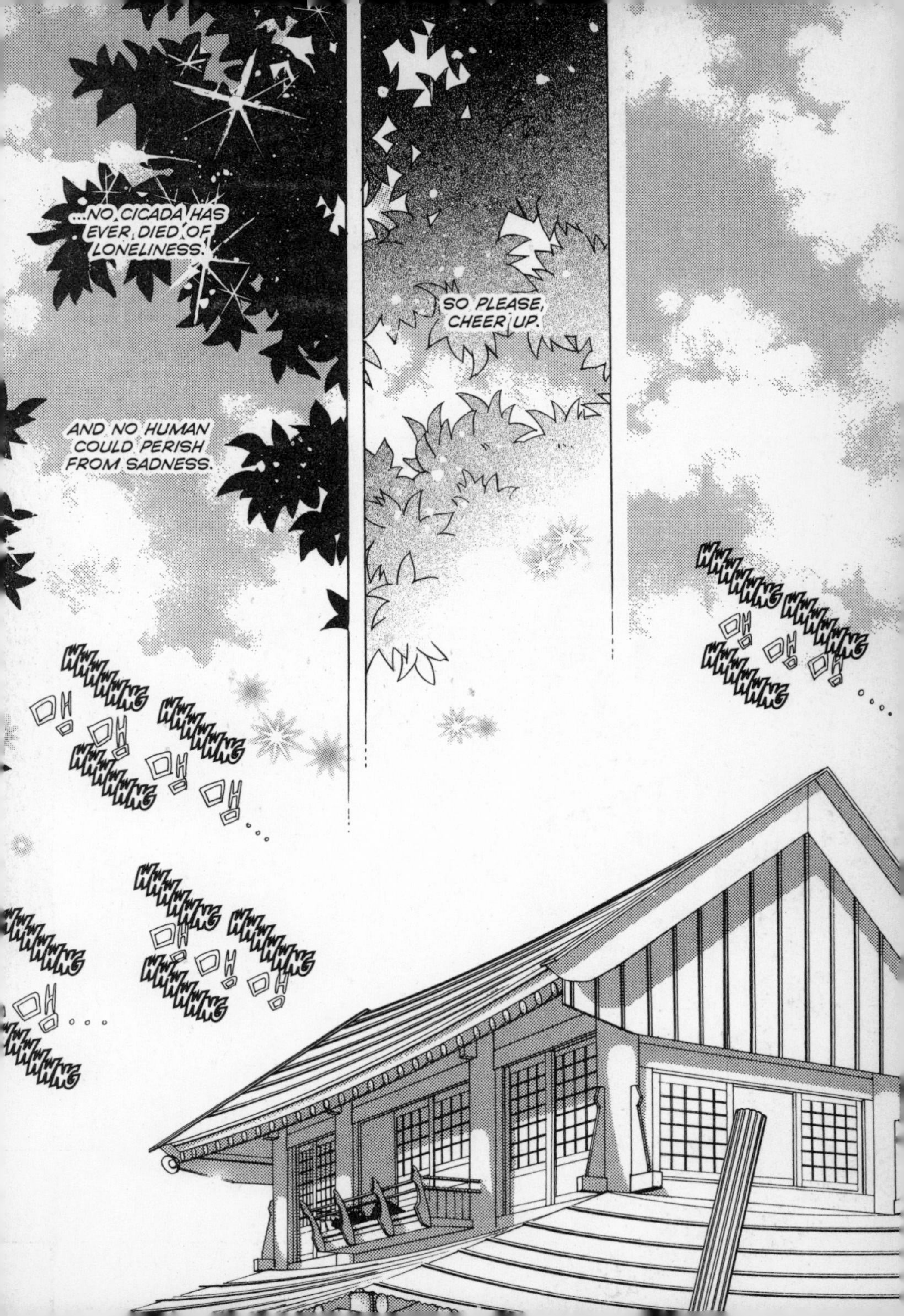
...NO CICADA HAS EVER DIED OF LONELINESS.
AND NO HUMAN COULD PERISH FROM SADNESS.
SO PLEASE, CHEER UP.
WHWHWHNG WHWHWHNG WHWHWHNG
OH! OH! OH!...
WHWHWHNG WHWHWHNG WHWHWHNG
OH! OH! OH!...
WHWHWHNG WHWHWHNG WHWHWHNG WHWHWHNG
OH! OH! OH!...

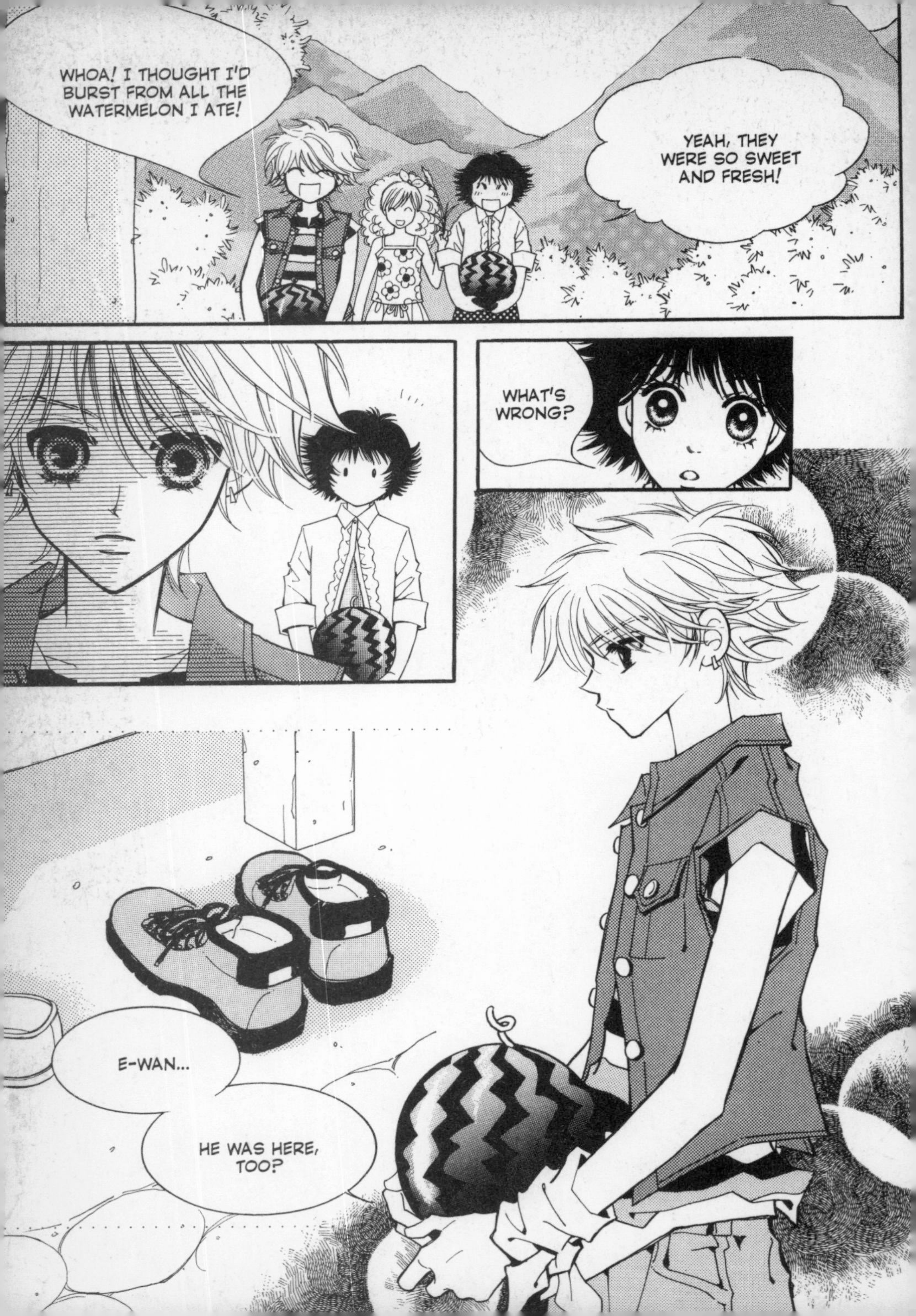
WHOA! I THOUGHT I'D BURST FROM ALL THE WATERMELON I ATE!
YEAH, THEY WERE SO SWEET AND FRESH!
WHAT'S WRONG?
E-WAN...
HE WAS HERE, TOO?

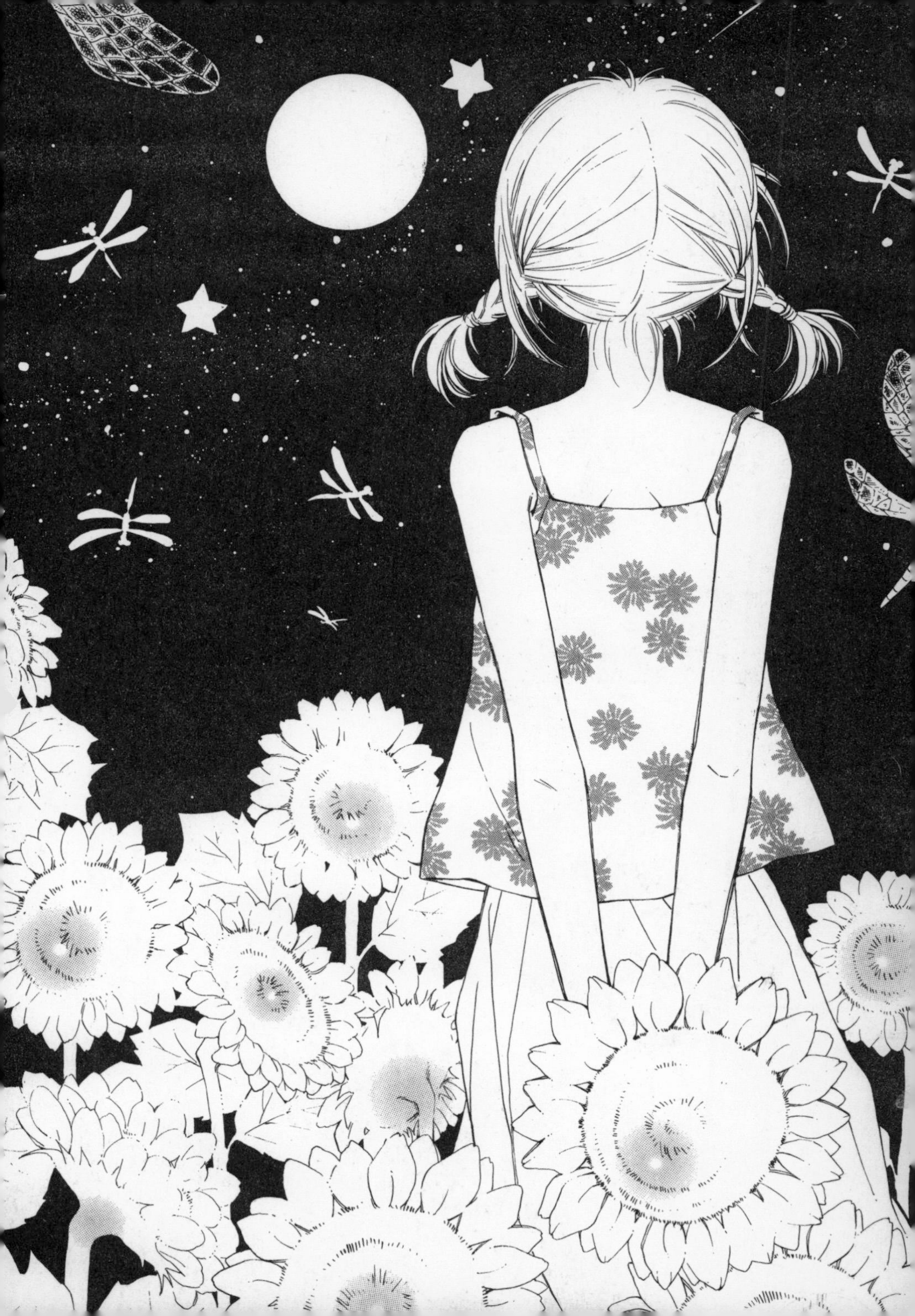

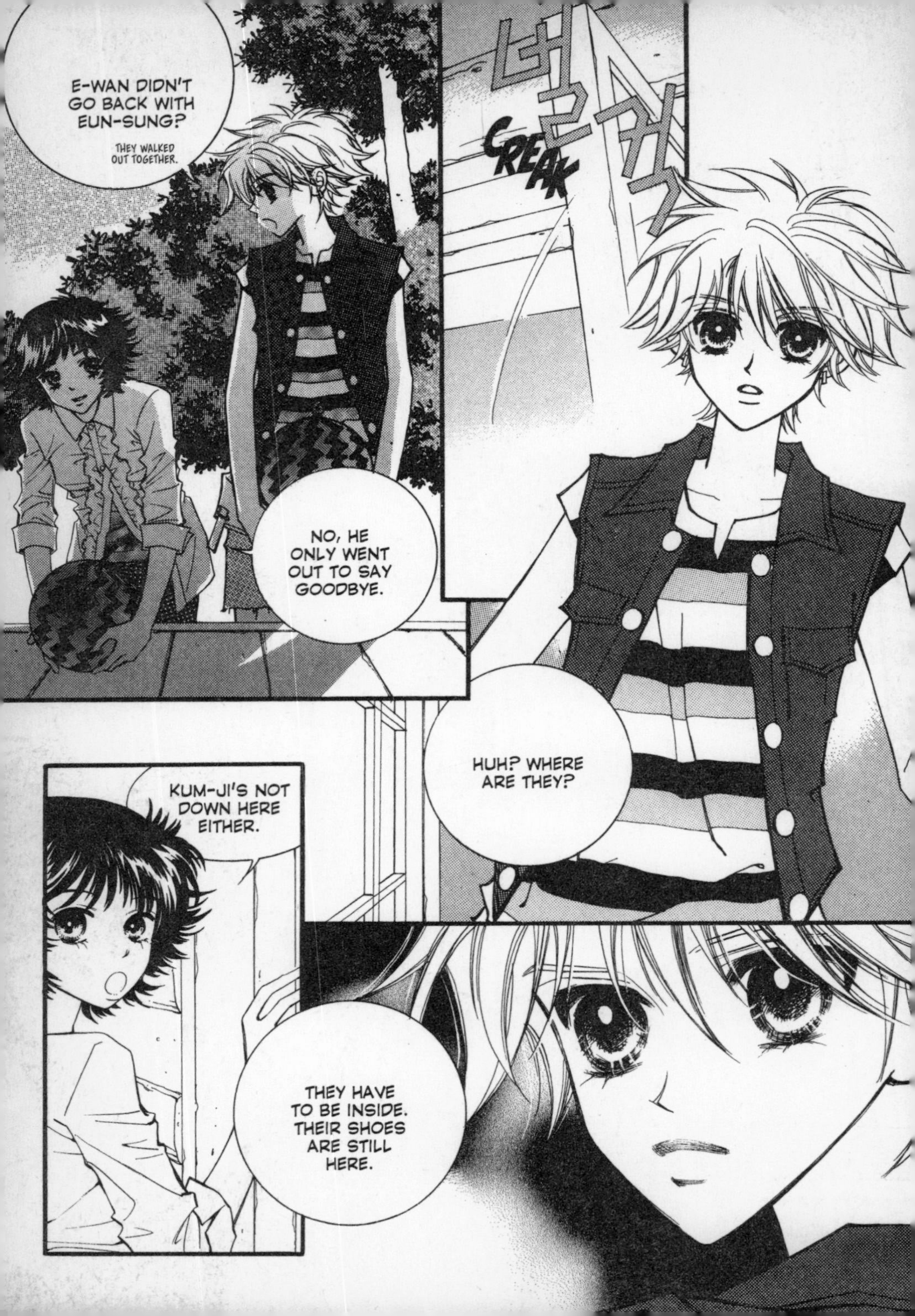
E-WAN DIDN'T GO BACK WITH EUN-SUNG?
THEY WALKED OUT TOGETHER.
NO, HE ONLY WENT OUT TO SAY GOODBYE.
CREAK
HUH? WHERE ARE THEY?
KUM-JI'S NOT DOWN HERE EITHER.
THEY HAVE TO BE INSIDE. THEIR SHOES ARE STILL HERE.

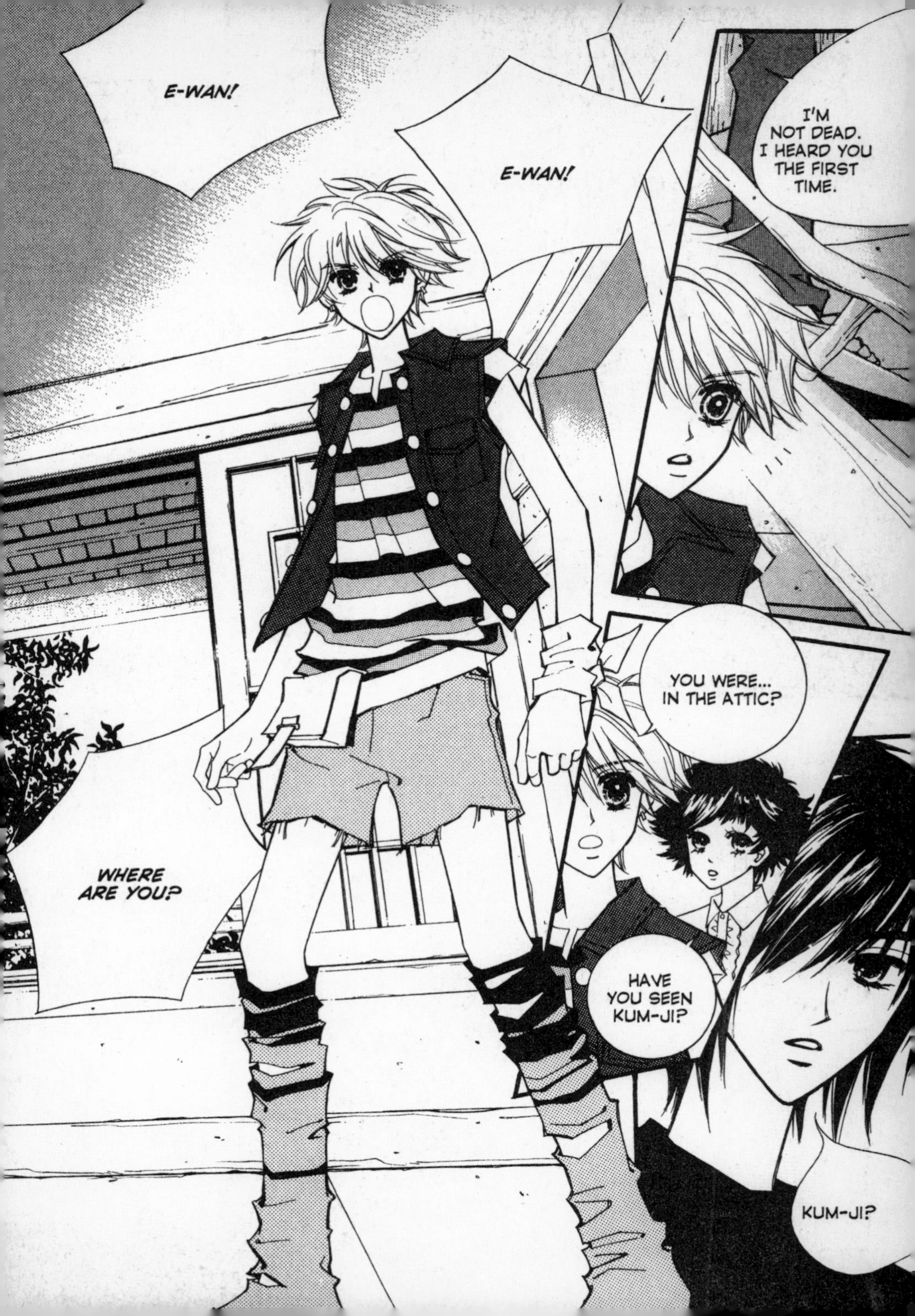
E-WAN!
E-WAN!
WHERE ARE YOU?
I'M NOT DEAD. I HEARD YOU THE FIRST TIME.
YOU WERE... IN THE ATTIC?
HAVE YOU SEEN KUM-JI?
KUM-JI?

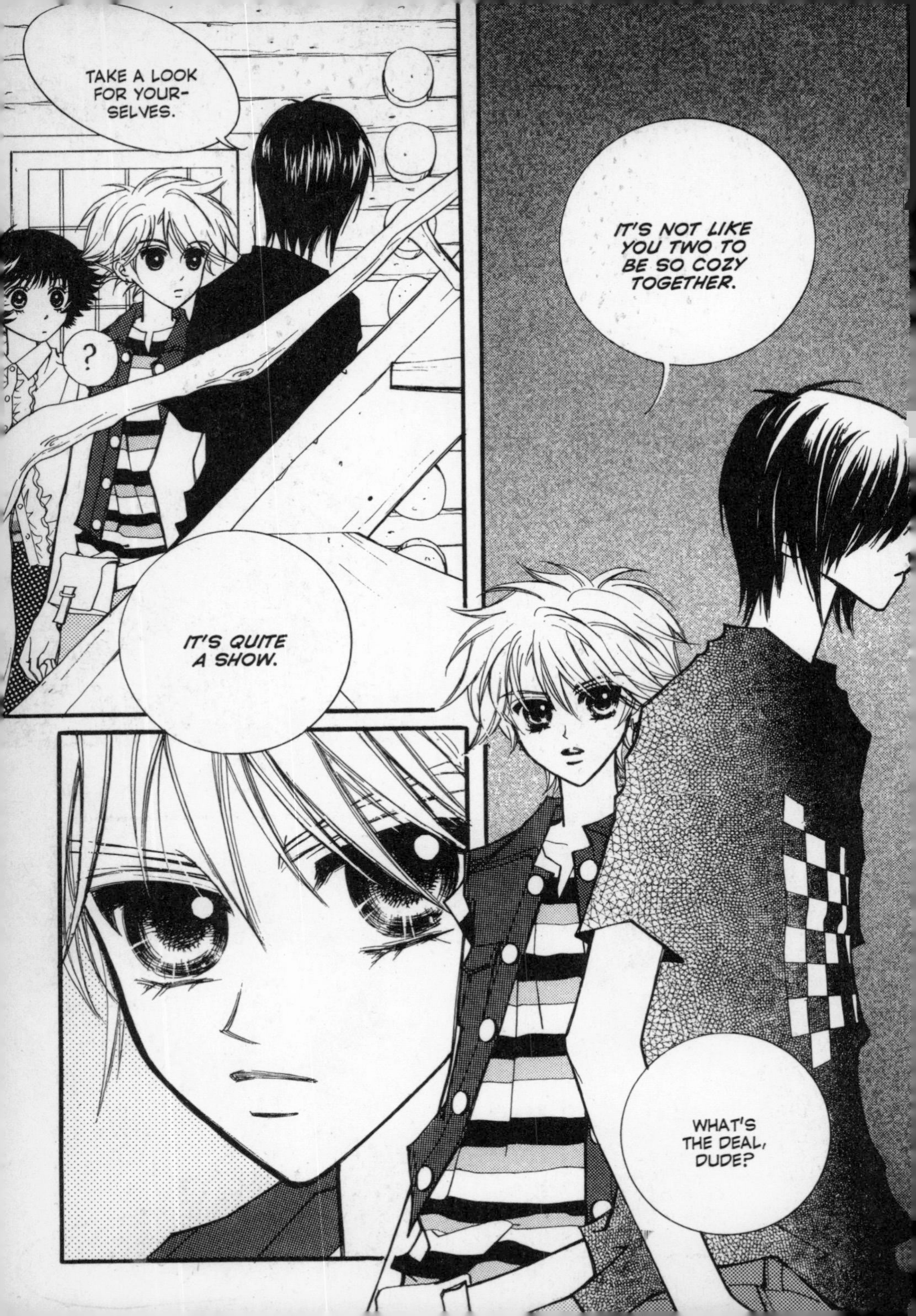
TAKE A LOOK FOR YOUR-SELVES.
?
IT'S QUITE A SHOW.
IT'S NOT LIKE YOU TWO TO BE SO COZY TOGETHER.
WHAT'S THE DEAL, DUDE?

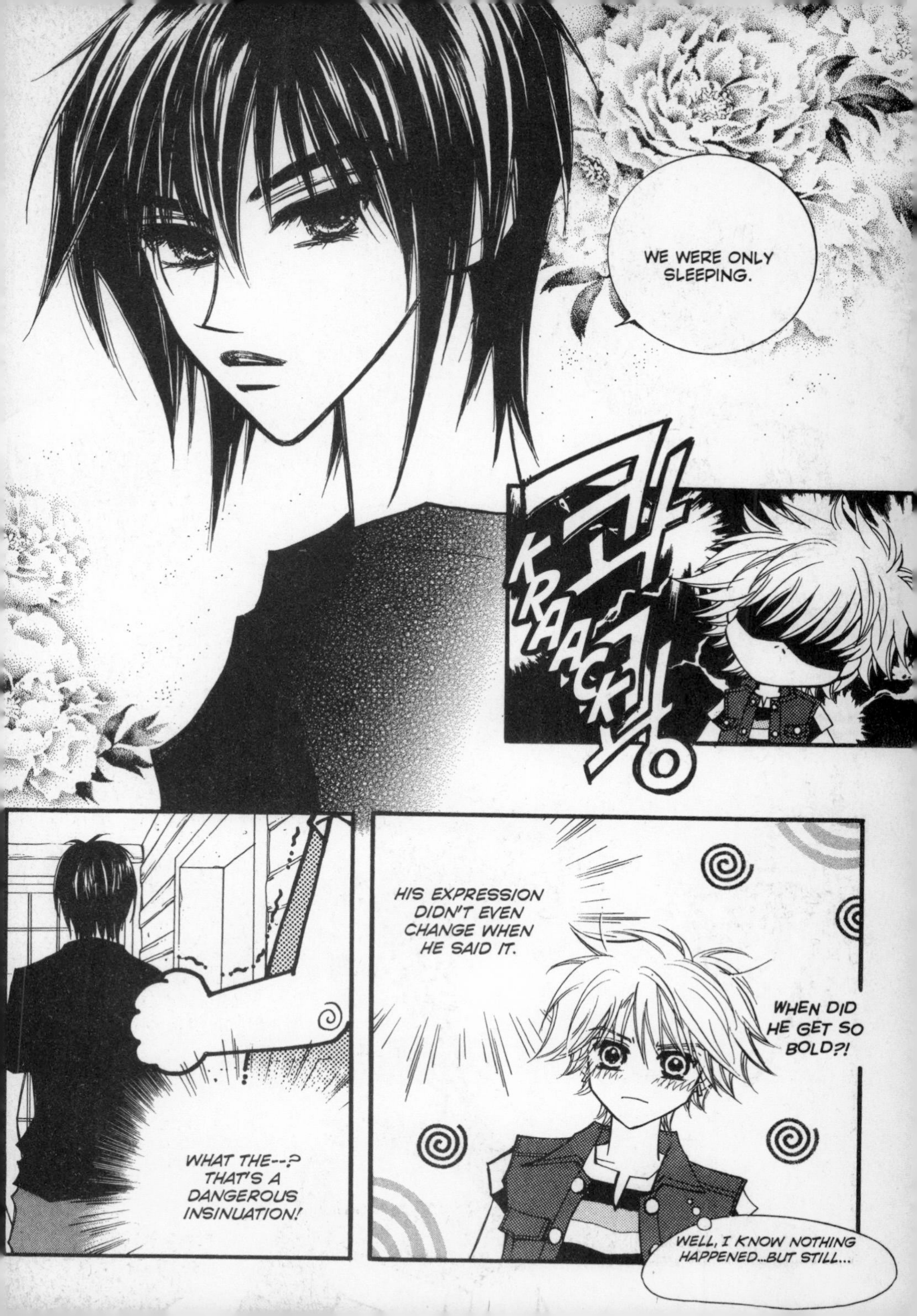
WE WERE ONLY SLEEPING.
KRAACK!
WHAT THE--? THAT'S A DANGEROUS INSINUATION!
HIS EXPRESSION DIDN'T EVEN CHANGE WHEN HE SAID IT.
WHEN DID HE GET SO BOLD?!
WELL, I KNOW NOTHING HAPPENED...BUT STILL...

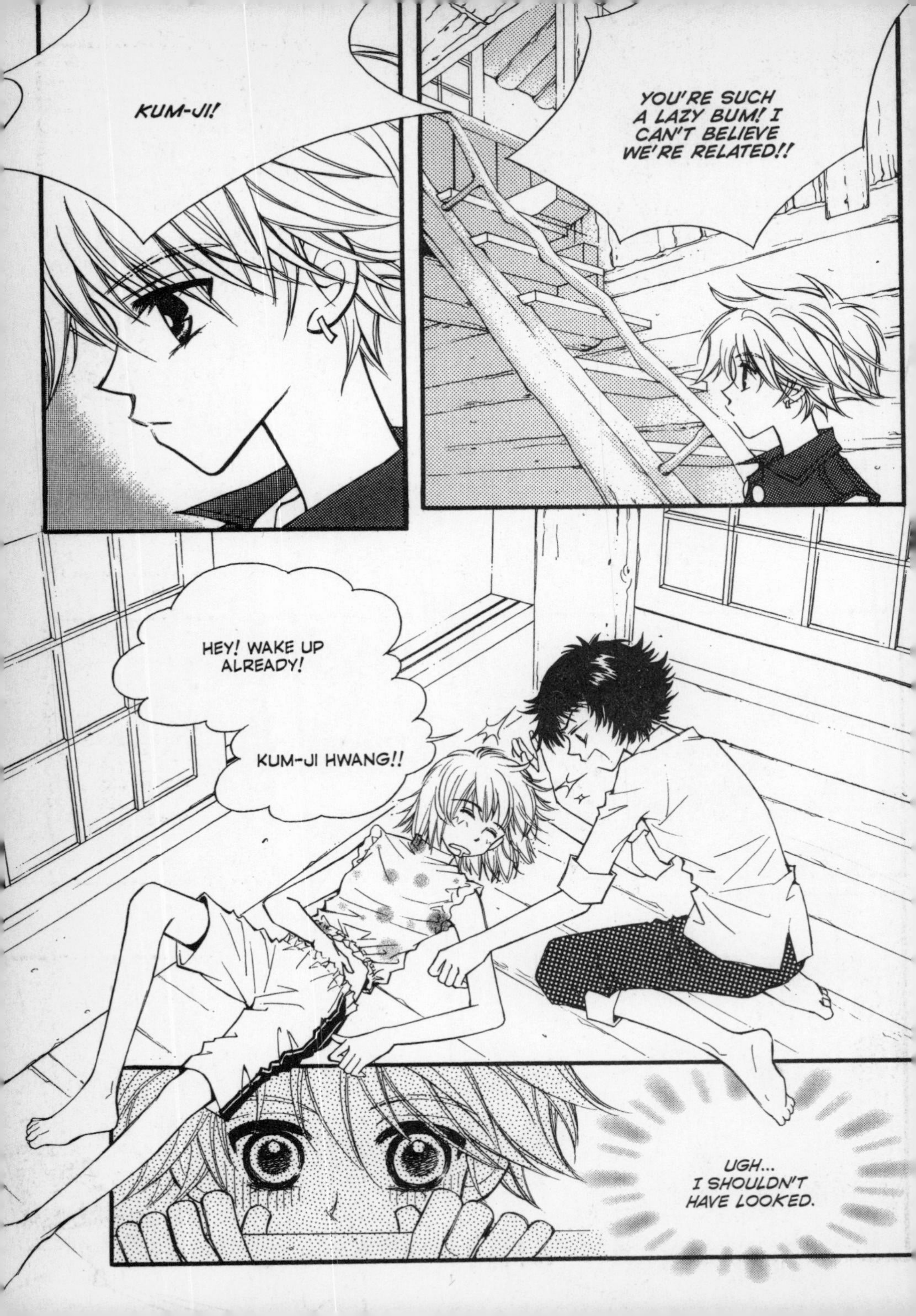
KUM-JI!
YOU'RE SUCH A LAZY BUM! I CAN'T BELIEVE WE'RE RELATED!!
HEY! WAKE UP ALREADY!
KUM-JI HWANG!!
UGH... I SHOULDN'T HAVE LOOKED.

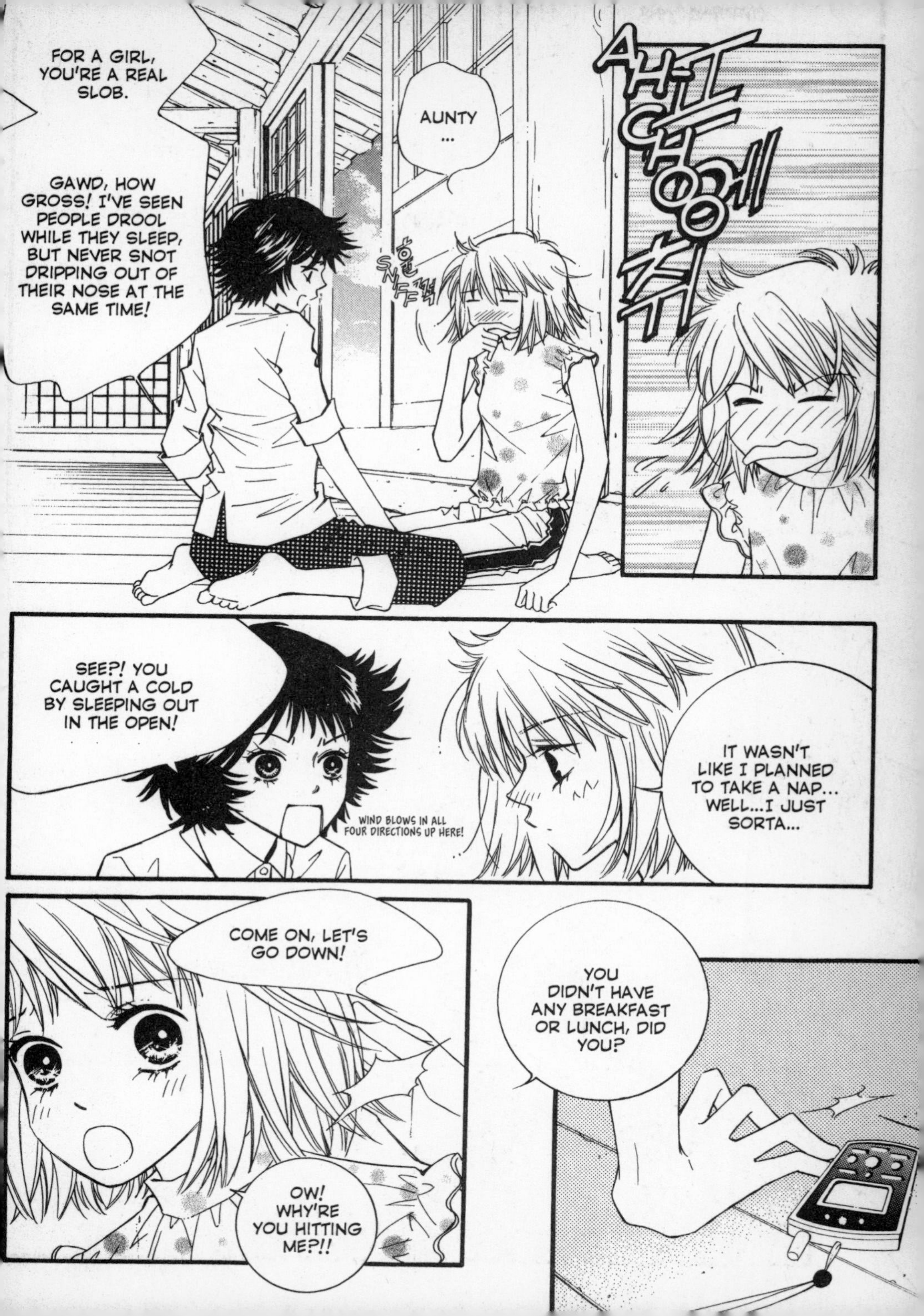
FOR A GIRL, YOU'RE A REAL SLOB.
AUNTY ...
GAWD, HOW GROSS! I'VE SEEN PEOPLE DROOL WHILE THEY SLEEP, BUT NEVER SNOT DRIPPING OUT OF THEIR NOSE AT THE SAME TIME!
SNIFF
AH-I CHOO!!
SEE?! YOU CAUGHT A COLD BY SLEEPING OUT IN THE OPEN!
WIND BLOWS IN ALL FOUR DIRECTIONS UP HERE!
IT WASN'T LIKE I PLANNED TO TAKE A NAP... WELL...I JUST SORTA...
COME ON, LET'S GO DOWN!
OW! WHY'RE YOU HITTING ME?!!
YOU DIDN'T HAVE ANY BREAKFAST OR LUNCH, DID YOU?

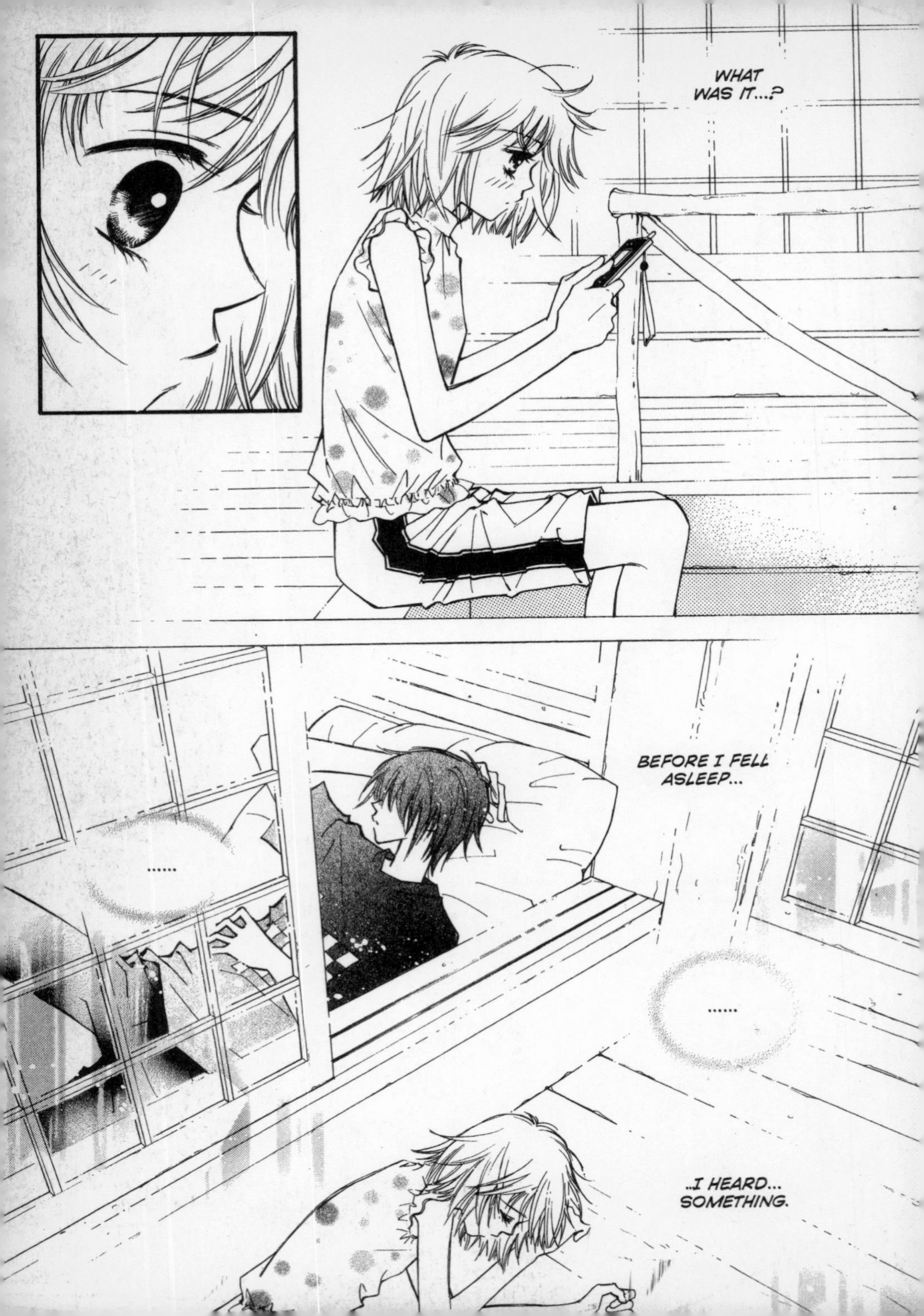
WHAT WAS IT...?
......
BEFORE I FELL ASLEEP...
......
...I HEARD... SOMETHING.

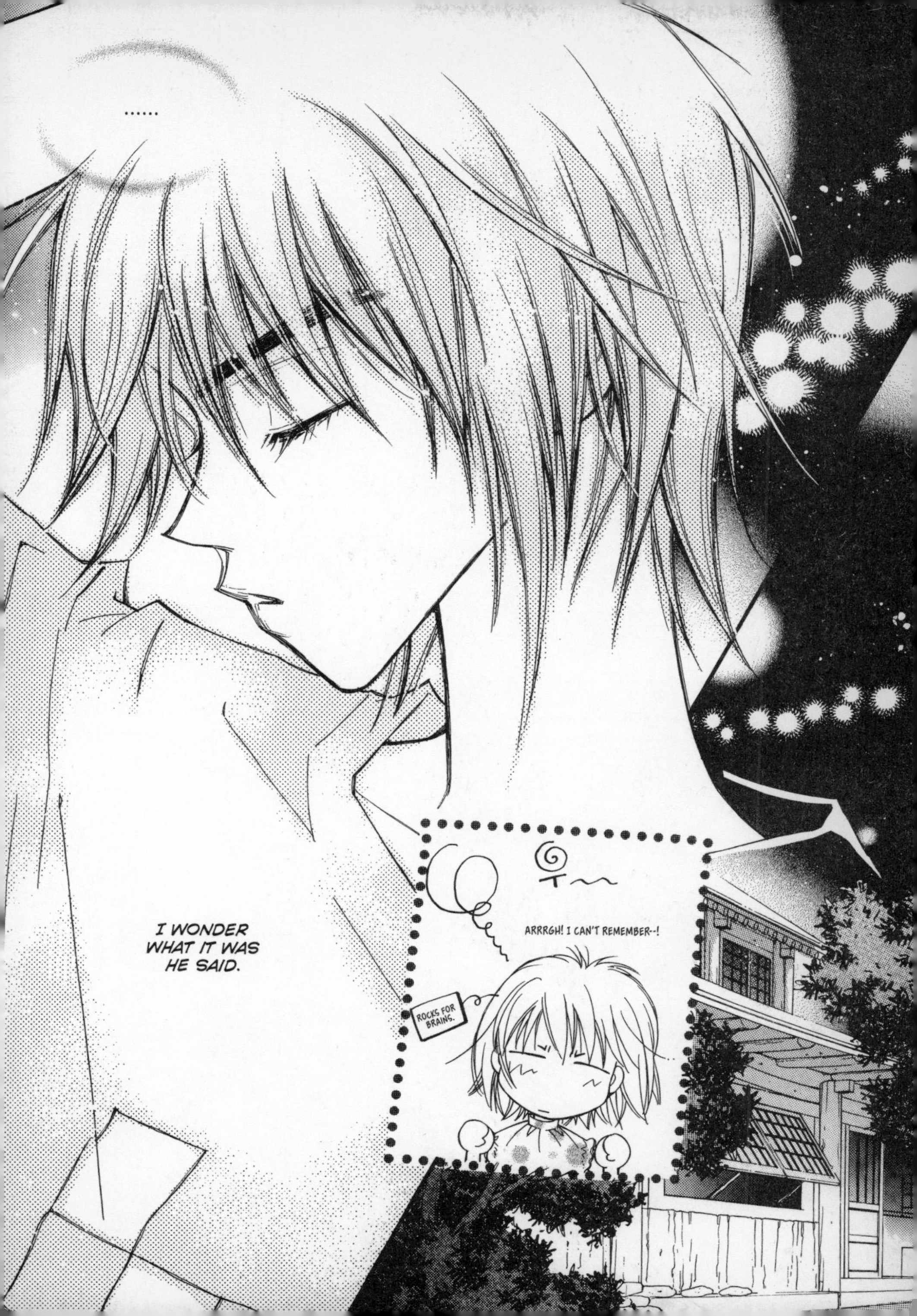
......
I WONDER WHAT IT WAS HE SAID.
ARRRGH! I CAN'T REMEMBER--!
ROCKS FOR BRAINS.

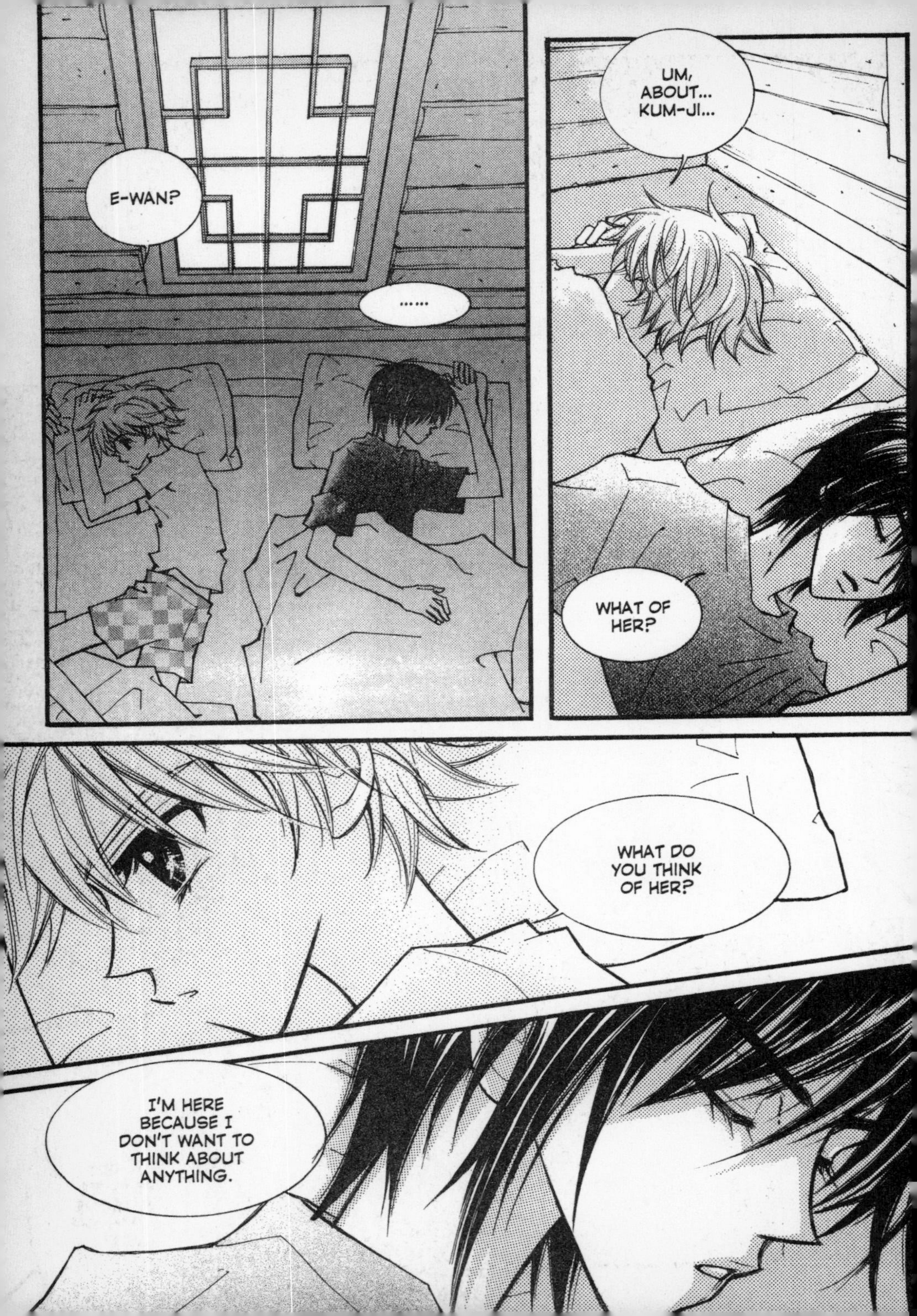
E-WAN?
......
UM, ABOUT... KUM-JI...
WHAT OF HER?
WHAT DO YOU THINK OF HER?
I'M HERE BECAUSE I DON'T WANT TO THINK ABOUT ANYTHING.

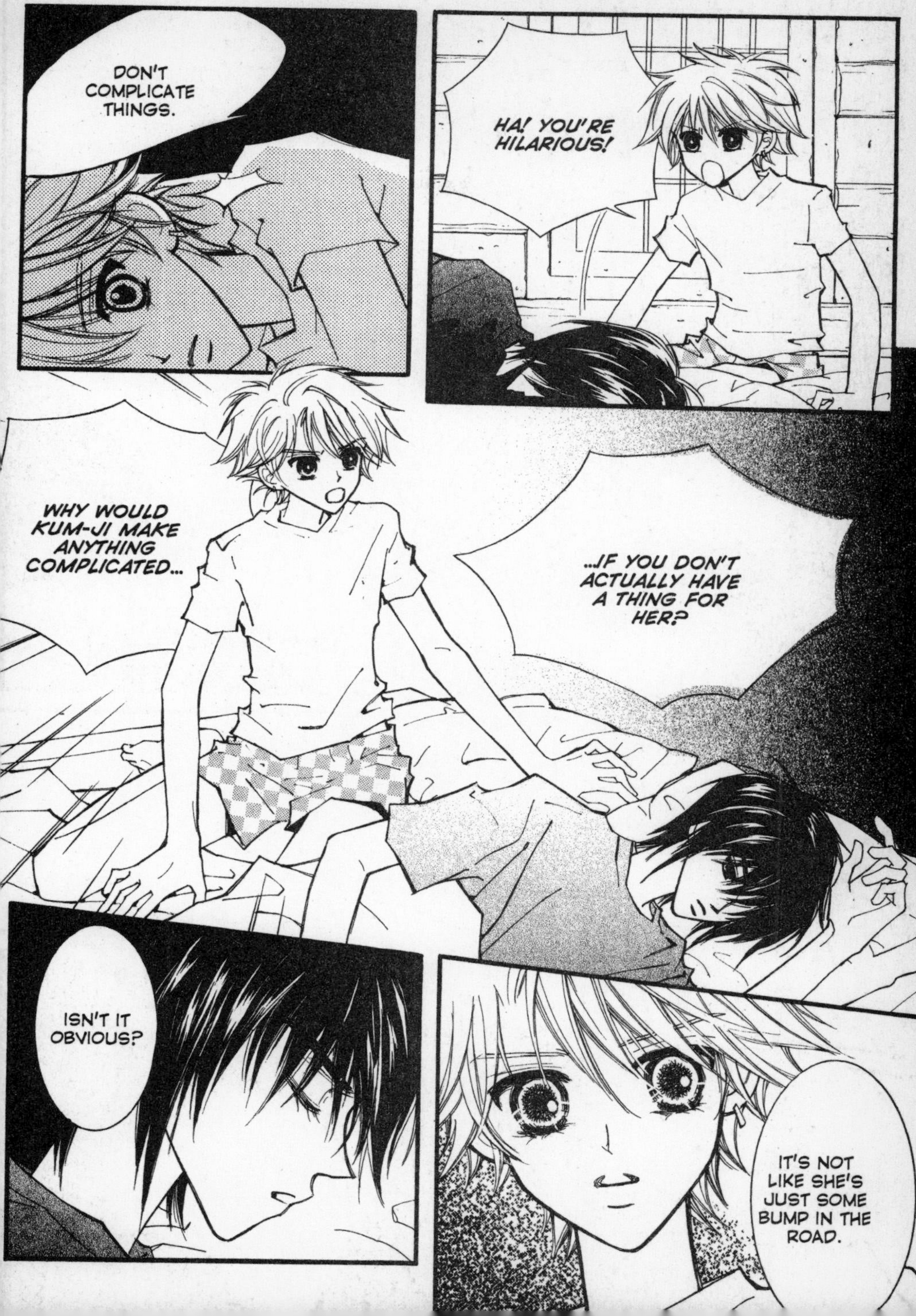
DON'T COMPLICATE THINGS.
HA! YOU'RE HILARIOUS!
WHY WOULD KUM-JI MAKE ANYTHING COMPLICATED...
...IF YOU DON'T ACTUALLY HAVE A THING FOR HER?
ISN'T IT OBVIOUS?
IT'S NOT LIKE SHE'S JUST SOME BUMP IN THE ROAD.

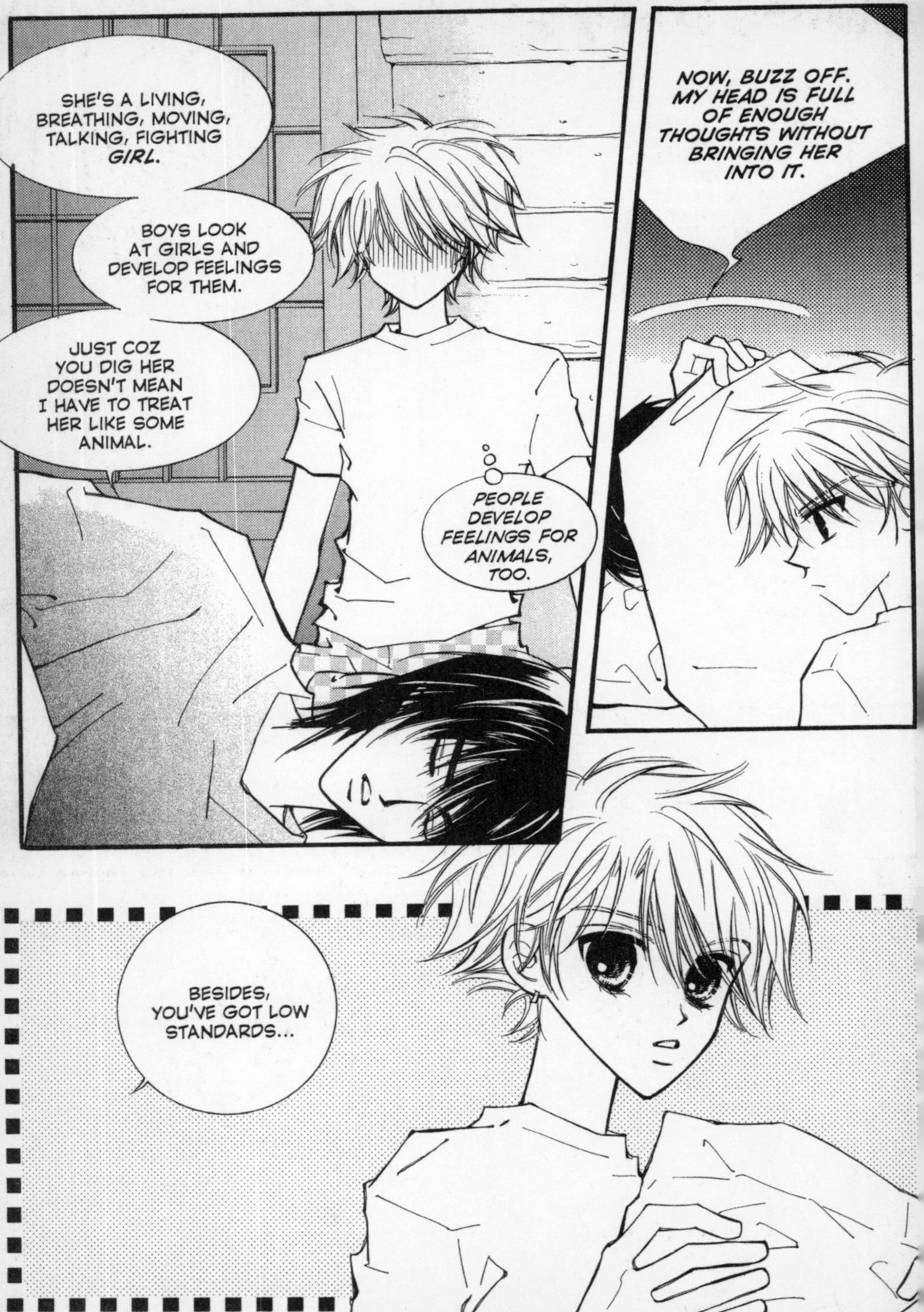
SHE'S A LIVING, BREATHING, MOVING, TALKING, FIGHTING GIRL.
BOYS LOOK AT GIRLS AND DEVELOP FEELINGS FOR THEM.
JUST COZ YOU DIG HER DOESN'T MEAN I HAVE TO TREAT HER LIKE SOME ANIMAL.
PEOPLE DEVELOP FEELINGS FOR ANIMALS, TOO.
NOW, BUZZ OFF. MY HEAD IS FULL OF ENOUGH THOUGHTS WITHOUT BRINGING HER INTO IT.
BESIDES, YOU'VE GOT LOW STANDARDS...

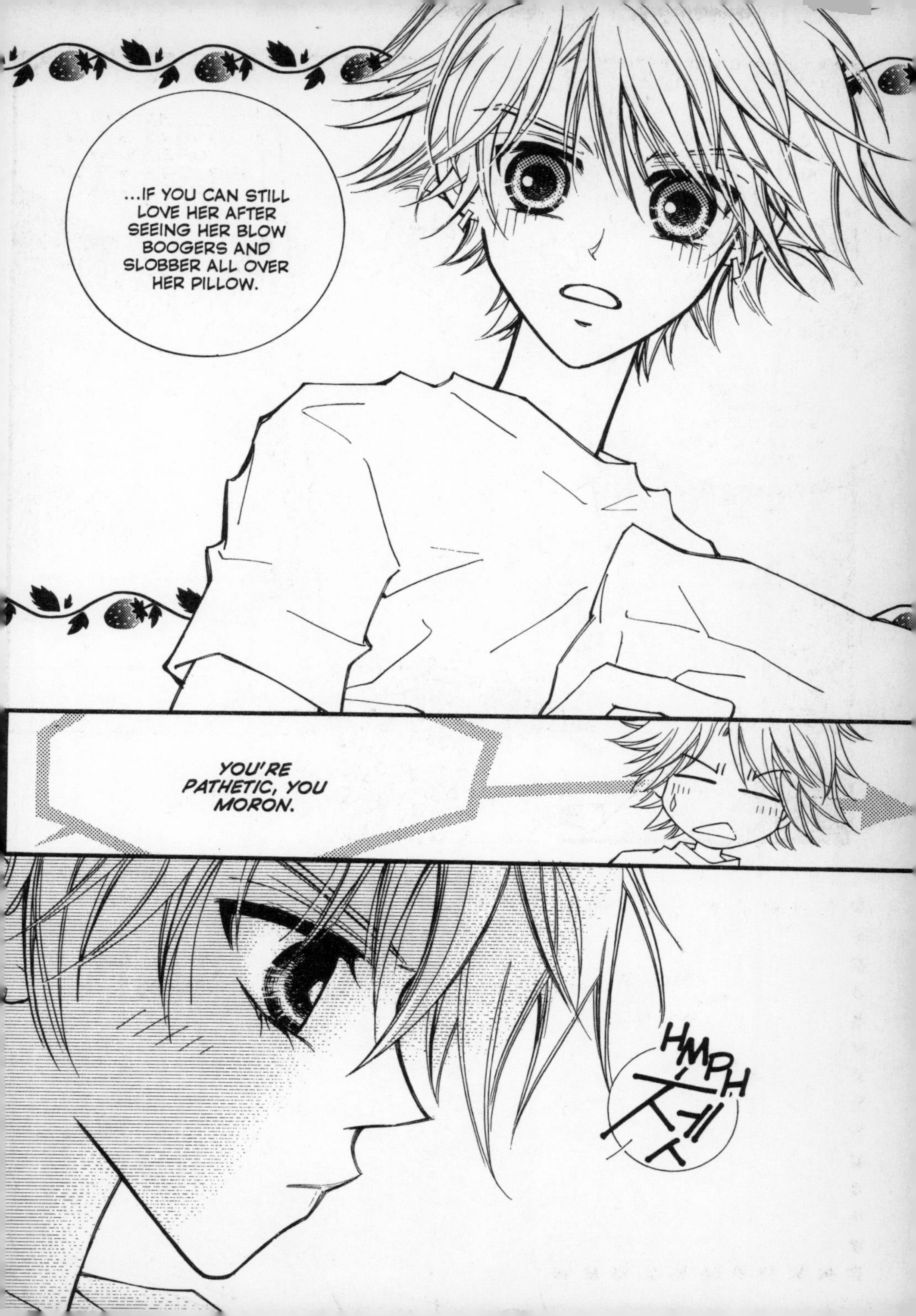
...IF YOU CAN STILL LOVE HER AFTER SEEING HER BLOW BOOGERS AND SLOBBER ALL OVER HER PILLOW.
YOU'RE PATHETIC, YOU MORON.
HMPH

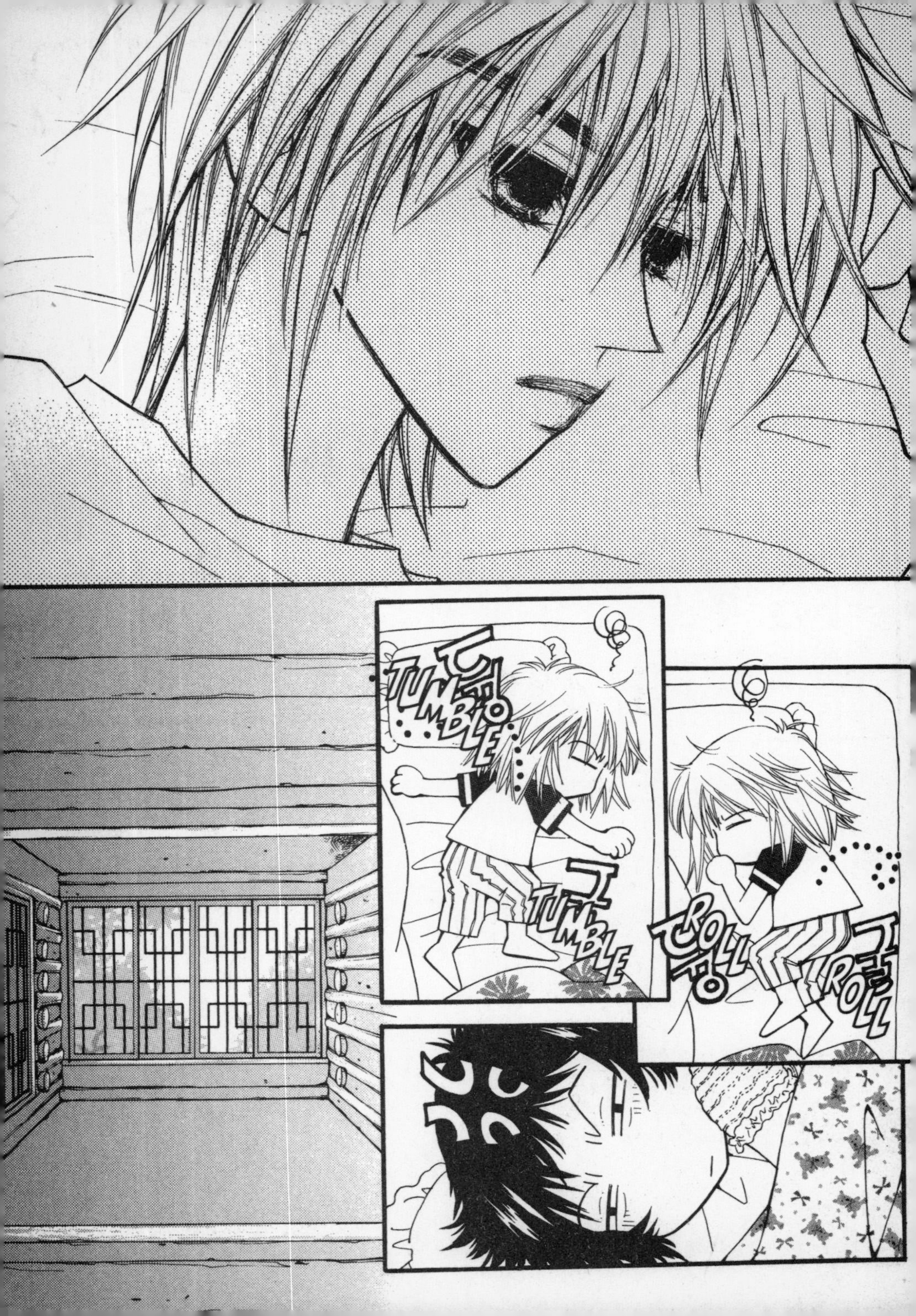
TUMBLE
TUMBLE
ROLL
ROLL

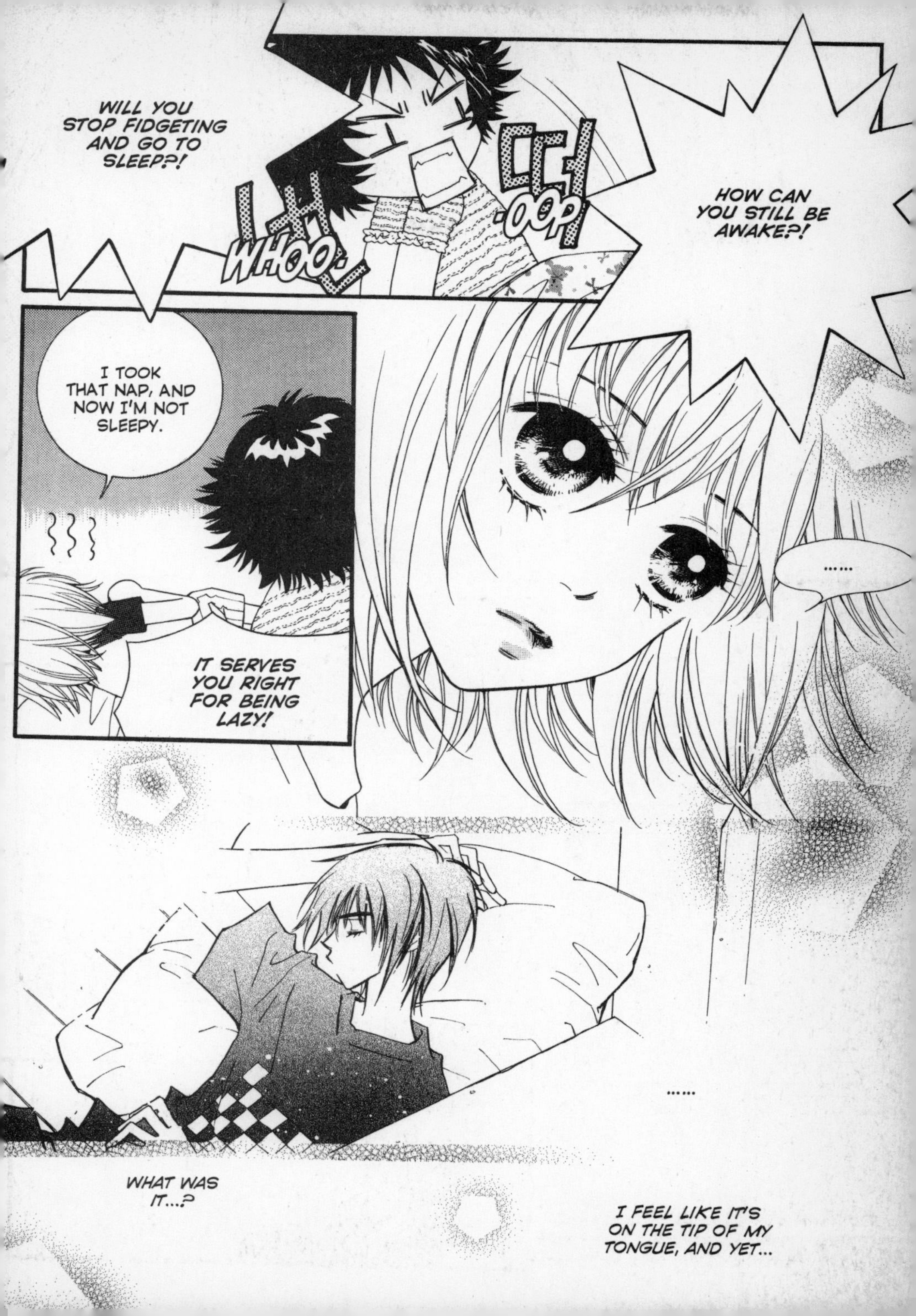
WILL YOU STOP FIDGETING AND GO TO SLEEP?!
WHOO-
-OOP
HOW CAN YOU STILL BE AWAKE?!
I TOOK THAT NAP, AND NOW I'M NOT SLEEPY.
IT SERVES YOU RIGHT FOR BEING LAZY!
......
......
WHAT WAS IT...?
I FEEL LIKE IT'S ON THE TIP OF MY TONGUE, AND YET...

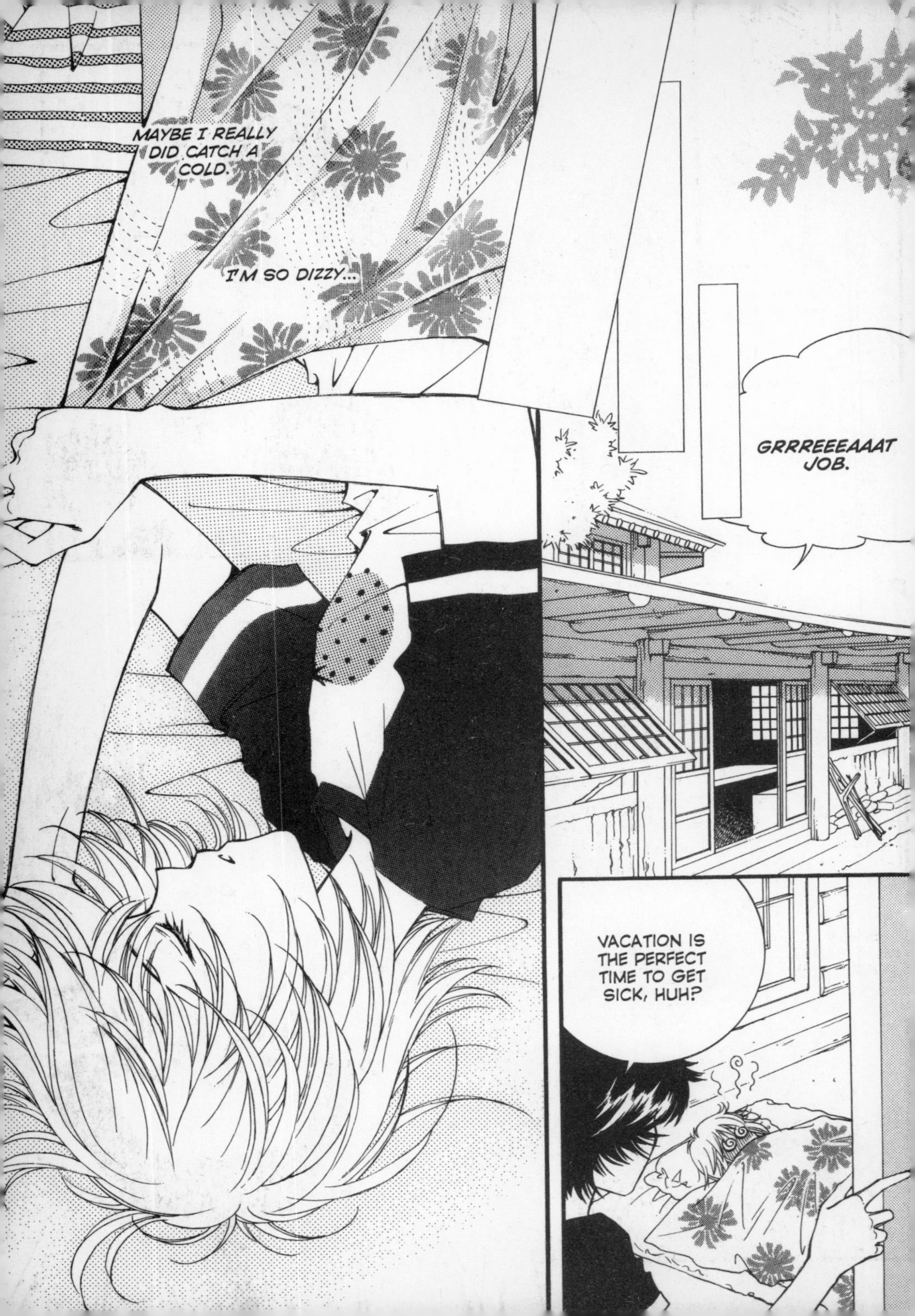
MAYBE I REALLY DID CATCH A COLD.
I'M SO DIZZY...
GRRREEEAAAT JOB.
VACATION IS THE PERFECT TIME TO GET SICK, HUH?

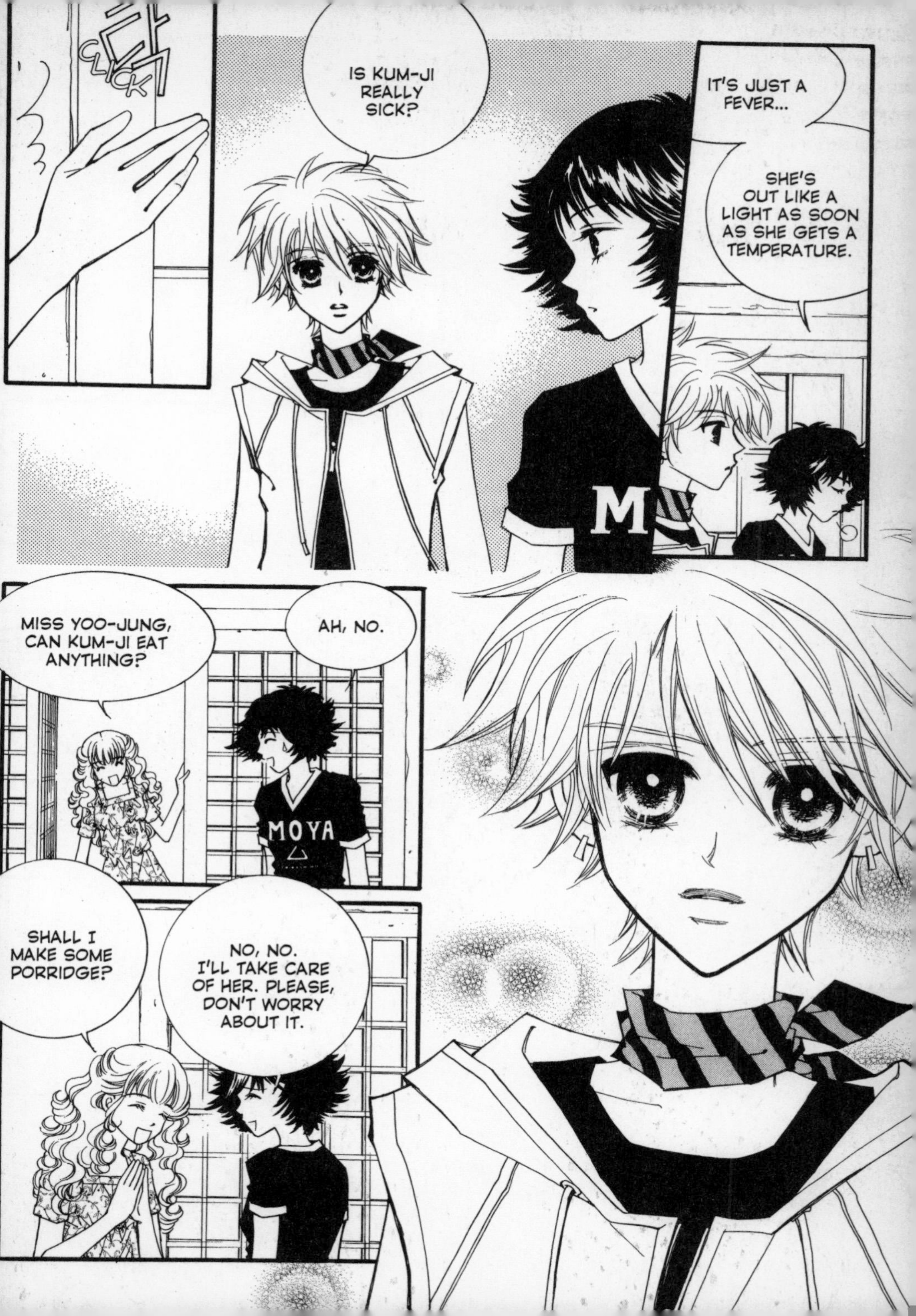
CLICK
IS KUM-JI REALLY SICK?
IT'S JUST A FEVER...
SHE'S OUT LIKE A LIGHT AS SOON AS SHE GETS A TEMPERATURE.
M
MISS YOO-JUNG, CAN KUM-JI EAT ANYTHING?
AH, NO.
MOYA
SHALL I MAKE SOME PORRIDGE?
NO, NO. I'LL TAKE CARE OF HER. PLEASE, DON'T WORRY ABOUT IT.

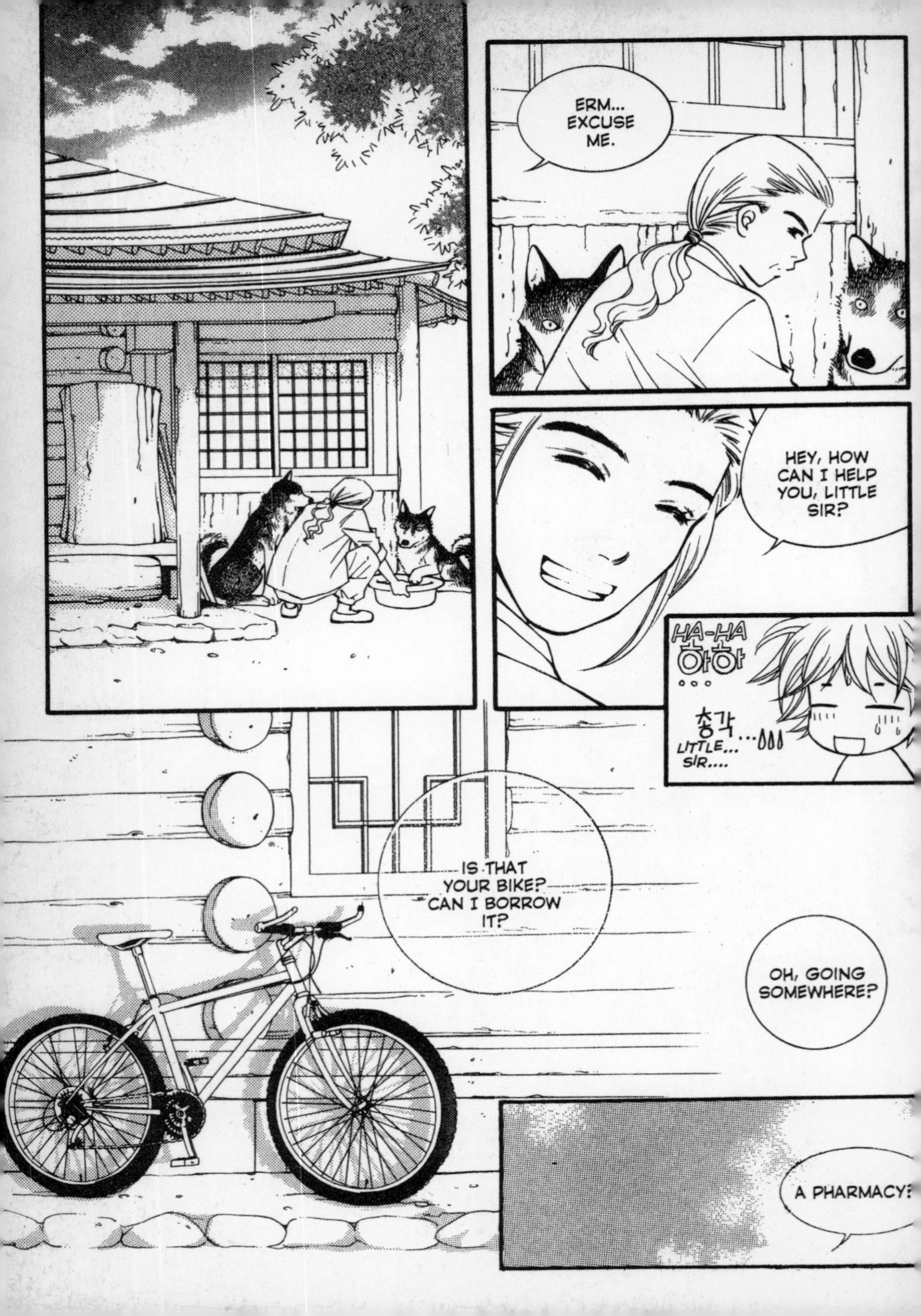
ERM... EXCUSE ME.
HEY, HOW CAN I HELP YOU, LITTLE SIR?
HA-HA
하하
...
총각...
LITTLE... SIR....
IS THAT YOUR BIKE? CAN I BORROW IT?
OH, GOING SOMEWHERE?
A PHARMACY?

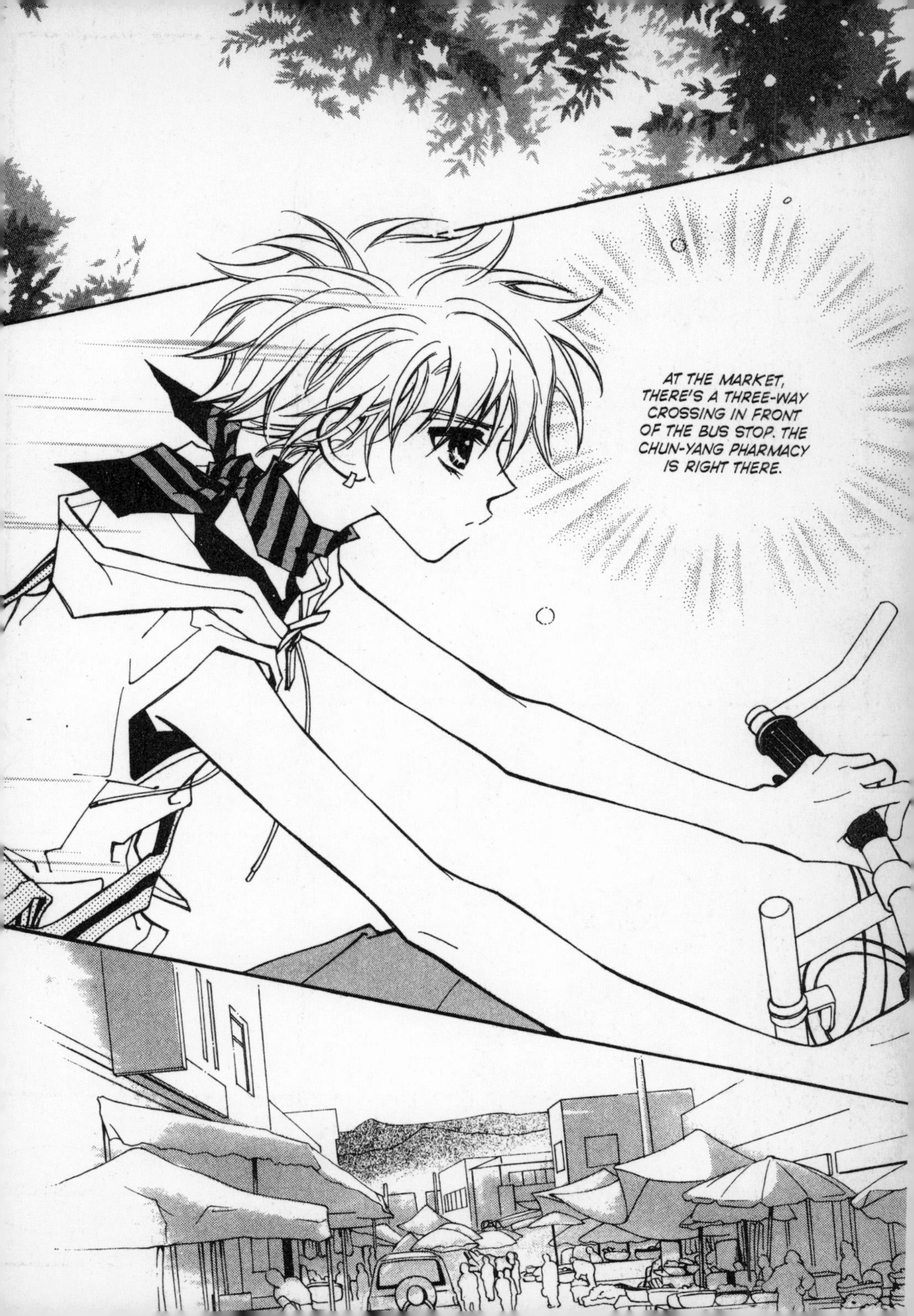
AT THE MARKET, THERE'S A THREE-WAY CROSSING IN FRONT OF THE BUS STOP. THE CHUN-YANG PHARMACY IS RIGHT THERE.

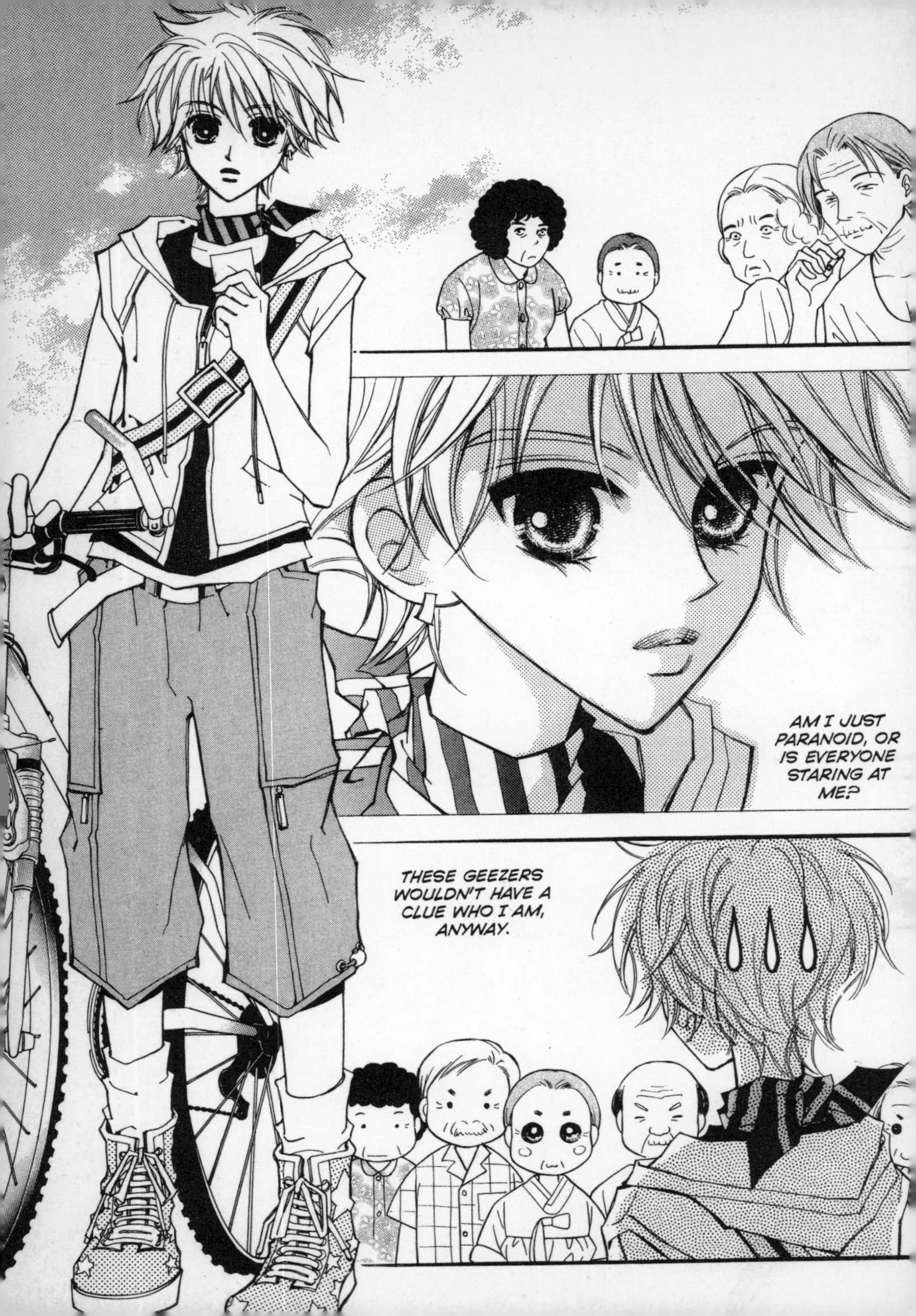
AM I JUST PARANOID, OR IS EVERYONE STARING AT ME?
THESE GEEZERS WOULDN'T HAVE A CLUE WHO I AM, ANYWAY.

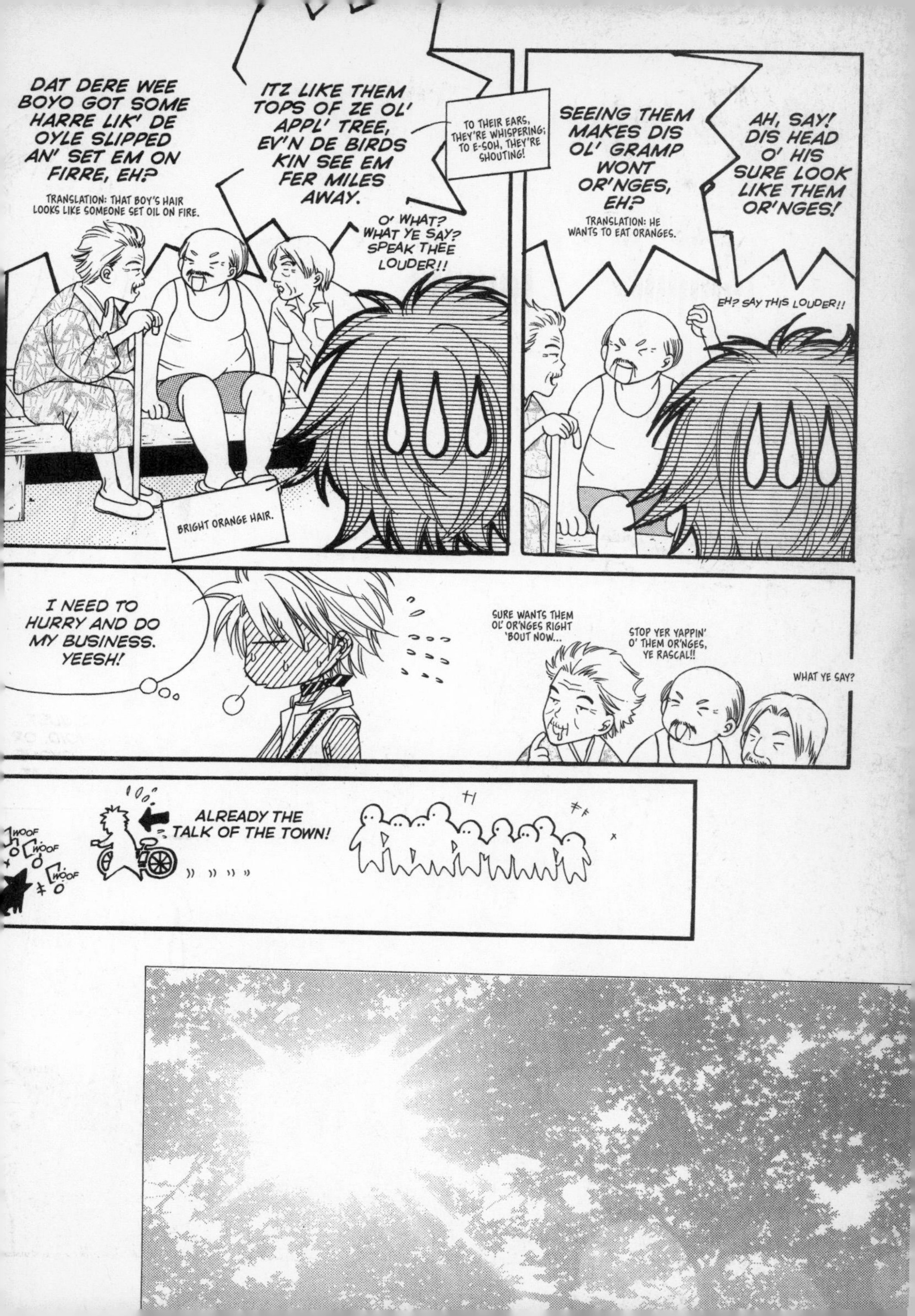
DAT DERE WEE BOYO GOT SOME HARRE LIK' DE OYLE SLIPPED AN' SET EM ON FIRRE, EH?
TRANSLATION: THAT BOY'S HAIR LOOKS LIKE SOMEONE SET OIL ON FIRE.
ITZ LIKE THEM TOPS OF ZE OL' APPL' TREE, EV'N DE BIRDS KIN SEE EM FER MILES AWAY.
TO THEIR EARS, THEY'RE WHISPERING; TO E-SOH, THEY'RE SHOUTING!
O' WHAT? WHAT YE SAY? SPEAK THEE LOUDER!!
BRIGHT ORANGE HAIR.
SEEING THEM MAKES DIS OL' GRAMP WONT OR'NGES, EH?
TRANSLATION: HE WANTS TO EAT ORANGES.
AH, SAY! DIS HEAD O' HIS SURE LOOK LIKE THEM OR'NGES!
EH? SAY THIS LOUDER!!
I NEED TO HURRY AND DO MY BUSINESS. YEESH!
SURE WANTS THEM OL' OR'NGES RIGHT 'BOUT NOW...
STOP YER YAPPIN' O' THEM OR'NGES, YE RASCAL!!
WHAT YE SAY?
WOOF
WOOF
WOOF
ALREADY THE TALK OF THE TOWN!

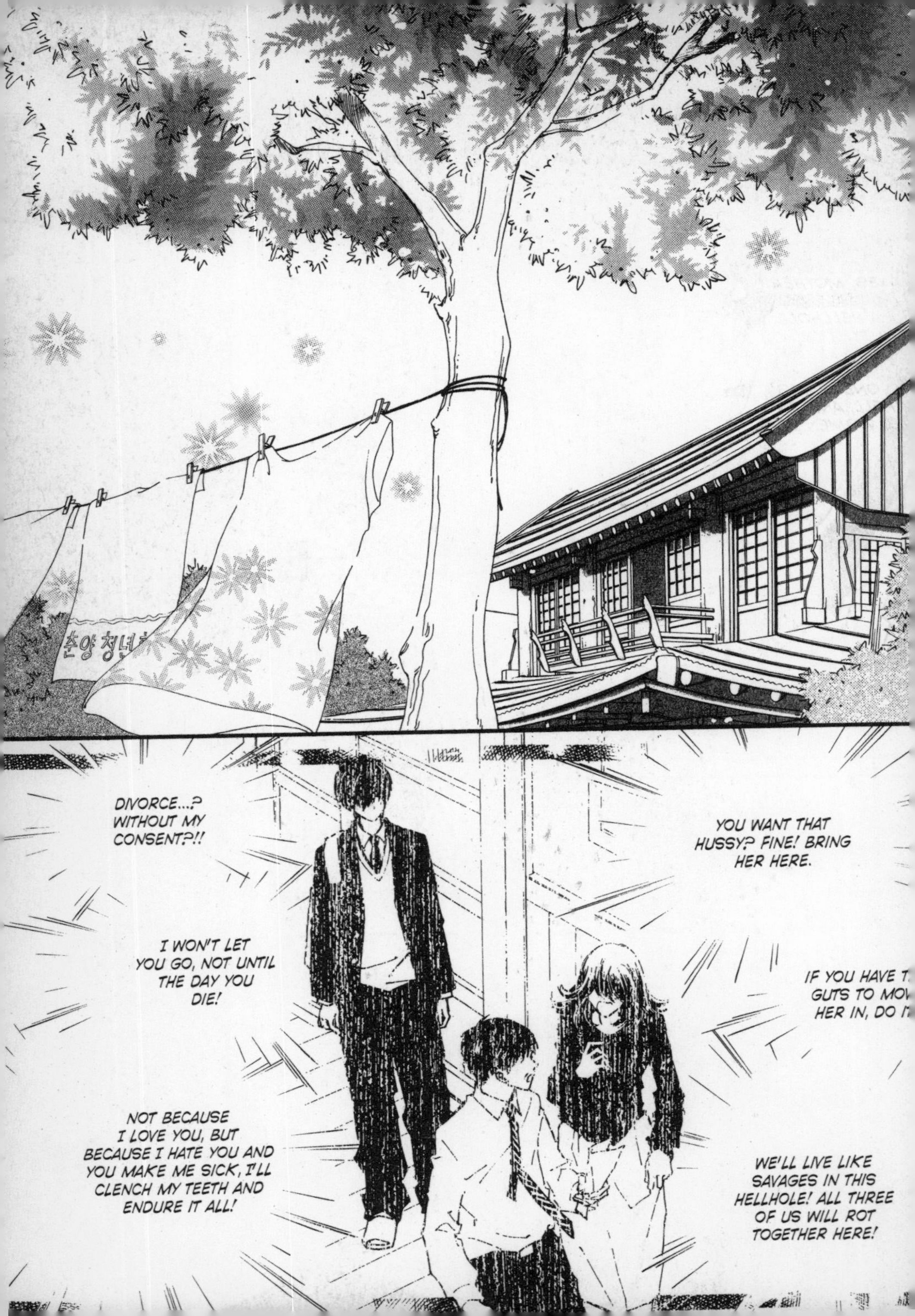

춘양 청년
DIVORCE...? WITHOUT MY CONSENT?!!
YOU WANT THAT HUSSY? FINE! BRING HER HERE.
I WON'T LET YOU GO, NOT UNTIL THE DAY YOU DIE!
IF YOU HAVE T GUTS TO MOV HER IN, DO I
NOT BECAUSE I LOVE YOU, BUT BECAUSE I HATE YOU AND YOU MAKE ME SICK, I'LL CLENCH MY TEETH AND ENDURE IT ALL!
WE'LL LIVE LIKE SAVAGES IN THIS HELLHOLE! ALL THREE OF US WILL ROT TOGETHER HERE!

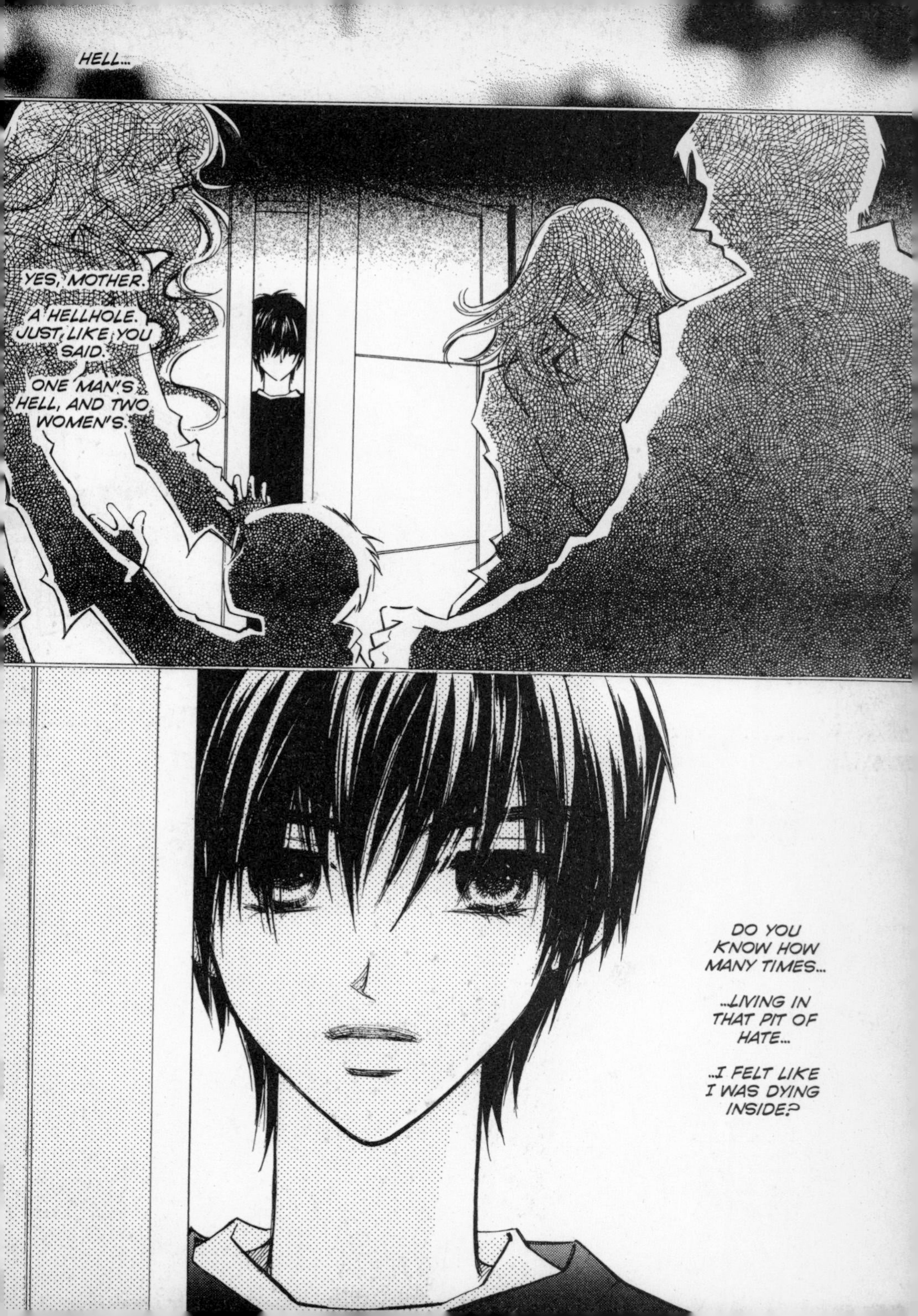
HELL...
YES, MOTHER.
A HELLHOLE. JUST LIKE YOU SAID.
ONE MAN'S HELL, AND TWO WOMEN'S.
DO YOU KNOW HOW MANY TIMES...
...LIVING IN THAT PIT OF HATE...
...I FELT LIKE I WAS DYING INSIDE?

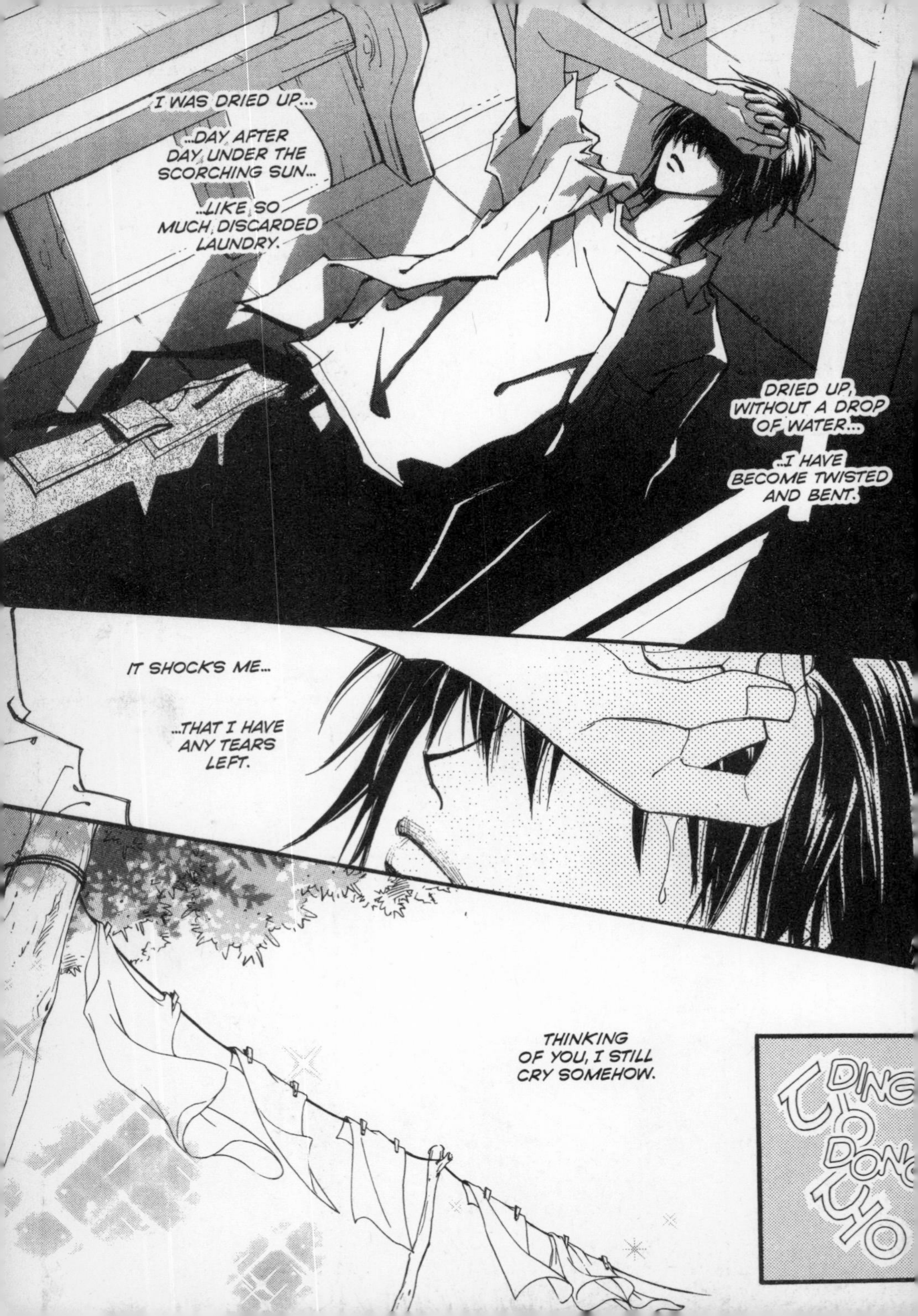
I WAS DRIED UP...
...DAY AFTER DAY UNDER THE SCORCHING SUN...
...LIKE SO MUCH DISCARDED LAUNDRY.
DRIED UP, WITHOUT A DROP OF WATER...
...I HAVE BECOME TWISTED AND BENT.
IT SHOCKS ME...
...THAT I HAVE ANY TEARS LEFT.
THINKING OF YOU, I STILL CRY SOMEHOW.
DING DONG

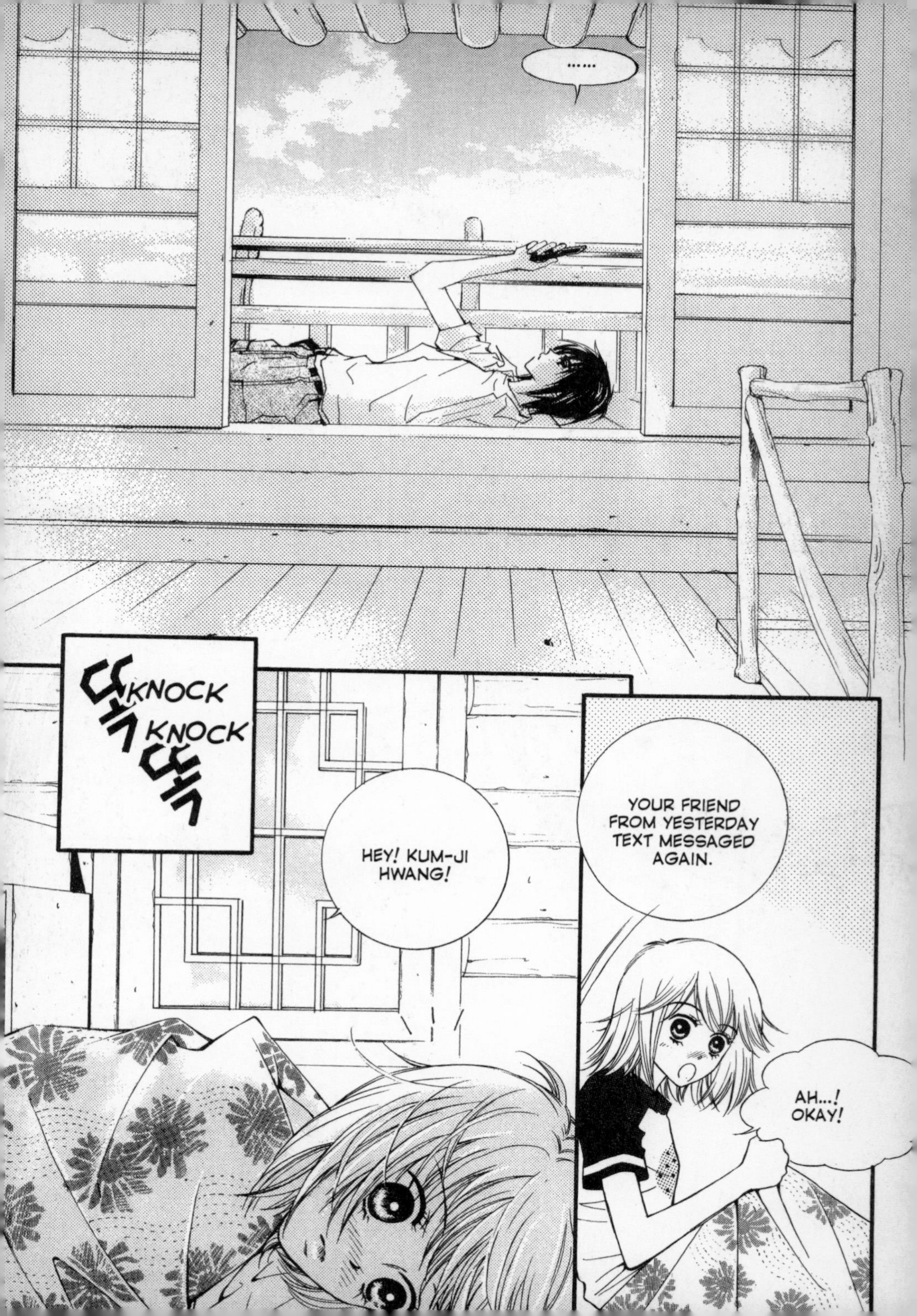

......
KNOCK KNOCK
HEY! KUM-JI HWANG!
YOUR FRIEND FROM YESTERDAY TEXT MESSAGED AGAIN.
AH...! OKAY!

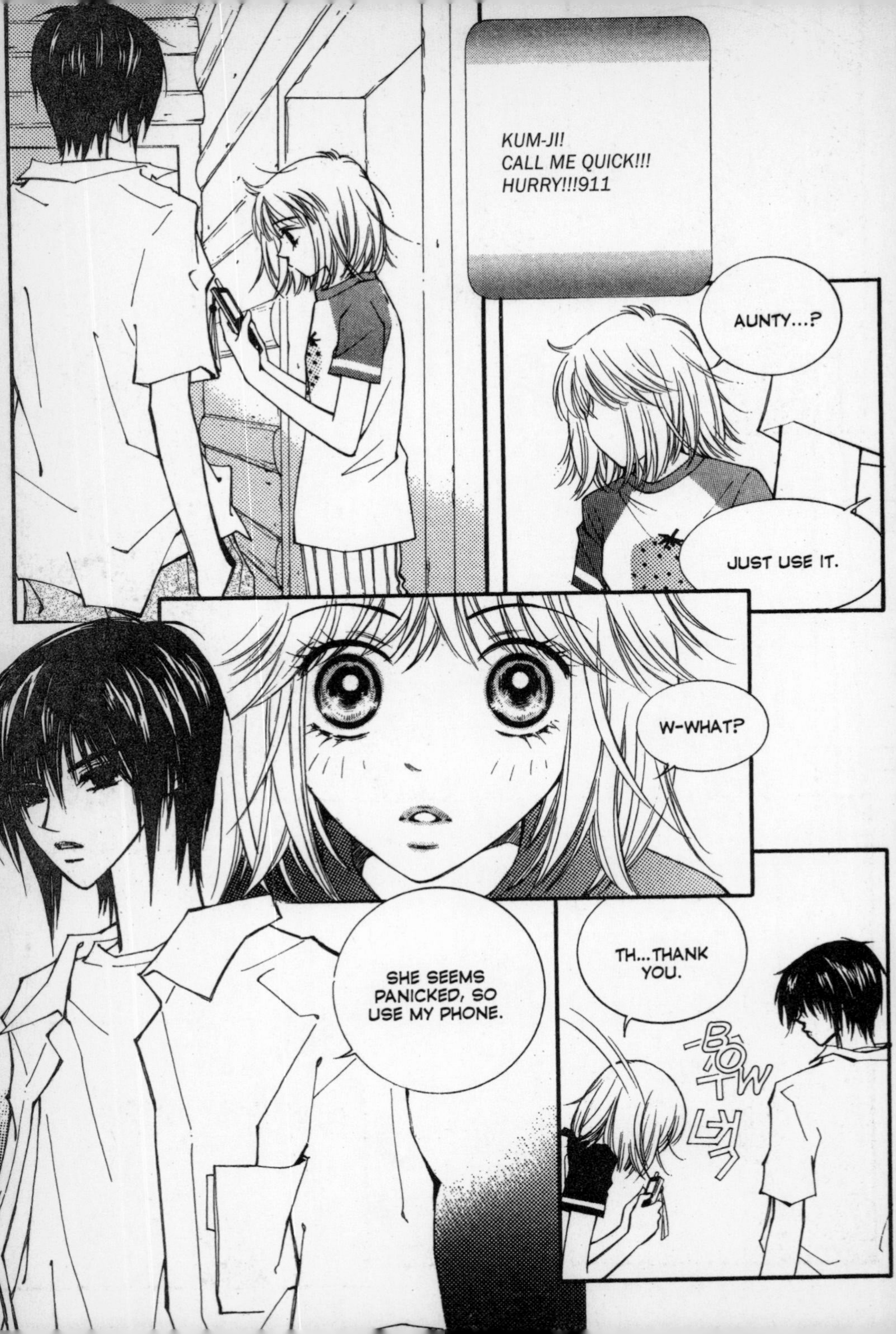
KUM-JI!
CALL ME QUICK!!!
HURRY!!!911
AUNTY...?
JUST USE IT.
W-WHAT?
SHE SEEMS PANICKED, SO USE MY PHONE.
TH...THANK YOU.
-BOW

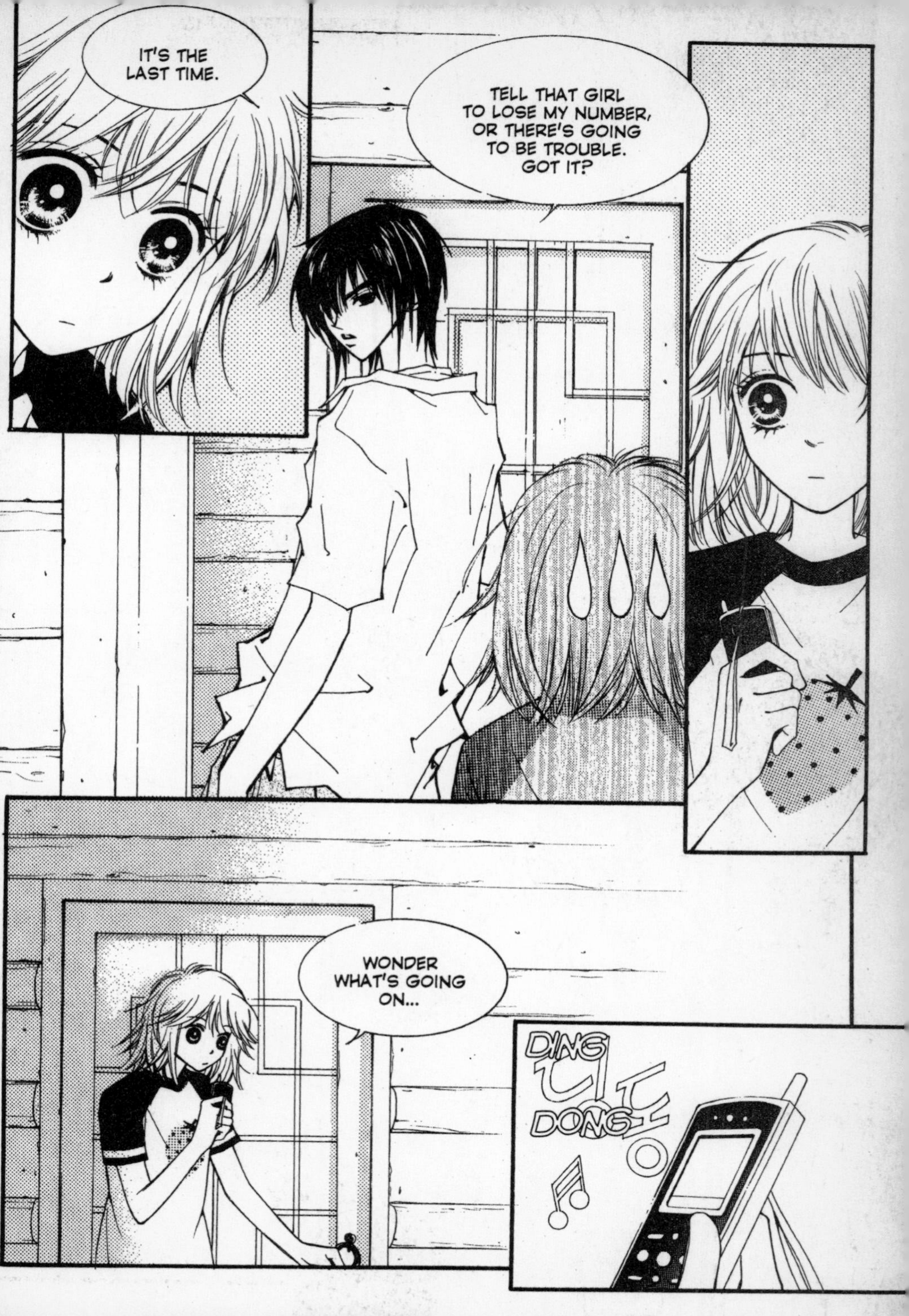
IT'S THE LAST TIME.
TELL THAT GIRL TO LOSE MY NUMBER, OR THERE'S GOING TO BE TROUBLE. GOT IT?
WONDER WHAT'S GOING ON...
DING DONG

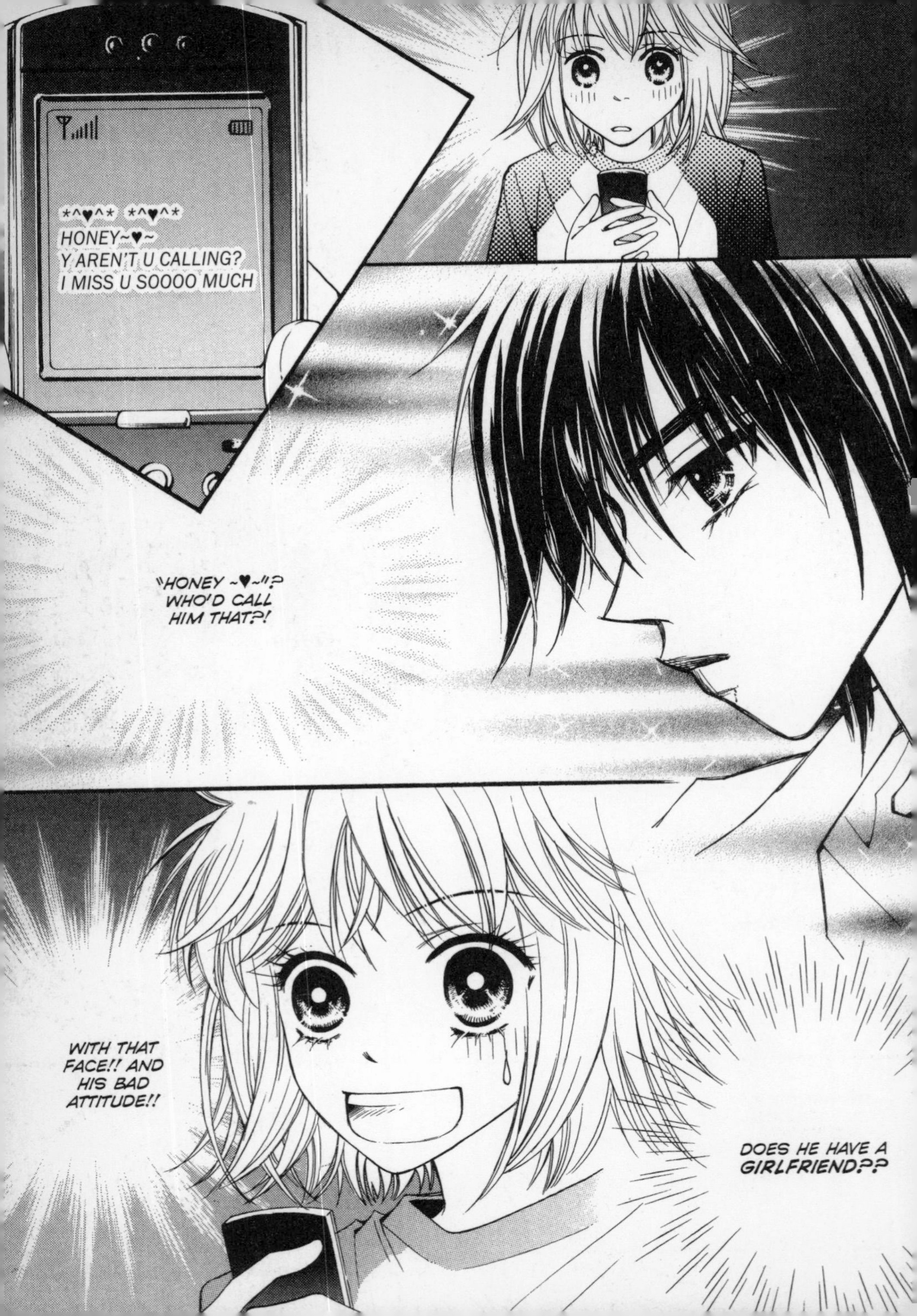
*^♥^* *^♥^*
HONEY~♥~
Y AREN'T U CALLING?
I MISS U SOOOO MUCH
"HONEY ~♥~"? WHO'D CALL HIM THAT?!
WITH THAT FACE!! AND HIS BAD ATTITUDE!!
DOES HE HAVE A GIRLFRIEND??

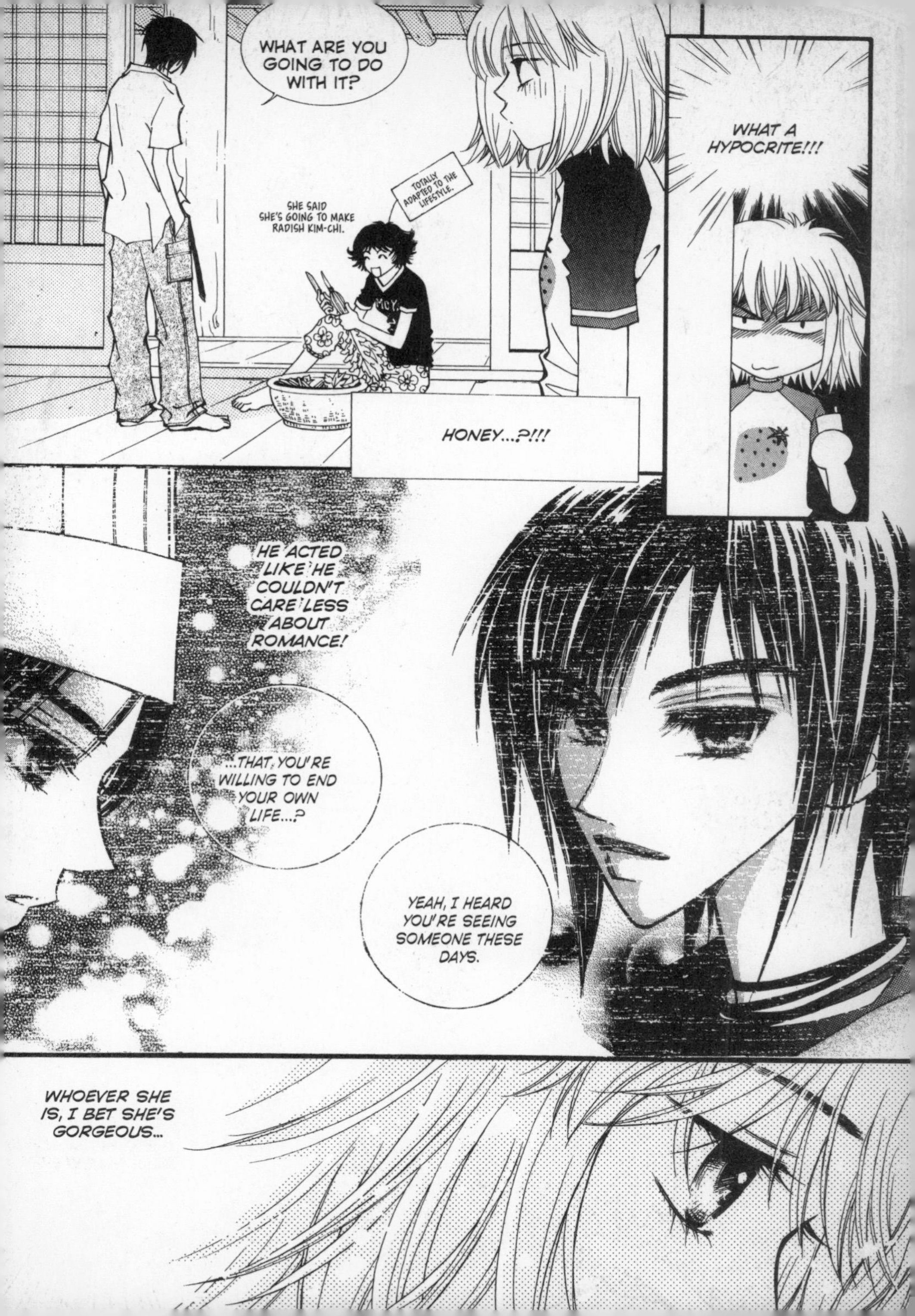
WHAT ARE YOU GOING TO DO WITH IT?
SHE SAID SHE'S GOING TO MAKE RADISH KIM-CHI.
TOTALLY ADAPTED TO THE LIFESTYLE.
HONEY...?!!!
WHAT A HYPOCRITE!!!
HE ACTED LIKE HE COULDN'T CARE LESS ABOUT ROMANCE!
...THAT YOU'RE WILLING TO END YOUR OWN LIFE...?
YEAH, I HEARD YOU'RE SEEING SOMEONE THESE DAYS.
WHOEVER SHE IS, I BET SHE'S GORGEOUS...

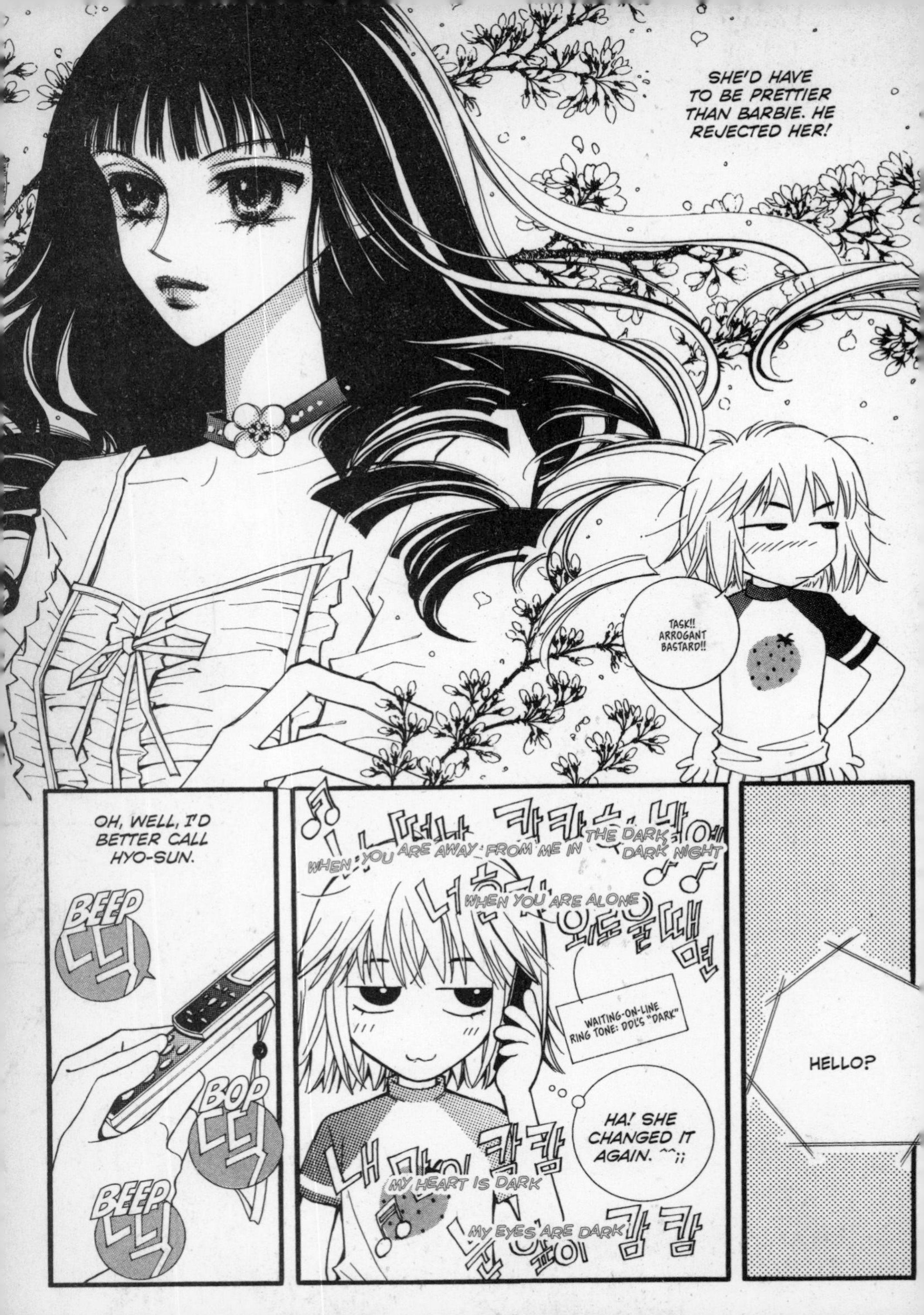
SHE'D HAVE TO BE PRETTIER THAN BARBIE. HE REJECTED HER!
TASK!! ARROGANT BASTARD!!
OH, WELL, I'D BETTER CALL HYO-SUN.
BEEP
BOP
BEEP
WHEN YOU ARE AWAY FROM ME IN THE DARK DARK NIGHT
WHEN YOU ARE ALONE
WAITING-ON-LINE RING TONE: DDL'S "DARK"
HA! SHE CHANGED IT AGAIN. ^^;;
MY HEART IS DARK
MY EYES ARE DARK
HELLO?

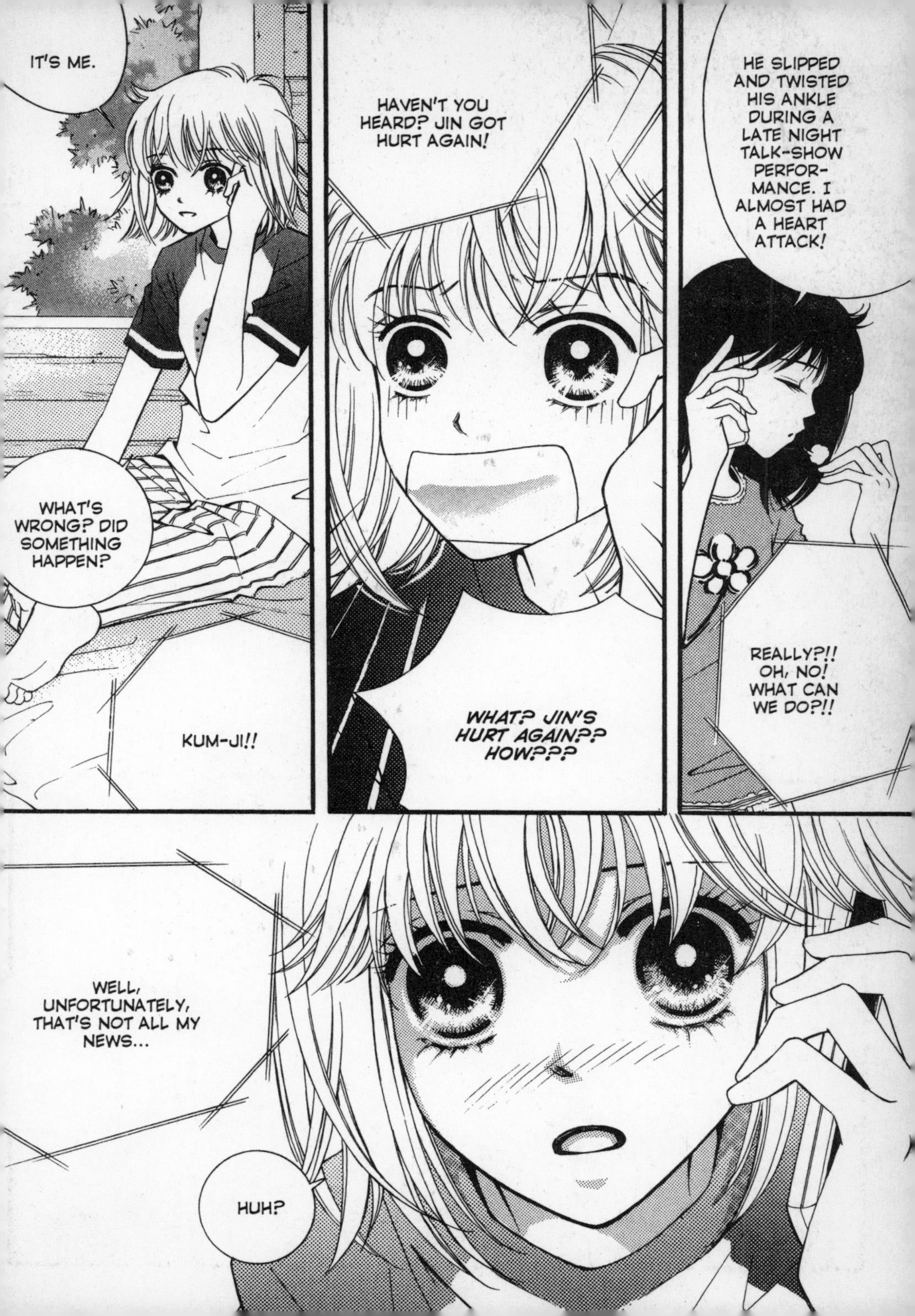
IT'S ME.
WHAT'S WRONG? DID SOMETHING HAPPEN?
KUM-JI!!
HAVEN'T YOU HEARD? JIN GOT HURT AGAIN!
WHAT? JIN'S HURT AGAIN?? HOW???
HE SLIPPED AND TWISTED HIS ANKLE DURING A LATE NIGHT TALK-SHOW PERFORMANCE. I ALMOST HAD A HEART ATTACK!
REALLY?!! OH, NO! WHAT CAN WE DO?!!
WELL, UNFORTUNATELY, THAT'S NOT ALL MY NEWS...
HUH?

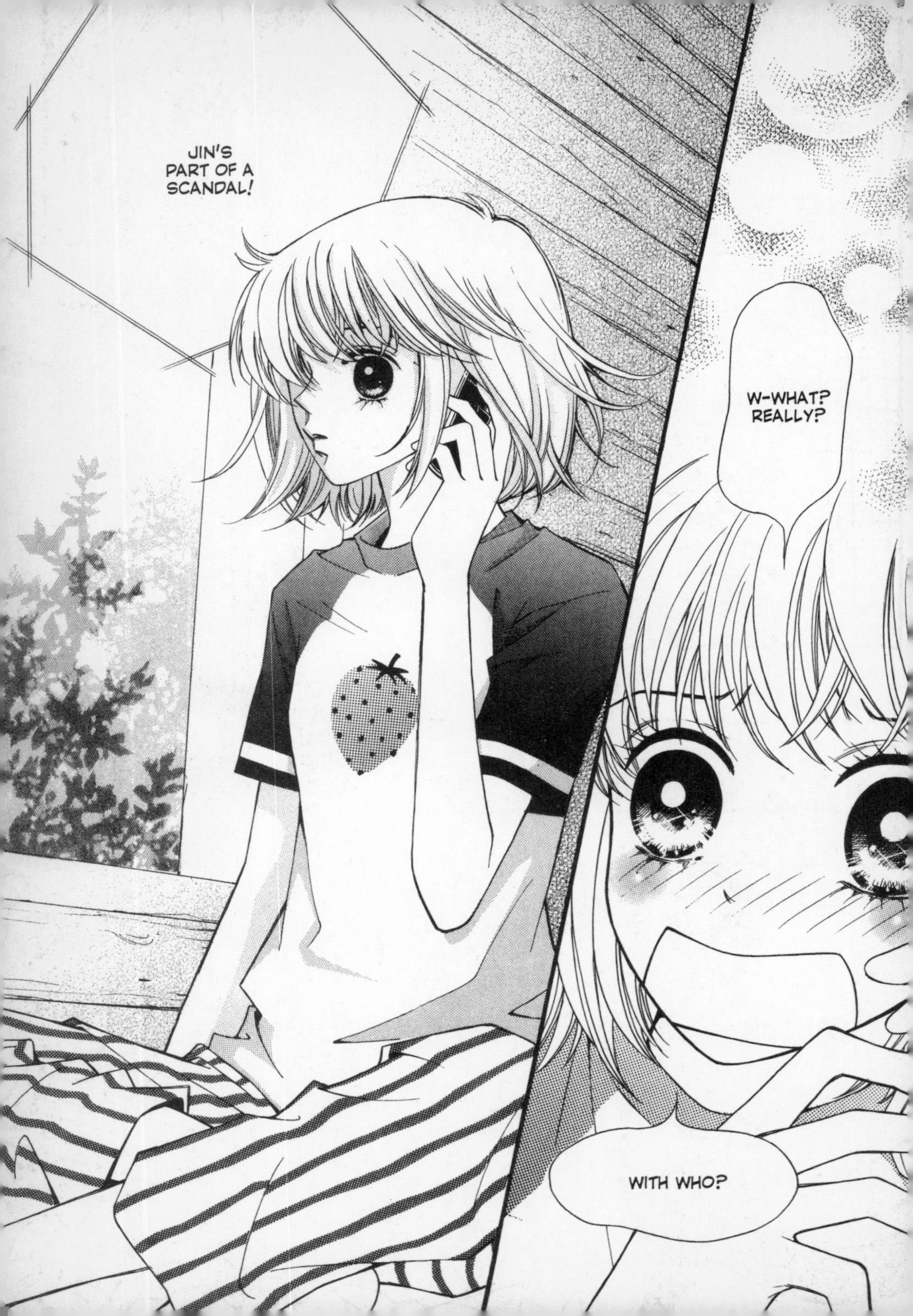
JIN'S PART OF A SCANDAL!
W-WHAT? REALLY?
WITH WHO?

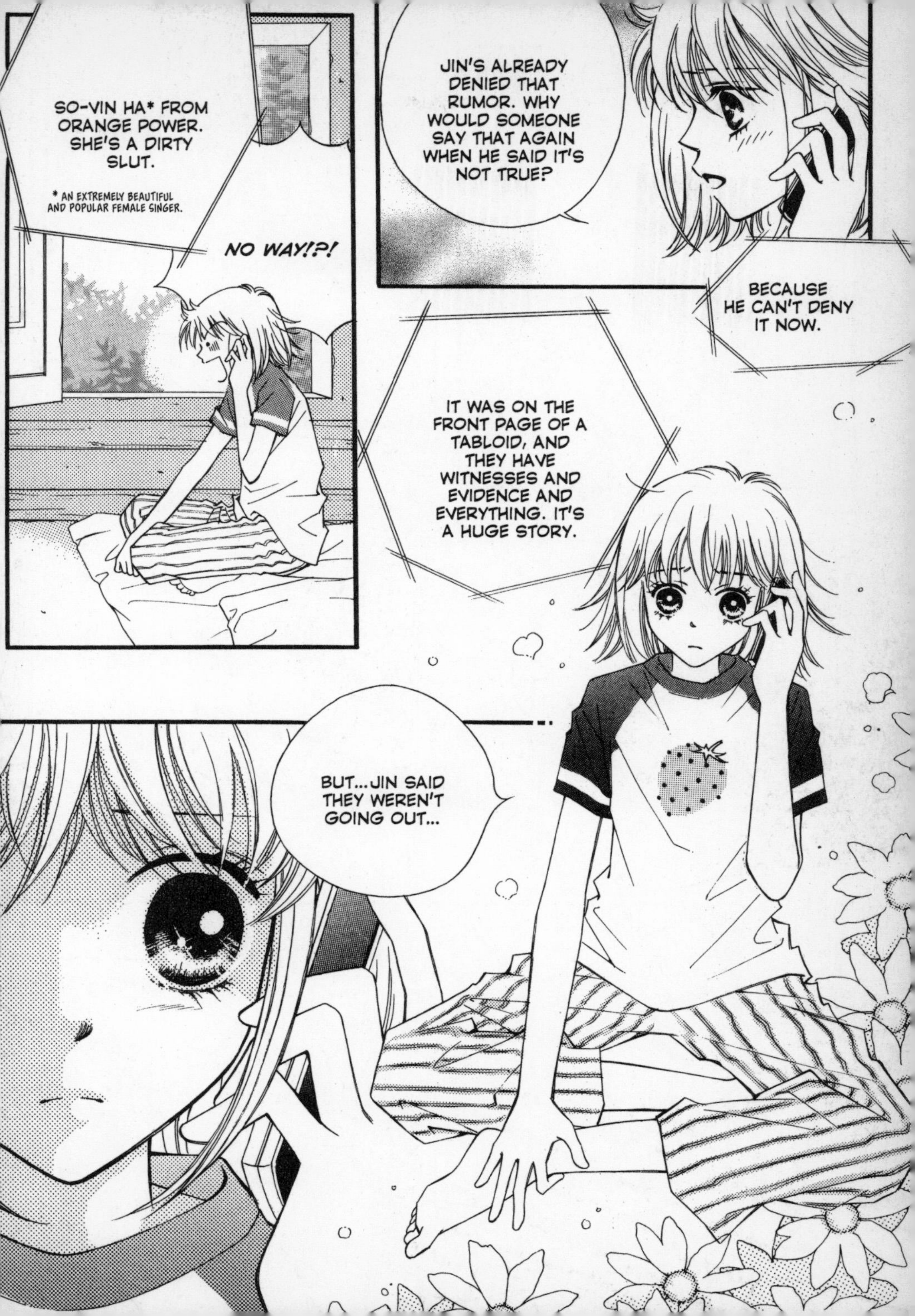
SO-VIN HA* FROM ORANGE POWER. SHE'S A DIRTY SLUT.
* AN EXTREMELY BEAUTIFUL AND POPULAR FEMALE SINGER.
NO WAY!?!
JIN'S ALREADY DENIED THAT RUMOR. WHY WOULD SOMEONE SAY THAT AGAIN WHEN HE SAID IT'S NOT TRUE?
BECAUSE HE CAN'T DENY IT NOW.
IT WAS ON THE FRONT PAGE OF A TABLOID, AND THEY HAVE WITNESSES AND EVIDENCE AND EVERYTHING. IT'S A HUGE STORY.
BUT...JIN SAID THEY WEREN'T GOING OUT...

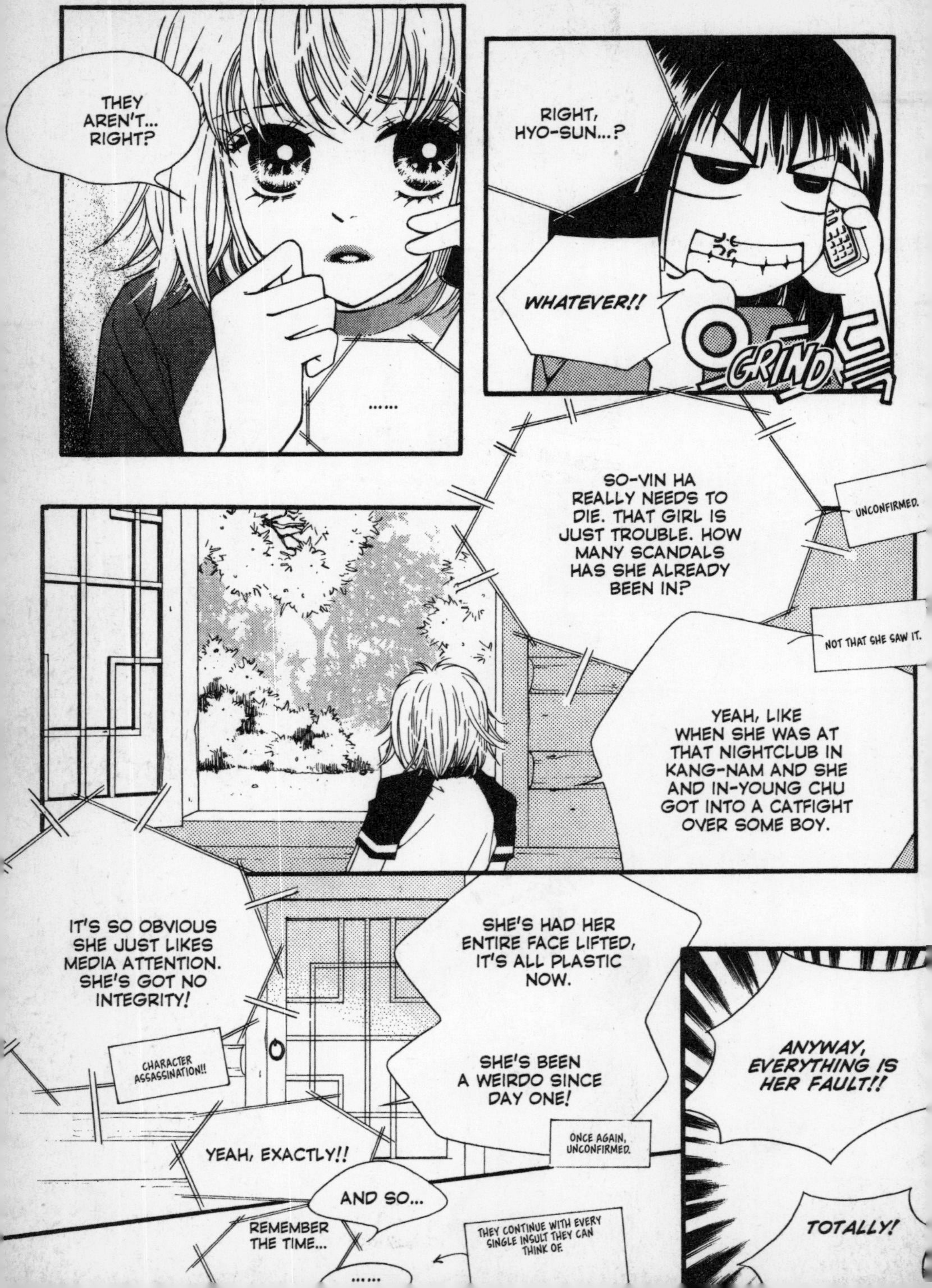
THEY AREN'T... RIGHT?
......
RIGHT, HYO-SUN...?
WHATEVER!!
GRIND
SO-VIN HA REALLY NEEDS TO DIE. THAT GIRL IS JUST TROUBLE. HOW MANY SCANDALS HAS SHE ALREADY BEEN IN?
UNCONFIRMED.
NOT THAT SHE SAW IT.
YEAH, LIKE WHEN SHE WAS AT THAT NIGHTCLUB IN KANG-NAM AND SHE AND IN-YOUNG CHU GOT INTO A CATFIGHT OVER SOME BOY.
IT'S SO OBVIOUS SHE JUST LIKES MEDIA ATTENTION. SHE'S GOT NO INTEGRITY!
CHARACTER ASSASSINATION!!
SHE'S HAD HER ENTIRE FACE LIFTED, IT'S ALL PLASTIC NOW.
SHE'S BEEN A WEIRDO SINCE DAY ONE!
ONCE AGAIN, UNCONFIRMED.
YEAH, EXACTLY!!
AND SO...
REMEMBER THE TIME...
THEY CONTINUE WITH EVERY SINGLE INSULT THEY CAN THINK OF.
......
ANYWAY, EVERYTHING IS HER FAULT!!
TOTALLY!

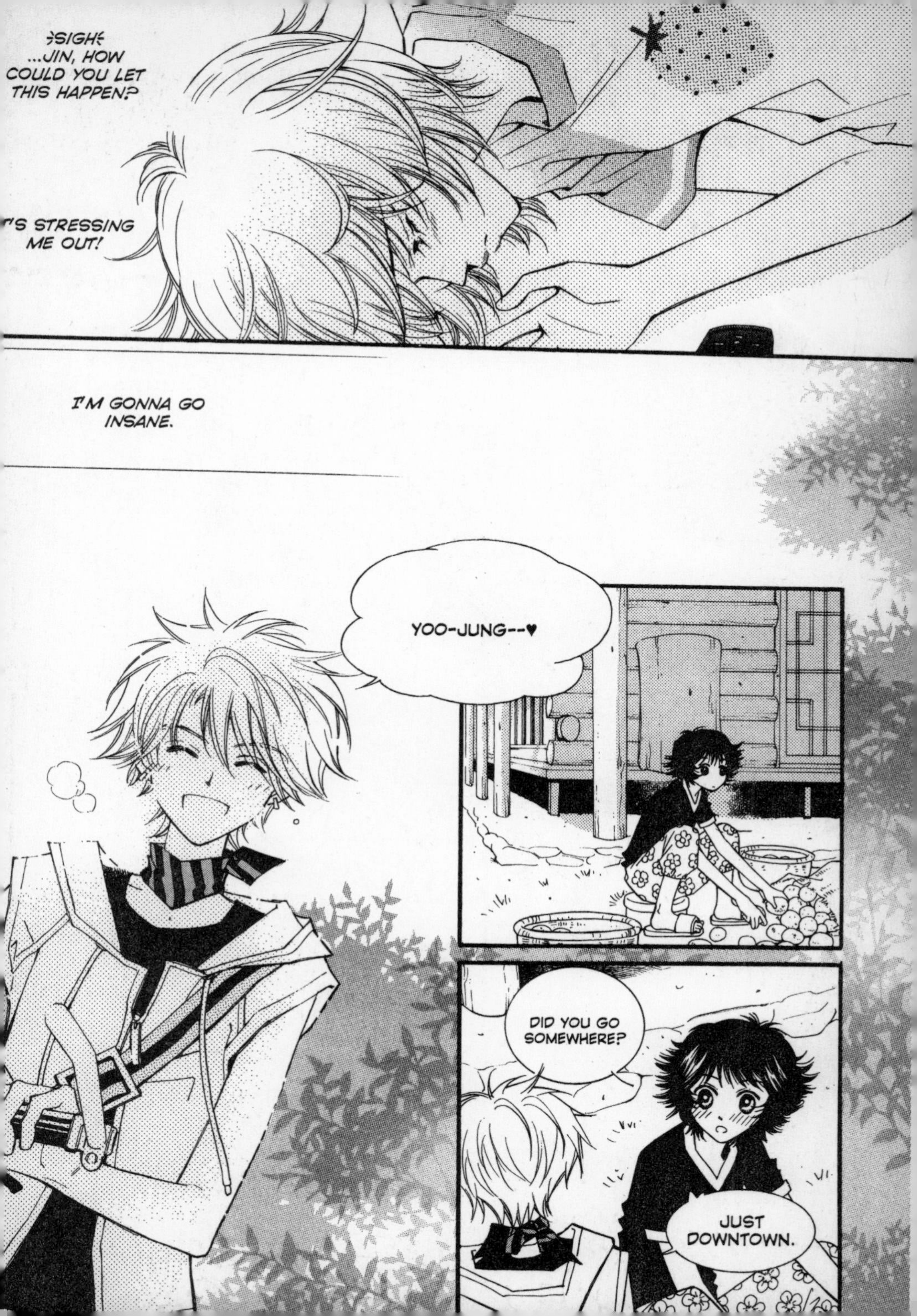

≯SIGH≮ ...JIN, HOW COULD YOU LET THIS HAPPEN?
'S STRESSING ME OUT!
I'M GONNA GO INSANE.
YOO-JUNG--♥
DID YOU GO SOMEWHERE?
JUST DOWNTOWN.

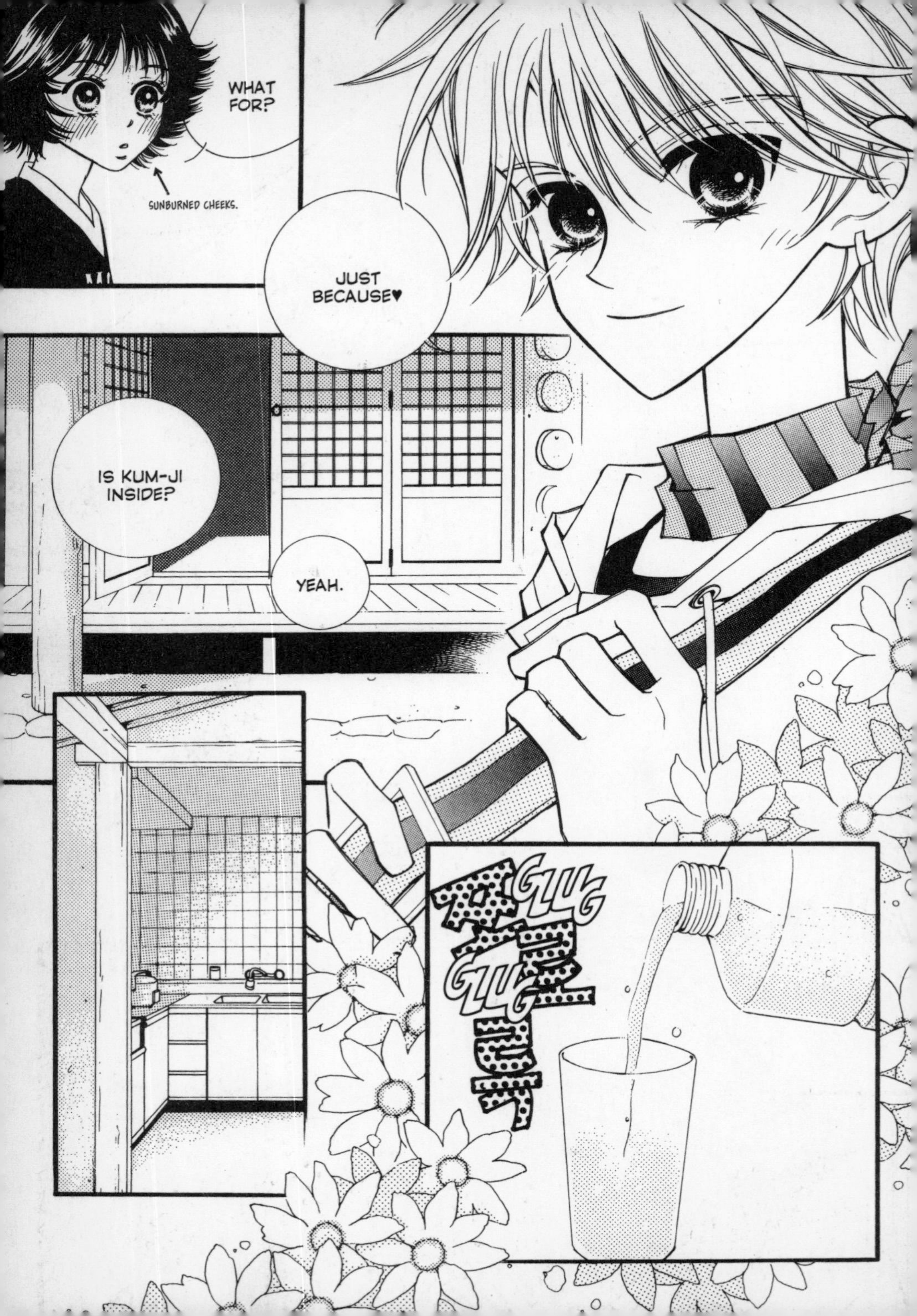
WHAT FOR?
SUNBURNED CHEEKS.
JUST BECAUSE♥
IS KUM-JI INSIDE?
YEAH.
GLUG
GLUG

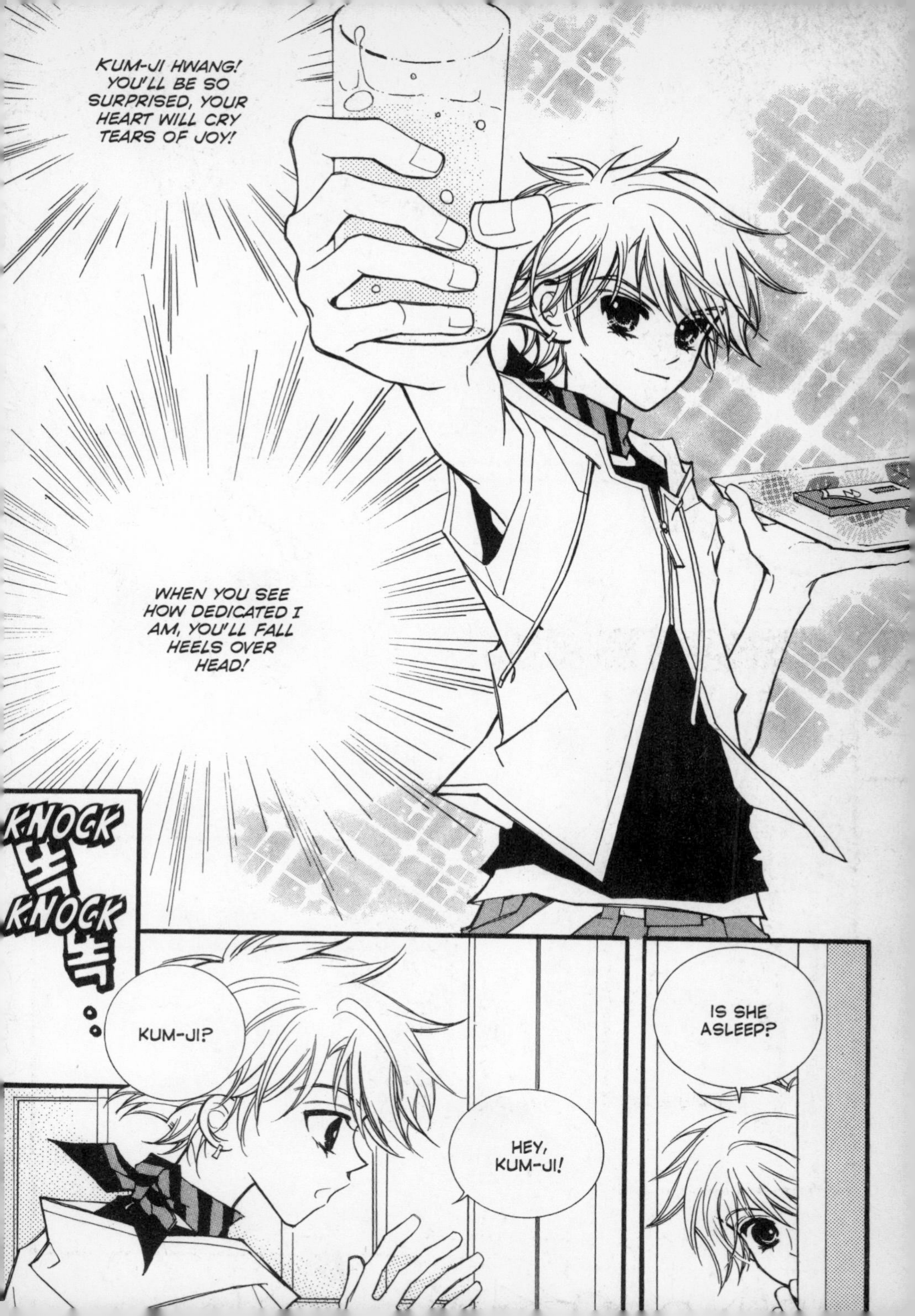
KUM-JI HWANG! YOU'LL BE SO SURPRISED, YOUR HEART WILL CRY TEARS OF JOY!
WHEN YOU SEE HOW DEDICATED I AM, YOU'LL FALL HEELS OVER HEAD!
KNOCK
KNOCK
KUM-JI?
HEY, KUM-JI!
IS SHE ASLEEP?

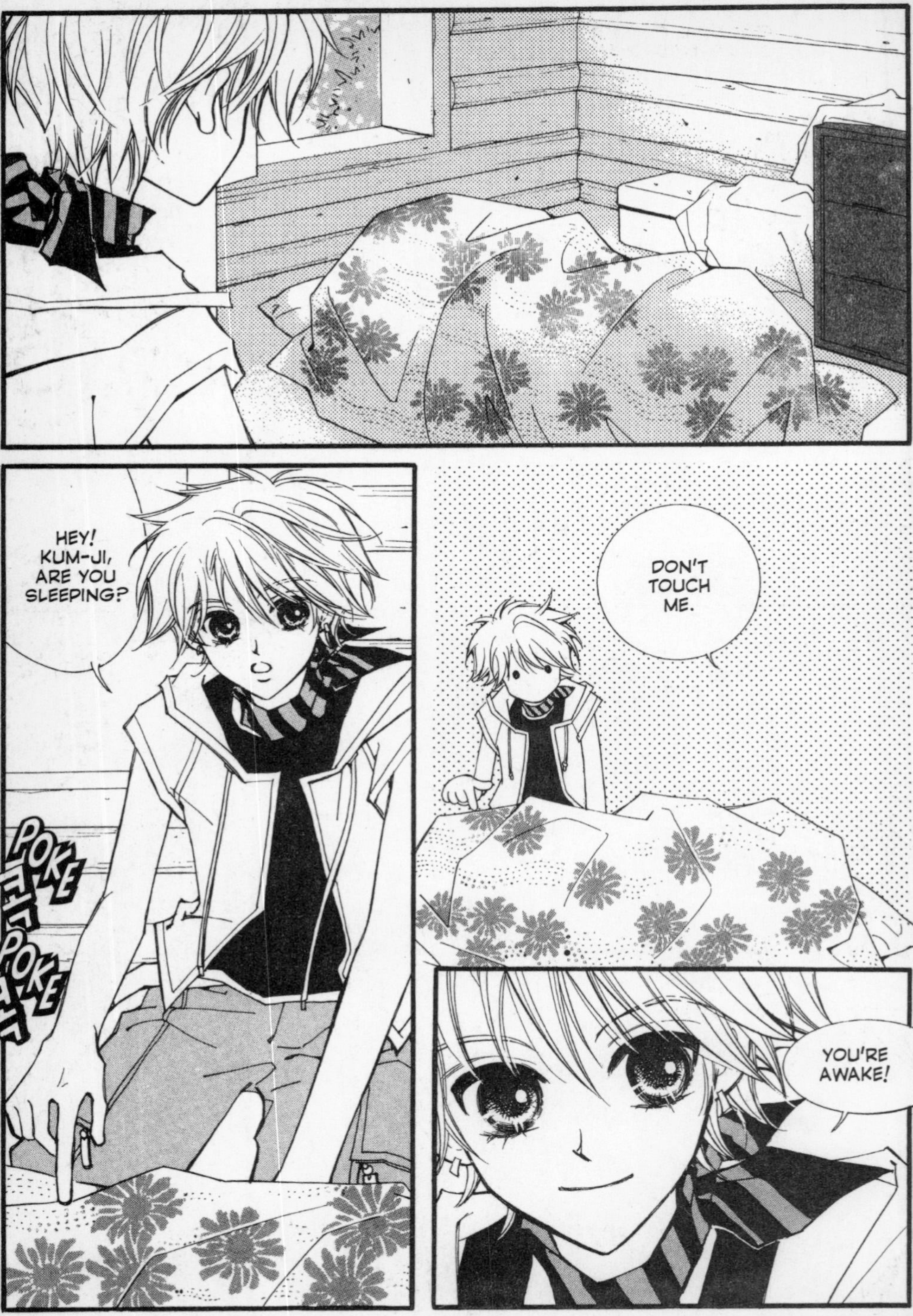
HEY! KUM-JI, ARE YOU SLEEPING?
POKE
POKE
DON'T TOUCH ME.
YOU'RE AWAKE!

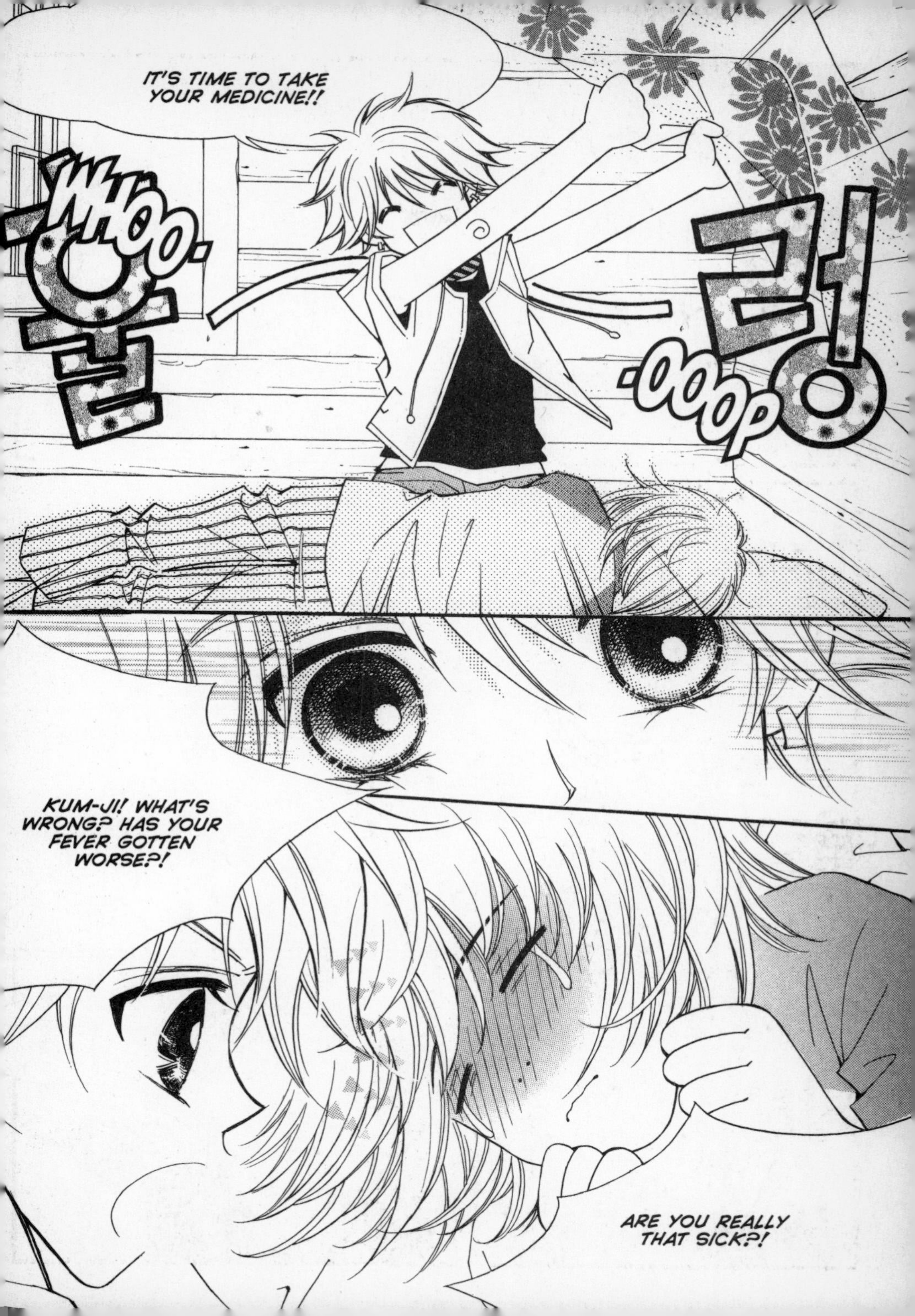
IT'S TIME TO TAKE YOUR MEDICINE!!
-WHOO-
-OOOP
KUM-JI! WHAT'S WRONG? HAS YOUR FEVER GOTTEN WORSE?!
ARE YOU REALLY THAT SICK?!

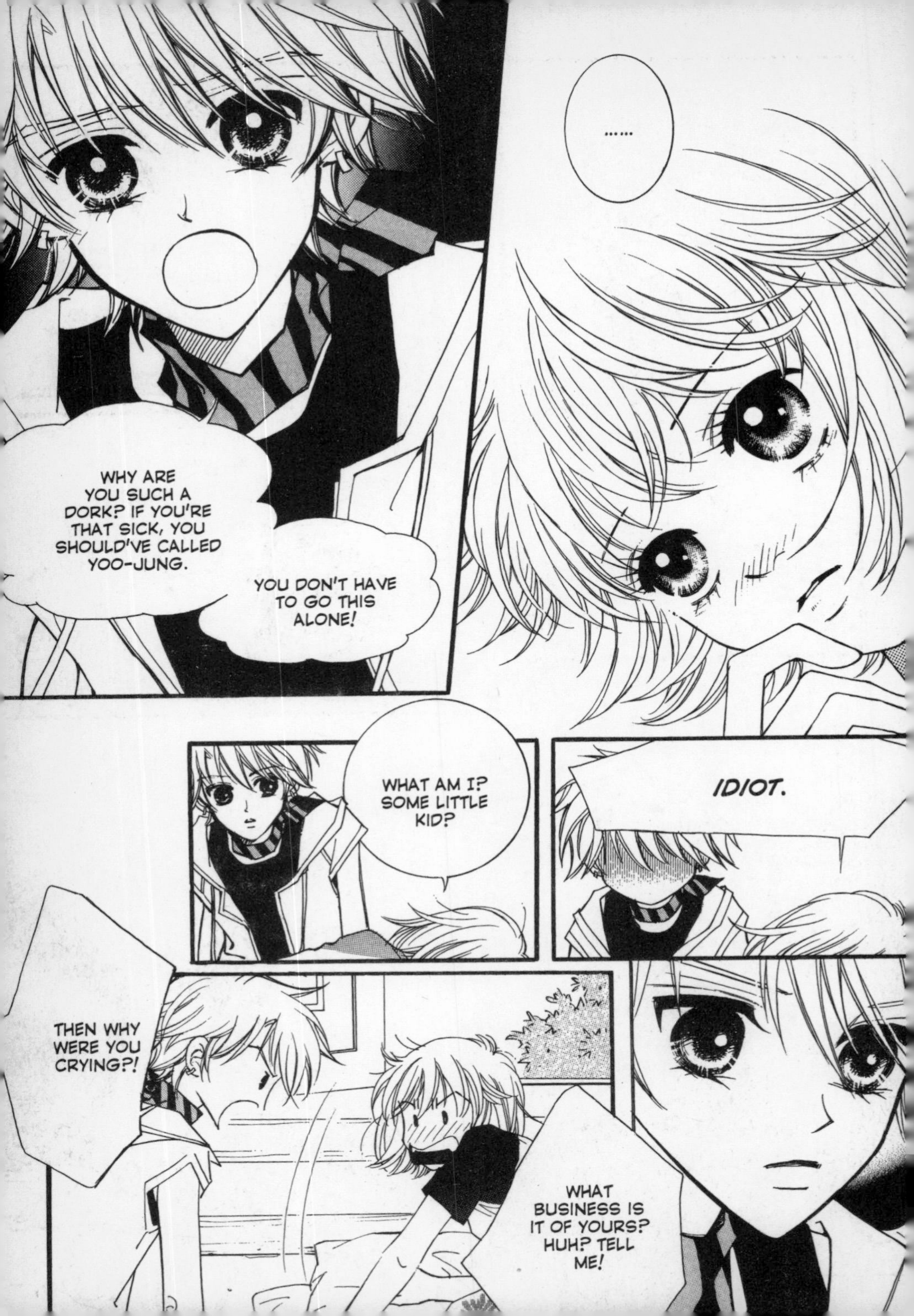
WHY ARE YOU SUCH A DORK? IF YOU'RE THAT SICK, YOU SHOULD'VE CALLED YOO-JUNG.
YOU DON'T HAVE TO GO THIS ALONE!
......
WHAT AM I? SOME LITTLE KID?
IDIOT.
THEN WHY WERE YOU CRYING?!
WHAT BUSINESS IS IT OF YOURS? HUH? TELL ME!

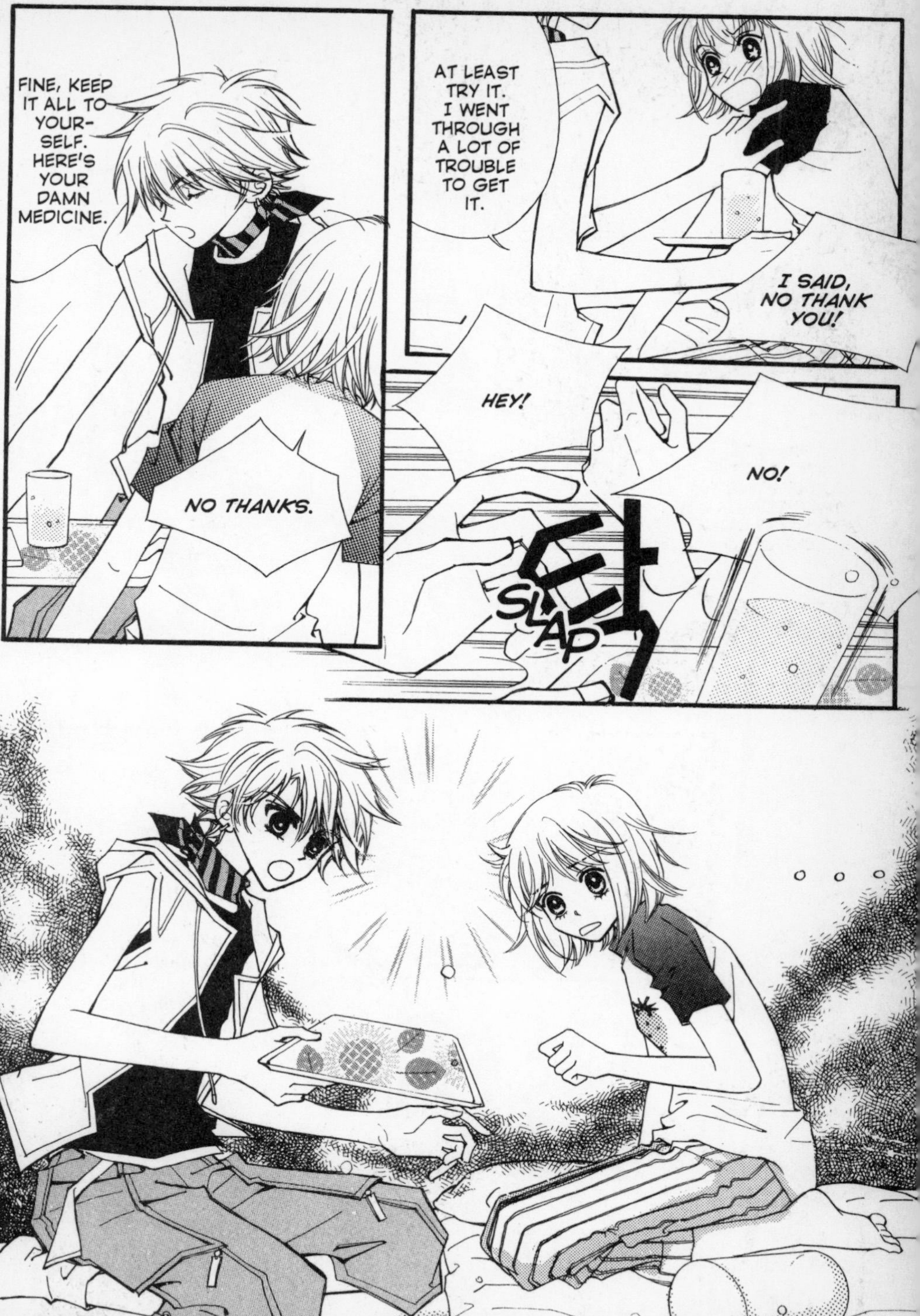
FINE, KEEP IT ALL TO YOUR-SELF. HERE'S YOUR DAMN MEDICINE.
NO THANKS.
AT LEAST TRY IT. I WENT THROUGH A LOT OF TROUBLE TO GET IT.
I SAID, NO THANK YOU!
HEY!
NO!
SLAP
...

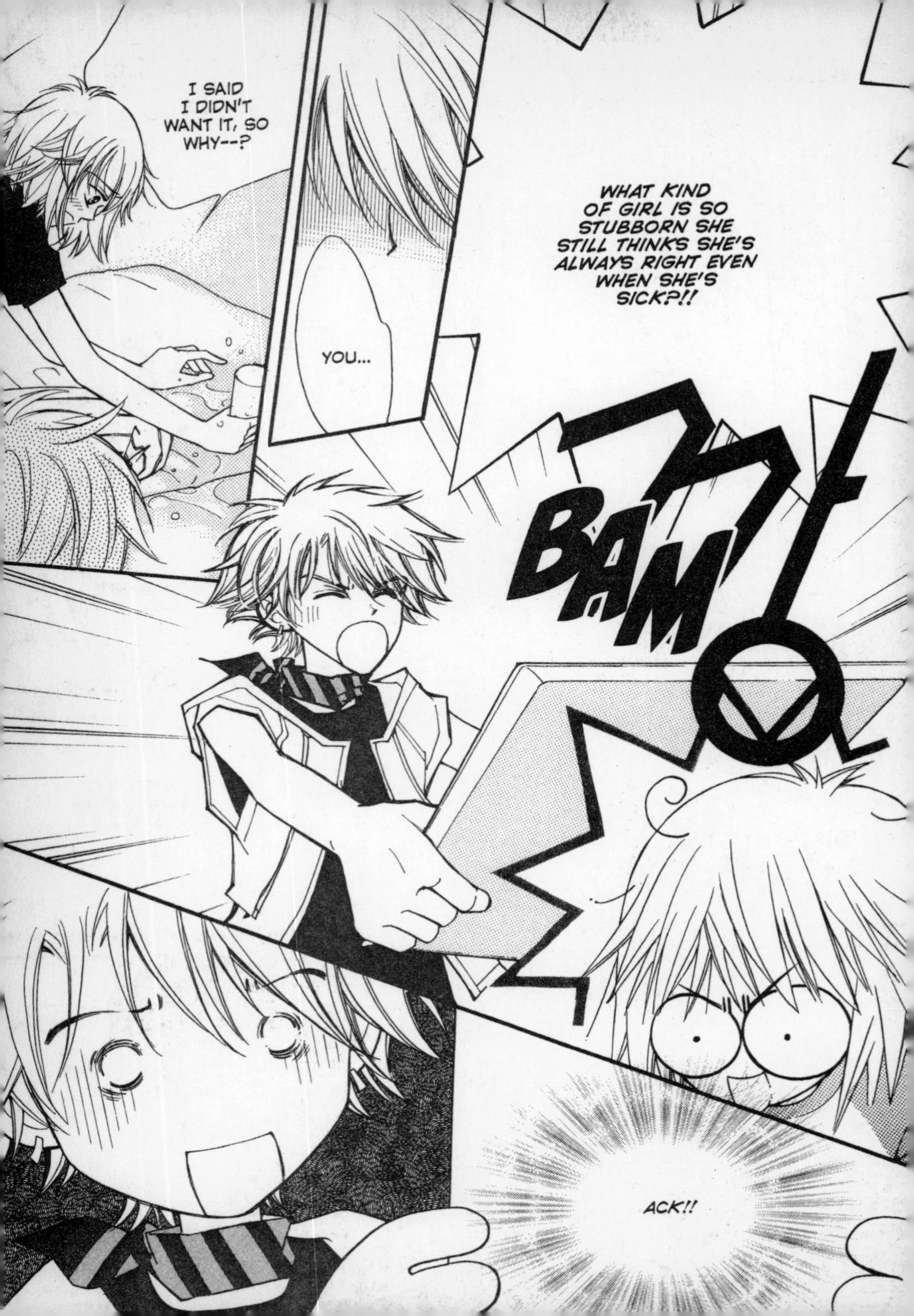
I SAID I DIDN'T WANT IT, SO WHY--?
YOU...
WHAT KIND OF GIRL IS SO STUBBORN SHE STILL THINKS SHE'S ALWAYS RIGHT EVEN WHEN SHE'S SICK?!!
BAM
ACK!!

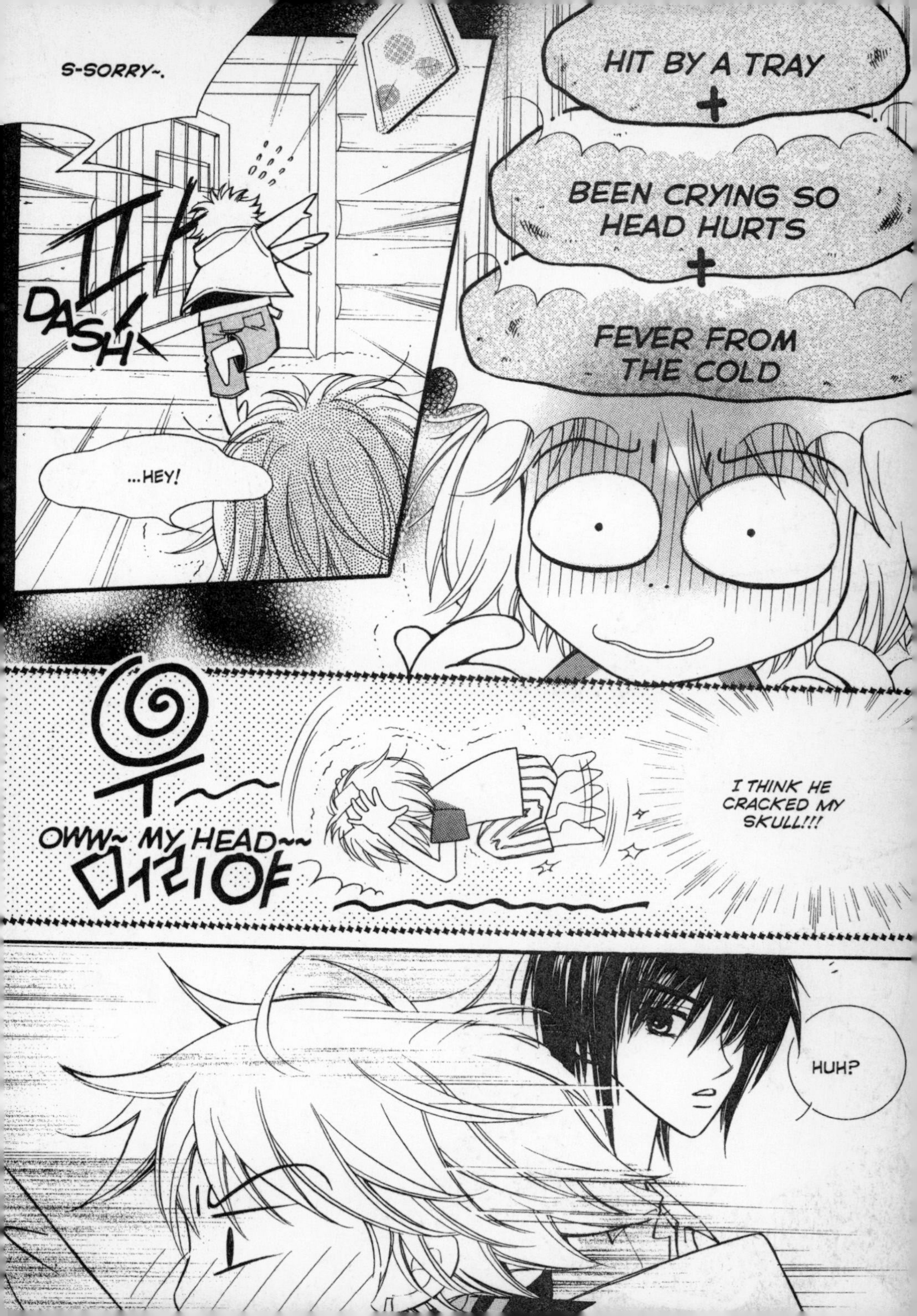
S-SORRY~.
DASH!
...HEY!
HIT BY A TRAY
+
BEEN CRYING SO HEAD HURTS
+
FEVER FROM THE COLD
OWW~ MY HEAD~~
우~ 머리야
I THINK HE CRACKED MY SKULL!!!
HUH?

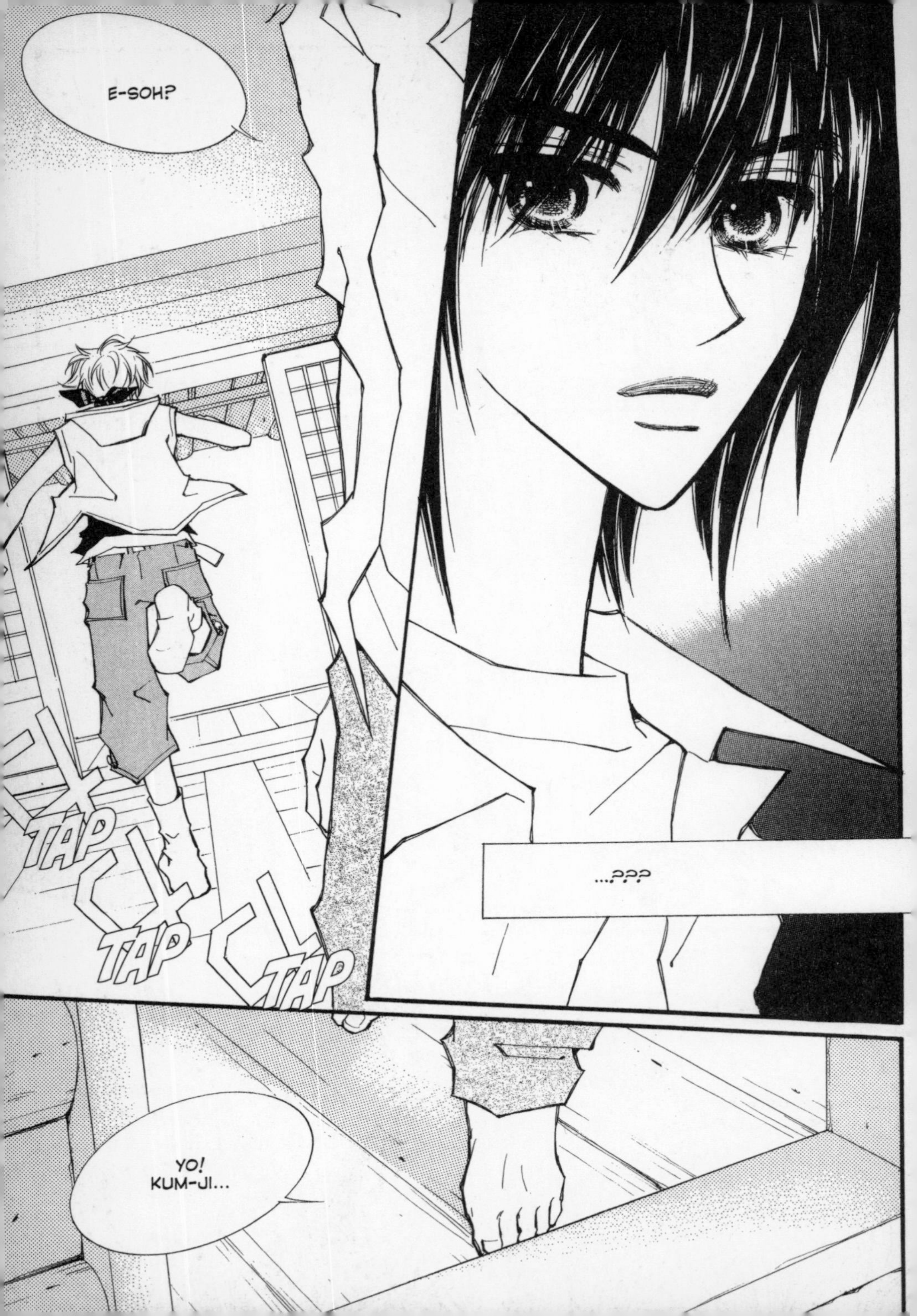
E-SOH?
TAP
TAP
TAP
...???
YO!
KUM-JI...

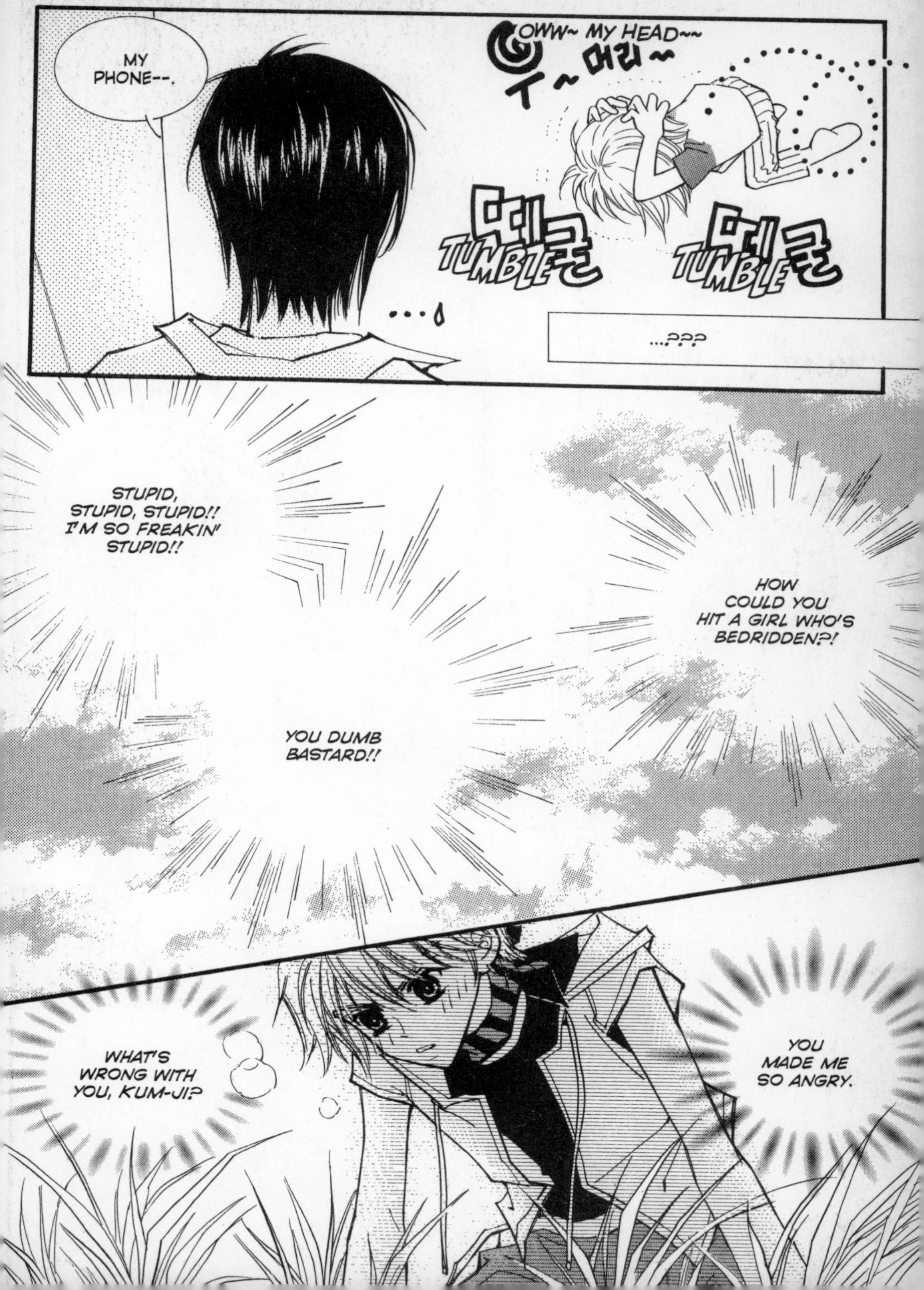
MY PHONE--.
OWW~ MY HEAD~~
아~머리~
데굴
TUMBLE
데굴
TUMBLE
...
...???
STUPID, STUPID, STUPID!! I'M SO FREAKIN' STUPID!!
HOW COULD YOU HIT A GIRL WHO'S BEDRIDDEN?!
YOU DUMB BASTARD!!
WHAT'S WRONG WITH YOU, KUM-JI?
YOU MADE ME SO ANGRY.

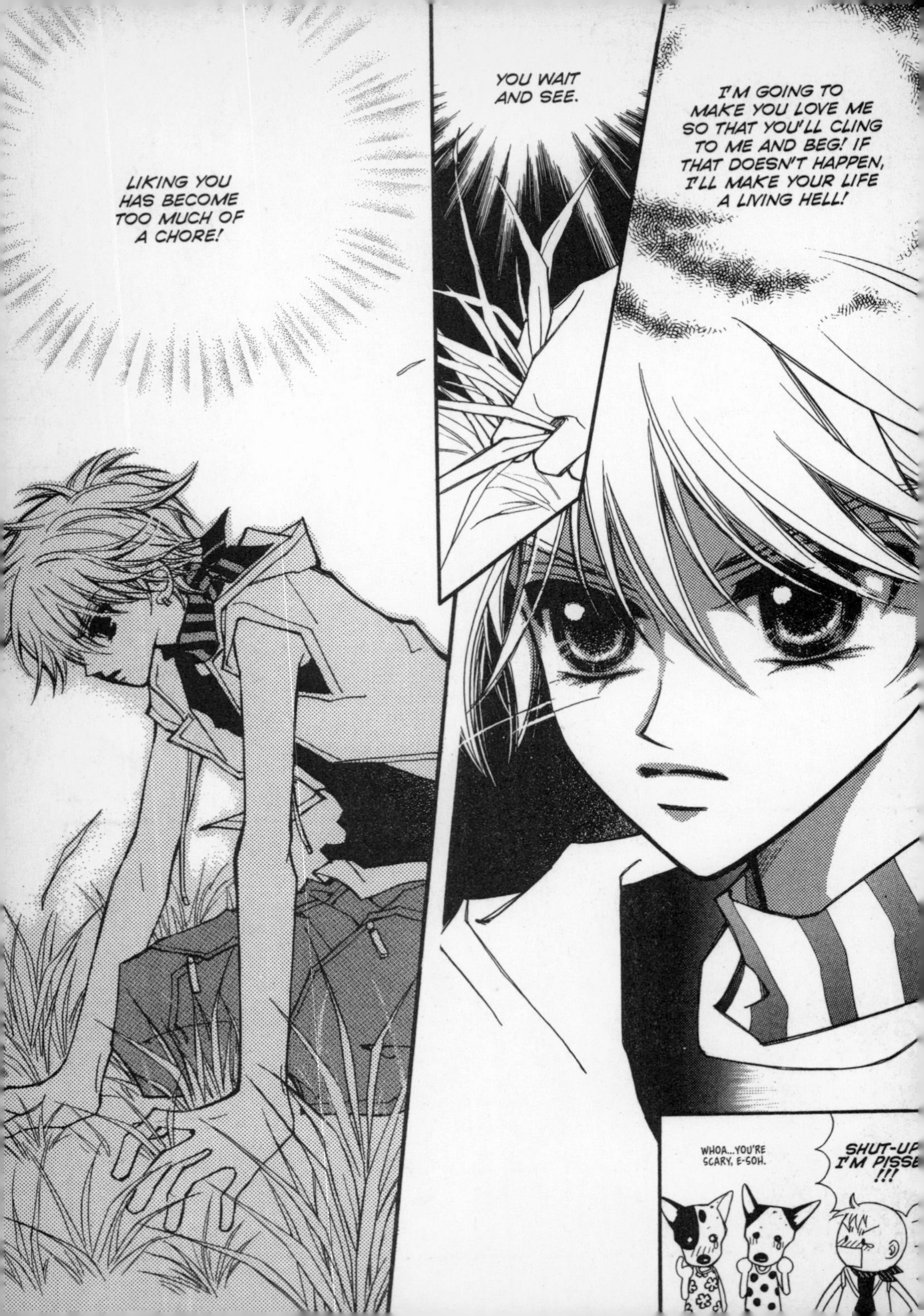
LIKING YOU HAS BECOME TOO MUCH OF A CHORE!
YOU WAIT AND SEE.
I'M GOING TO MAKE YOU LOVE ME SO THAT YOU'LL CLING TO ME AND BEG! IF THAT DOESN'T HAPPEN, I'LL MAKE YOUR LIFE A LIVING HELL!
WHOA...YOU'RE SCARY, E-SOH.
SHUT-UP
I'M PISSE
!!!

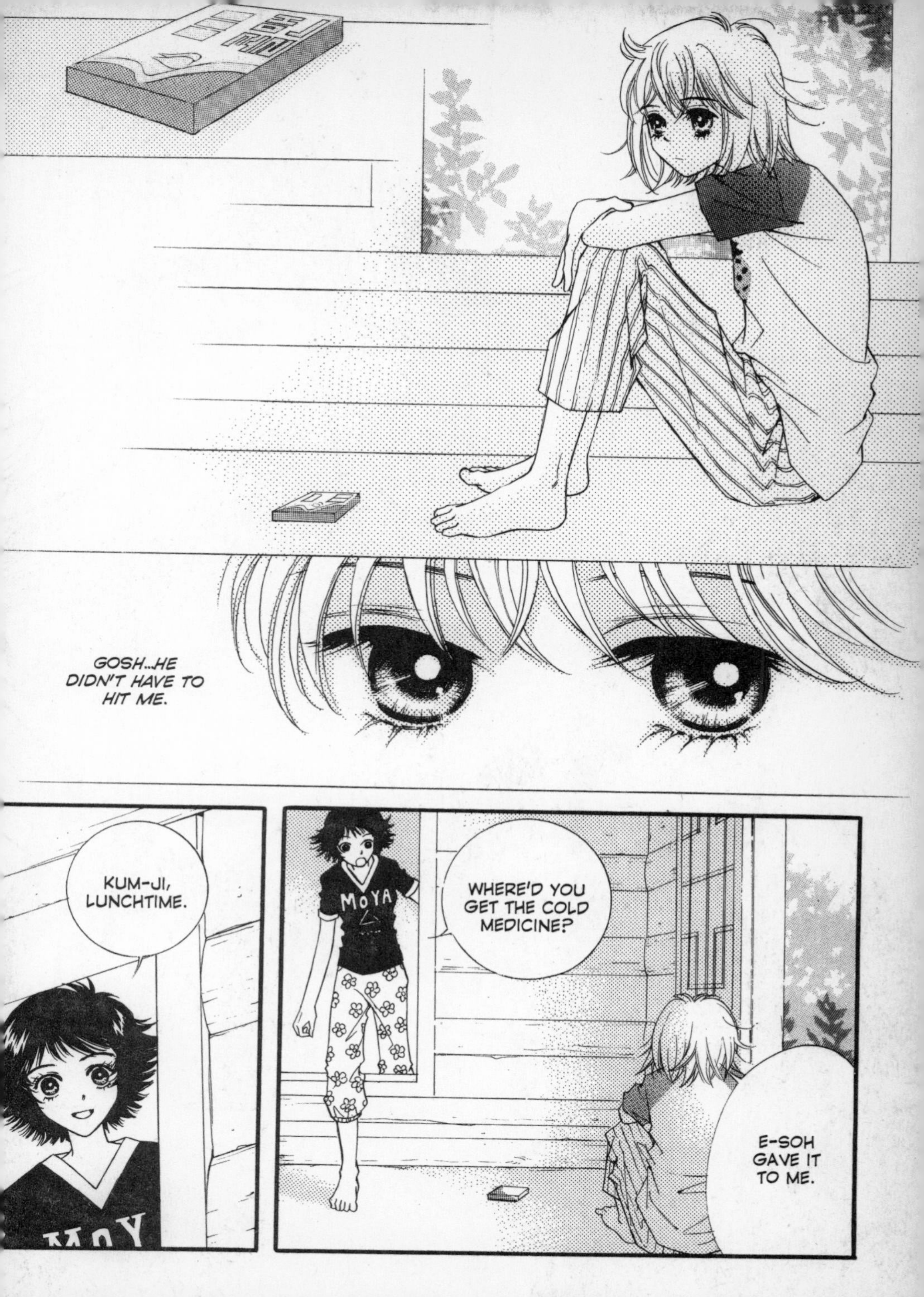
GOSH...HE DIDN'T HAVE TO HIT ME.
KUM-JI, LUNCHTIME.
WHERE'D YOU GET THE COLD MEDICINE?
E-SOH GAVE IT TO ME.

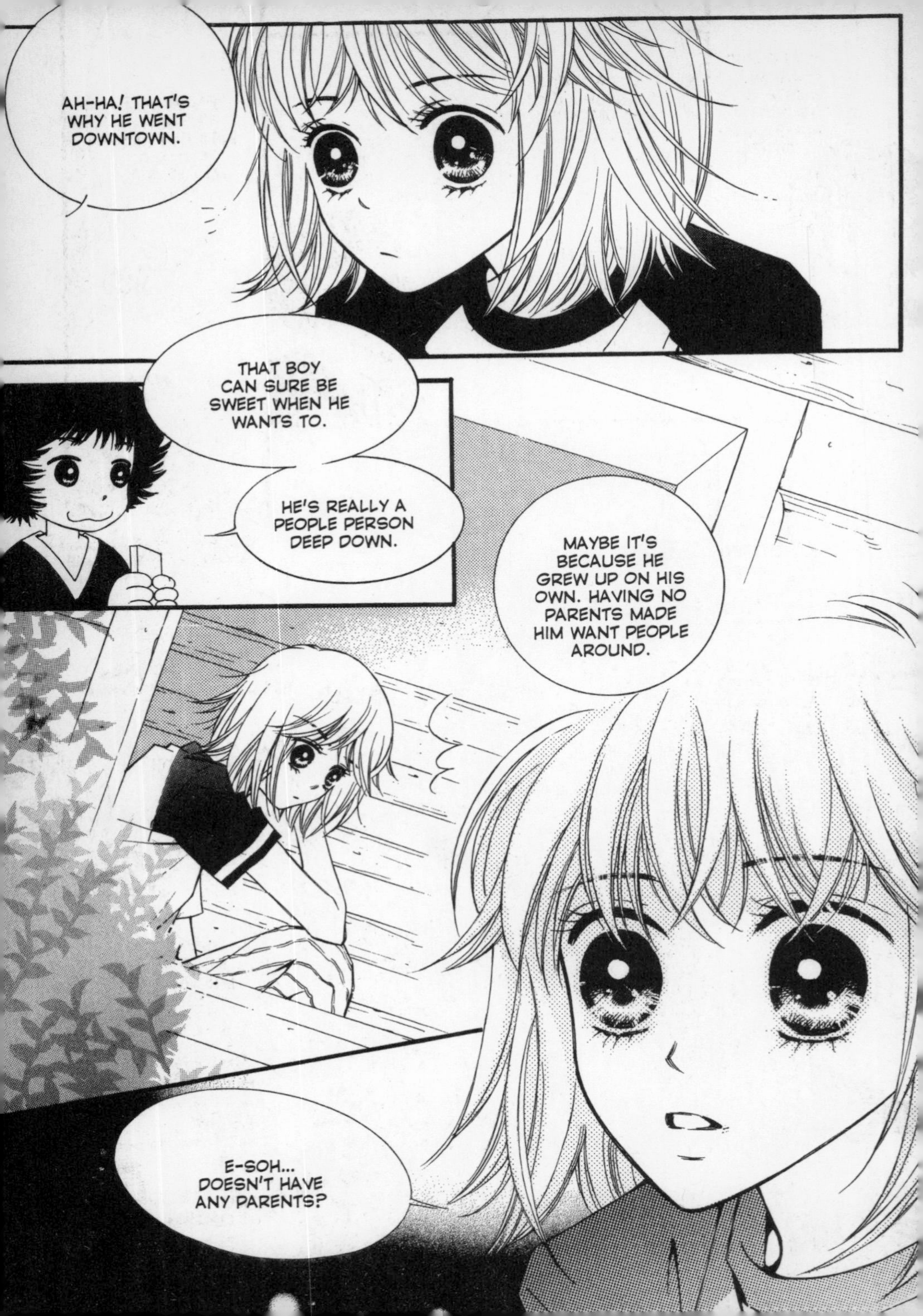
AH-HA! THAT'S WHY HE WENT DOWNTOWN.
THAT BOY CAN SURE BE SWEET WHEN HE WANTS TO.
HE'S REALLY A PEOPLE PERSON DEEP DOWN.
MAYBE IT'S BECAUSE HE GREW UP ON HIS OWN. HAVING NO PARENTS MADE HIM WANT PEOPLE AROUND.
E-SOH... DOESN'T HAVE ANY PARENTS?

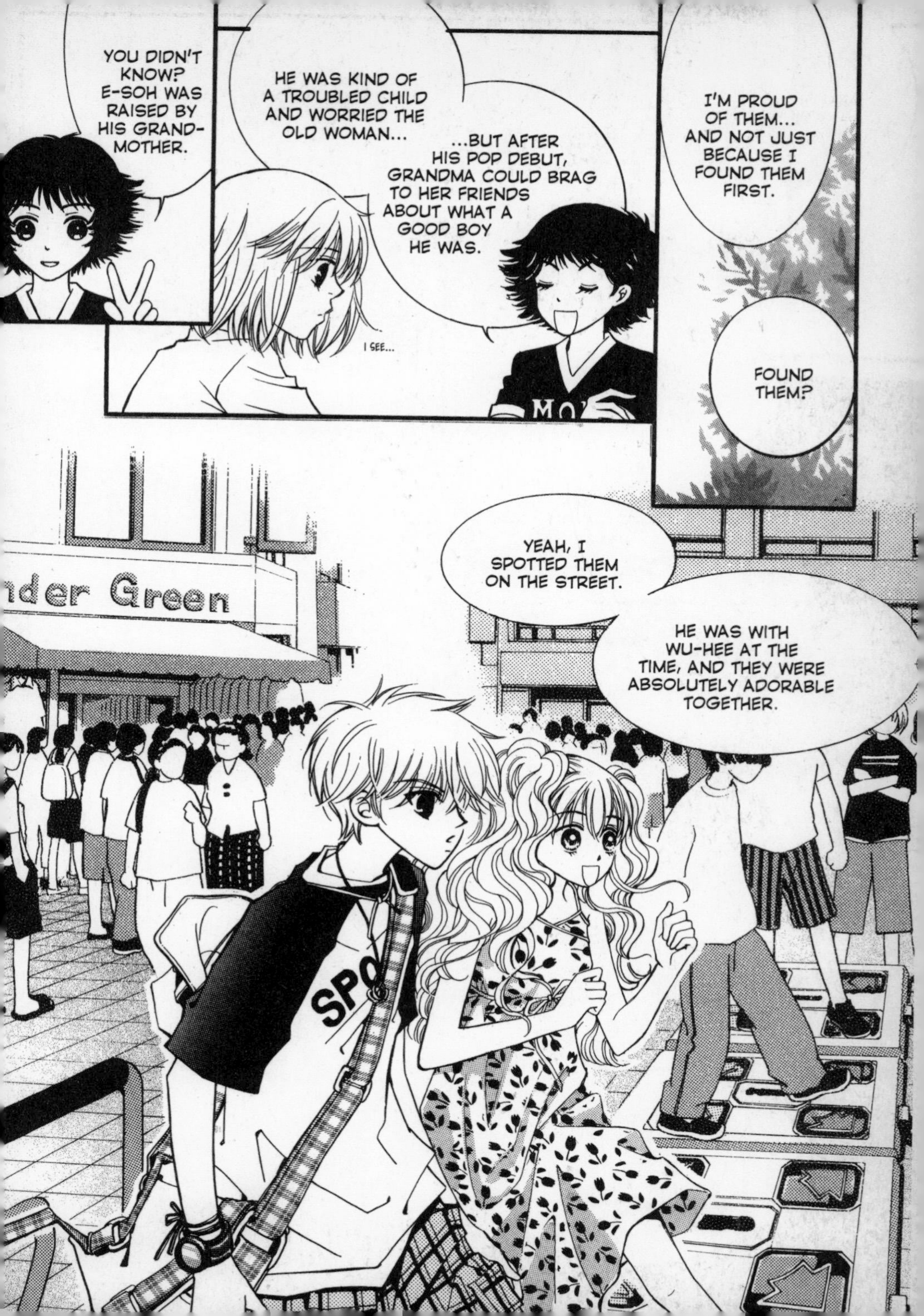
YOU DIDN'T KNOW? E-SOH WAS RAISED BY HIS GRAND-MOTHER.
HE WAS KIND OF A TROUBLED CHILD AND WORRIED THE OLD WOMAN...
...BUT AFTER HIS POP DEBUT, GRANDMA COULD BRAG TO HER FRIENDS ABOUT WHAT A GOOD BOY HE WAS.
I SEE...
I'M PROUD OF THEM... AND NOT JUST BECAUSE I FOUND THEM FIRST.
FOUND THEM?
nder Green
YEAH, I SPOTTED THEM ON THE STREET.
HE WAS WITH WU-HEE AT THE TIME, AND THEY WERE ABSOLUTELY ADORABLE TOGETHER.

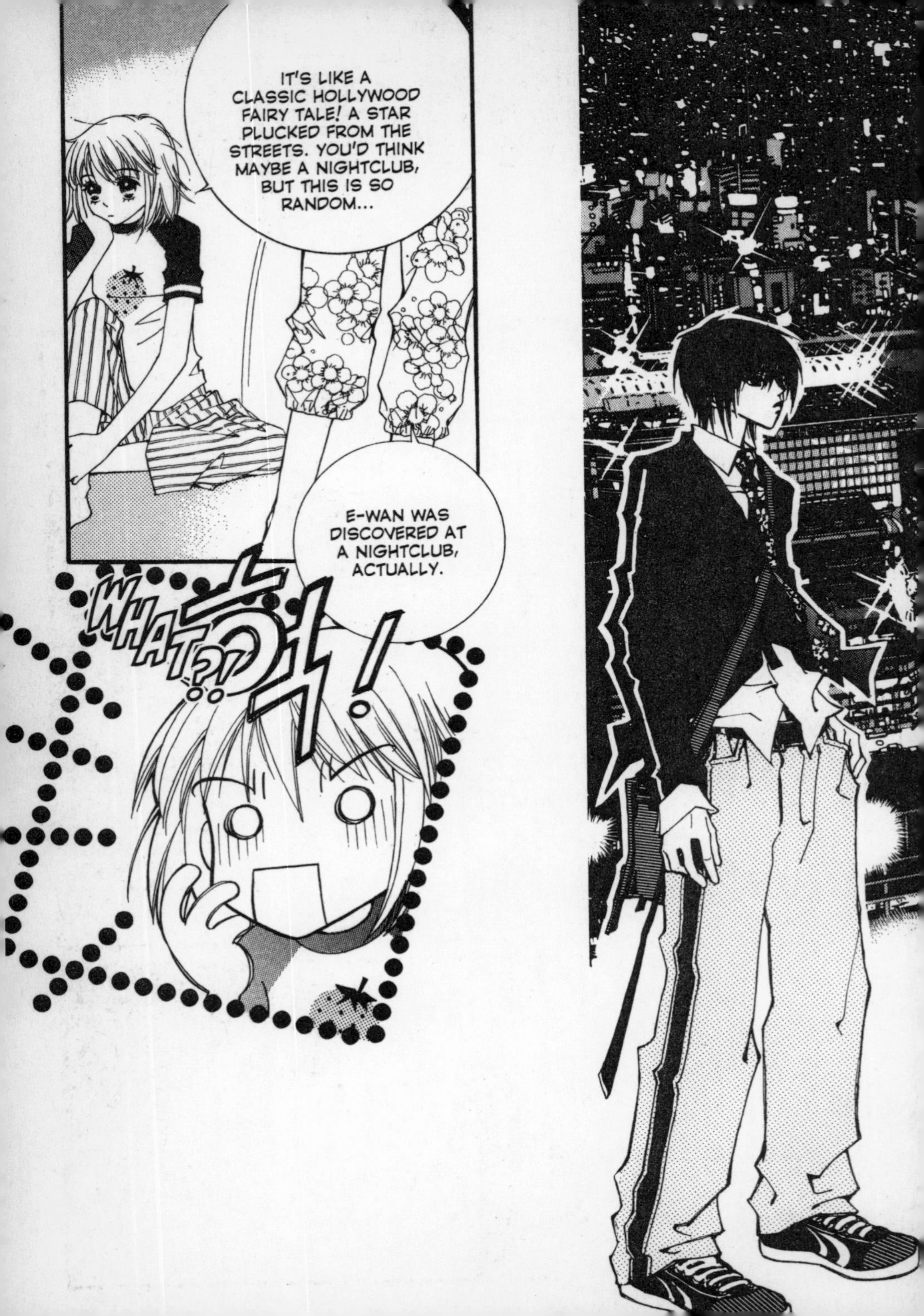
IT'S LIKE A CLASSIC HOLLYWOOD FAIRY TALE! A STAR PLUCKED FROM THE STREETS. YOU'D THINK MAYBE A NIGHTCLUB, BUT THIS IS SO RANDOM...
E-WAN WAS DISCOVERED AT A NIGHTCLUB, ACTUALLY.
WHAT?!

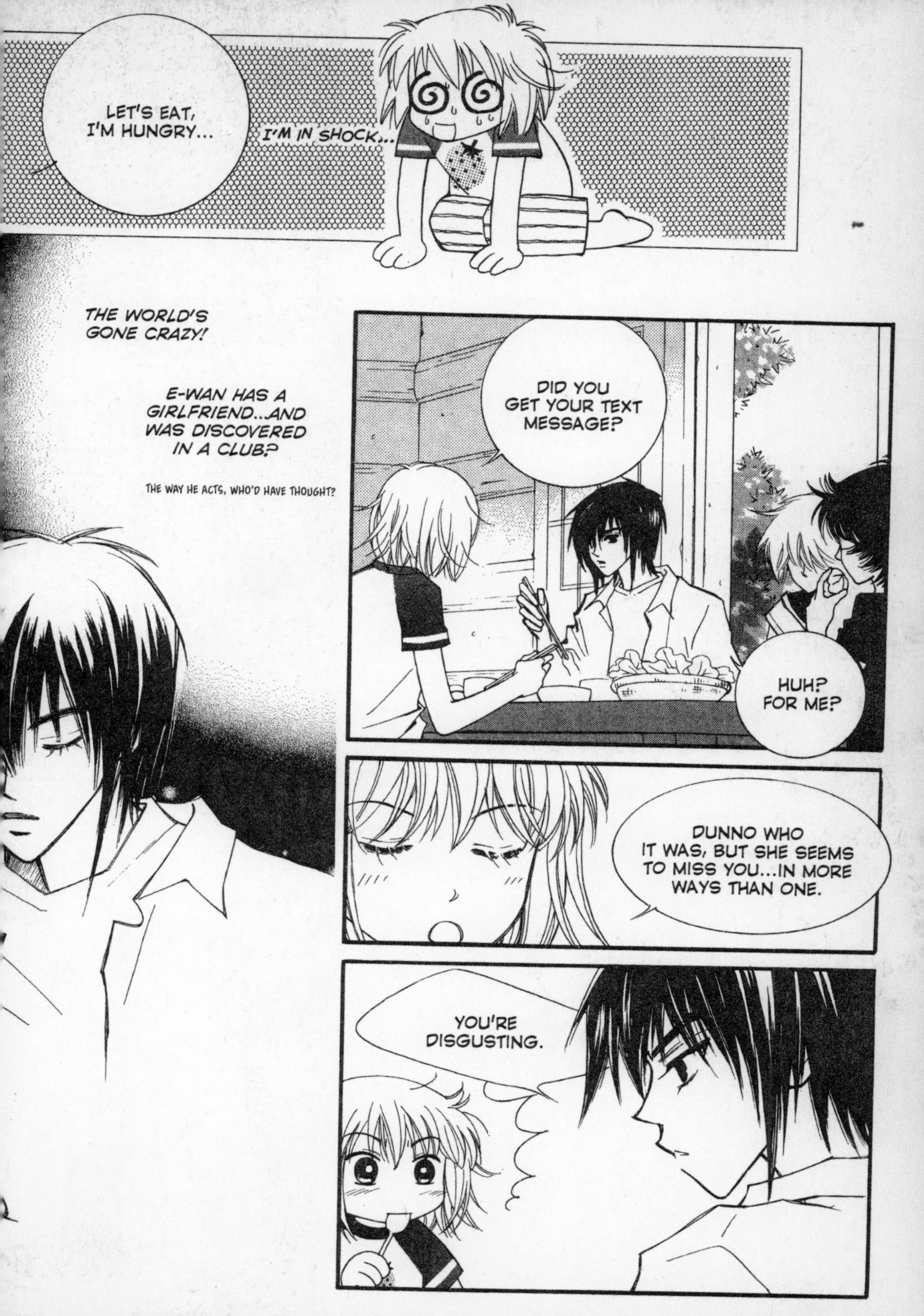
LET'S EAT, I'M HUNGRY...
I'M IN SHOCK...
THE WORLD'S GONE CRAZY!
E-WAN HAS A GIRLFRIEND...AND WAS DISCOVERED IN A CLUB?
THE WAY HE ACTS, WHO'D HAVE THOUGHT?
DID YOU GET YOUR TEXT MESSAGE?
HUH? FOR ME?
DUNNO WHO IT WAS, BUT SHE SEEMS TO MISS YOU...IN MORE WAYS THAN ONE.
YOU'RE DISGUSTING.

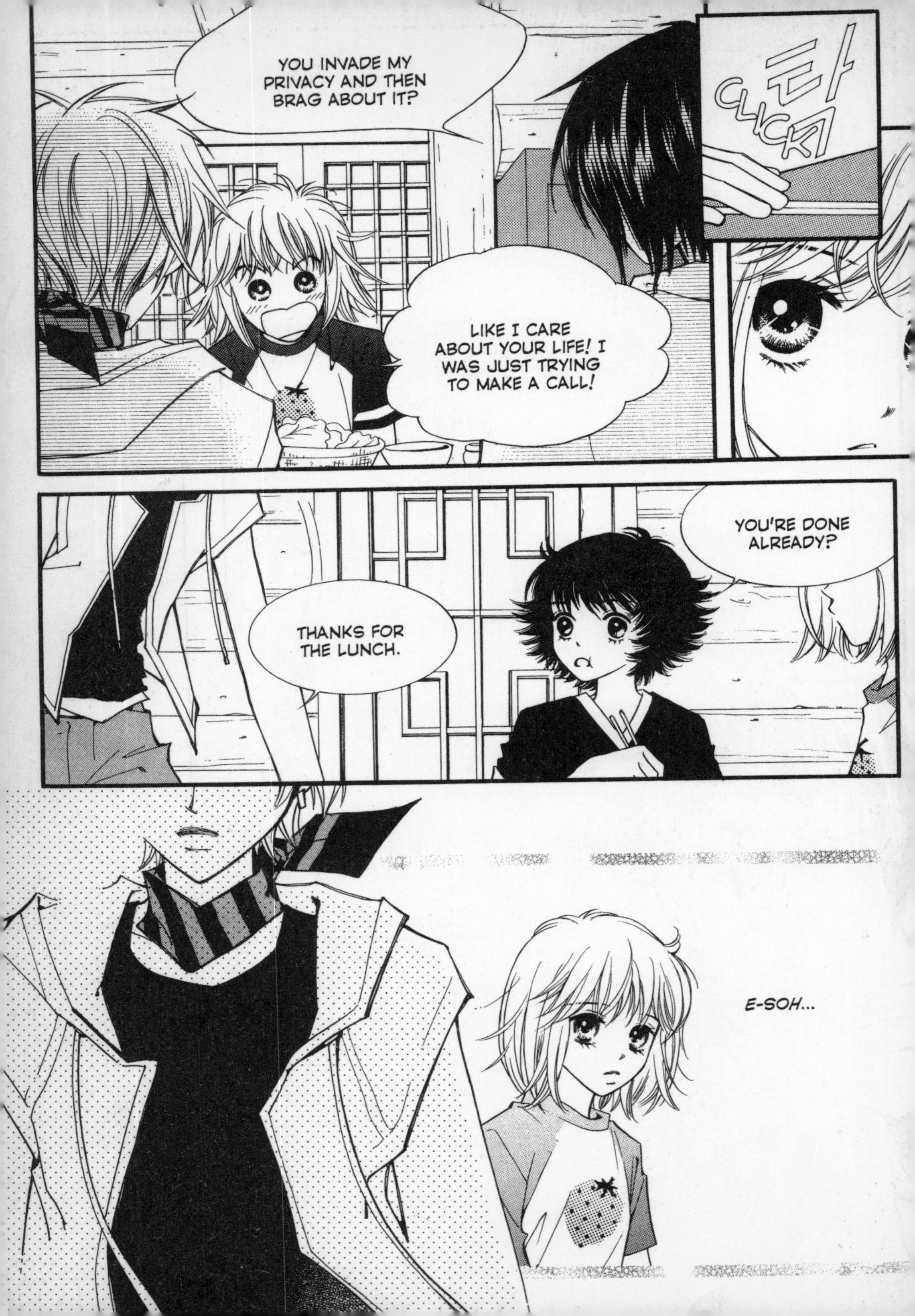
YOU INVADE MY PRIVACY AND THEN BRAG ABOUT IT?
LIKE I CARE ABOUT YOUR LIFE! I WAS JUST TRYING TO MAKE A CALL!
CLICK
YOU'RE DONE ALREADY?
THANKS FOR THE LUNCH.
E-SOH...

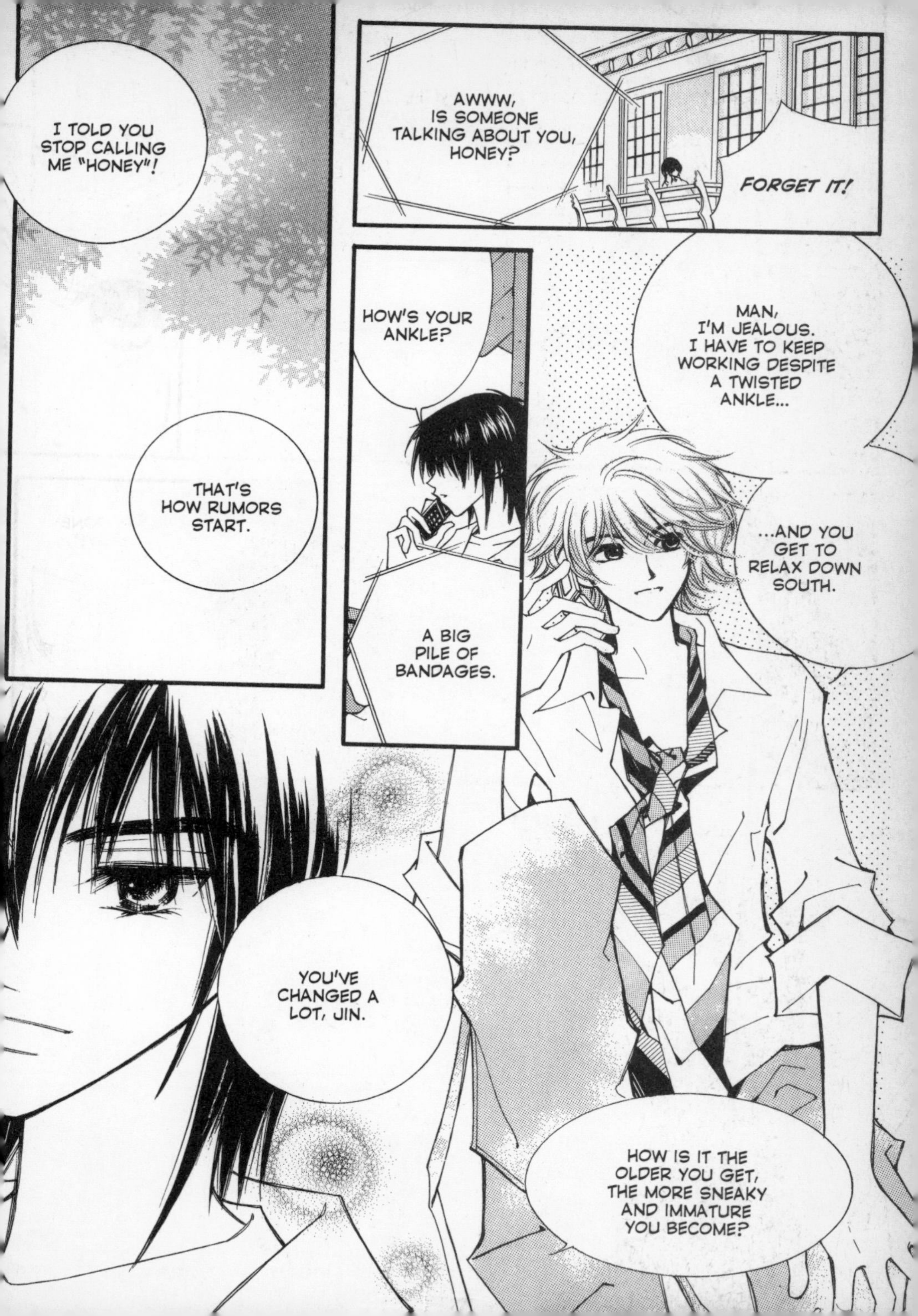
I TOLD YOU STOP CALLING ME "HONEY"!
THAT'S HOW RUMORS START.
AWWW, IS SOMEONE TALKING ABOUT YOU, HONEY?
FORGET IT!
HOW'S YOUR ANKLE?
A BIG PILE OF BANDAGES.
MAN, I'M JEALOUS. I HAVE TO KEEP WORKING DESPITE A TWISTED ANKLE...
...AND YOU GET TO RELAX DOWN SOUTH.
YOU'VE CHANGED A LOT, JIN.
HOW IS IT THE OLDER YOU GET, THE MORE SNEAKY AND IMMATURE YOU BECOME?

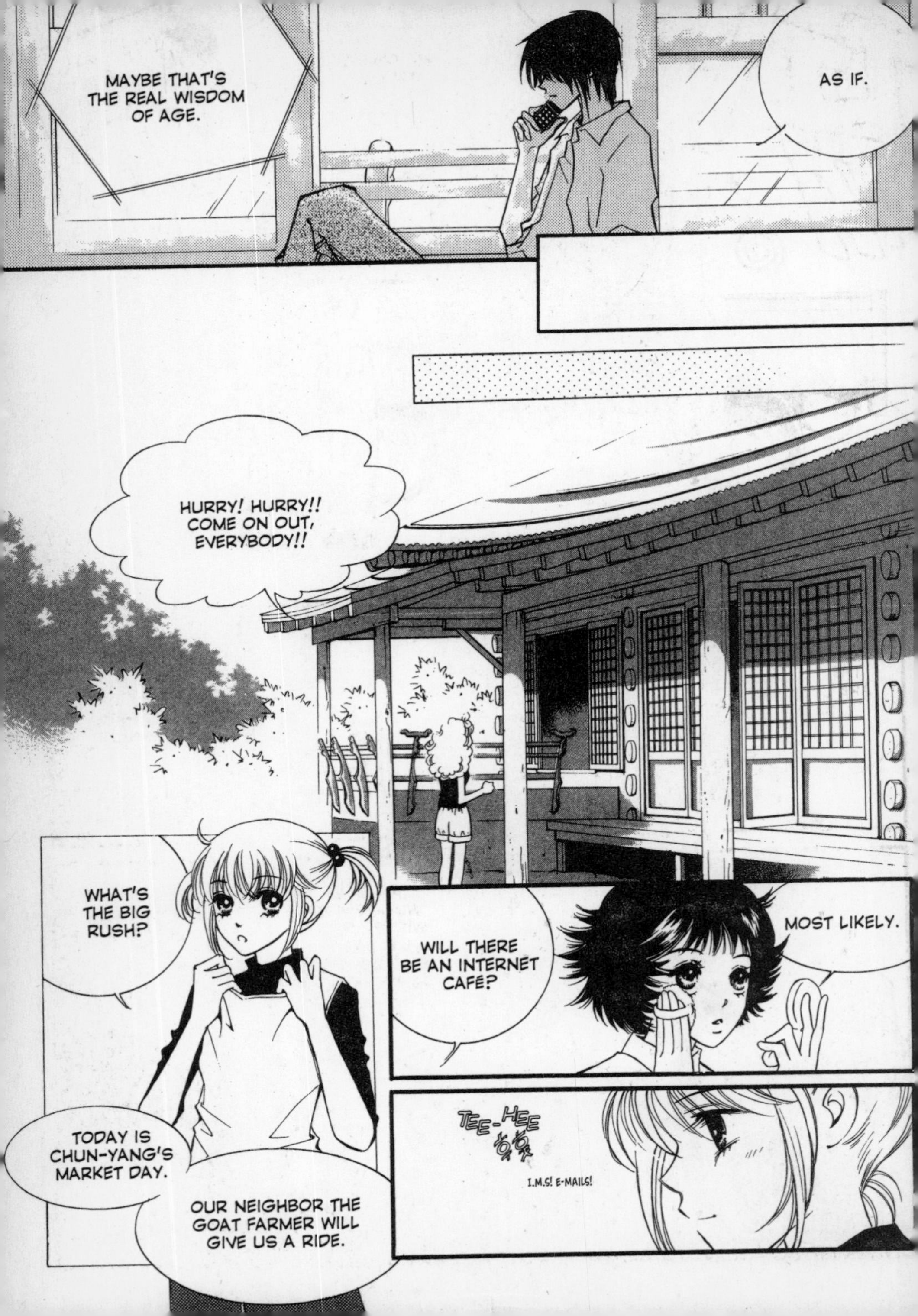

MAYBE THAT'S THE REAL WISDOM OF AGE.
AS IF.
HURRY! HURRY!! COME ON OUT, EVERYBODY!!
WHAT'S THE BIG RUSH?
TODAY IS CHUN-YANG'S MARKET DAY.
OUR NEIGHBOR THE GOAT FARMER WILL GIVE US A RIDE.
WILL THERE BE AN INTERNET CAFÉ?
MOST LIKELY.
TEE-HEE
I.M.S! E-MAILS!

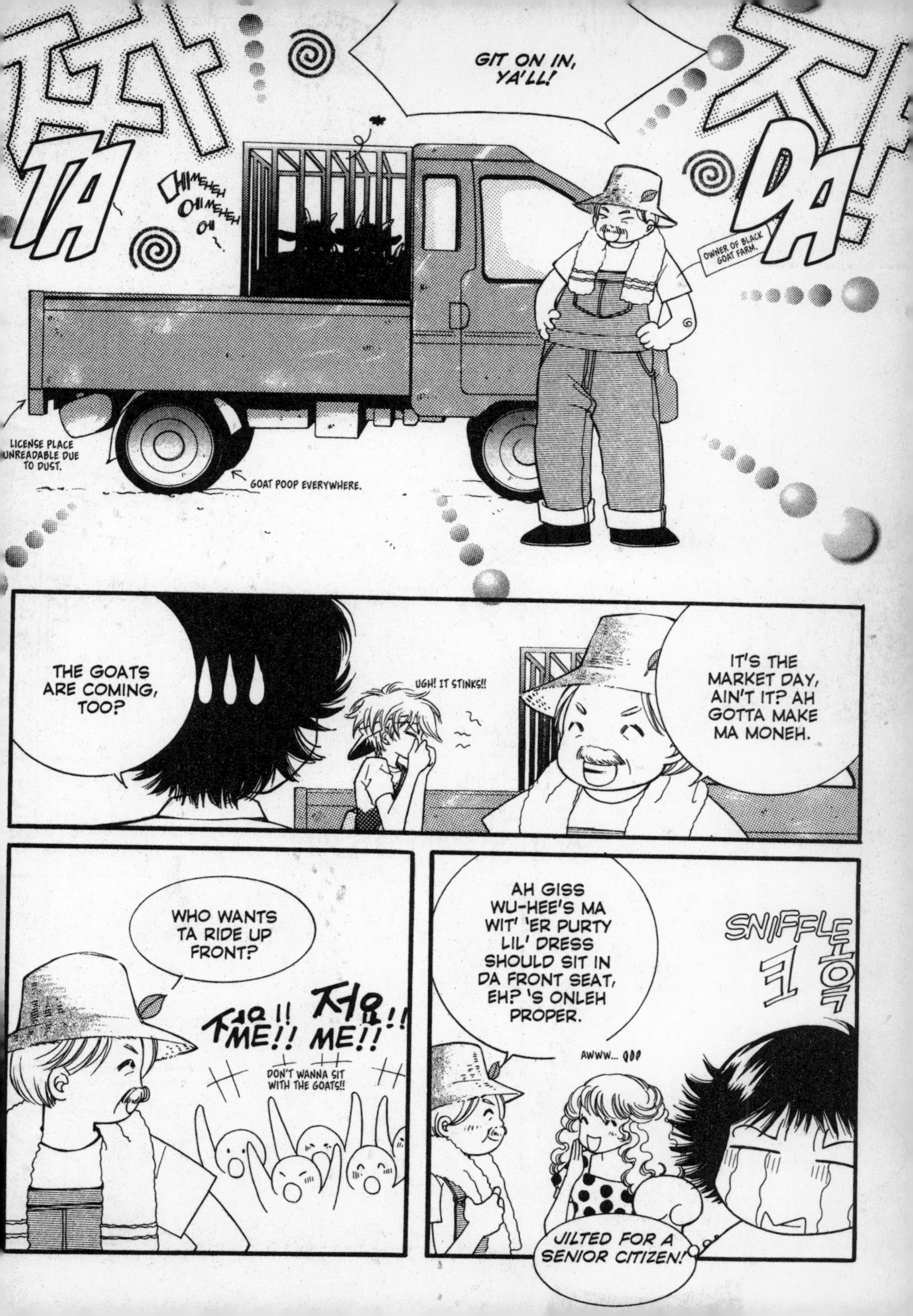
TA
CHIMEHEH
CHIMEHEH
CH!
GIT ON IN, YA'LL!
DA!
OWNER OF BLACK GOAT FARM.
LICENSE PLACE UNREADABLE DUE TO DUST.
GOAT POOP EVERYWHERE.
THE GOATS ARE COMING, TOO?
UGH! IT STINKS!!
IT'S THE MARKET DAY, AIN'T IT? AH GOTTA MAKE MA MONEH.
WHO WANTS TA RIDE UP FRONT?
저요!! ME!!
저요!! ME!!
DON'T WANNA SIT WITH THE GOATS!!
AH GISS WU-HEE'S MA WIT' 'ER PURTY LIL' DRESS SHOULD SIT IN DA FRONT SEAT, EH? 'S ONLEH PROPER.
SNIFFLE
AWWW...
JILTED FOR A SENIOR CITIZEN!

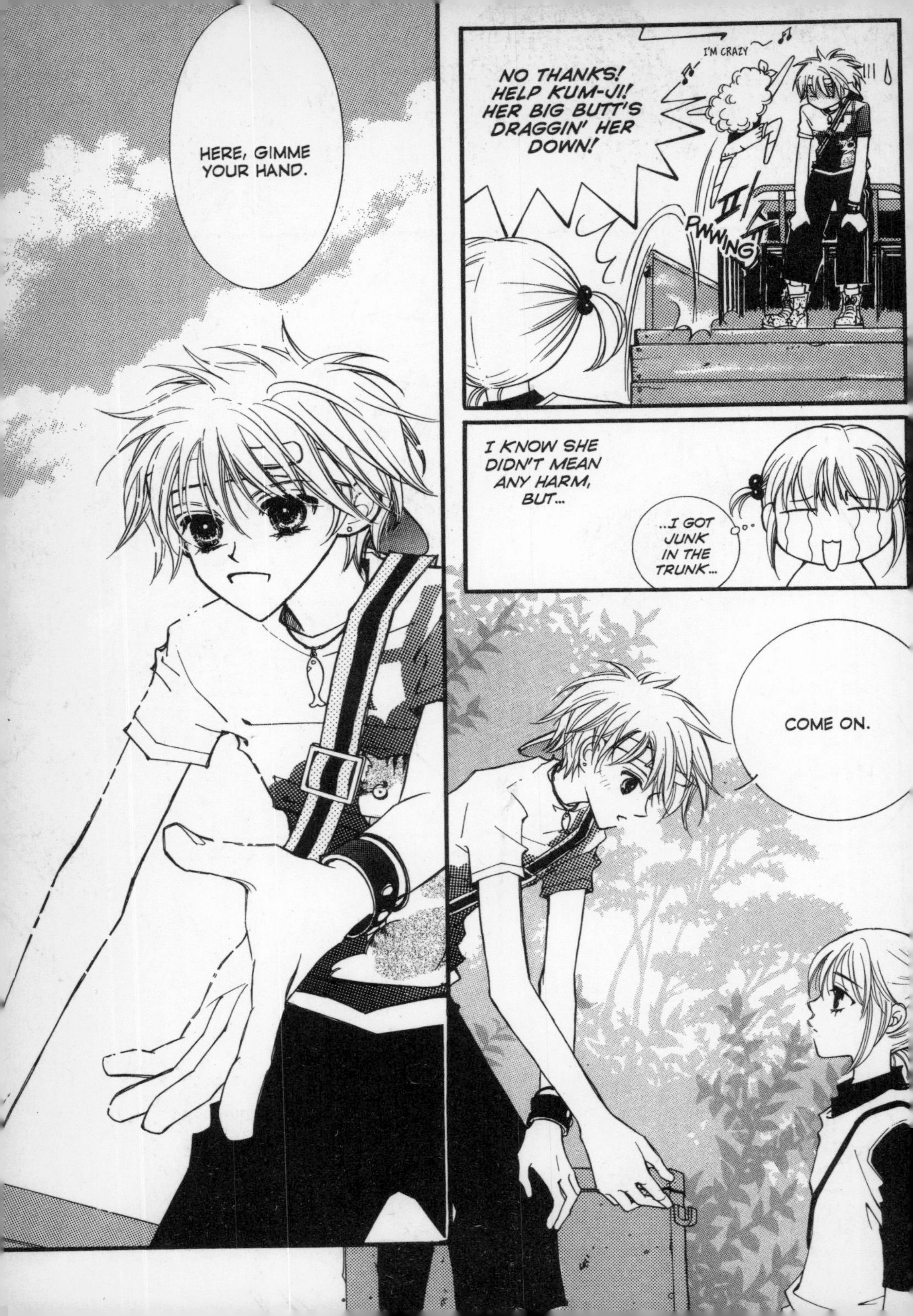
HERE, GIMME YOUR HAND.
NO THANKS! HELP KUM-JI! HER BIG BUTT'S DRAGGIN' HER DOWN!
I'M CRAZY
PWWING
I KNOW SHE DIDN'T MEAN ANY HARM, BUT...
...I GOT JUNK IN THE TRUNK...
COME ON.

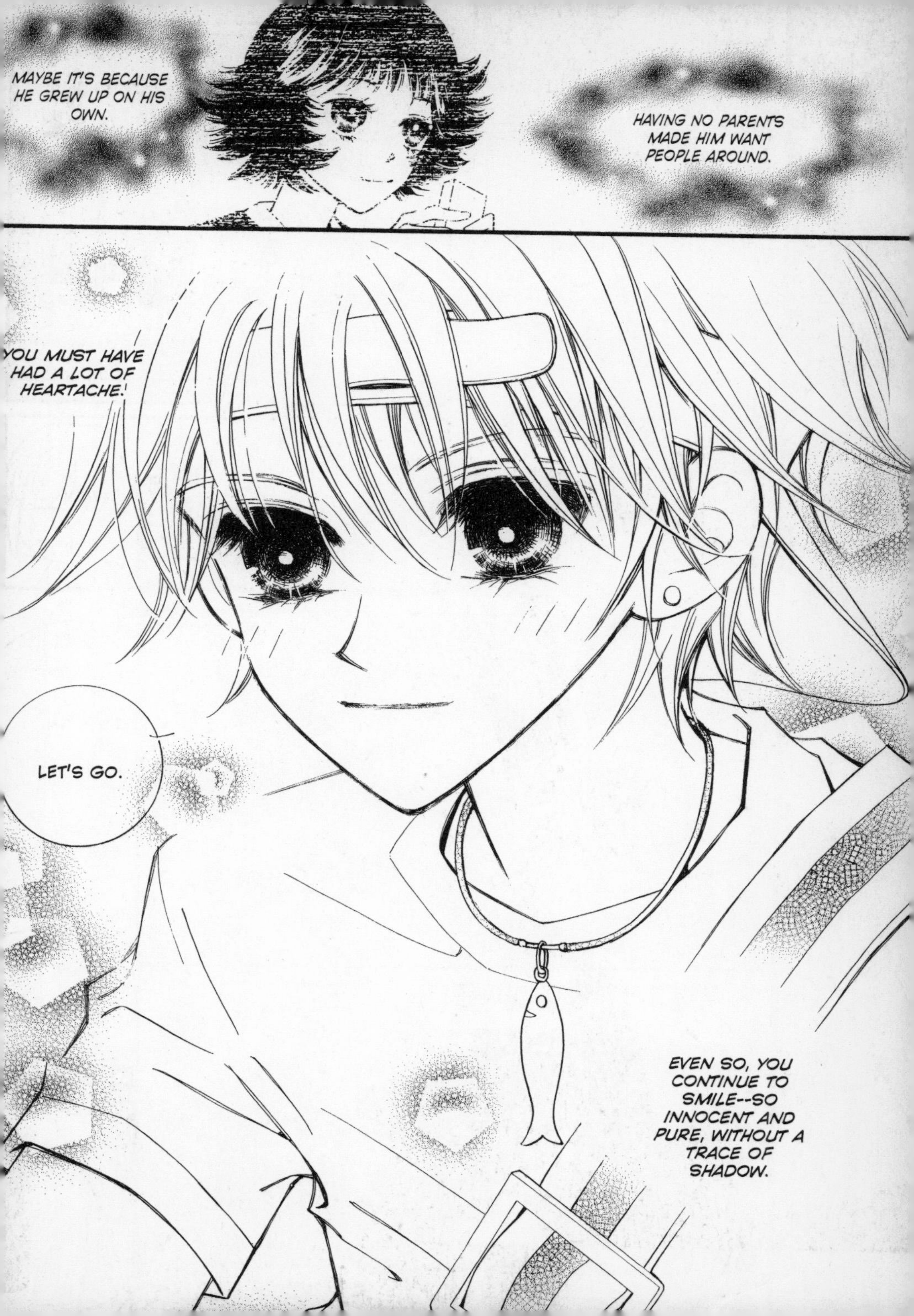
MAYBE IT'S BECAUSE HE GREW UP ON HIS OWN.
HAVING NO PARENTS MADE HIM WANT PEOPLE AROUND.
YOU MUST HAVE HAD A LOT OF HEARTACHE.
LET'S GO.
EVEN SO, YOU CONTINUE TO SMILE--SO INNOCENT AND PURE, WITHOUT A TRACE OF SHADOW.

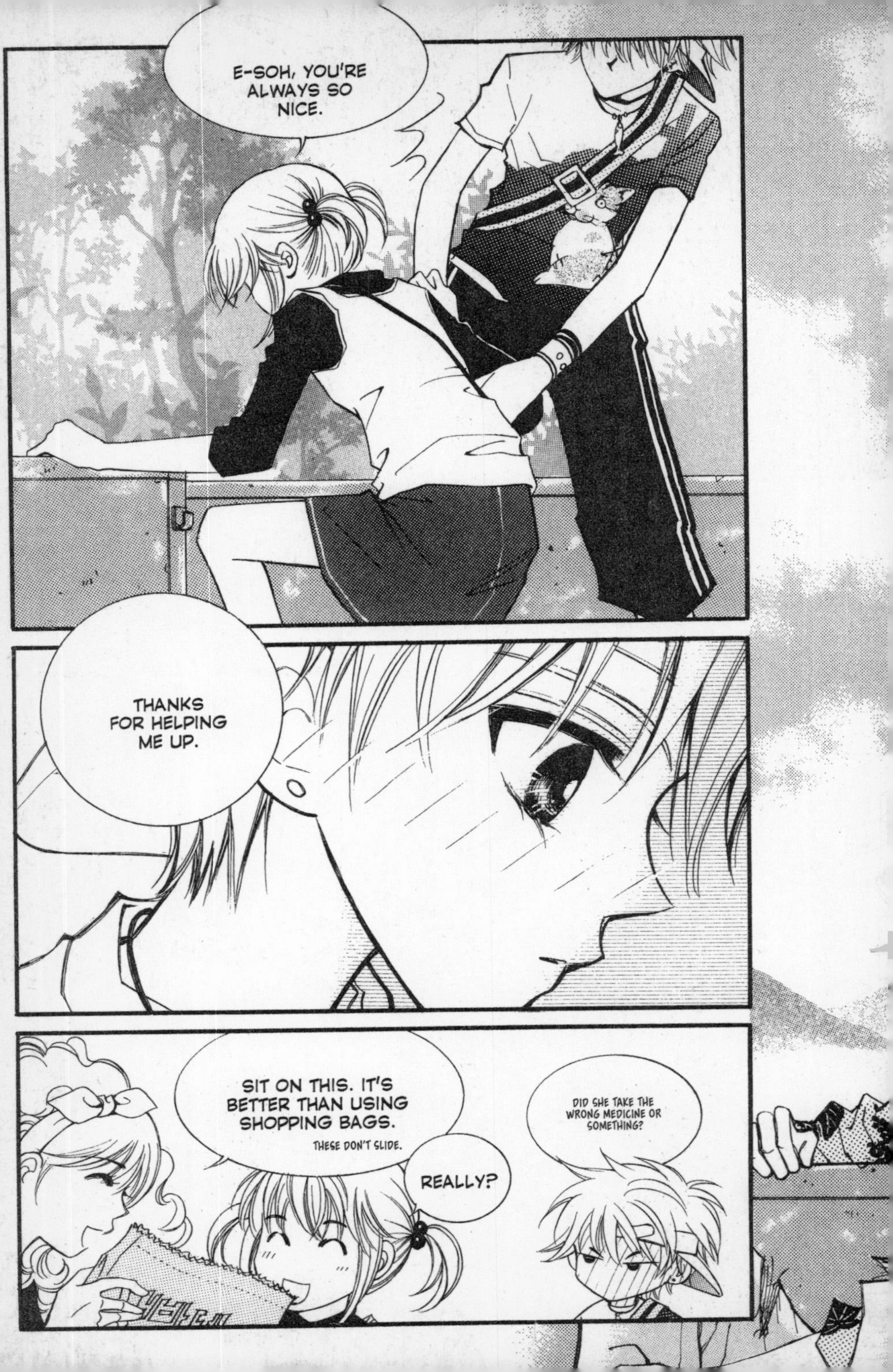
E-SOH, YOU'RE ALWAYS SO NICE.
THANKS FOR HELPING ME UP.
SIT ON THIS. IT'S BETTER THAN USING SHOPPING BAGS.
THESE DON'T SLIDE.
REALLY?
DID SHE TAKE THE WRONG MEDICINE OR SOMETHING?

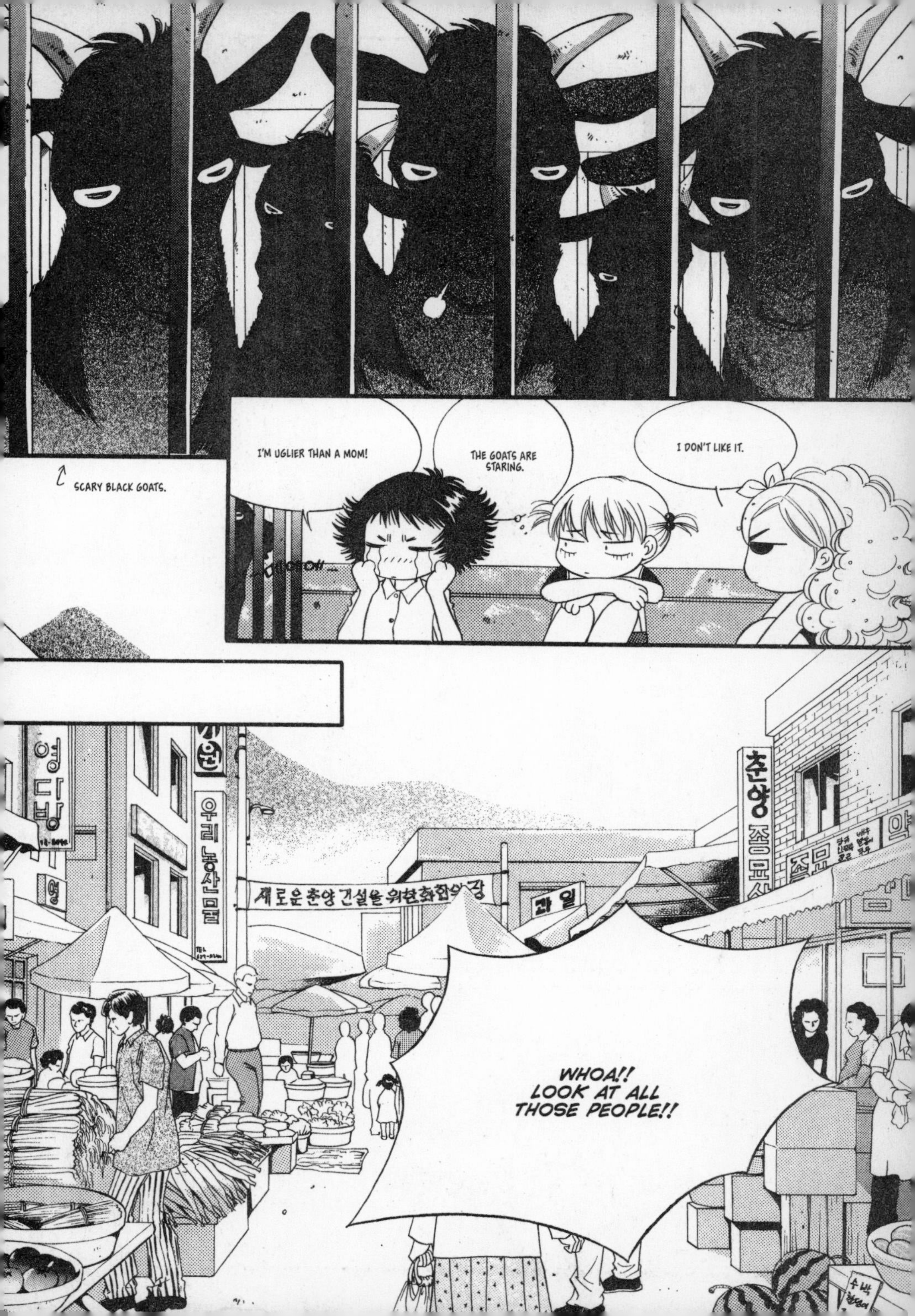
SCARY BLACK GOATS.
I'M UGLIER THAN A MOM!
THE GOATS ARE STARING.
I DON'T LIKE IT.
우리농산물
과일
WHOA!! LOOK AT ALL THOSE PEOPLE!!

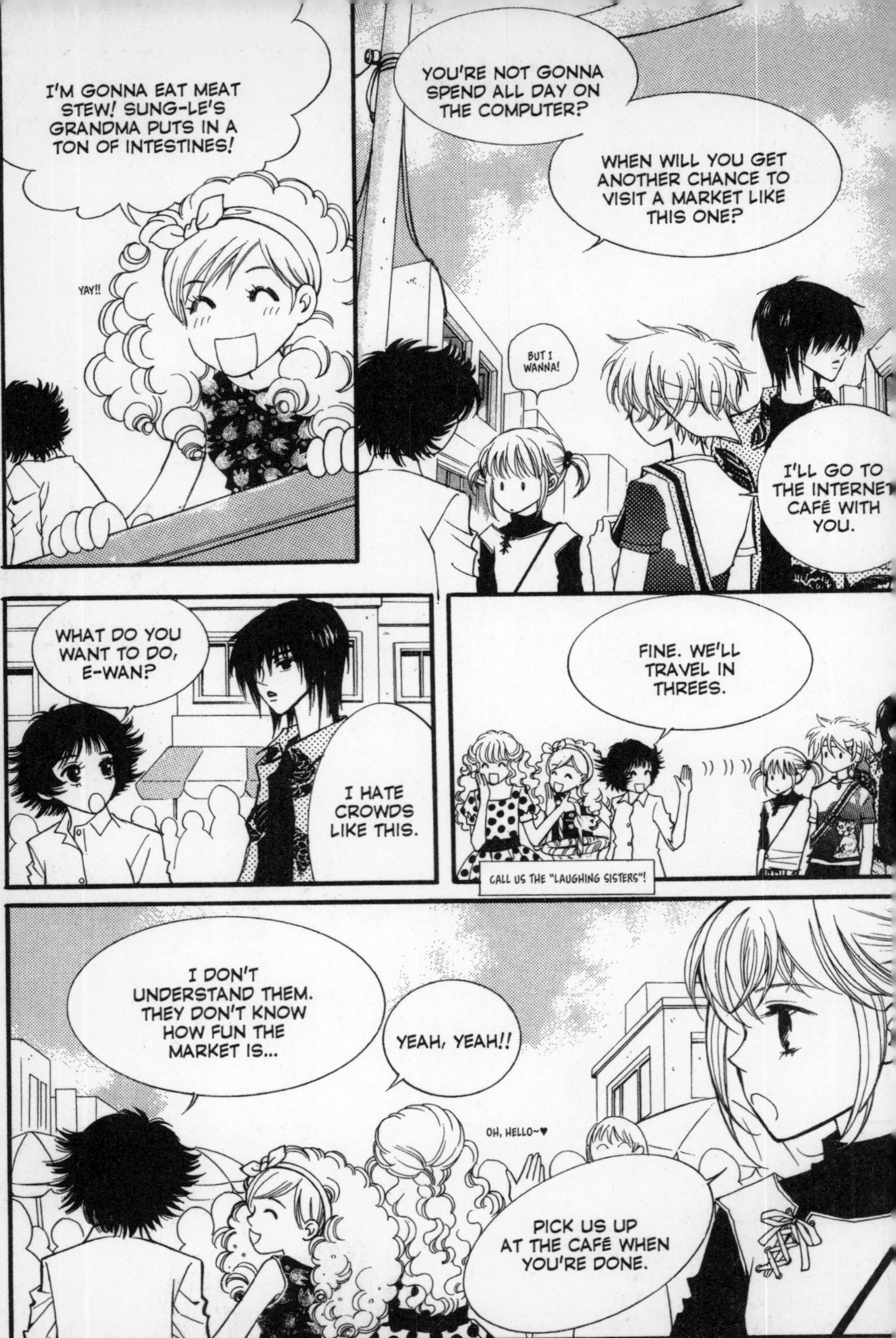
I'M GONNA EAT MEAT STEW! SUNG-LE'S GRANDMA PUTS IN A TON OF INTESTINES!
YAY!!
YOU'RE NOT GONNA SPEND ALL DAY ON THE COMPUTER?
WHEN WILL YOU GET ANOTHER CHANCE TO VISIT A MARKET LIKE THIS ONE?
BUT I WANNA!
I'LL GO TO THE INTERNET CAFÉ WITH YOU.
WHAT DO YOU WANT TO DO, E-WAN?
I HATE CROWDS LIKE THIS.
FINE. WE'LL TRAVEL IN THREES.
CALL US THE "LAUGHING SISTERS"!
I DON'T UNDERSTAND THEM. THEY DON'T KNOW HOW FUN THE MARKET IS...
YEAH, YEAH!!
OH, HELLO~♥
PICK US UP AT THE CAFÉ WHEN YOU'RE DONE.

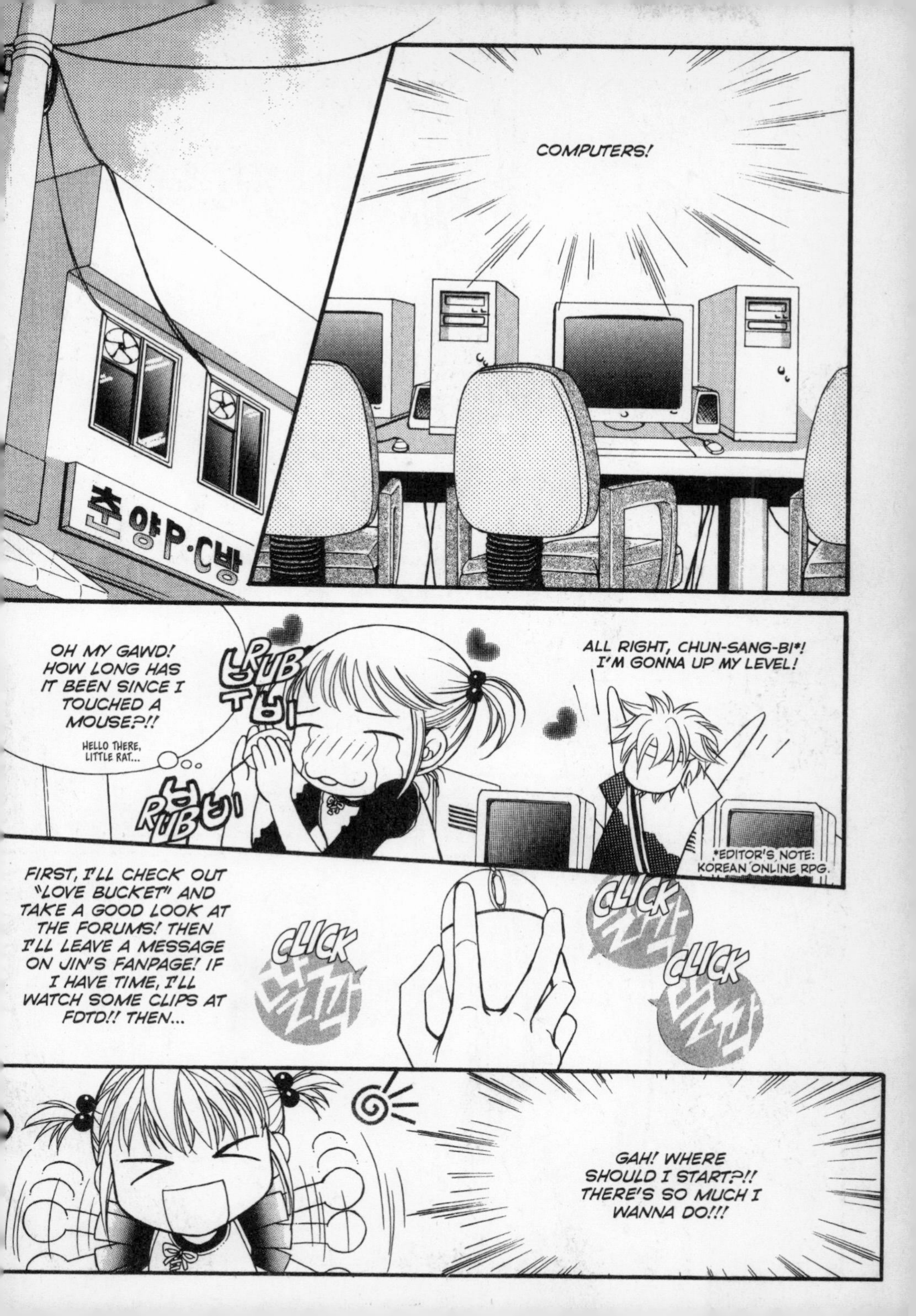

춘양P·C방
COMPUTERS!
OH MY GAWD! HOW LONG HAS IT BEEN SINCE I TOUCHED A MOUSE?!!
RUB
RUB
HELLO THERE, LITTLE RAT...
ALL RIGHT, CHUN-SANG-BI*! I'M GONNA UP MY LEVEL!
*EDITOR'S NOTE: KOREAN ONLINE RPG.
FIRST, I'LL CHECK OUT "LOVE BUCKET" AND TAKE A GOOD LOOK AT THE FORUMS! THEN I'LL LEAVE A MESSAGE ON JIN'S FANPAGE! IF I HAVE TIME, I'LL WATCH SOME CLIPS AT FDTD!! THEN...
CLICK
CLICK
CLICK
GAH! WHERE SHOULD I START?!! THERE'S SO MUCH I WANNA DO!!!

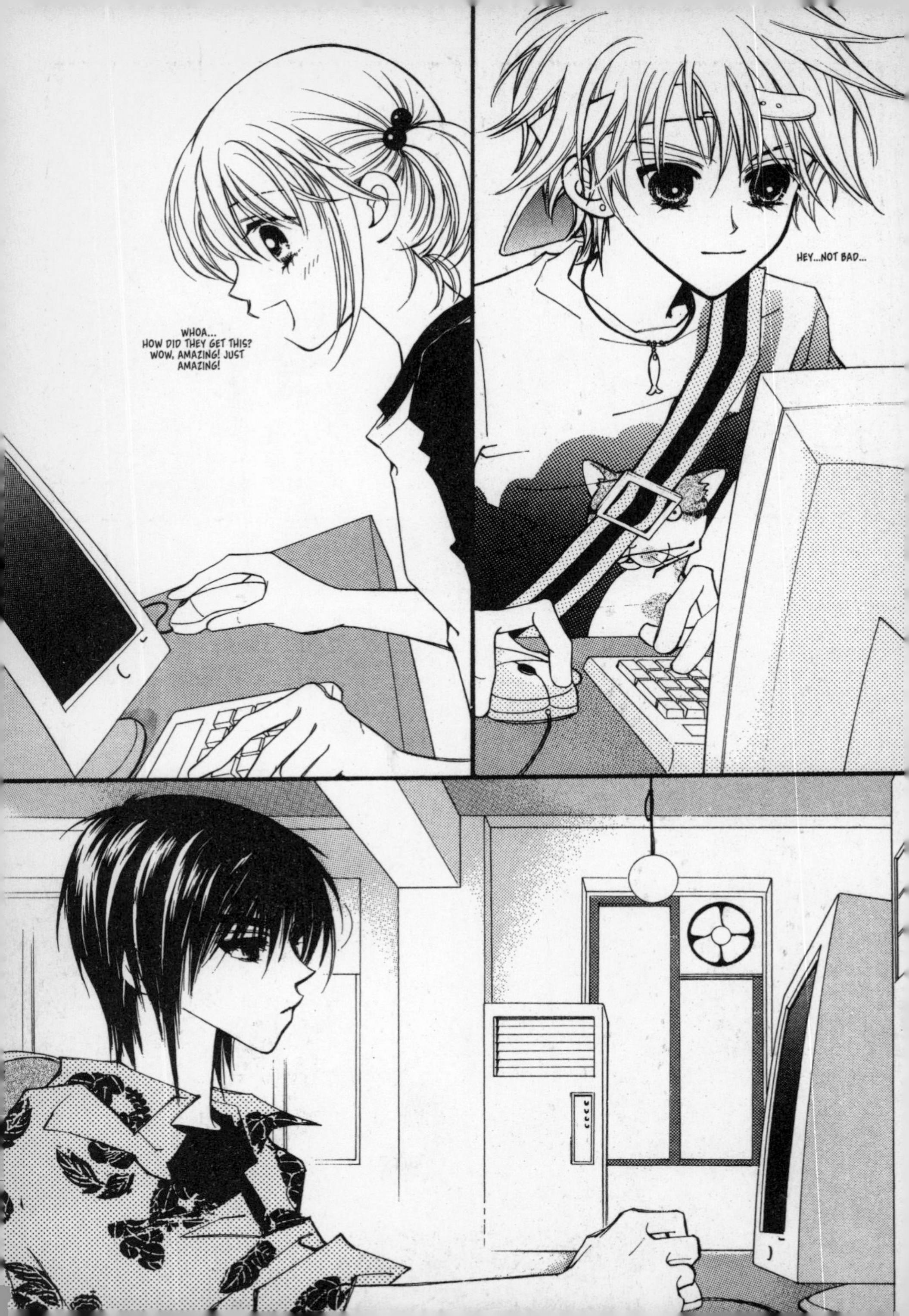
WHOA... HOW DID THEY GET THIS? WOW, AMAZING! JUST AMAZING!
HEY...NOT BAD...

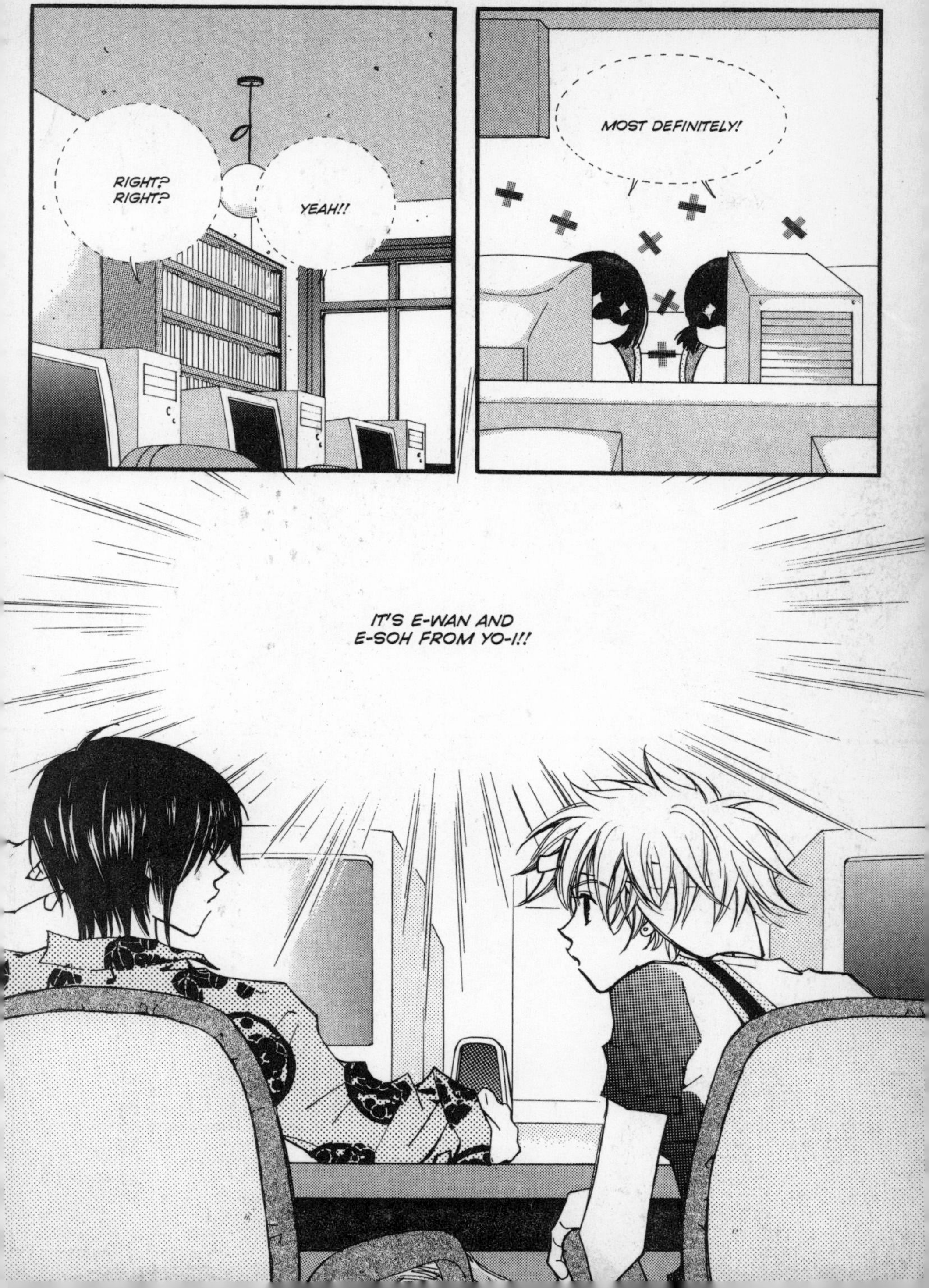
RIGHT? RIGHT?
YEAH!!
MOST DEFINITELY!
IT'S E-WAN AND E-SOH FROM YO-I!!

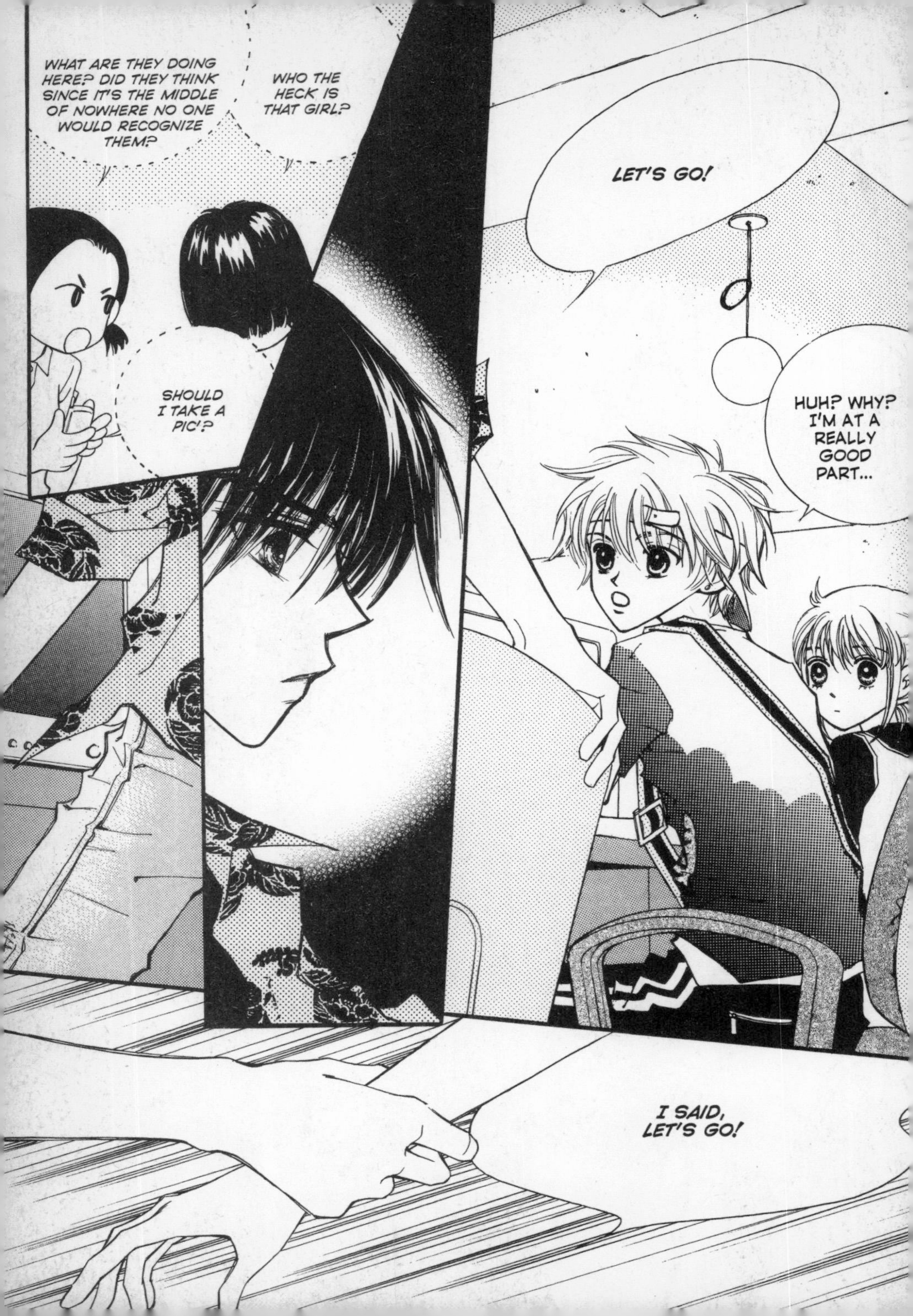
WHAT ARE THEY DOING HERE? DID THEY THINK SINCE IT'S THE MIDDLE OF NOWHERE NO ONE WOULD RECOGNIZE THEM?
WHO THE HECK IS THAT GIRL?
SHOULD I TAKE A PIC'?
LET'S GO!
HUH? WHY? I'M AT A REALLY GOOD PART...
I SAID, LET'S GO!

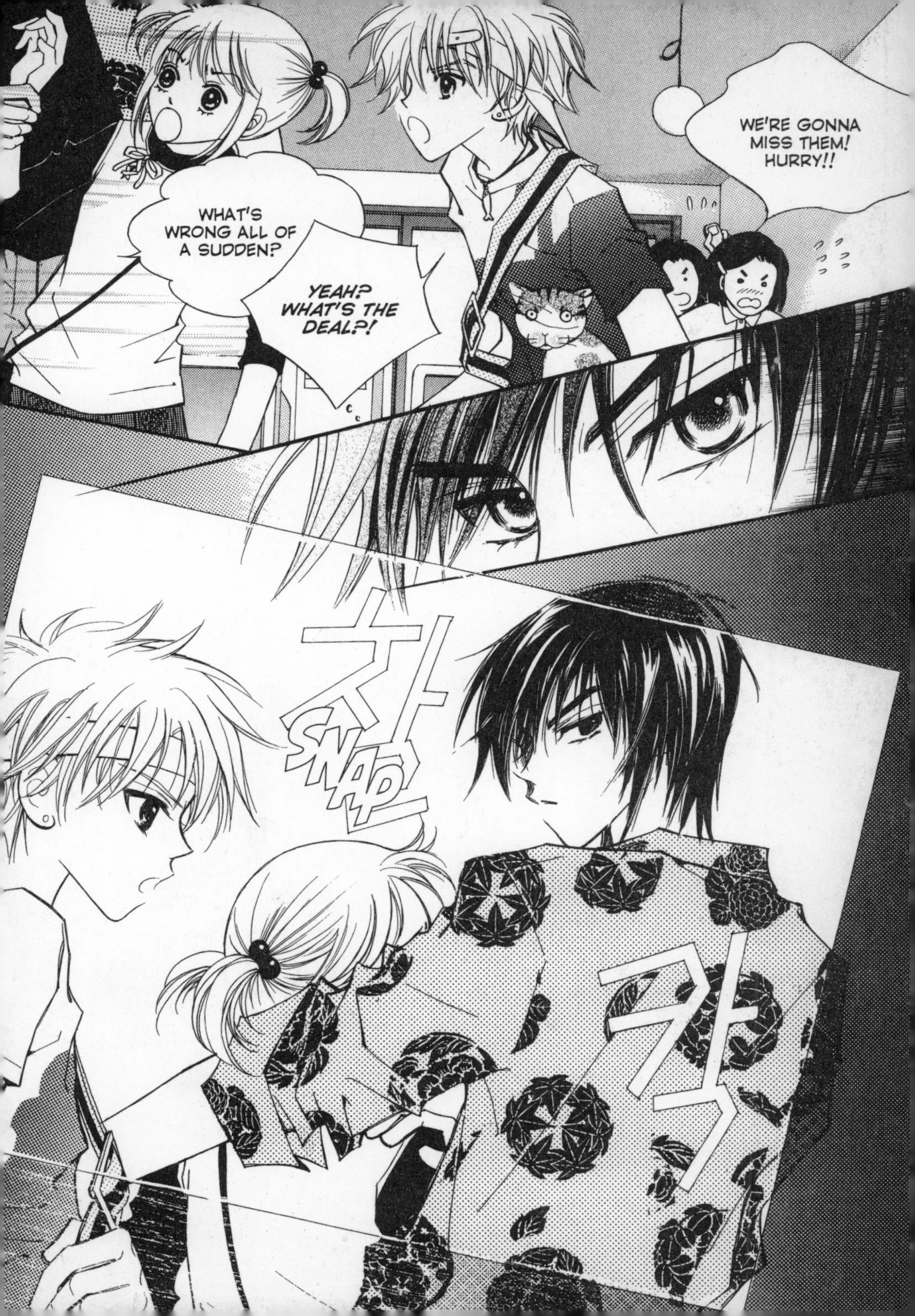
WHAT'S WRONG ALL OF A SUDDEN?
YEAH? WHAT'S THE DEAL?!
WE'RE GONNA MISS THEM! HURRY!!
SNAP

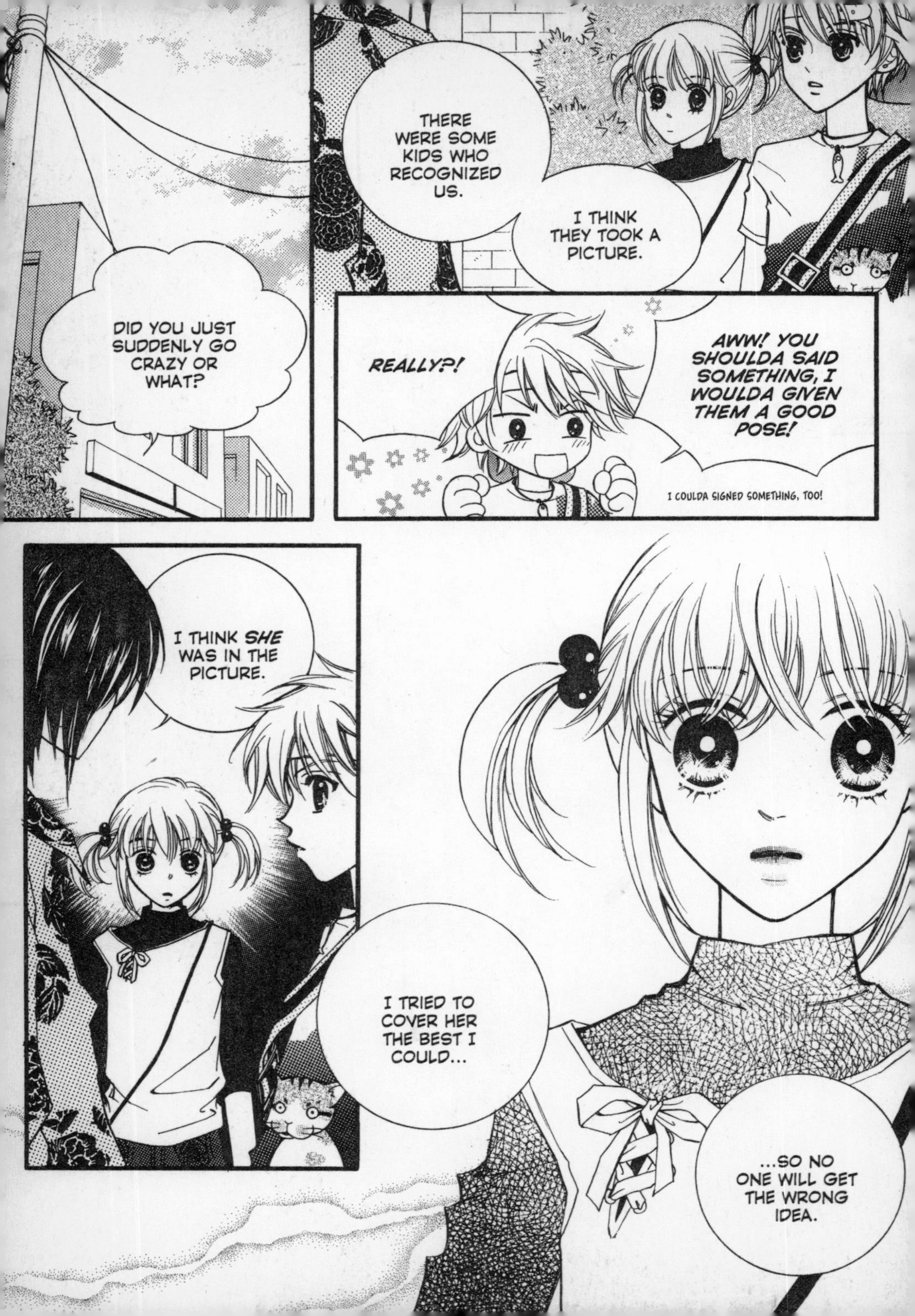
DID YOU JUST SUDDENLY GO CRAZY OR WHAT?
THERE WERE SOME KIDS WHO RECOGNIZED US.
I THINK THEY TOOK A PICTURE.
REALLY?!
AWW! YOU SHOULDA SAID SOMETHING, I WOULDA GIVEN THEM A GOOD POSE!
I COULDA SIGNED SOMETHING, TOO!
I THINK SHE WAS IN THE PICTURE.
I TRIED TO COVER HER THE BEST I COULD...
...SO NO ONE WILL GET THE WRONG IDEA.

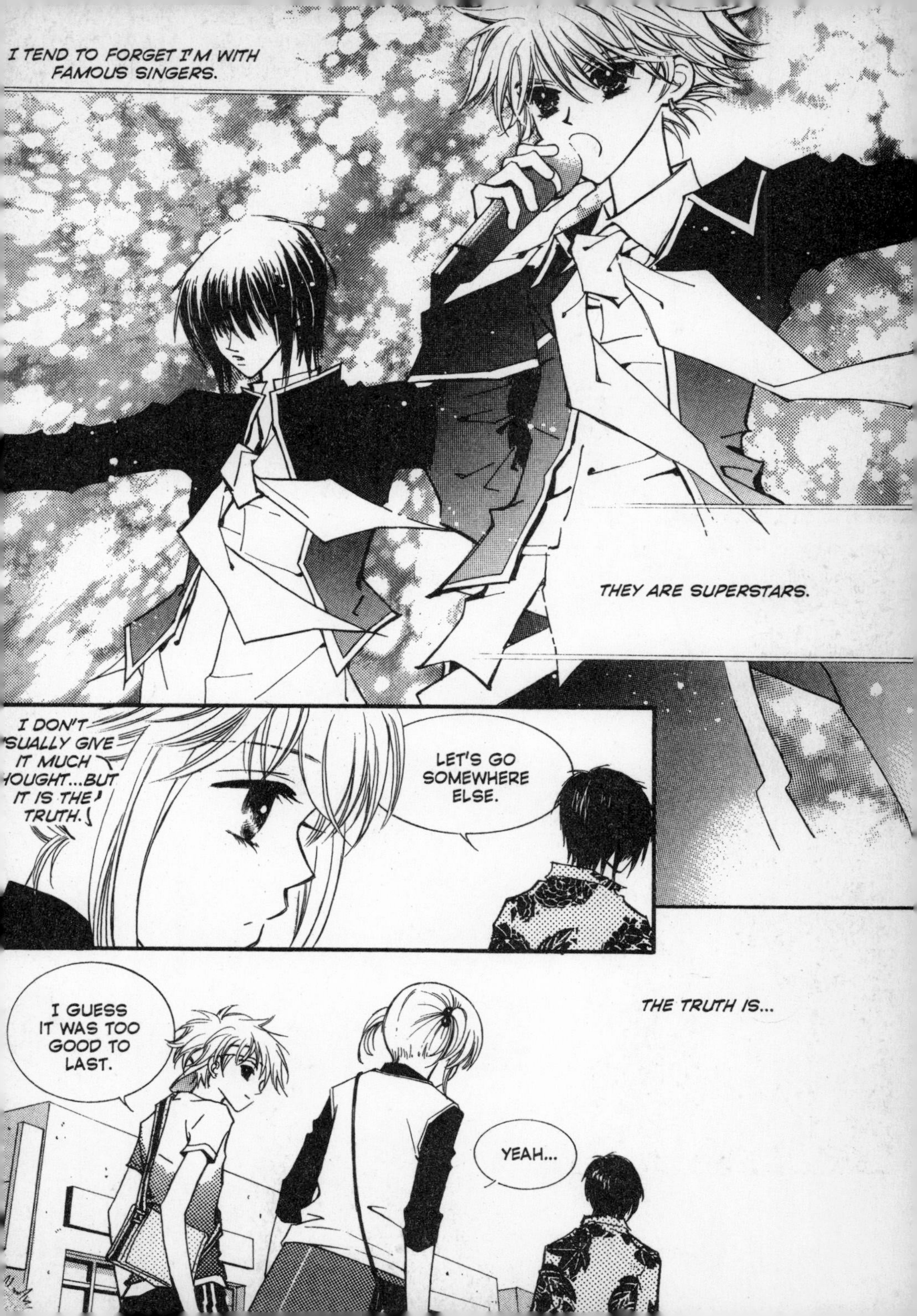
I TEND TO FORGET I'M WITH FAMOUS SINGERS.
THEY ARE SUPERSTARS.
I DON'T 'SUALLY GIVE IT MUCH HOUGHT...BUT IT IS THE TRUTH.
LET'S GO SOMEWHERE ELSE.
I GUESS IT WAS TOO GOOD TO LAST.
THE TRUTH IS...
YEAH...

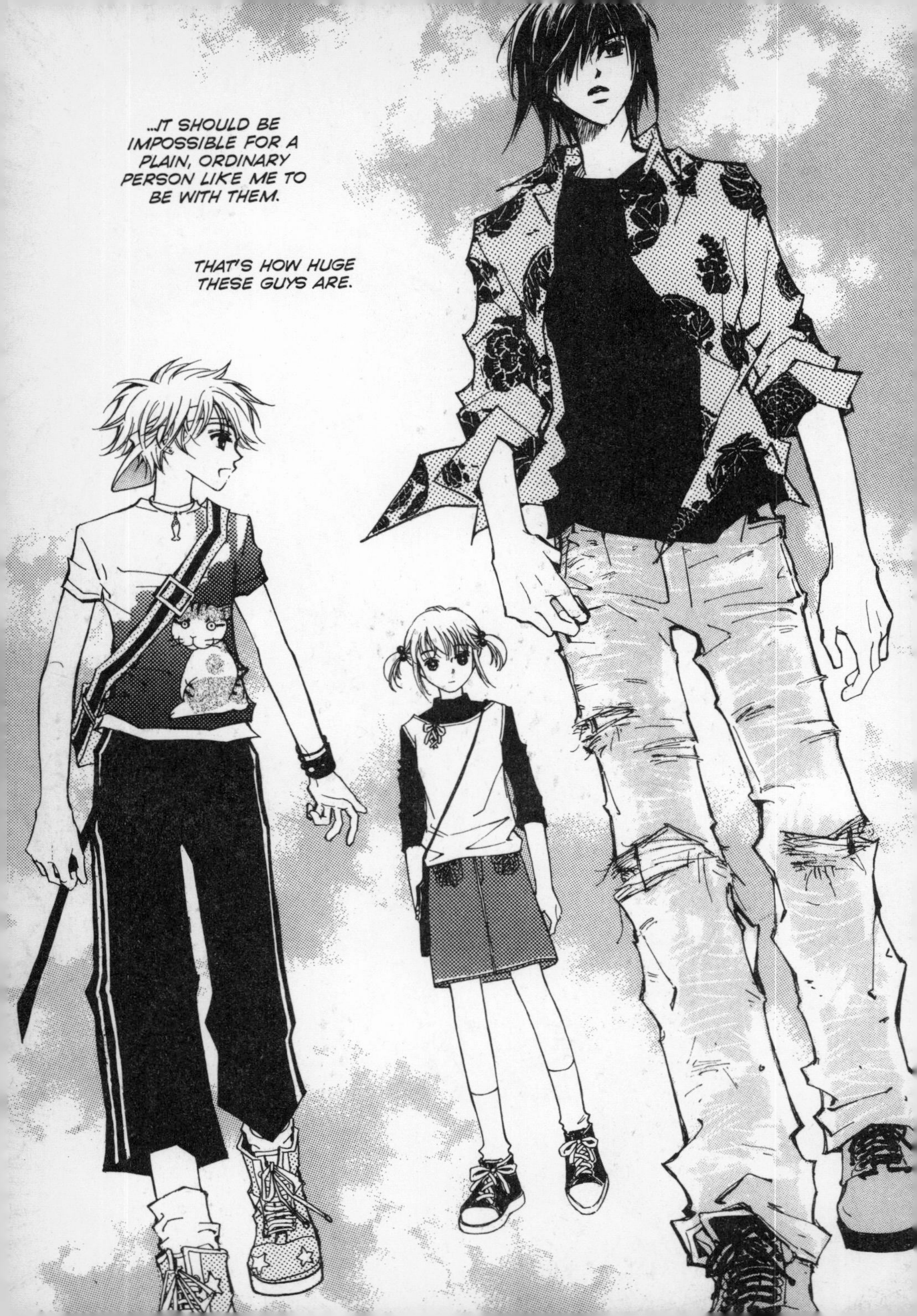
...IT SHOULD BE IMPOSSIBLE FOR A PLAIN, ORDINARY PERSON LIKE ME TO BE WITH THEM.
THAT'S HOW HUGE THESE GUYS ARE.

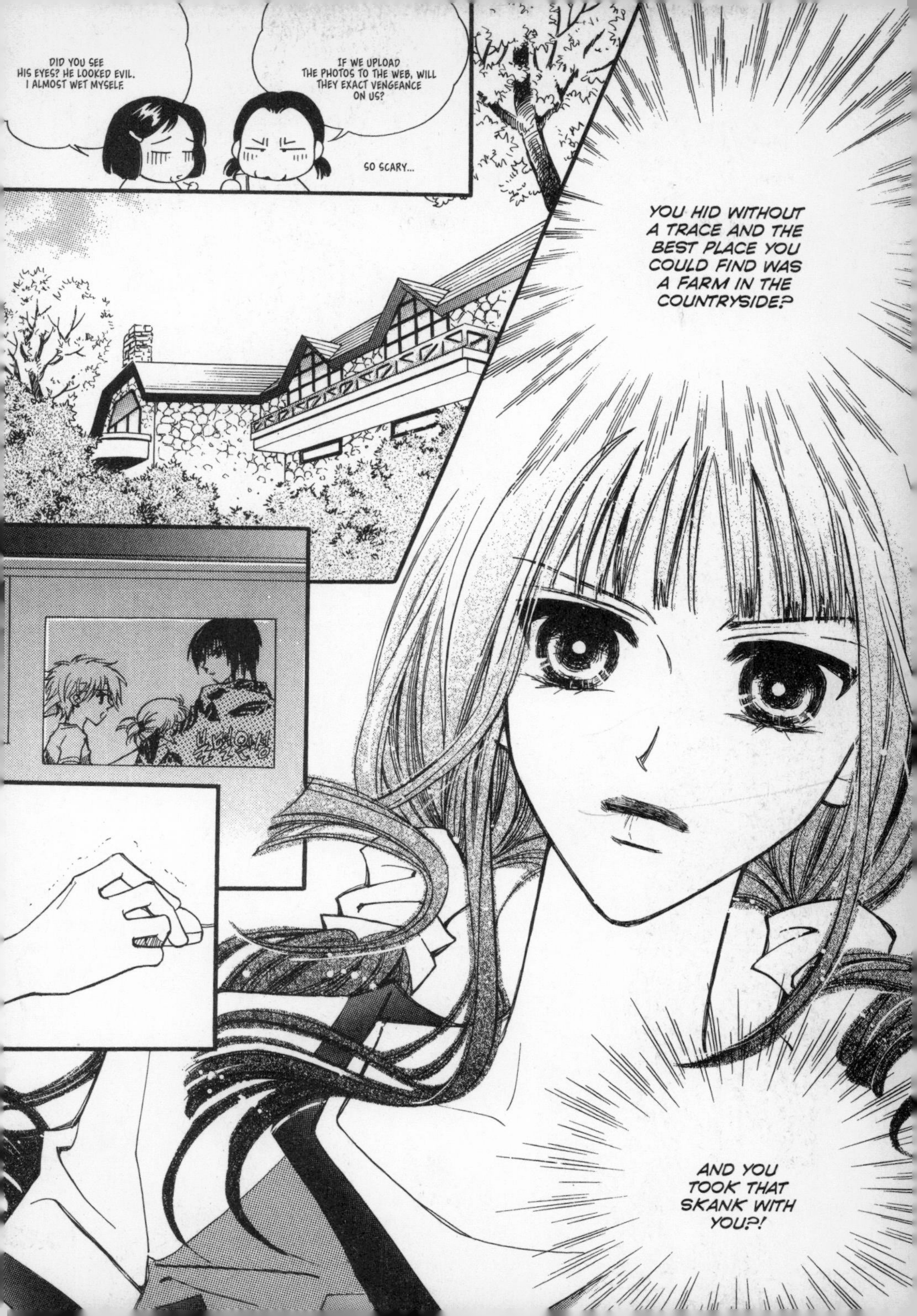
DID YOU SEE HIS EYES? HE LOOKED EVIL. I ALMOST WET MYSELF.
IF WE UPLOAD THE PHOTOS TO THE WEB, WILL THEY EXACT VENGEANCE ON US?
SO SCARY...
YOU HID WITHOUT A TRACE AND THE BEST PLACE YOU COULD FIND WAS A FARM IN THE COUNTRYSIDE?
AND YOU TOOK THAT SKANK WITH YOU?!

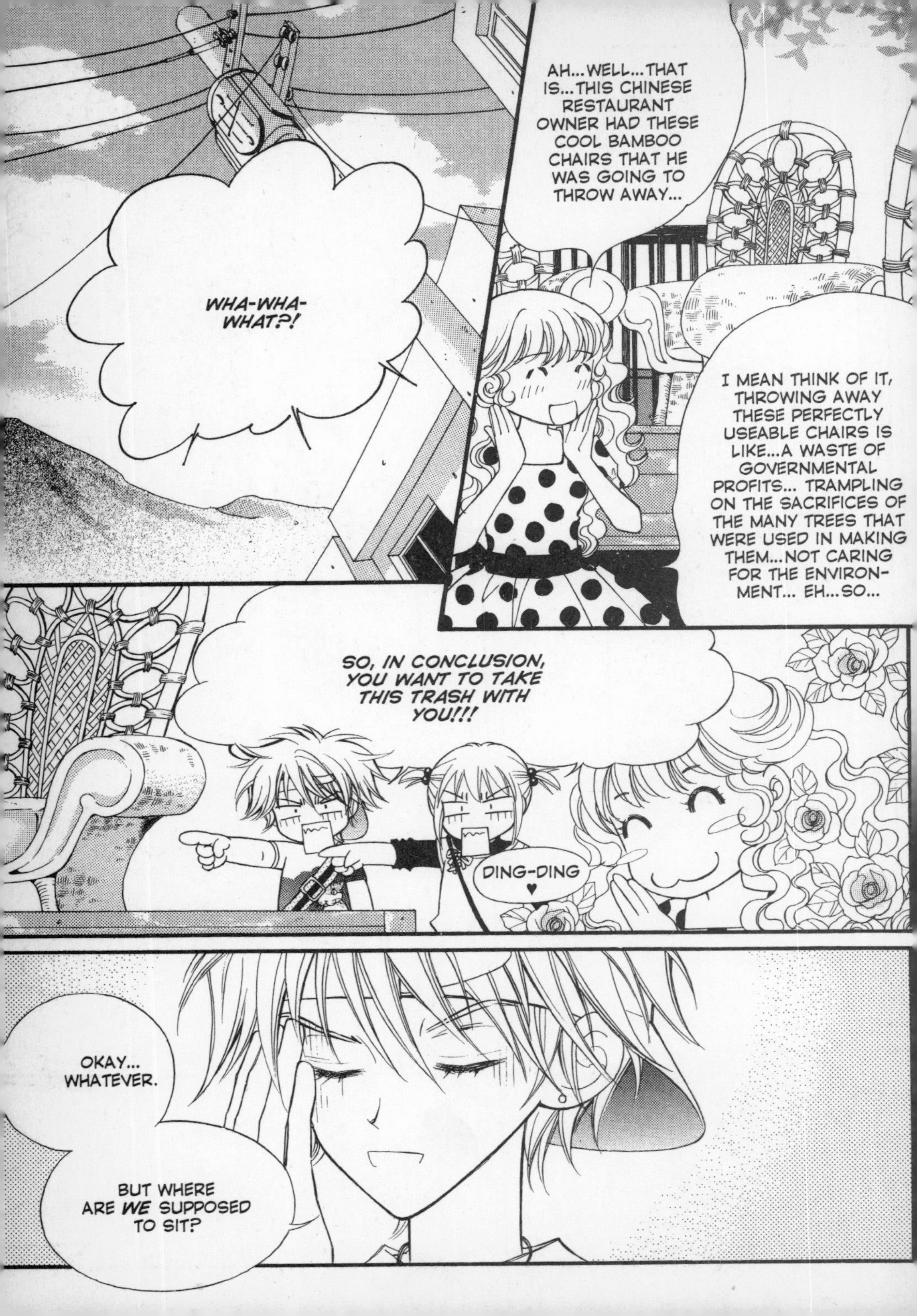
WHA-WHA-WHAT?!
AH...WELL...THAT IS...THIS CHINESE RESTAURANT OWNER HAD THESE COOL BAMBOO CHAIRS THAT HE WAS GOING TO THROW AWAY...
I MEAN THINK OF IT, THROWING AWAY THESE PERFECTLY USEABLE CHAIRS IS LIKE...A WASTE OF GOVERNMENTAL PROFITS... TRAMPLING ON THE SACRIFICES OF THE MANY TREES THAT WERE USED IN MAKING THEM...NOT CARING FOR THE ENVIRONMENT... EH...SO...
SO, IN CONCLUSION, YOU WANT TO TAKE THIS TRASH WITH YOU!!!
DING-DING ♥
OKAY... WHATEVER.
BUT WHERE ARE *WE* SUPPOSED TO SIT?

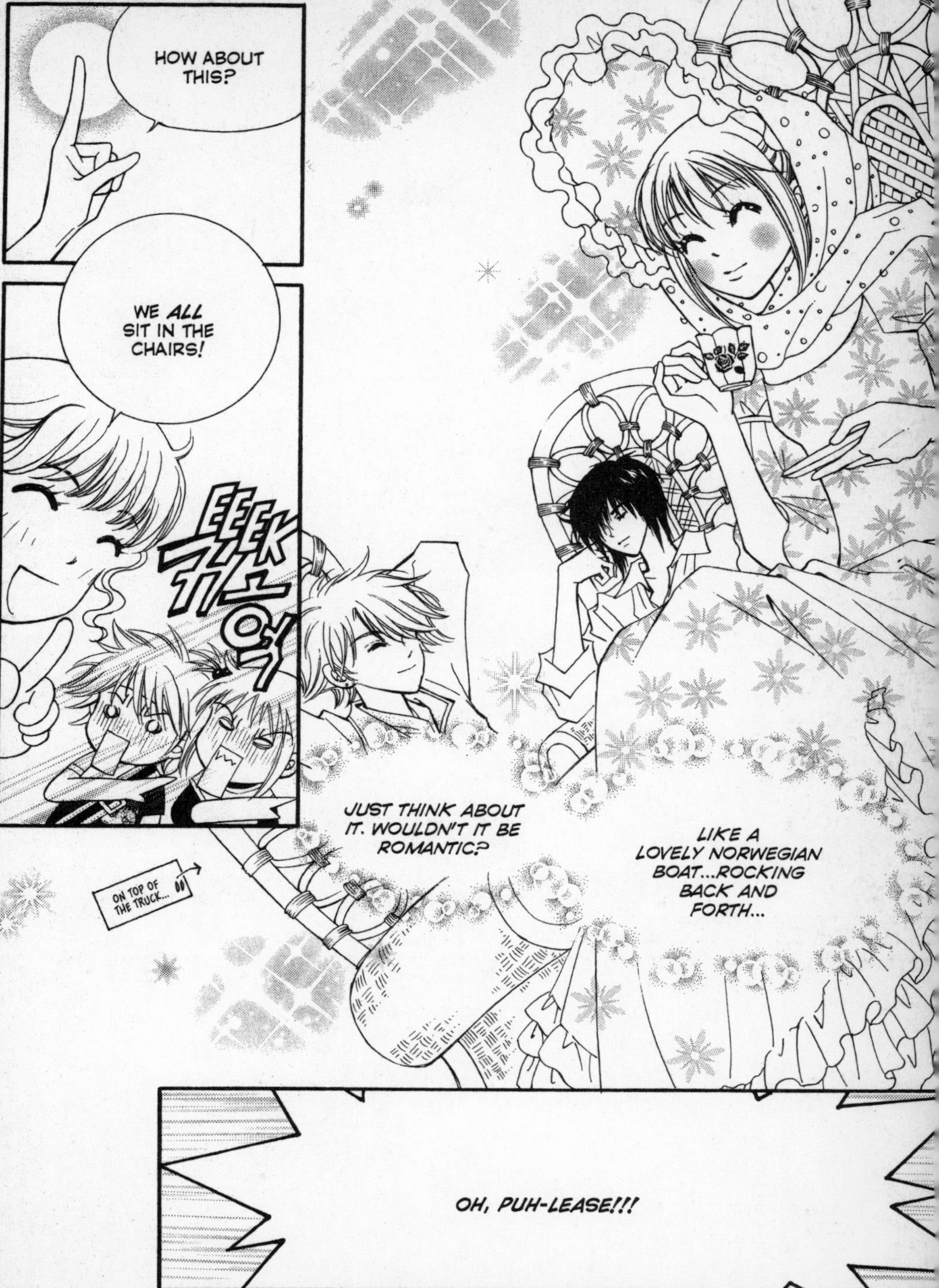
HOW ABOUT THIS?
WE ALL SIT IN THE CHAIRS!
EEEK
JUST THINK ABOUT IT. WOULDN'T IT BE ROMANTIC?
ON TOP OF THE TRUCK...
LIKE A LOVELY NORWEGIAN BOAT...ROCKING BACK AND FORTH...
OH, PUH-LEASE!!!

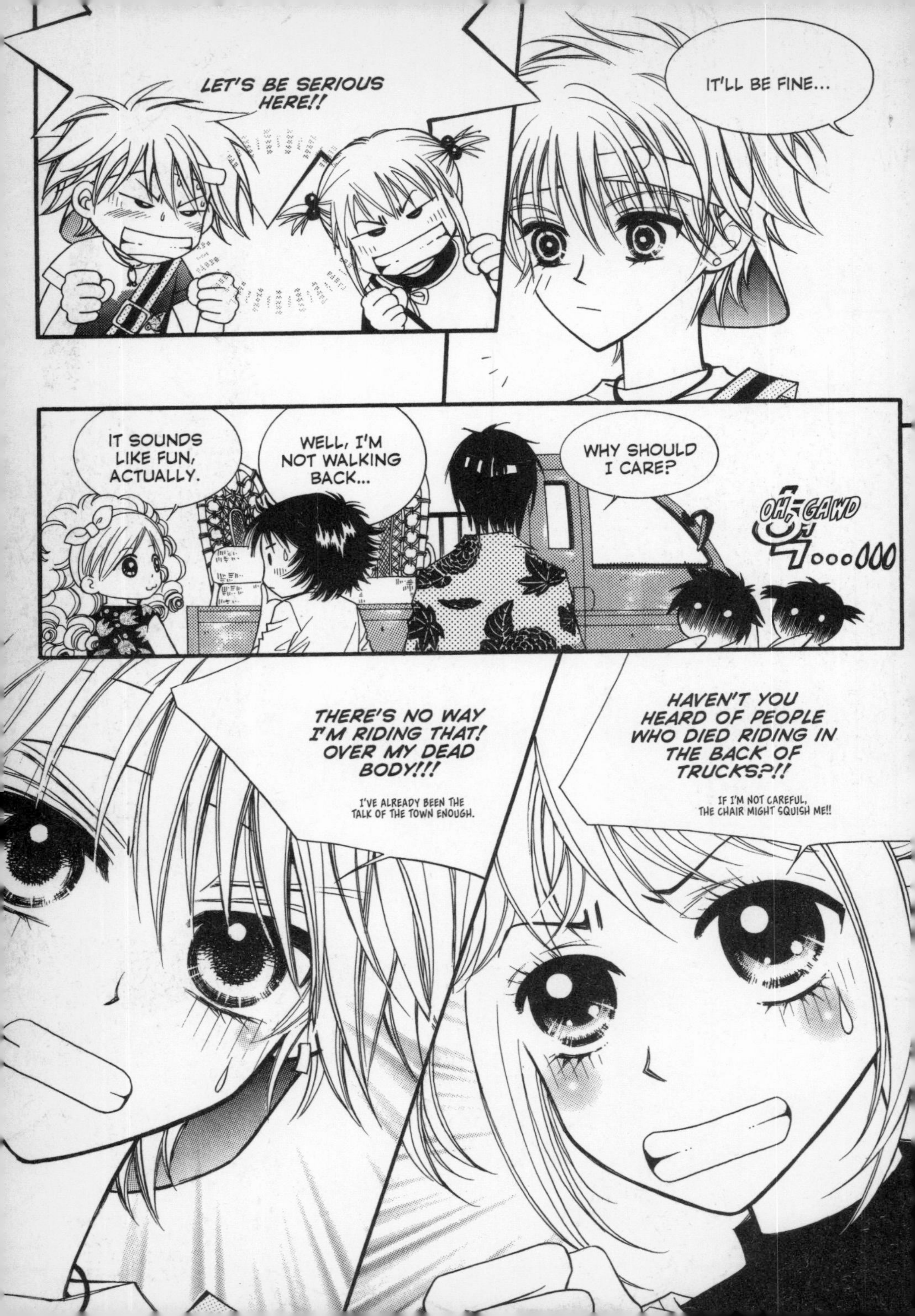
LET'S BE SERIOUS HERE!!
IT'LL BE FINE...
IT SOUNDS LIKE FUN, ACTUALLY.
WELL, I'M NOT WALKING BACK...
WHY SHOULD I CARE?
OH, GAWD
THERE'S NO WAY I'M RIDING THAT! OVER MY DEAD BODY!!!
I'VE ALREADY BEEN THE TALK OF THE TOWN ENOUGH.
HAVEN'T YOU HEARD OF PEOPLE WHO DIED RIDING IN THE BACK OF TRUCKS?!!
IF I'M NOT CAREFUL, THE CHAIR MIGHT SQUISH ME!!

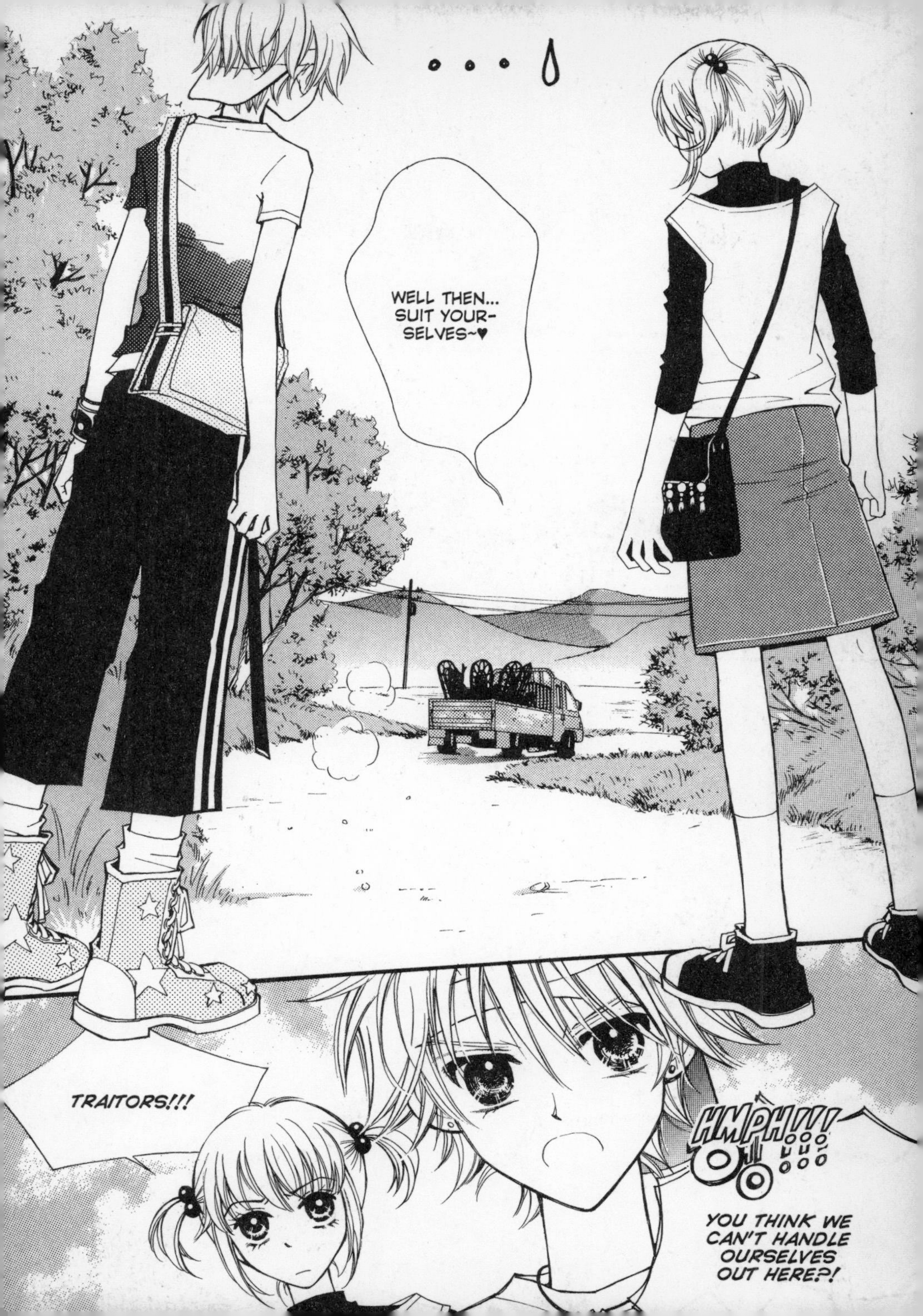
...
WELL THEN... SUIT YOUR-SELVES~♥
TRAITORS!!!
HMPH!!!
YOU THINK WE CAN'T HANDLE OURSELVES OUT HERE?!

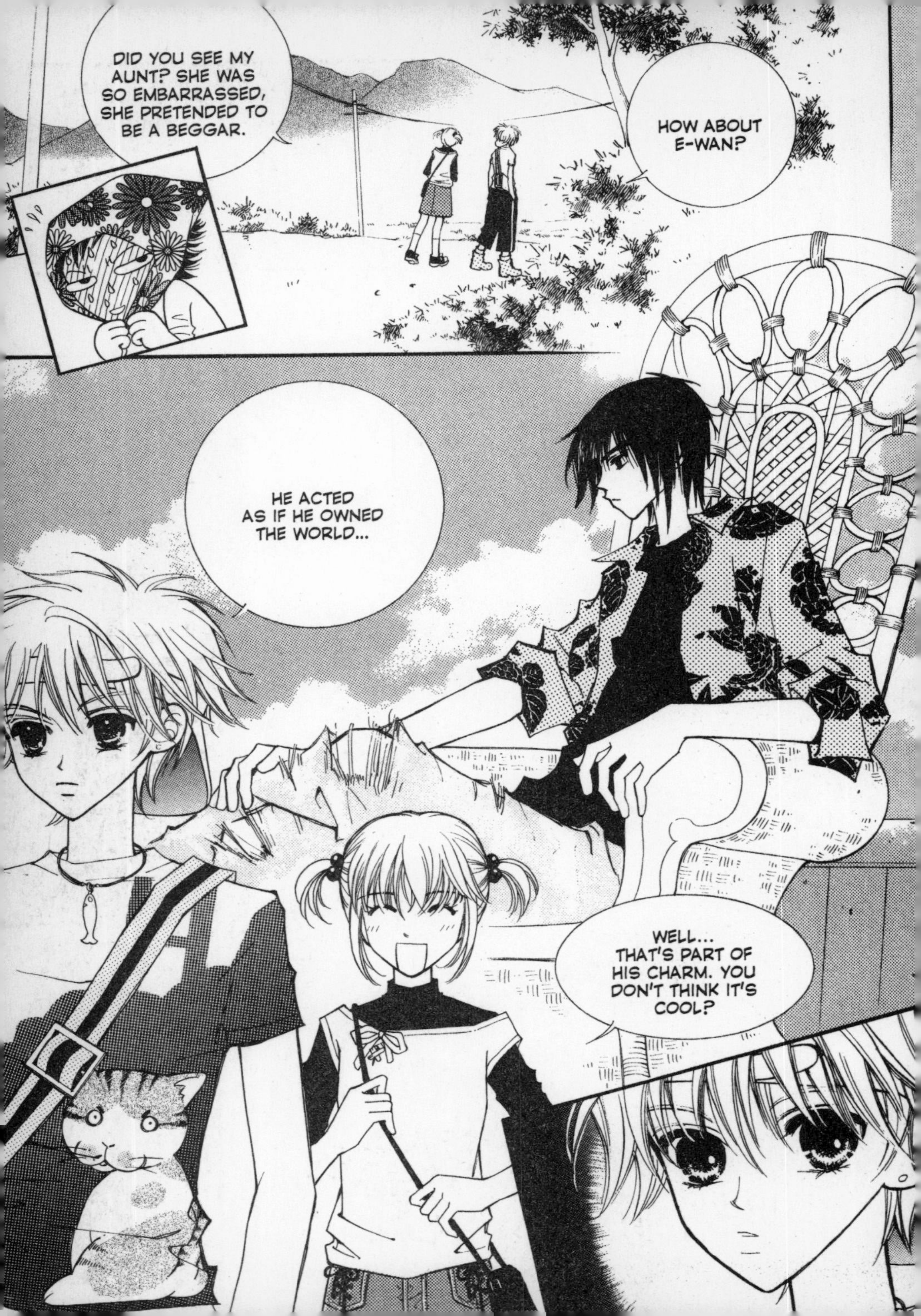
DID YOU SEE MY AUNT? SHE WAS SO EMBARRASSED, SHE PRETENDED TO BE A BEGGAR.
HOW ABOUT E-WAN?
HE ACTED AS IF HE OWNED THE WORLD...
WELL... THAT'S PART OF HIS CHARM. YOU DON'T THINK IT'S COOL?

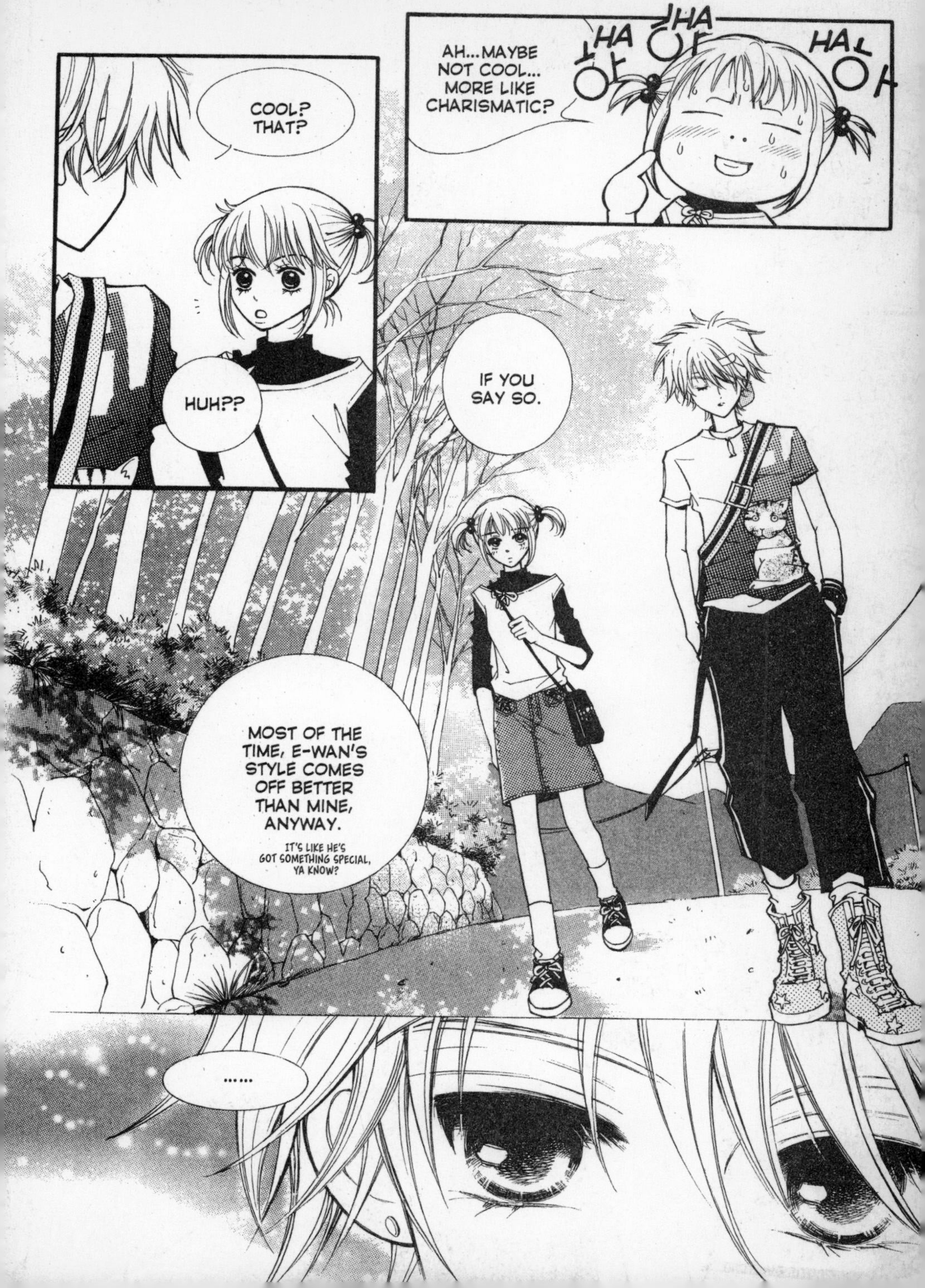
COOL? THAT?
HUH??
AH...MAYBE NOT COOL... MORE LIKE CHARISMATIC?
HA HA HA
IF YOU SAY SO.
MOST OF THE TIME, E-WAN'S STYLE COMES OFF BETTER THAN MINE, ANYWAY.
IT'S LIKE HE'S GOT SOMETHING SPECIAL, YA KNOW?
......

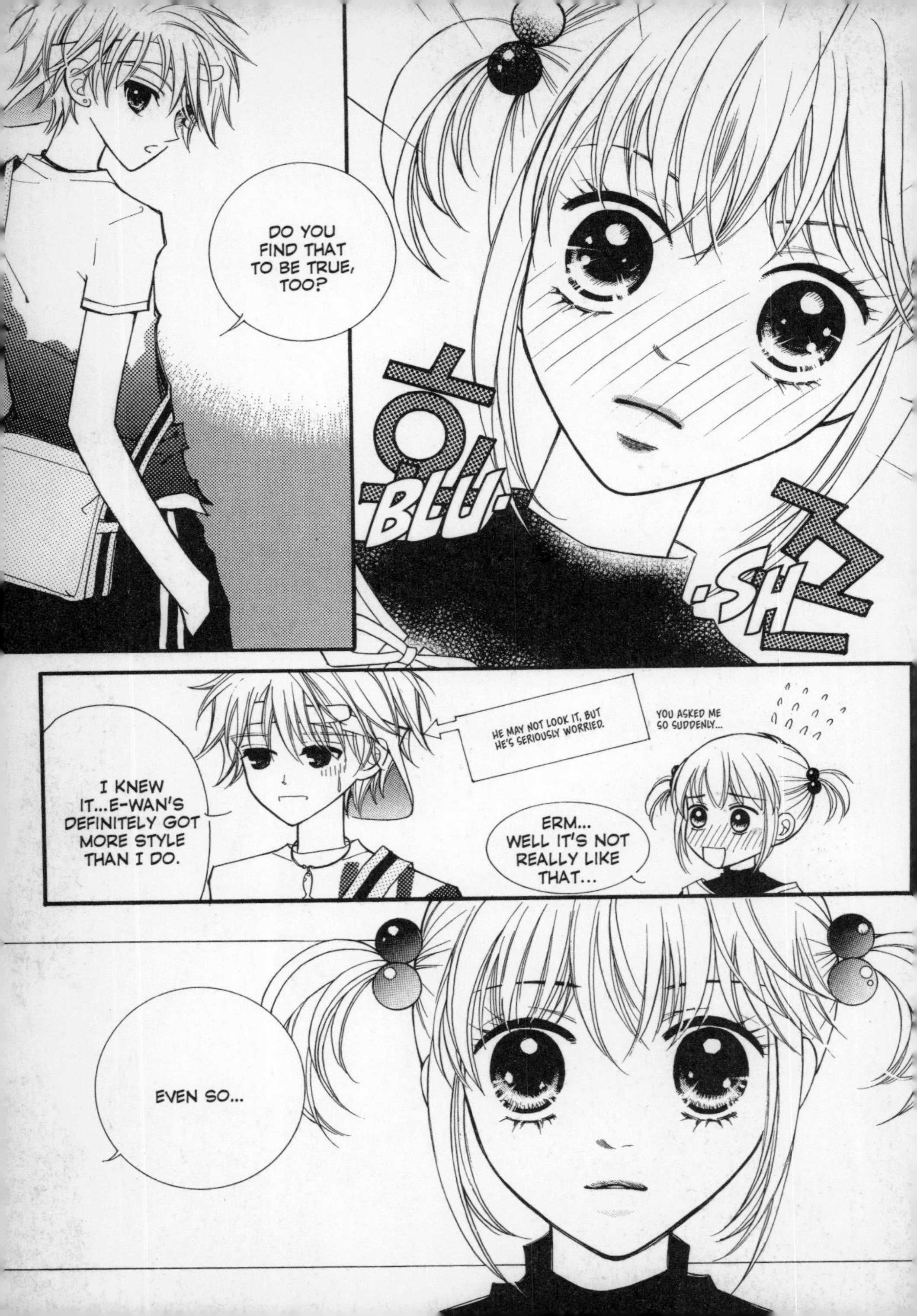
DO YOU FIND THAT TO BE TRUE, TOO?
BLU-
-SH
I KNEW IT...E-WAN'S DEFINITELY GOT MORE STYLE THAN I DO.
HE MAY NOT LOOK IT, BUT HE'S SERIOUSLY WORRIED.
YOU ASKED ME SO SUDDENLY...
ERM... WELL IT'S NOT REALLY LIKE THAT...
EVEN SO...

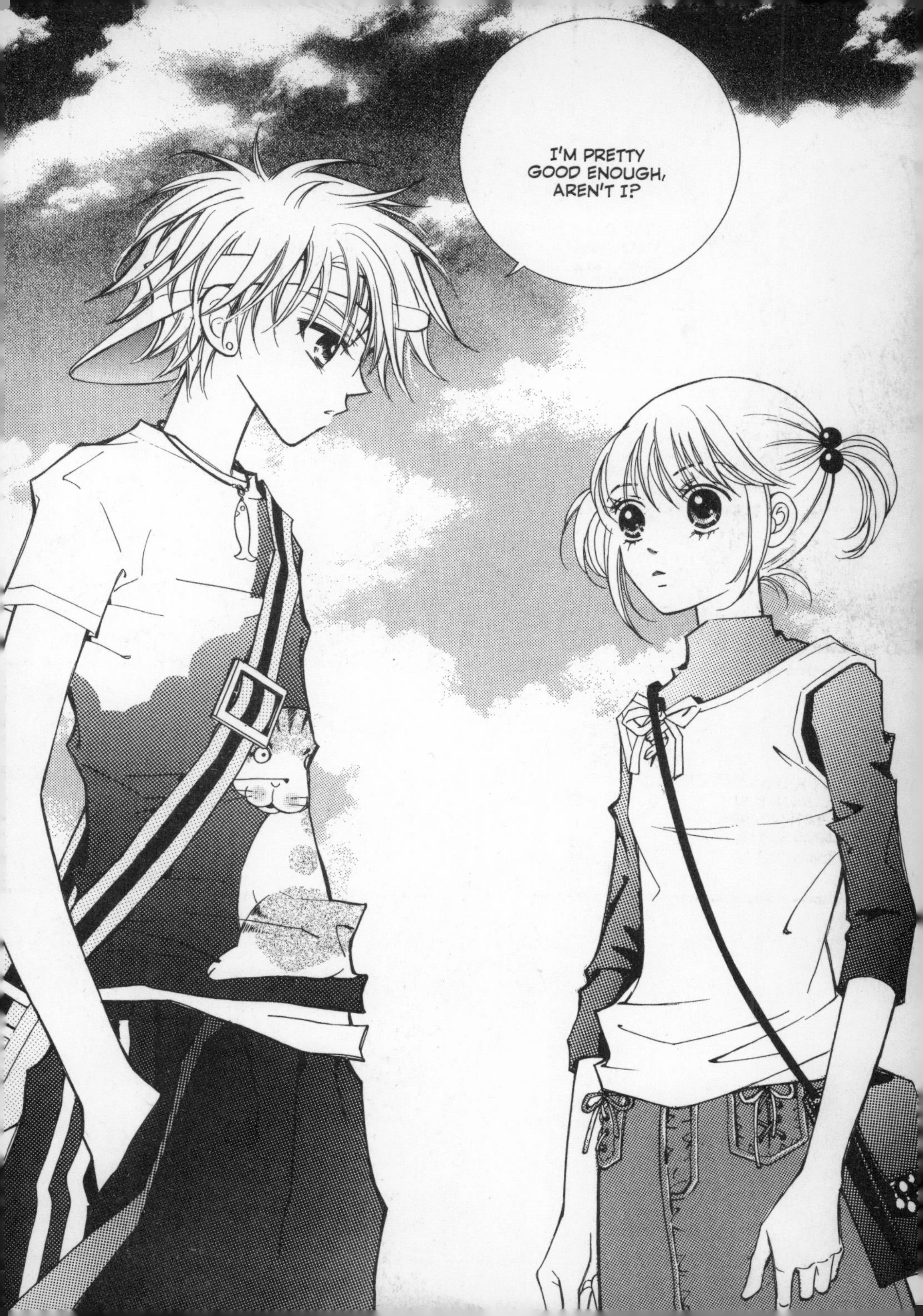
I'M PRETTY GOOD ENOUGH, AREN'T I?

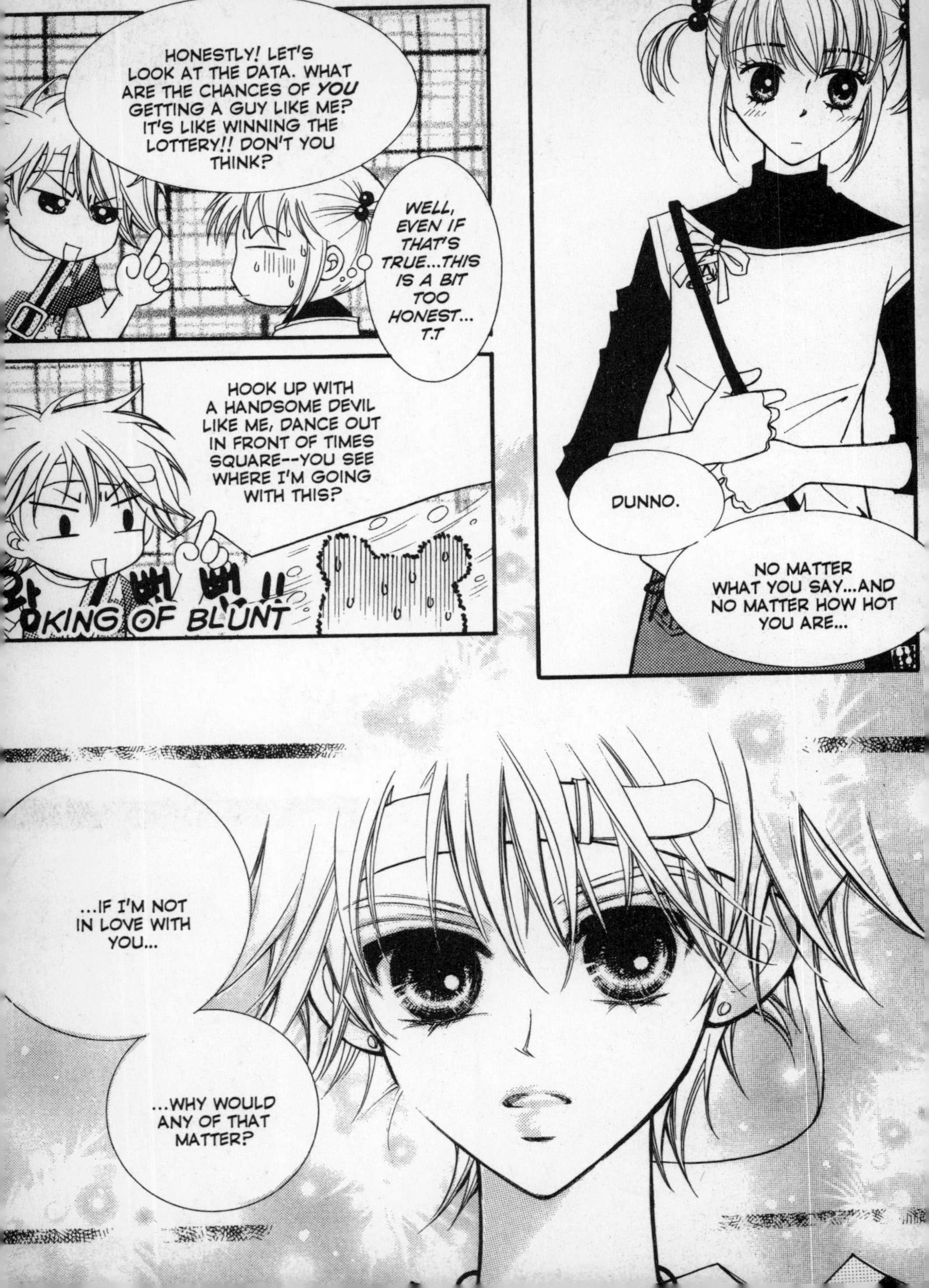
HONESTLY! LET'S LOOK AT THE DATA. WHAT ARE THE CHANCES OF *YOU* GETTING A GUY LIKE ME? IT'S LIKE WINNING THE LOTTERY!! DON'T YOU THINK?
WELL, EVEN IF THAT'S TRUE...THIS IS A BIT TOO HONEST... T.T
HOOK UP WITH A HANDSOME DEVIL LIKE ME, DANCE OUT IN FRONT OF TIMES SQUARE--YOU SEE WHERE I'M GOING WITH THIS?
KING OF BLUNT
DUNNO.
NO MATTER WHAT YOU SAY...AND NO MATTER HOW HOT YOU ARE...
...IF I'M NOT IN LOVE WITH YOU...
...WHY WOULD ANY OF THAT MATTER?

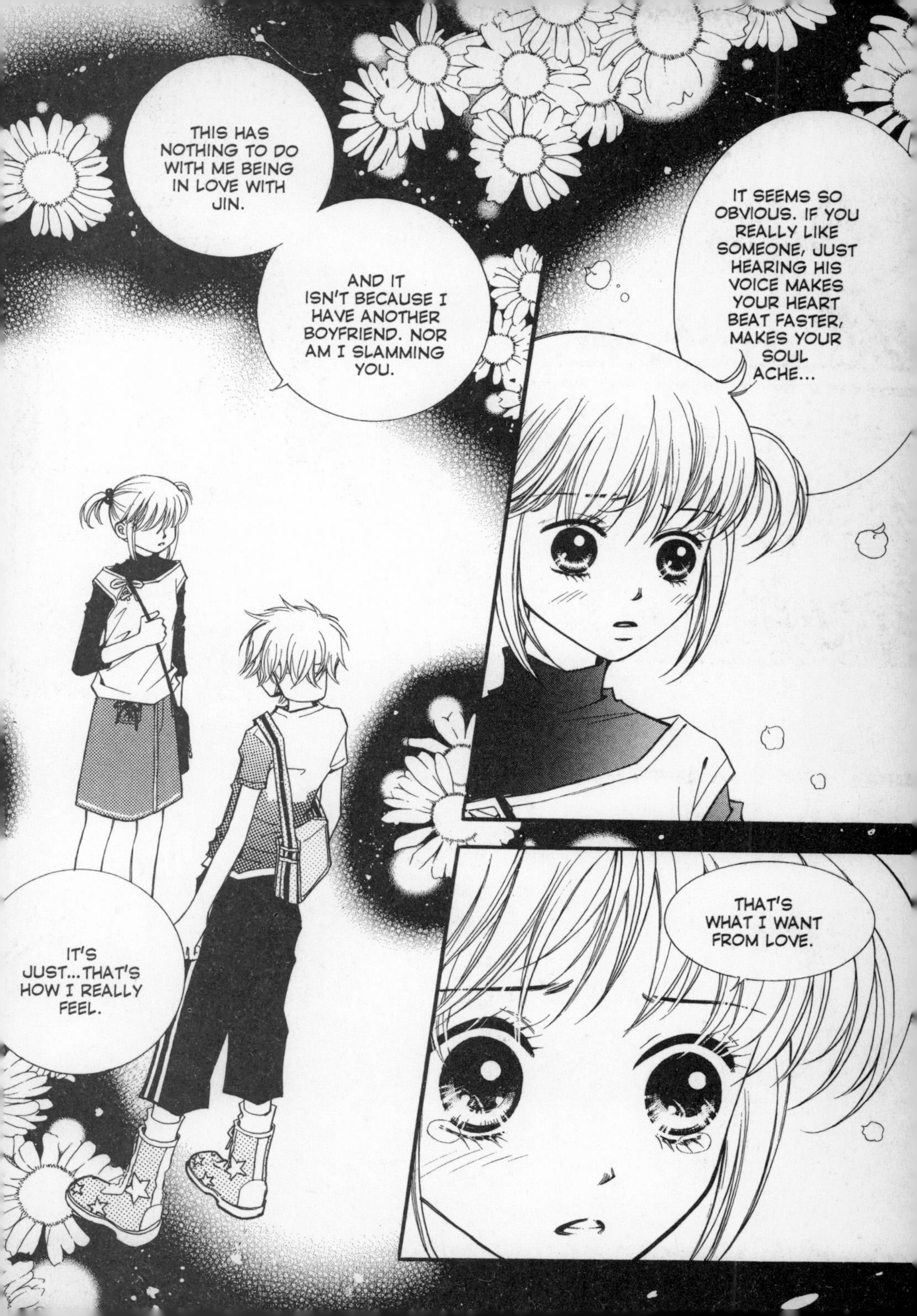
THIS HAS NOTHING TO DO WITH ME BEING IN LOVE WITH JIN.
AND IT ISN'T BECAUSE I HAVE ANOTHER BOYFRIEND. NOR AM I SLAMMING YOU.
IT'S JUST...THAT'S HOW I REALLY FEEL.
IT SEEMS SO OBVIOUS. IF YOU REALLY LIKE SOMEONE, JUST HEARING HIS VOICE MAKES YOUR HEART BEAT FASTER, MAKES YOUR SOUL ACHE...
THAT'S WHAT I WANT FROM LOVE.

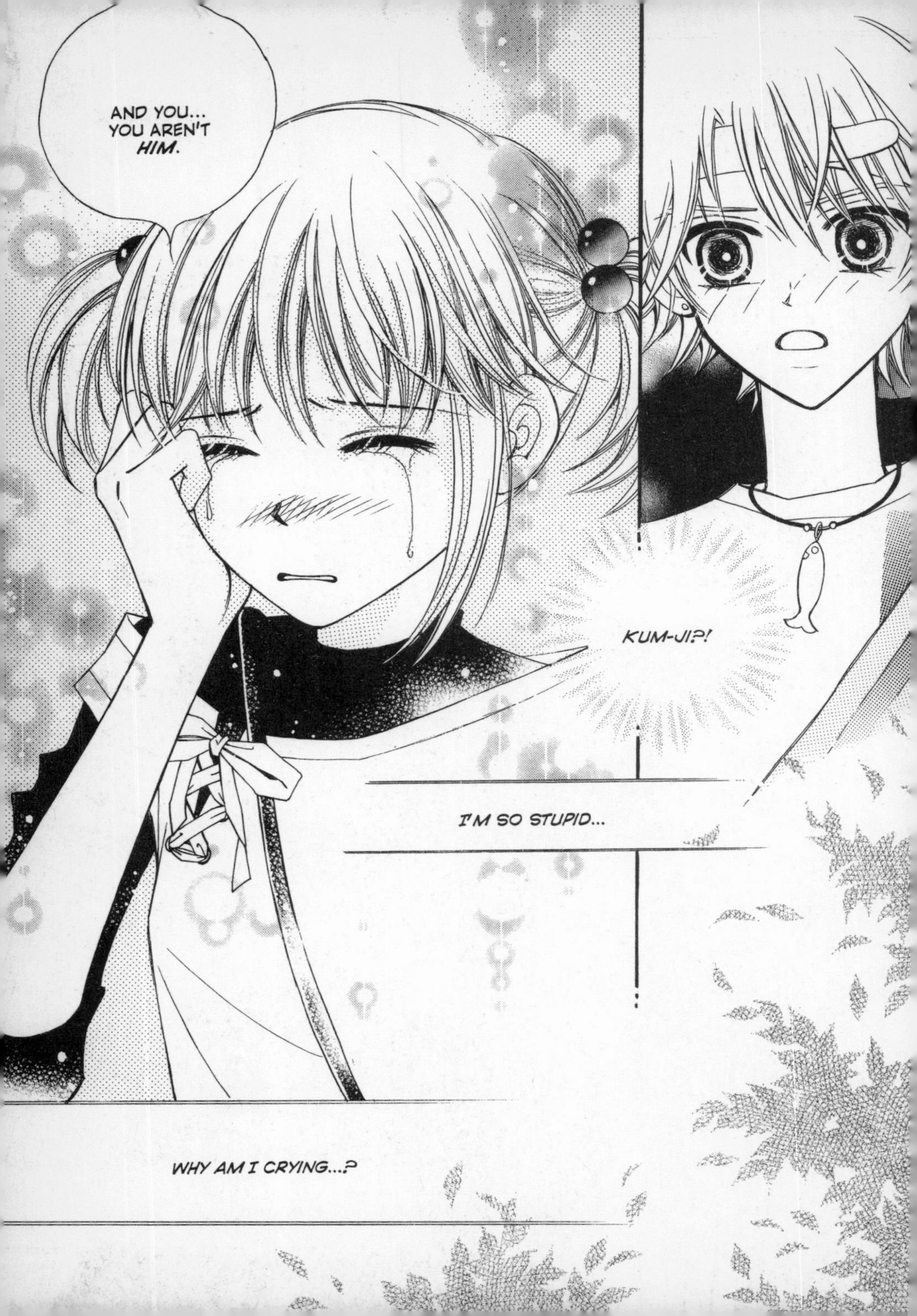
AND YOU... YOU AREN'T HIM.
KUM-JI?!
I'M SO STUPID...
WHY AM I CRYING...?

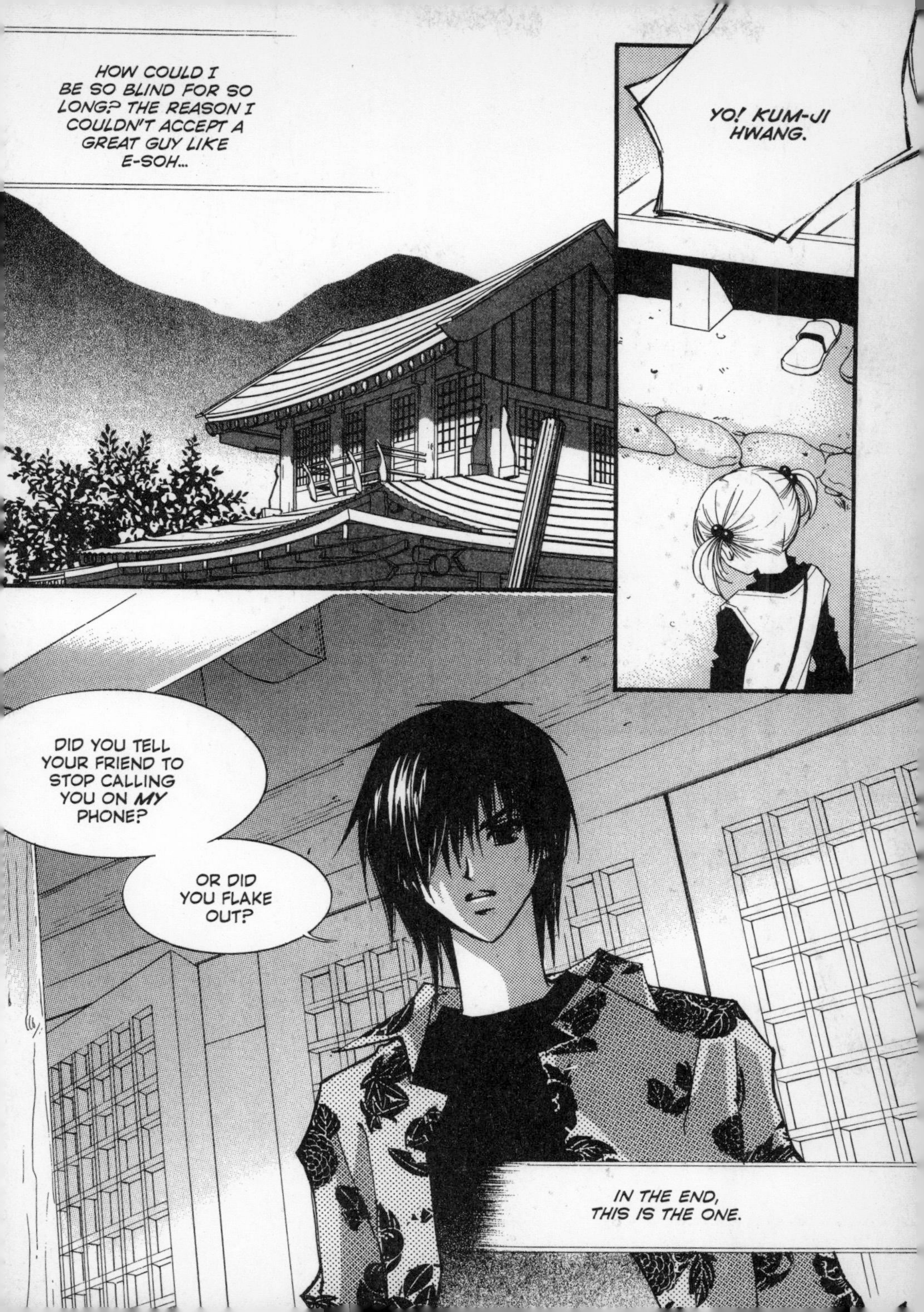
HOW COULD I BE SO BLIND FOR SO LONG? THE REASON I COULDN'T ACCEPT A GREAT GUY LIKE E-SOH...
YO! KUM-JI HWANG.
DID YOU TELL YOUR FRIEND TO STOP CALLING YOU ON *MY* PHONE?
OR DID YOU FLAKE OUT?
IN THE END, THIS IS THE ONE.

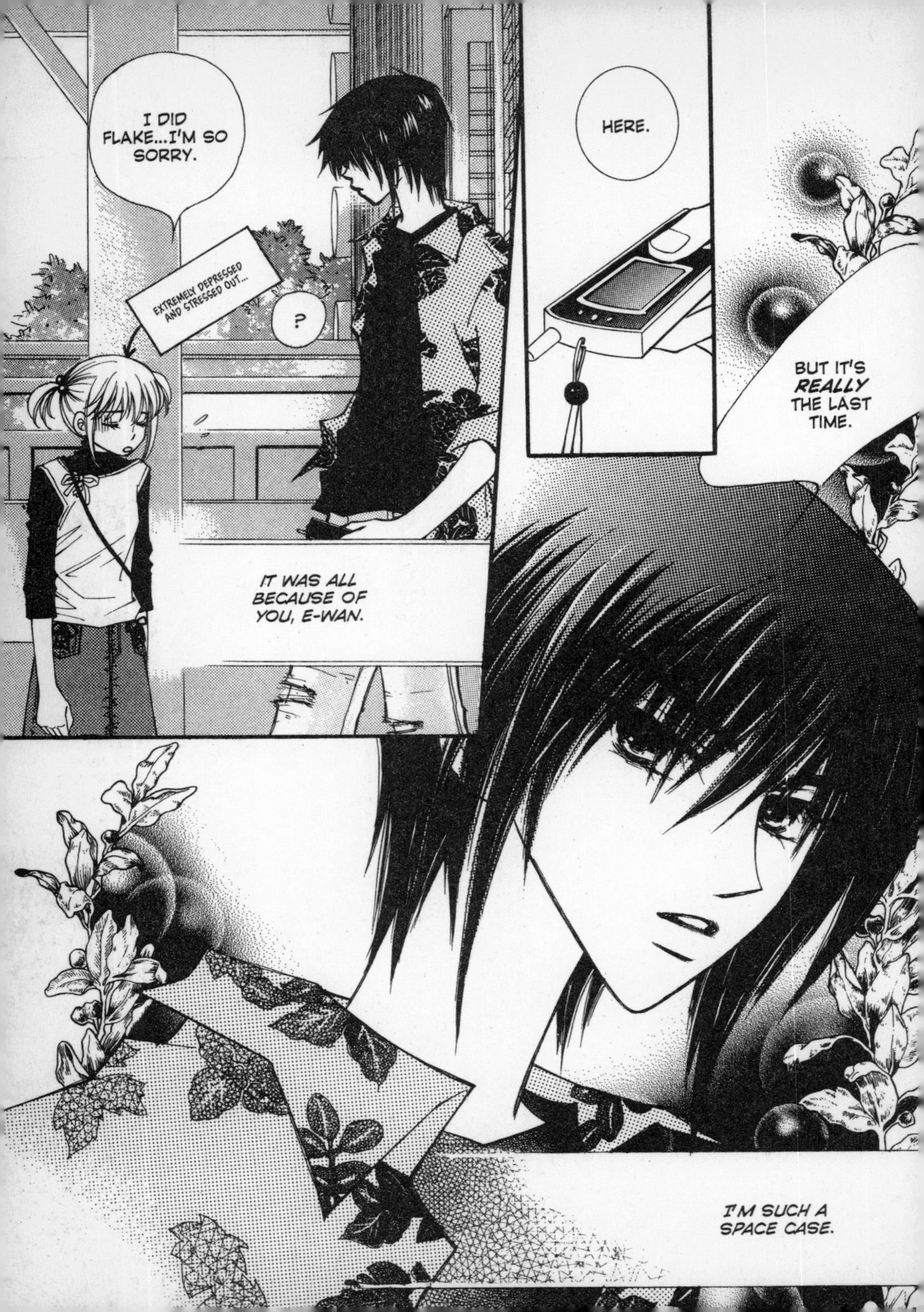
I DID FLAKE...I'M SO SORRY.
EXTREMELY DEPRESSED AND STRESSED OUT...
?
IT WAS ALL BECAUSE OF YOU, E-WAN.
HERE.
BUT IT'S REALLY THE LAST TIME.
I'M SUCH A SPACE CASE.

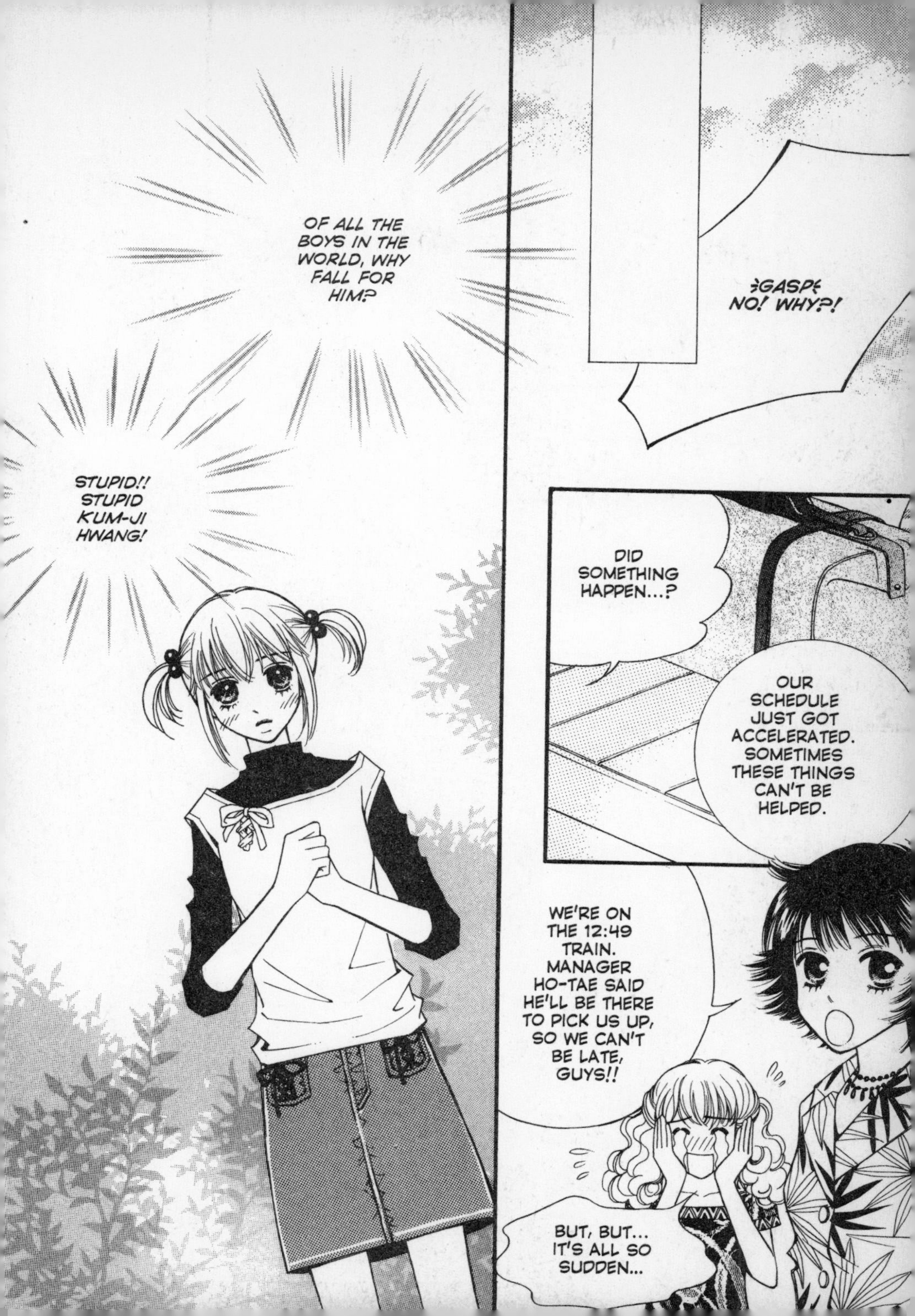
OF ALL THE BOYS IN THE WORLD, WHY FALL FOR HIM?
STUPID!! STUPID KUM-JI HWANG!
:GASP: NO! WHY?!
DID SOMETHING HAPPEN...?
OUR SCHEDULE JUST GOT ACCELERATED. SOMETIMES THESE THINGS CAN'T BE HELPED.
WE'RE ON THE 12:49 TRAIN. MANAGER HO-TAE SAID HE'LL BE THERE TO PICK US UP, SO WE CAN'T BE LATE, GUYS!!
BUT, BUT... IT'S ALL SO SUDDEN...

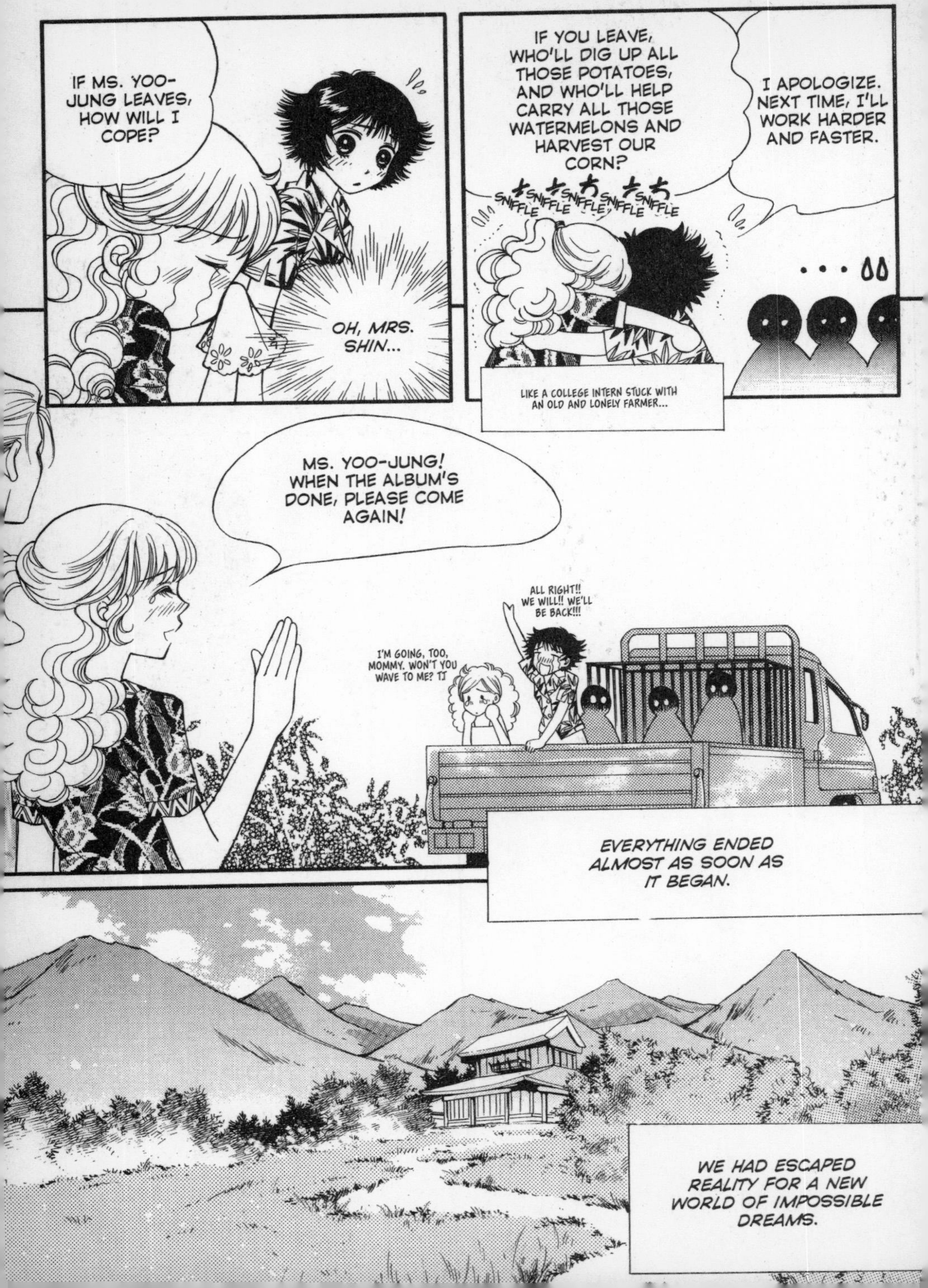
IF MS. YOO-JUNG LEAVES, HOW WILL I COPE?
OH, MRS. SHIN...
IF YOU LEAVE, WHO'LL DIG UP ALL THOSE POTATOES, AND WHO'LL HELP CARRY ALL THOSE WATERMELONS AND HARVEST OUR CORN?
SNIFFLE SNIFFLE SNIFFLE SNIFFLE SNIFFLE
I APOLOGIZE. NEXT TIME, I'LL WORK HARDER AND FASTER.
LIKE A COLLEGE INTERN STUCK WITH AN OLD AND LONELY FARMER...
...
MS. YOO-JUNG! WHEN THE ALBUM'S DONE, PLEASE COME AGAIN!
I'M GOING, TOO, MOMMY. WON'T YOU WAVE TO ME? TJ
ALL RIGHT!! WE WILL!! WE'LL BE BACK!!!
EVERYTHING ENDED ALMOST AS SOON AS IT BEGAN.
WE HAD ESCAPED REALITY FOR A NEW WORLD OF IMPOSSIBLE DREAMS.

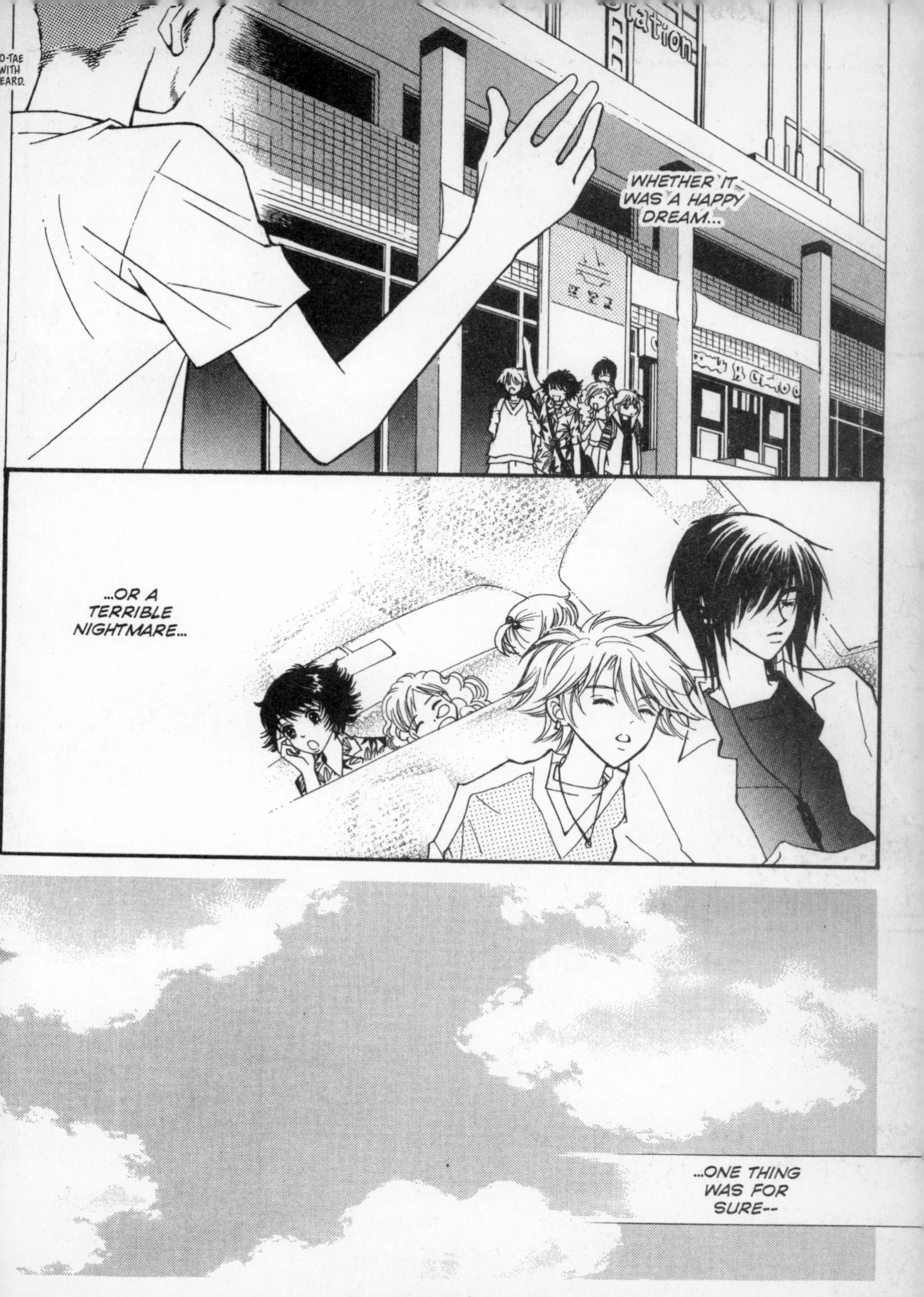
WHETHER IT WAS A HAPPY DREAM...
...OR A TERRIBLE NIGHTMARE...
...ONE THING WAS FOR SURE--

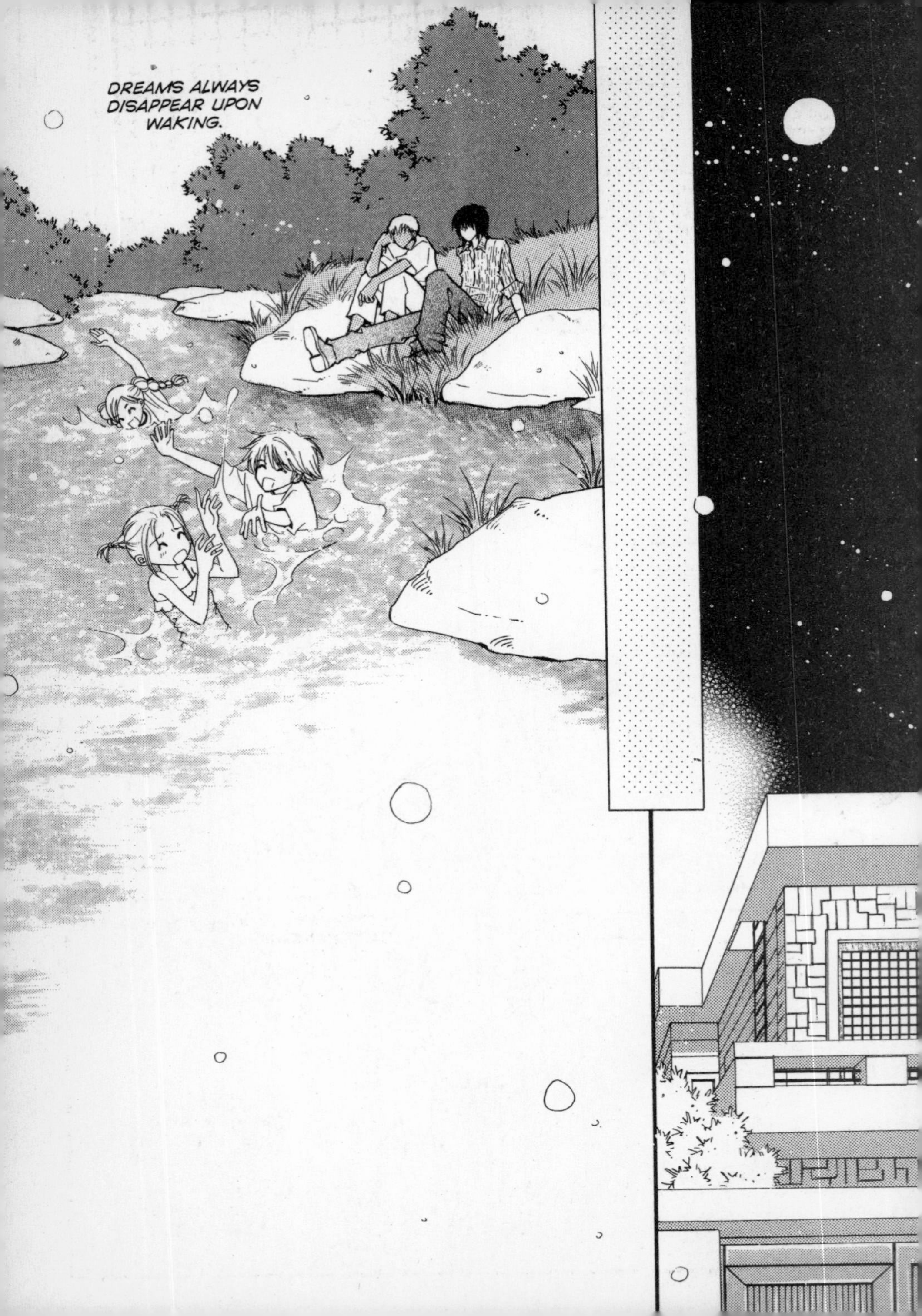
DREAMS ALWAYS DISAPPEAR UPON WAKING.

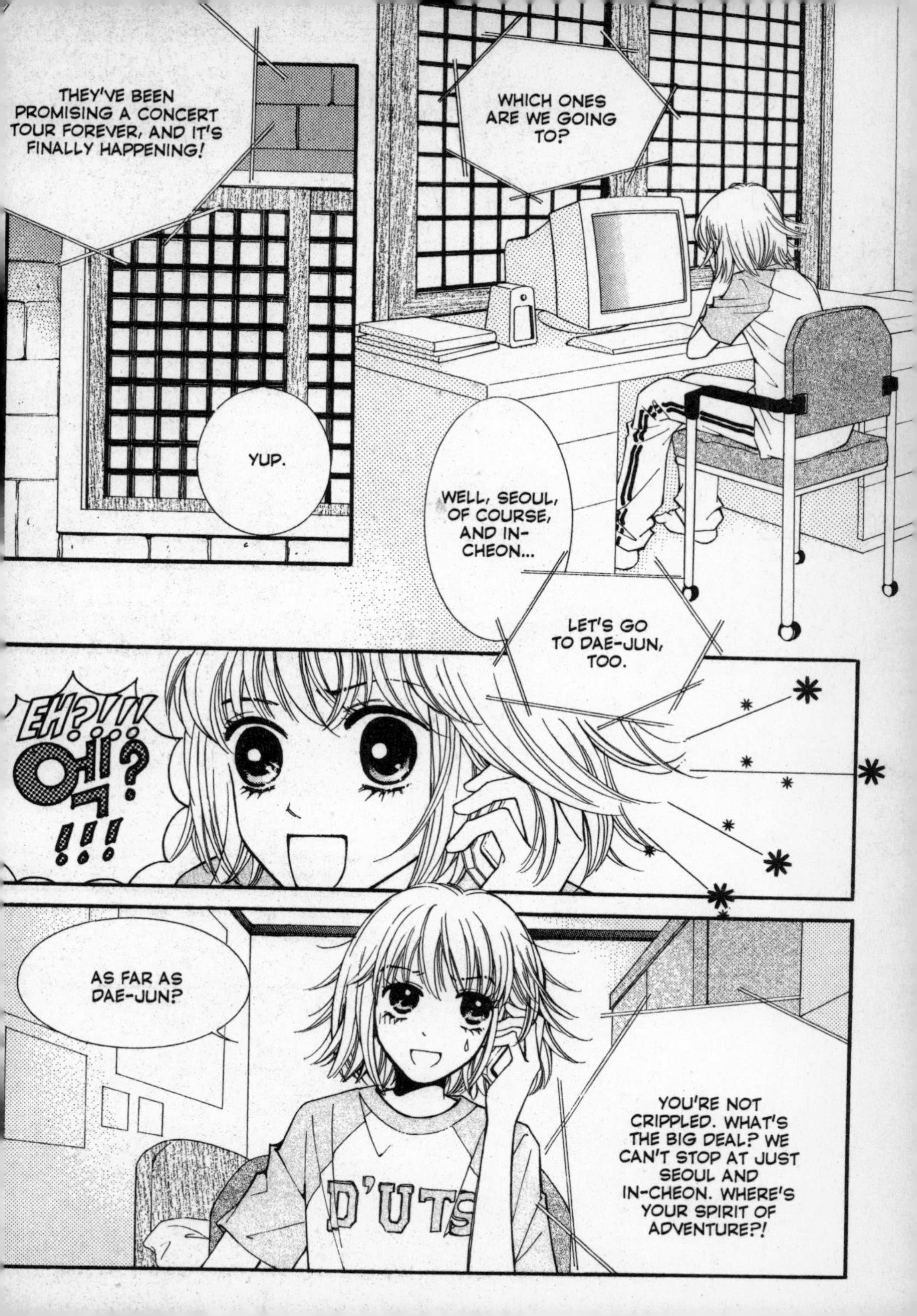
THEY'VE BEEN PROMISING A CONCERT TOUR FOREVER, AND IT'S FINALLY HAPPENING!
YUP.
WHICH ONES ARE WE GOING TO?
WELL, SEOUL, OF COURSE, AND IN-CHEON...
LET'S GO TO DAE-JUN, TOO.
EH?!!!
에?!!!
AS FAR AS DAE-JUN?
YOU'RE NOT CRIPPLED. WHAT'S THE BIG DEAL? WE CAN'T STOP AT JUST SEOUL AND IN-CHEON. WHERE'S YOUR SPIRIT OF ADVENTURE?!
D'UTS

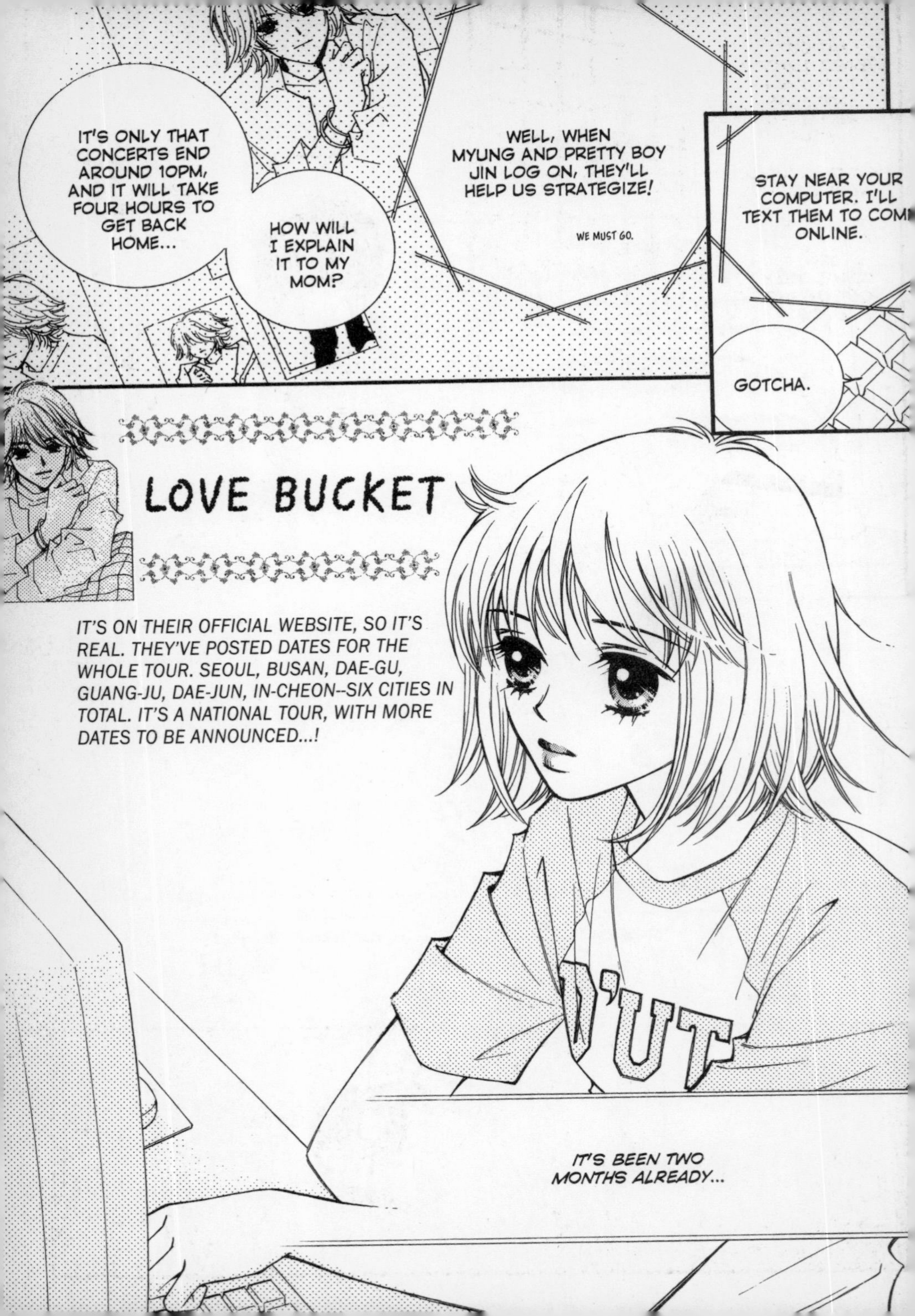
IT'S ONLY THAT CONCERTS END AROUND 10PM, AND IT WILL TAKE FOUR HOURS TO GET BACK HOME...
HOW WILL I EXPLAIN IT TO MY MOM?
WELL, WHEN MYUNG AND PRETTY BOY JIN LOG ON, THEY'LL HELP US STRATEGIZE!
WE MUST GO.
STAY NEAR YOUR COMPUTER. I'LL TEXT THEM TO COM ONLINE.
GOTCHA.
LOVE BUCKET
IT'S ON THEIR OFFICIAL WEBSITE, SO IT'S REAL. THEY'VE POSTED DATES FOR THE WHOLE TOUR. SEOUL, BUSAN, DAE-GU, GUANG-JU, DAE-JUN, IN-CHEON--SIX CITIES IN TOTAL. IT'S A NATIONAL TOUR, WITH MORE DATES TO BE ANNOUNCED...!
D'UT
IT'S BEEN TWO MONTHS ALREADY...

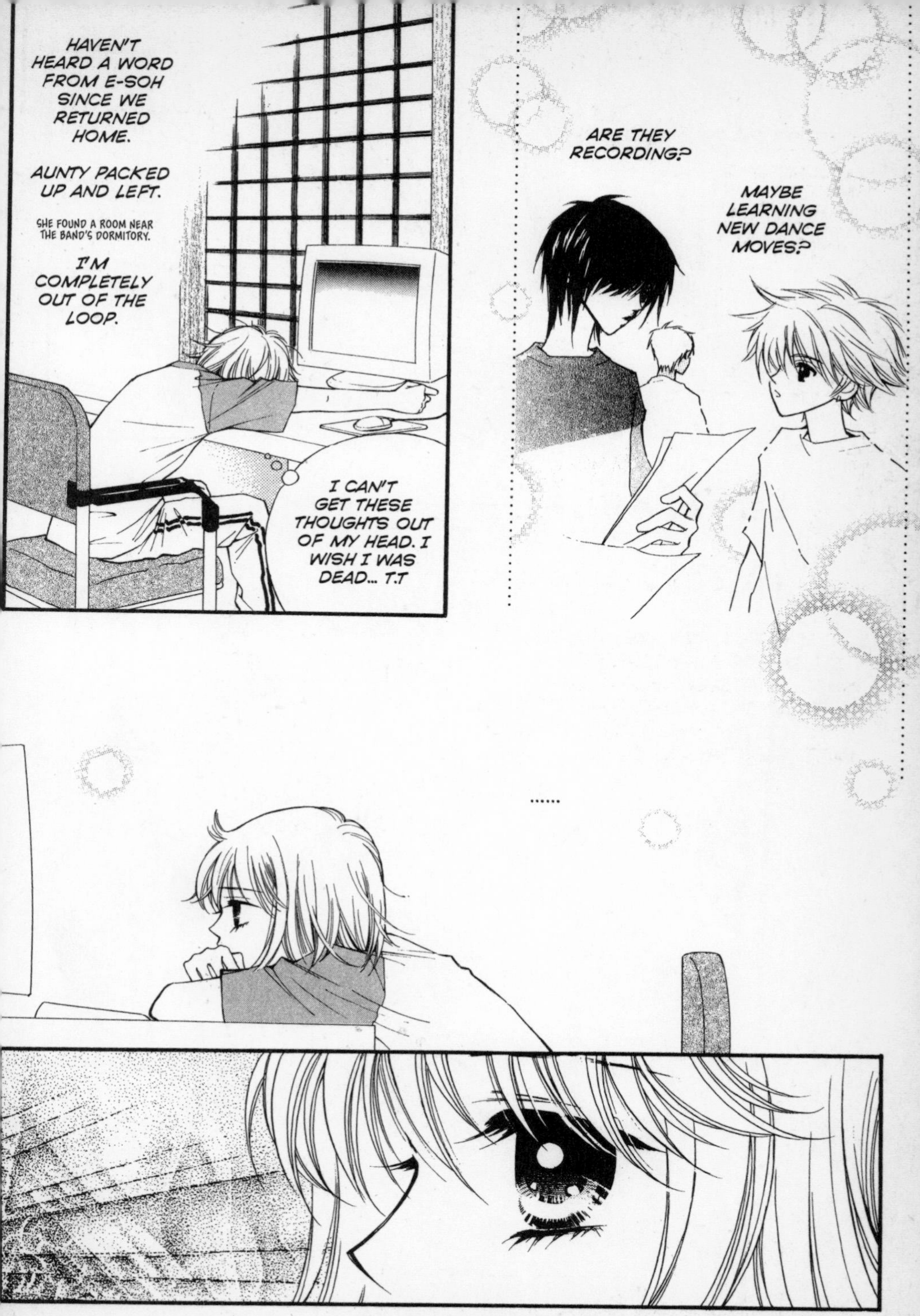
HAVEN'T HEARD A WORD FROM E-SOH SINCE WE RETURNED HOME.
AUNTY PACKED UP AND LEFT.
SHE FOUND A ROOM NEAR THE BAND'S DORMITORY.
I'M COMPLETELY OUT OF THE LOOP.
I CAN'T GET THESE THOUGHTS OUT OF MY HEAD. I WISH I WAS DEAD... T.T
ARE THEY RECORDING?
MAYBE LEARNING NEW DANCE MOVES?
......

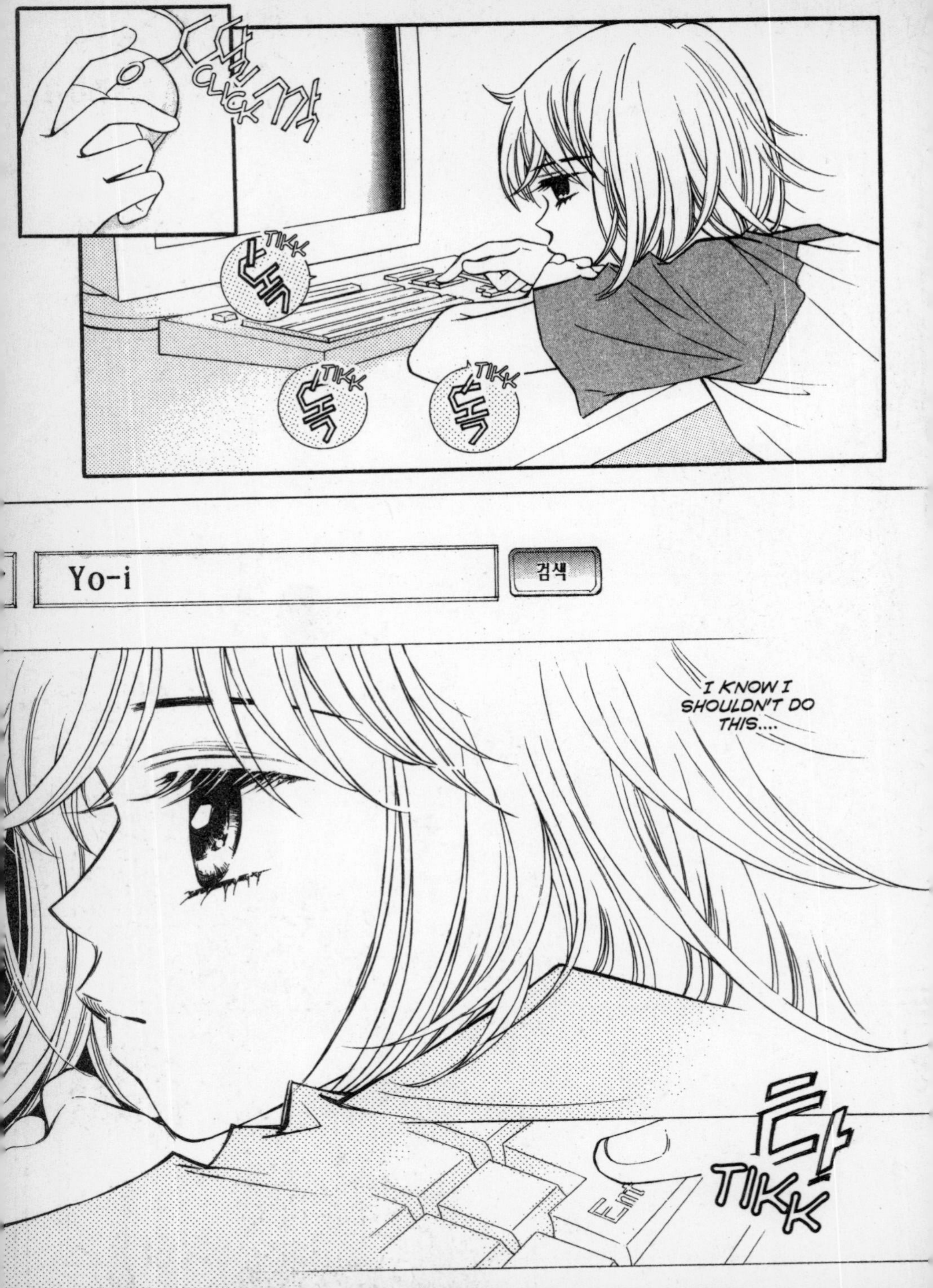
CLICK
TIKK
TIKK
TIKK
Yo-i
검색
I KNOW I SHOULDN'T DO THIS....
탁
TIKK

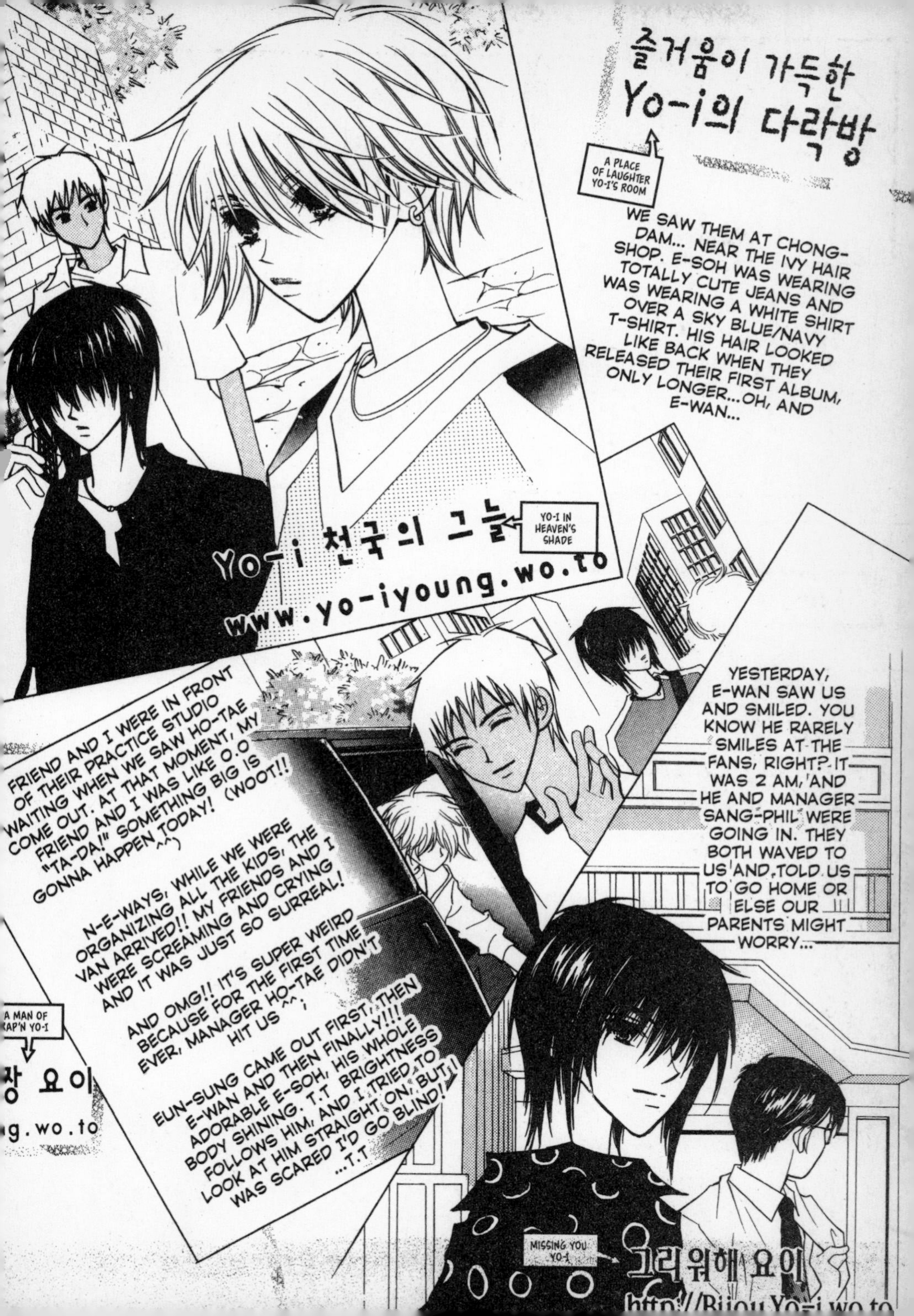

즐거움이 가득한
Yo-i의 다락방
A PLACE OF LAUGHTER YO-I'S ROOM
WE SAW THEM AT CHONG-DAM... NEAR THE IVY HAIR SHOP. E-SOH WAS WEARING TOTALLY CUTE JEANS AND WAS WEARING A WHITE SHIRT OVER A SKY BLUE/NAVY T-SHIRT. HIS HAIR LOOKED LIKE BACK WHEN THEY RELEASED THEIR FIRST ALBUM, ONLY LONGER...OH, AND E-WAN...
Yo-i 천국의 그늘
YO-I IN HEAVEN'S SHADE
www.yo-iyoung.wo.to
FRIEND AND I WERE IN FRONT OF THEIR PRACTICE STUDIO WAITING WHEN WE SAW HO-TAE COME OUT. AT THAT MOMENT, MY FRIEND AND I WAS LIKE O.O "TA-DA!" SOMETHING BIG IS GONNA HAPPEN TODAY! (WOOT!! ^^)
N-E-WAYS, WHILE WE WERE ORGANIZING ALL THE KIDS, THE VAN ARRIVED!! MY FRIENDS AND I WERE SCREAMING AND CRYING AND IT WAS JUST SO SURREAL!
AND OMG!! IT'S SUPER WEIRD BECAUSE FOR THE FIRST TIME EVER, MANAGER HO-TAE DIDN'T HIT US ^^;
EUN-SUNG CAME OUT FIRST, THEN E-WAN AND THEN FINALLY!!! ADORABLE E-SOH, HIS WHOLE BODY SHINING. T.T BRIGHTNESS FOLLOWS HIM, AND I TRIED TO LOOK AT HIM STRAIGHT ON, BUT I WAS SCARED I'D GO BLIND! ...T.T
YESTERDAY, E-WAN SAW US AND SMILED. YOU KNOW HE RARELY SMILES AT THE FANS, RIGHT? IT WAS 2 AM, AND HE AND MANAGER SANG-PHIL WERE GOING IN. THEY BOTH WAVED TO US AND TOLD US TO GO HOME OR ELSE OUR PARENTS MIGHT WORRY...
A MAN OF
AP'N YO-I
장 요이
g.wo.to
MISSING YOU YO-I
그리워해 요이
http://Bijou Yo-i wo to

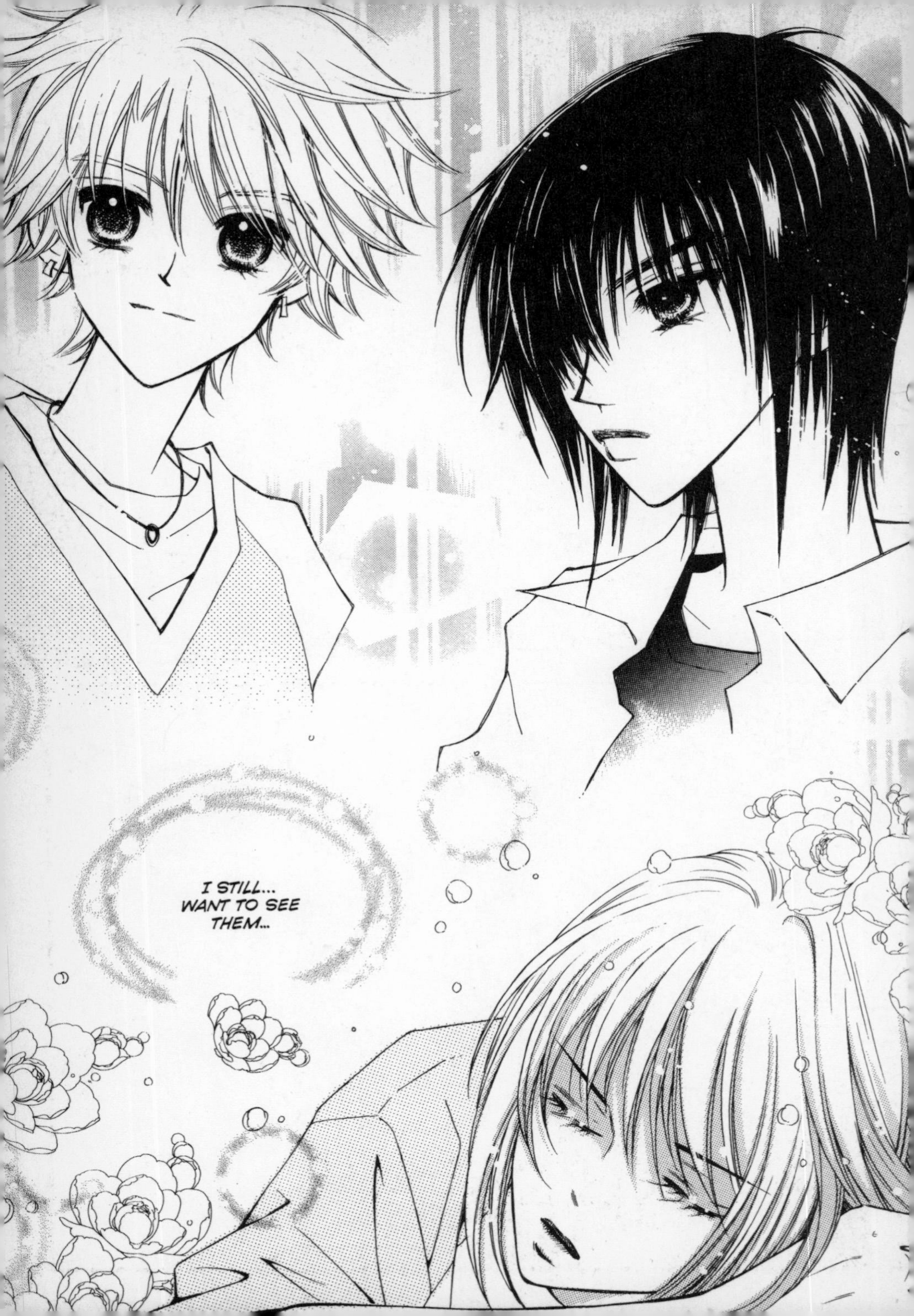
I STILL... WANT TO SEE THEM...

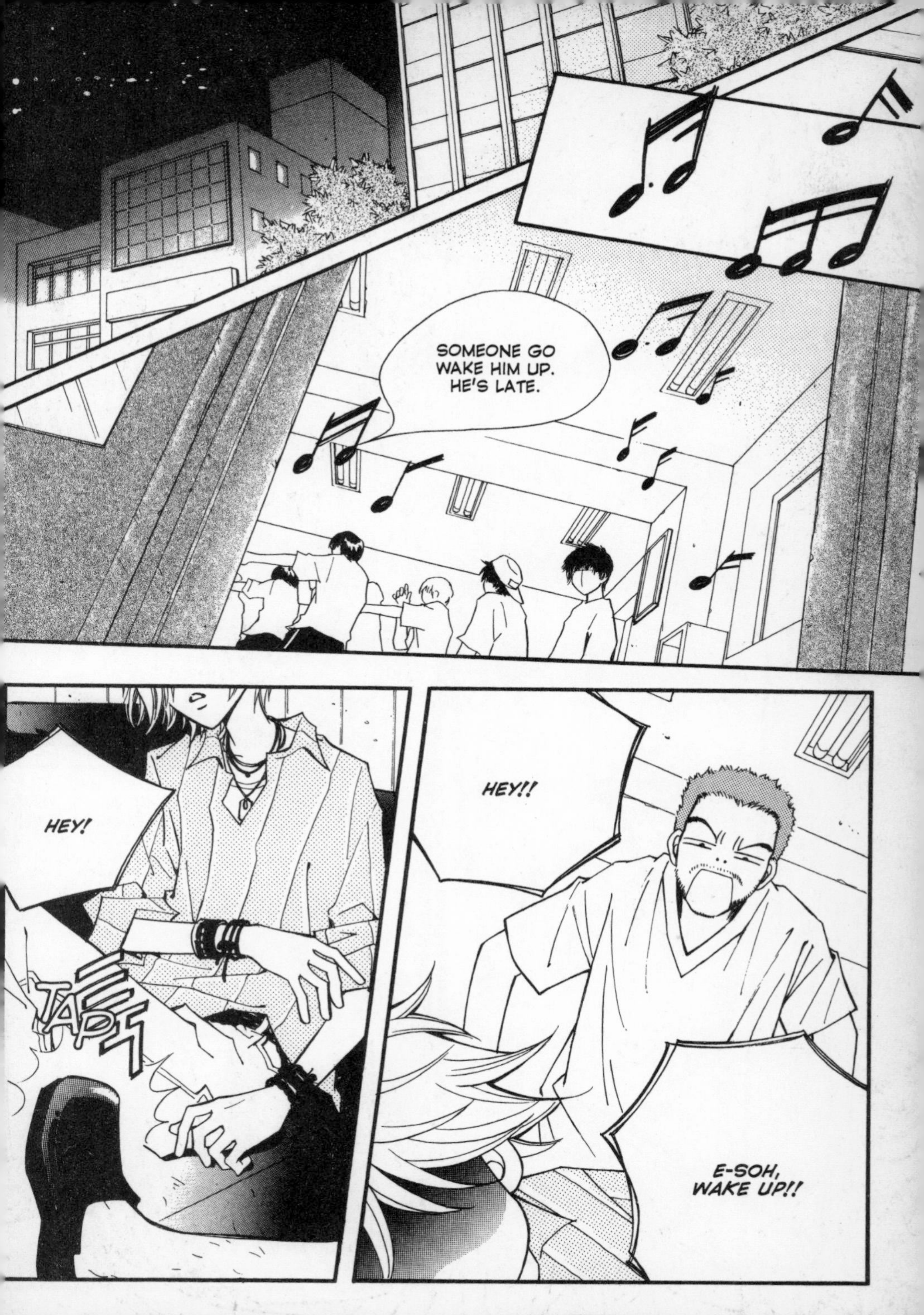

SOMEONE GO WAKE HIM UP. HE'S LATE.
HEY!
TAP
HEY!!
E-SOH, WAKE UP!!

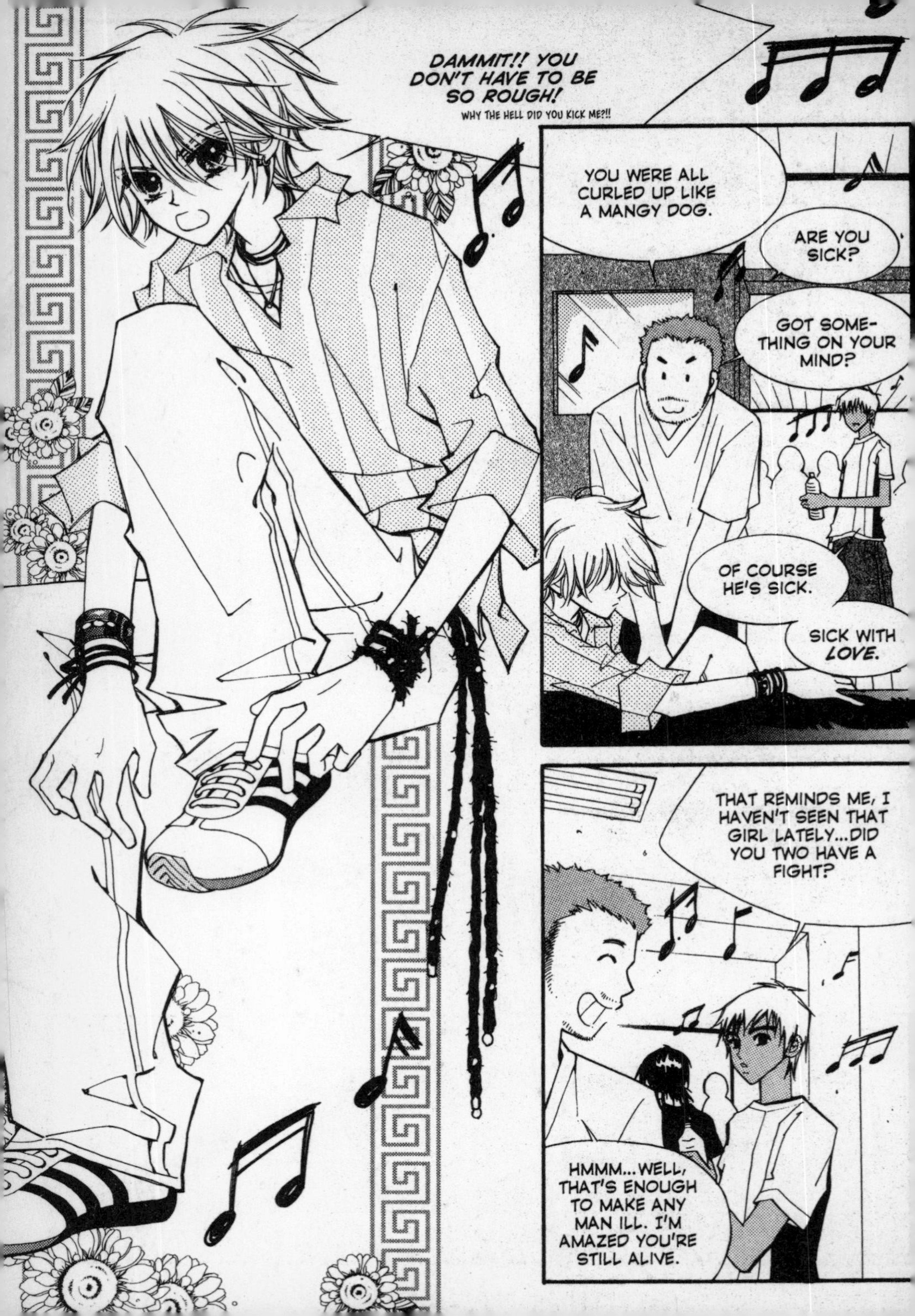
DAMMIT!! YOU DON'T HAVE TO BE SO ROUGH!
WHY THE HELL DID YOU KICK ME?!!
YOU WERE ALL CURLED UP LIKE A MANGY DOG.
ARE YOU SICK?
GOT SOME-THING ON YOUR MIND?
OF COURSE HE'S SICK.
SICK WITH LOVE.
THAT REMINDS ME, I HAVEN'T SEEN THAT GIRL LATELY...DID YOU TWO HAVE A FIGHT?
HMMM...WELL, THAT'S ENOUGH TO MAKE ANY MAN ILL. I'M AMAZED YOU'RE STILL ALIVE.

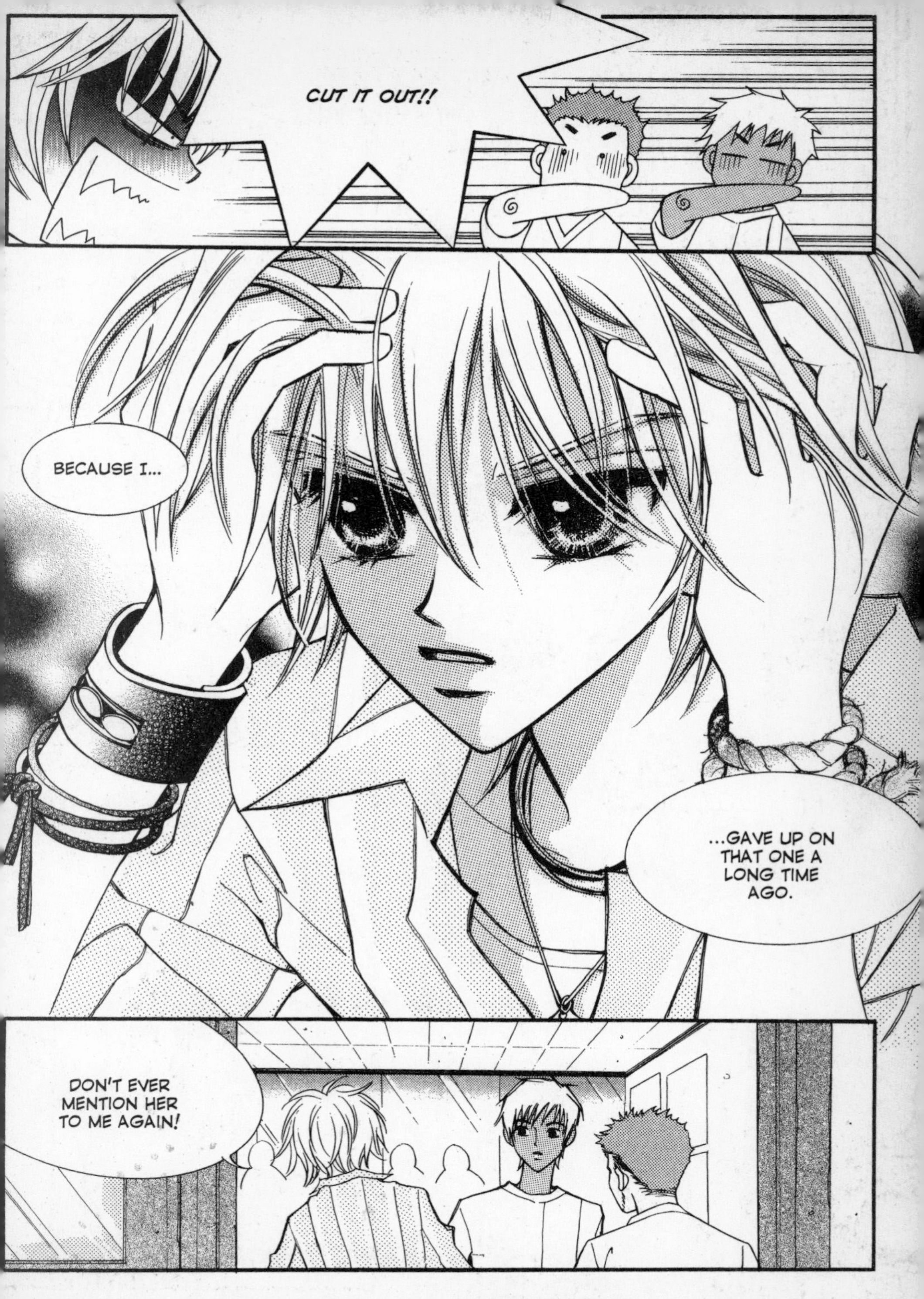
CUT IT OUT!!
BECAUSE I...
...GAVE UP ON THAT ONE A LONG TIME AGO.
DON'T EVER MENTION HER TO ME AGAIN!

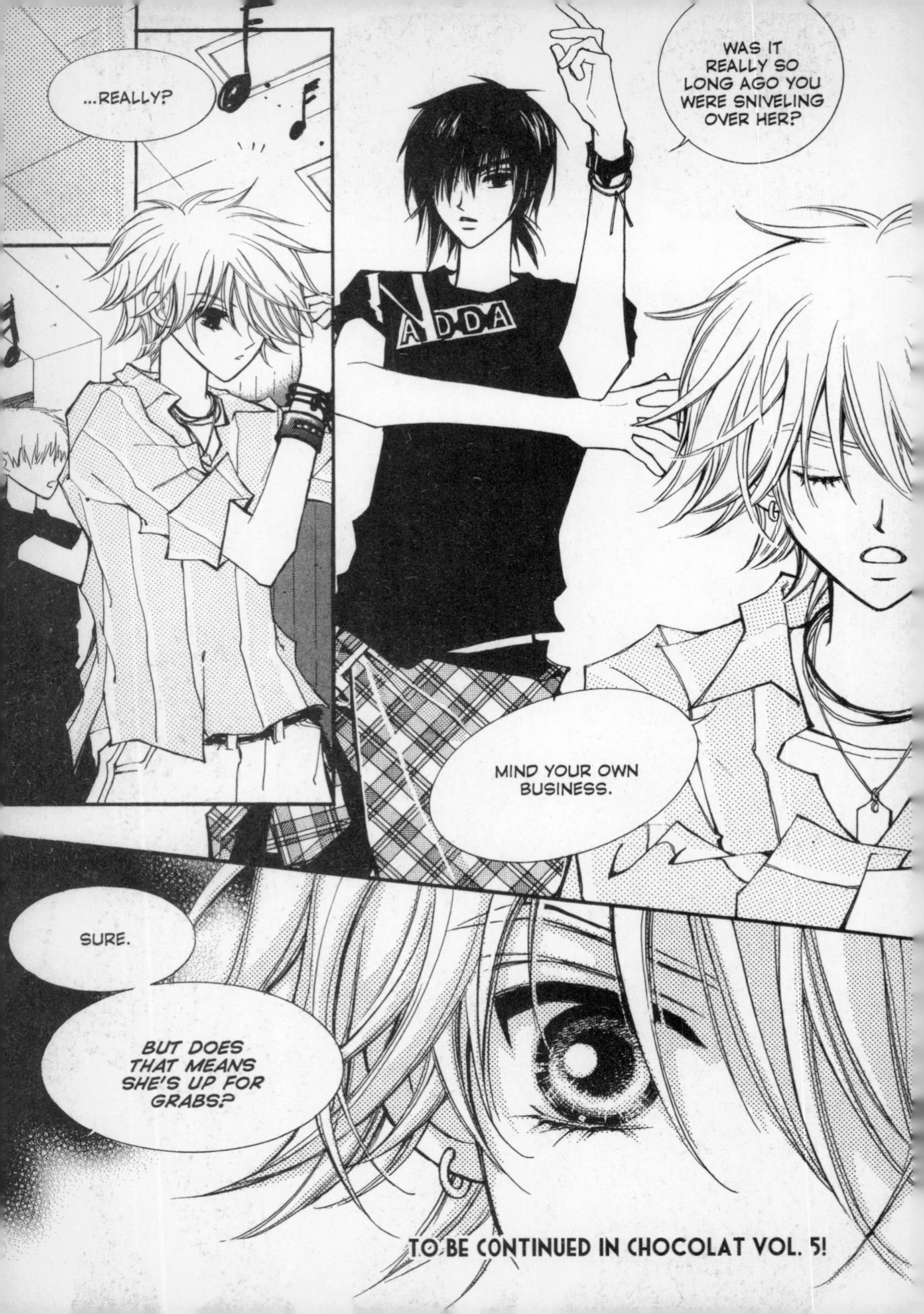

...REALLY?
WAS IT REALLY SO LONG AGO YOU WERE SNIVELING OVER HER?
ADDA
MIND YOUR OWN BUSINESS.
SURE.
BUT DOES THAT MEANS SHE'S UP FOR GRABS?
TO BE CONTINUED IN CHOCOLAT VOL. 5!

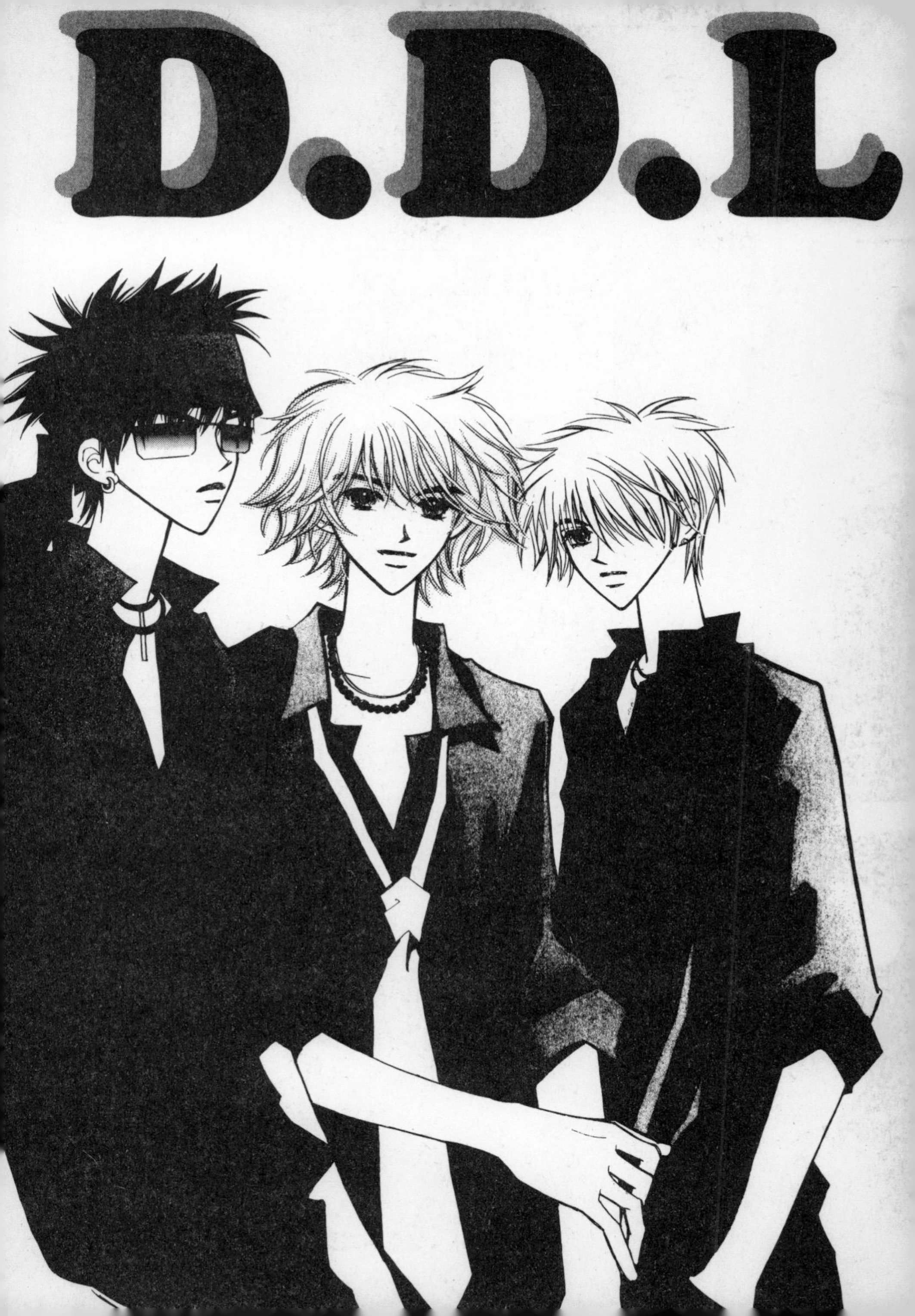
D.D.L

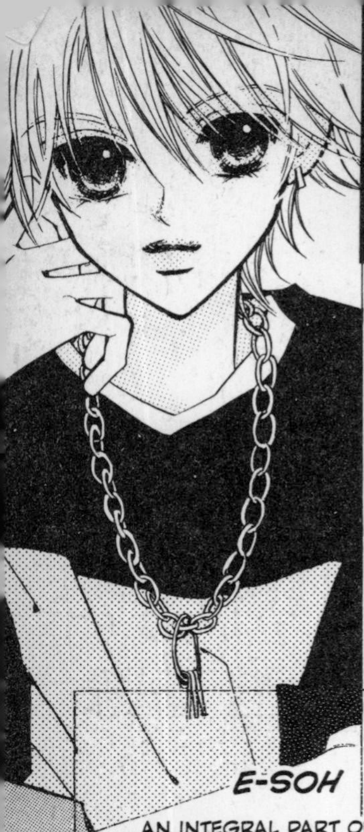

O, X QUIZ: WHAT IS THE BEAT OF YOUR HEART TELLING YOU?

1. IS THERE ANY FEMALE STAR YOU REALLY WANT TO BE IN A SERIOUS RELATIONSHIP WITH?
O — JIN, ANDY, FUU
X — E-WAN, EUN-SUNG, E-SOH...WU-HEE (HOW CAN A GIRL FLIRT WITH ANOTHER GIRL...? T.T)

2. LOOKS OVER PERSONALITY?
O — E-WAN (... -.-;;;)
X — EVERYONE ELSE

3. IS THERE ANY TIME YOU HATE BEING A STAR?
O — EVERYONE EXCEPT WU-HEE
X — WU-HEE (BUT IT'S FUN... ^^;;)

4. LOVE AND WORK: IF I MUST CHOOSE, I'LL CHOOSE WORK!
O — JIN, FUU, EUN-SUNG
X — ANDY, E-SOH
NO ANSWER — E-WAN (DOESN'T CARE FOR EITHER), WU-HEE (CAN'T DECIDE)

5. IF I LIKE A FAN, I WILL DATE HIM/HER.
O — JIN, ANDY, E-SOH (IT'S OKAY IF SHE'S FAN OF SOMEONE ELSE...RIGHT?...@.@;;) ,WU-HEE
X — E-WAN, EUN-SUNG, FUU

E-SOH

AN INTEGRAL PART OF YO-I. HE'S KNOWN TO BE PRETTY SELF-CENTERED AND IS OFTEN IMMATURE, BUT WHEN IT COMES TO LOVE, HE'S AN EXTREMELY PASSIONATE BOY WHO WILL GO THROUGH THE FIRES OF HELL FOR A KISS. FALLING IN LOVE WITH KUM-JI IS CAUSING HIM TO GROW UP FAST.

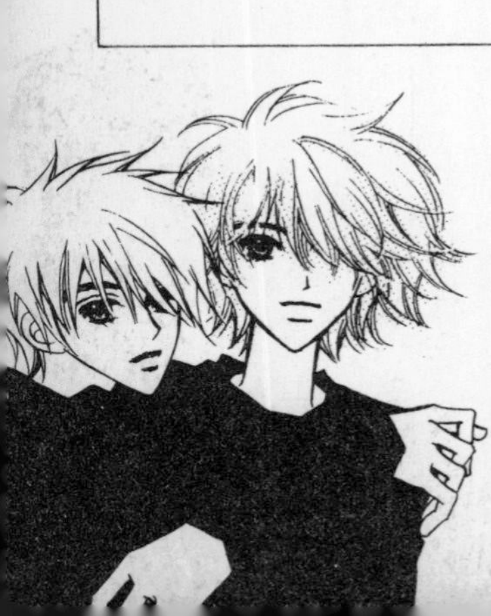

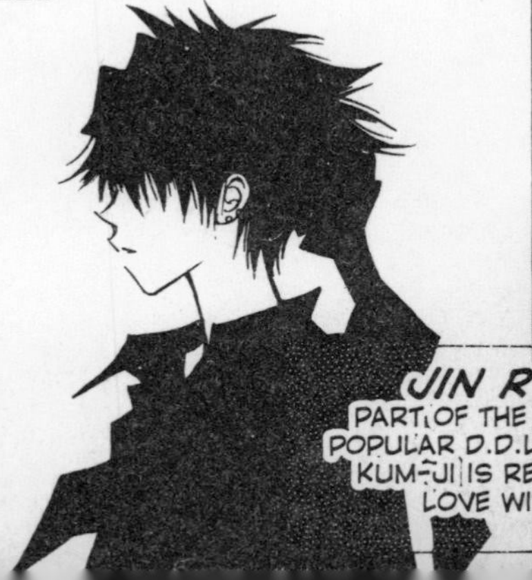

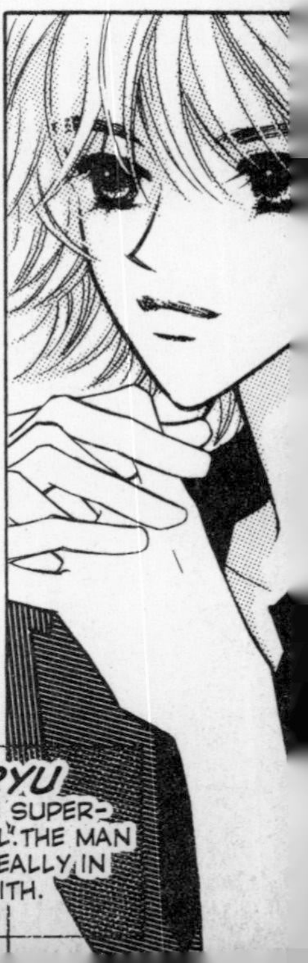

JIN RYU

PART OF THE SUPER-POPULAR D.D.L. THE MAN KUM-JI IS REALLY IN LOVE WITH.

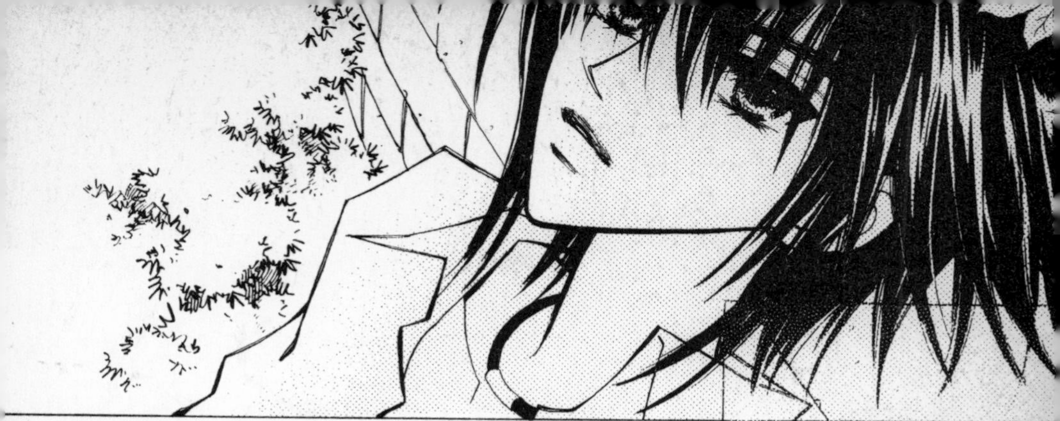

6. ACTUALLY, I HAVE A GIRL/BOYFRIEND RIGHT NOW...
O — JIN, ANDY, E-SOH
X — FUU, E-WAN, EUN-SUNG, WU-HEE

7. WITHIN THIS LAST YEAR, I'VE BEEN REJECTED.
O — ANDY, E-SOH (... T.T)
X — JIN, FUU, E-WAN, EUN-SUNG, WU-HEE (IF THEY NEVER START ANYTHING, THERE'S NO WAY TO GET DUMPED...)

8. WITHIN THIS LAST YEAR, YOU'VE KISSED SOMEONE.
O — JIN, ANDY, E-WAN, E-SOH, WU-HEE
X — FUU, EUN-SUNG (WHAT THE HELL IS WRONG WITH US...?)

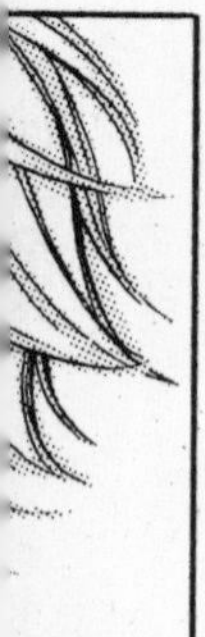

9. THERE'S SOMEONE IN YOUR RIVAL GROUP YOU WANT IN YOUR OWN TEAM.
O — JIN, FUU
X — EVERYONE ELSE (WHO? WHO DO YOU WANT? PLEASE TELL US!)

10. THERE'S SOMEONE IN MY TEAM I WANT OUT.
... (EVERYONE CHOOSES "NO COMMENT." T.T)

E-WAN
THE OTHER SIDE OF YO-I. FAMILY PROBLEMS CAUSED HIM TO HAVE A REBELLIOUS PERIOD, AND THAT'S WHEN EUN-SUNG AND JIN BOTH BROUGHT HIM TO THE ATTENTION OF YO-I'S RECORD LABEL. HIS BIZARRE INTERACTIONS WITH KUM-JI MAKE E-SOH NERVOUS; HOWEVER, HE'S DEAD LAST WHEN IT COMES TO UNDERSTANDING HIS OWN EMOTIONS.

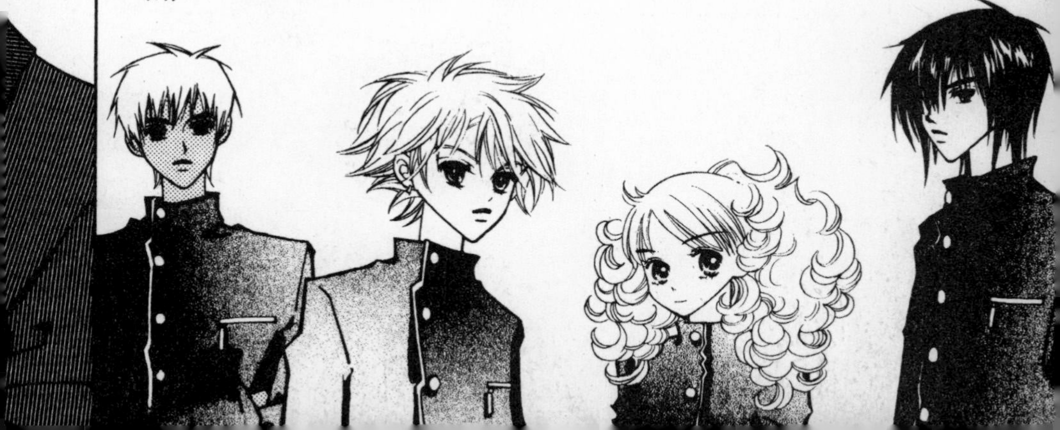

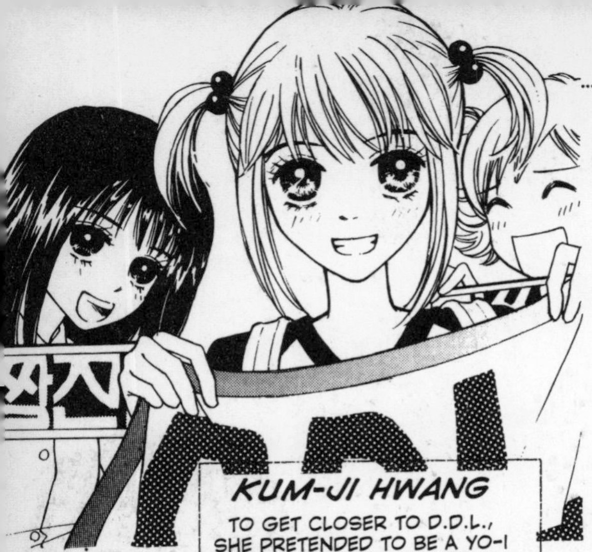

D.D.L

KUM-JI HWANG

TO GET CLOSER TO D.D.L., SHE PRETENDED TO BE A YO-I FAN AND JOINED THEIR FANCLUB. LITTLE DID SHE KNOW, SHE'D CAPTURE E-SOH'S HEART. UNFORTUNATELY, HER OWN HEART IS FLUTTERING IN AN UNFORESEEN DIRECTION...

WE MET AT D.D.L.'S CONCERTS!

THESE THREE D.D.L. DEVOTEES ORIGINALLY MET BY GOING TO ALL THE SAME EVENTS. KUM-JI HWANG, HYO-SUN KANG, AND MYUNG SONG REALLY LOVE D.D.L. WHILE WE WERE TAKING PICTURES, THEY KEPT SAYING, "WHEN THE BOOK COMES OUT, WILL THE BOYS SEE IT?" AND "PLEASE TAKE GOOD PICTURES OF US!" AND "WE NEED TO LOOK GOOD," ETC. WHEN THE MUSIC STARTED, THEY WERE SCREAMING AT THE TOP OF THEIR LUNGS. THEIR ENTHUSIASM WAS REFRESHING.

D.D.L. FANS VS. YO-I FANS

PLEASE MEET THE YO-I FANCLUB PRESIDENT, CHAE-RYUN YANG.

CHAE-RYUN IS SEEMINGLY KNOWN BY EVERYBODY, AND SHE'S BEST REMEMBERED FOR HER BEAUTY. MANY BELIEVE SHE COULD BE A STAR IN HER OWN RIGHT, BUT SHE SAYS SHE'D RATHER CONTINUE TO FOLLOW HER BELOVED IDOLS.

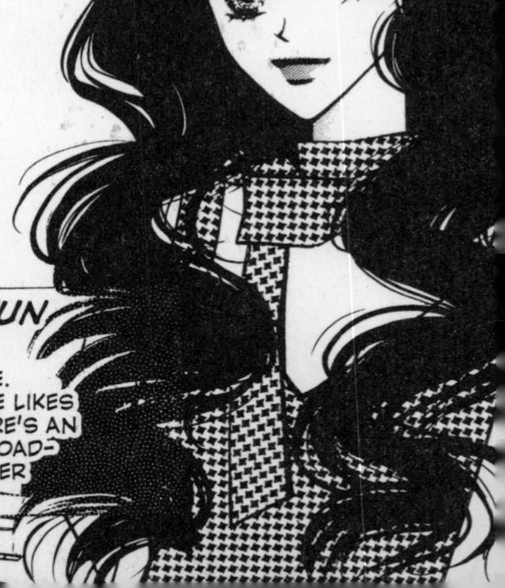

CHAE-RYUN YANG

AKA BARBIE. PERSONALLY SHE LIKES E-WAN, BUT THERE'S AN UNEXPECTED ROADBLOCK ON HER JOURNEY.

Yo-i

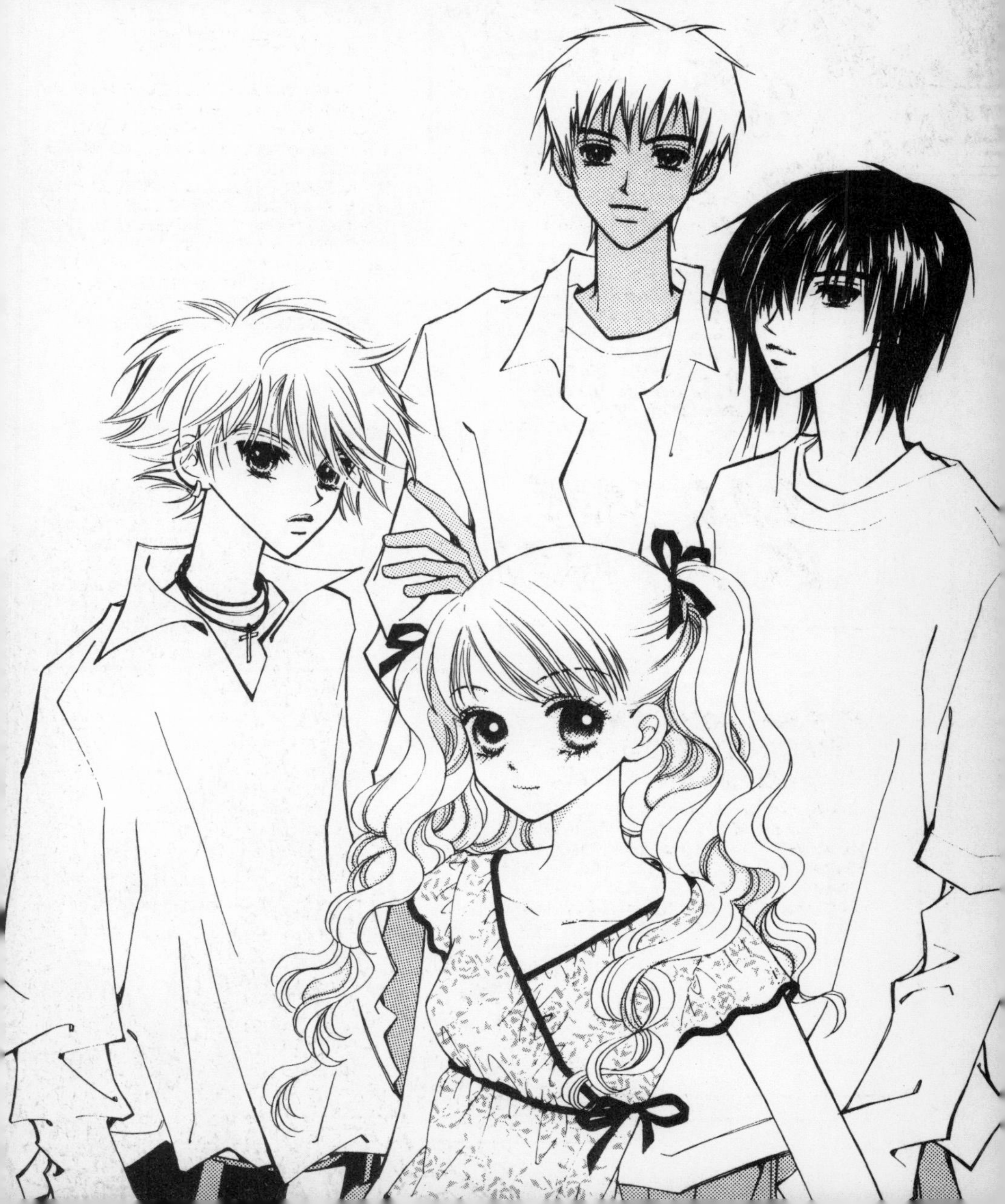

IF I HAD 600 UK...

EDITOR'S NOTE: 10 UK = 1 BILLION
$1.00 = APPROXIMATELY W1,000

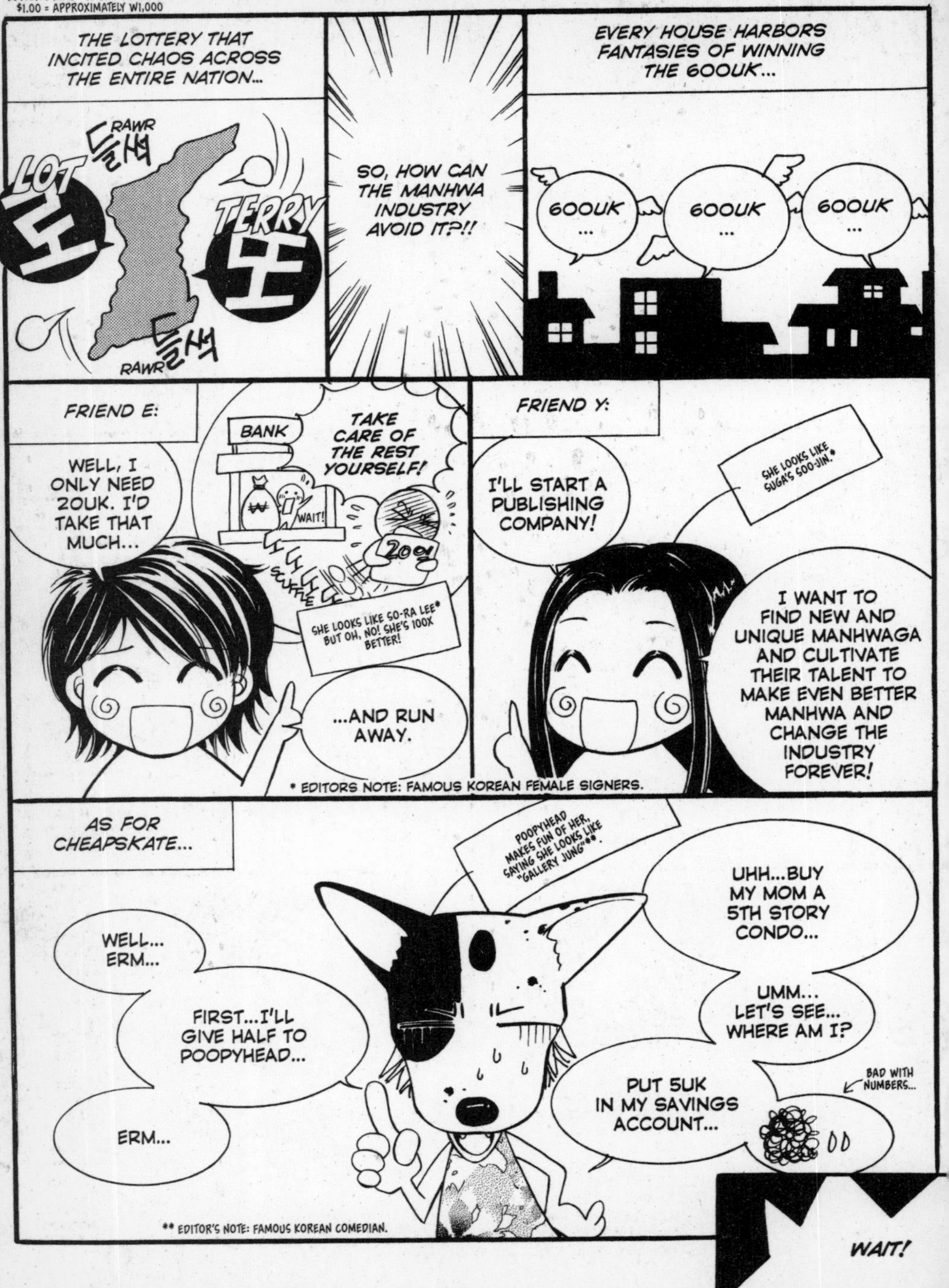

THE LOTTERY THAT INCITED CHAOS ACROSS THE ENTIRE NATION...
RAWR
LOT
TERRY
RAWR
SO, HOW CAN THE MANHWA INDUSTRY AVOID IT?!!
EVERY HOUSE HARBORS FANTASIES OF WINNING THE 600UK...
600UK ...
600UK ...
600UK ...
FRIEND E:
WELL, I ONLY NEED 20UK. I'D TAKE THAT MUCH...
TAKE CARE OF THE REST YOURSELF!
BANK
WAIT!
SCUFFLE
SHE LOOKS LIKE SO-RA LEE* BUT OH, NO! SHE'S 100X BETTER!
...AND RUN AWAY.
FRIEND Y:
I'LL START A PUBLISHING COMPANY!
SHE LOOKS LIKE SUGA'S SOO-JIN.*
I WANT TO FIND NEW AND UNIQUE MANHWAGA AND CULTIVATE THEIR TALENT TO MAKE EVEN BETTER MANHWA AND CHANGE THE INDUSTRY FOREVER!
* EDITORS NOTE: FAMOUS KOREAN FEMALE SIGNERS.
AS FOR CHEAPSKATE...
POOPYHEAD MAKES FUN OF HER, SAYING SHE LOOKS LIKE "GALLERY JUNG"**.
WELL... ERM...
FIRST...I'LL GIVE HALF TO POOPYHEAD...
ERM...
UHH...BUY MY MOM A 5TH STORY CONDO...
UMM... LET'S SEE... WHERE AM I?
PUT 5UK IN MY SAVINGS ACCOUNT...
BAD WITH NUMBERS...
** EDITOR'S NOTE: FAMOUS KOREAN COMEDIAN.
WAIT!

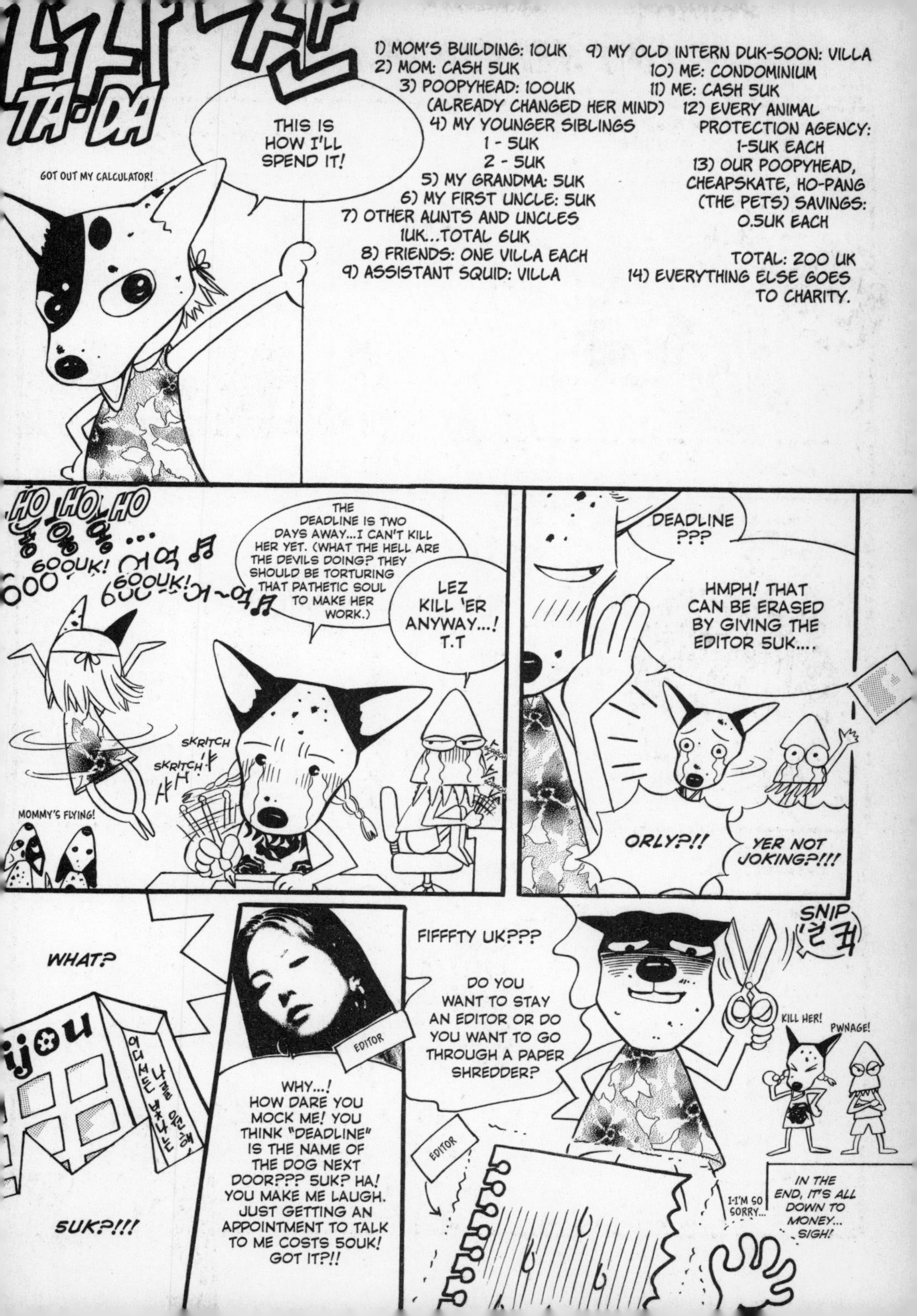
TA-DA
GOT OUT MY CALCULATOR!
THIS IS HOW I'LL SPEND IT!
1) MOM'S BUILDING: 10UK
2) MOM: CASH 5UK
3) POOPYHEAD: 100UK (ALREADY CHANGED HER MIND)
4) MY YOUNGER SIBLINGS 1 - 5UK 2 - 5UK
5) MY GRANDMA: 5UK
6) MY FIRST UNCLE: 5UK
7) OTHER AUNTS AND UNCLES 1UK...TOTAL 6UK
8) FRIENDS: ONE VILLA EACH
9) ASSISTANT SQUID: VILLA
9) MY OLD INTERN DUK-SOON: VILLA
10) ME: CONDOMINIUM
11) ME: CASH 5UK
12) EVERY ANIMAL PROTECTION AGENCY: 1-5UK EACH
13) OUR POOPYHEAD, CHEAPSKATE, HO-PANG (THE PETS) SAVINGS: 0.5UK EACH
TOTAL: 200 UK
14) EVERYTHING ELSE GOES TO CHARITY.
HO HO HO
600UK! 600UK!
THE DEADLINE IS TWO DAYS AWAY...I CAN'T KILL HER YET. (WHAT THE HELL ARE THE DEVILS DOING? THEY SHOULD BE TORTURING THAT PATHETIC SOUL TO MAKE HER WORK.)
LEZ KILL 'ER ANYWAY...! T.T
SKRITCH SKRITCH
MOMMY'S FLYING!
DEADLINE ???
HMPH! THAT CAN BE ERASED BY GIVING THE EDITOR 5UK....
ORLY?!!
YER NOT JOKING?!!!
WHAT?
SUK?!!!
EDITOR
WHY...! HOW DARE YOU MOCK ME! YOU THINK "DEADLINE" IS THE NAME OF THE DOG NEXT DOOR??? 5UK? HA! YOU MAKE ME LAUGH. JUST GETTING AN APPOINTMENT TO TALK TO ME COSTS 50UK! GOT IT?!!
FIFFFTY UK???
DO YOU WANT TO STAY AN EDITOR OR DO YOU WANT TO GO THROUGH A PAPER SHREDDER?
SNIP
EDITOR
I-I'M SO SORRY...
KILL HER!
PWNAGE!
IN THE END, IT'S ALL DOWN TO MONEY... SIGH!

THE STUDIO'S BIG BANG EVENT...

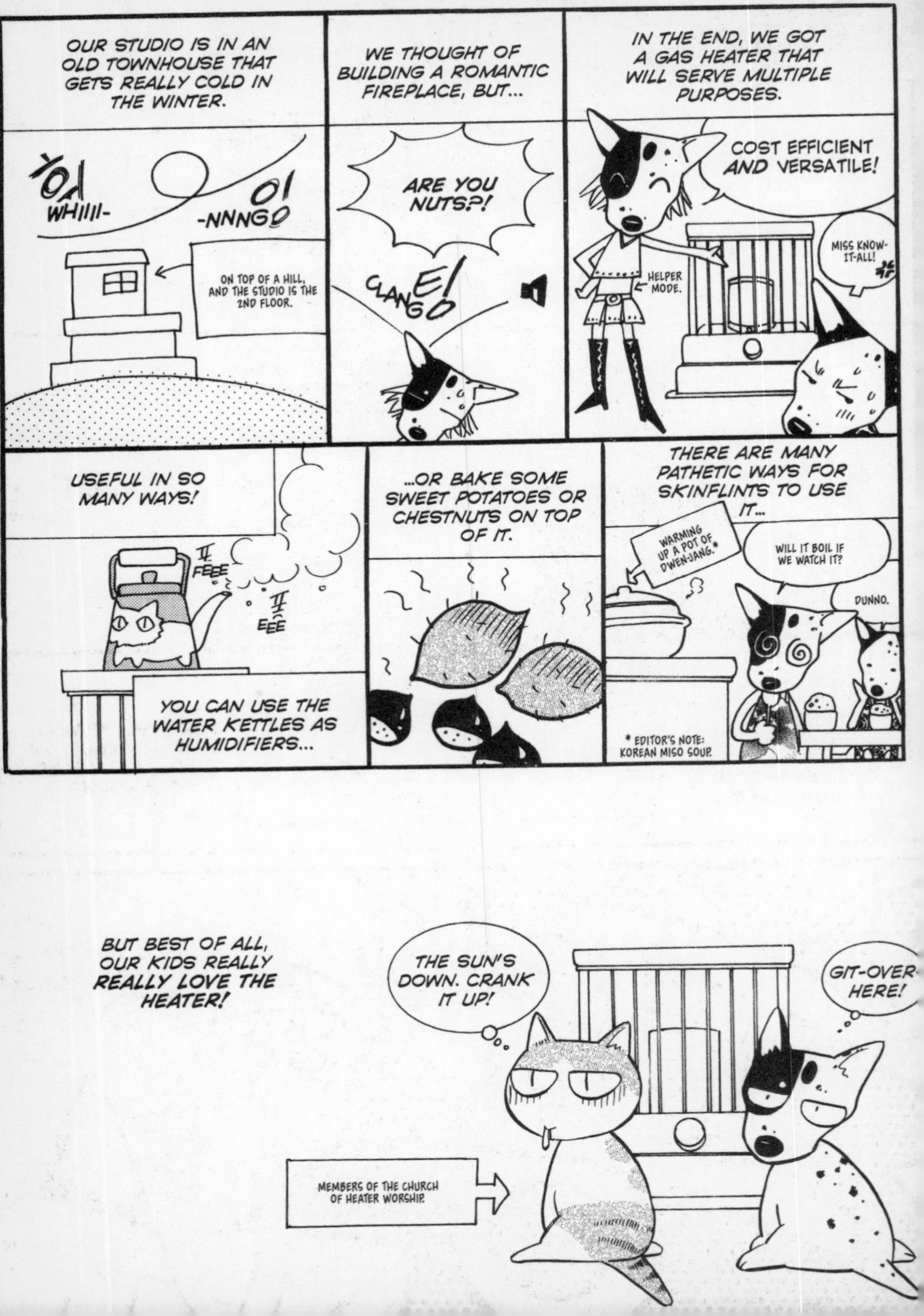

OUR STUDIO IS IN AN OLD TOWNHOUSE THAT GETS REALLY COLD IN THE WINTER.
WHIIII-
-NNNG
ON TOP OF A HILL, AND THE STUDIO IS THE 2ND FLOOR.
WE THOUGHT OF BUILDING A ROMANTIC FIREPLACE, BUT...
ARE YOU NUTS?!
CLANG
IN THE END, WE GOT A GAS HEATER THAT WILL SERVE MULTIPLE PURPOSES.
COST EFFICIENT AND VERSATILE!
HELPER MODE.
MISS KNOW-IT-ALL!
USEFUL IN SO MANY WAYS!
FEEE
EEE
YOU CAN USE THE WATER KETTLES AS HUMIDIFIERS...
...OR BAKE SOME SWEET POTATOES OR CHESTNUTS ON TOP OF IT.
THERE ARE MANY PATHETIC WAYS FOR SKINFLINTS TO USE IT...
WARMING UP A POT OF DWEN-JANG.*
WILL IT BOIL IF WE WATCH IT?
DUNNO.
* EDITOR'S NOTE: KOREAN MISO SOUP.
BUT BEST OF ALL, OUR KIDS REALLY REALLY LOVE THE HEATER!
THE SUN'S DOWN. CRANK IT UP!
GIT-OVER HERE!
MEMBERS OF THE CHURCH OF HEATER WORSHIP.

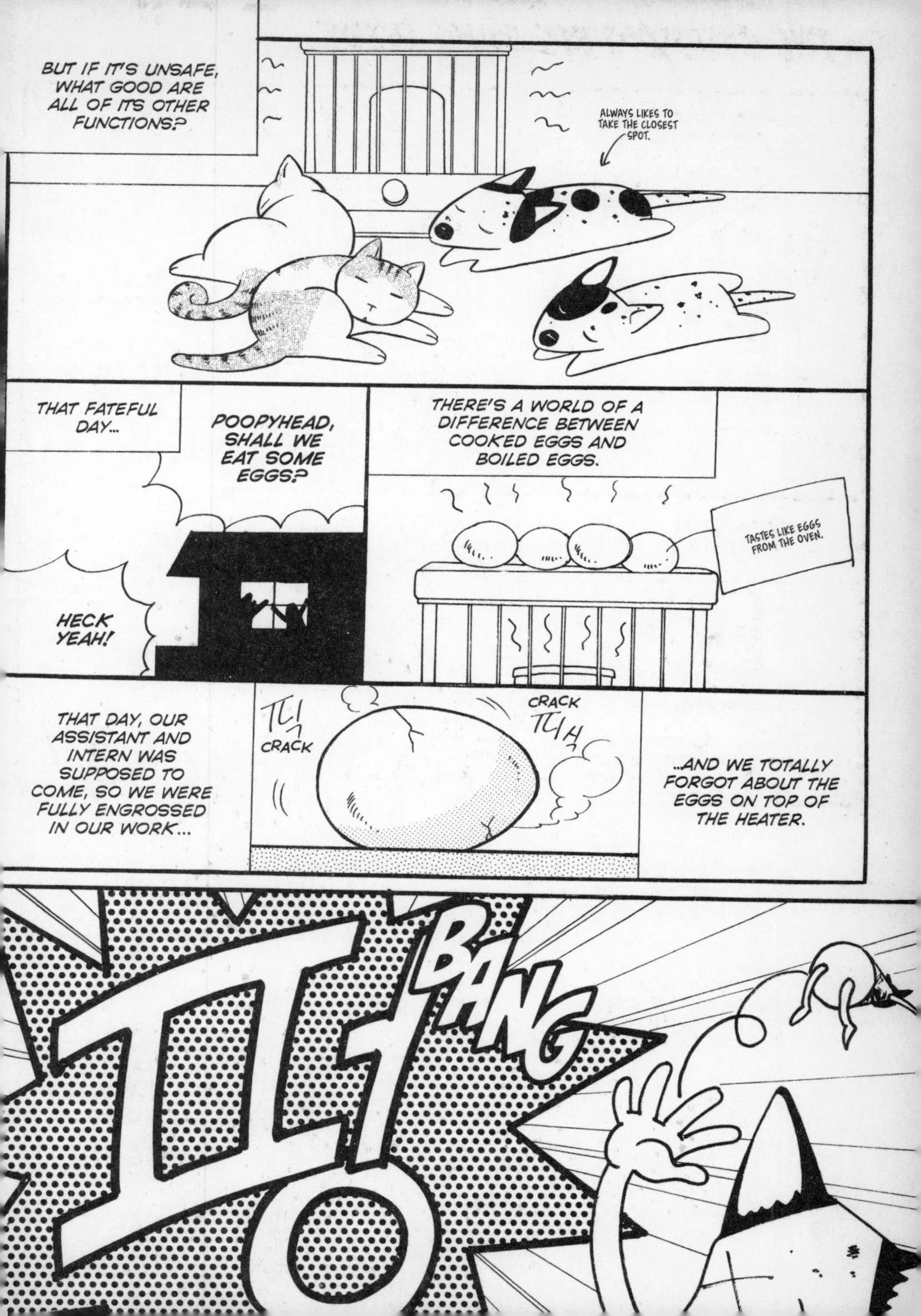
BUT IF IT'S UNSAFE, WHAT GOOD ARE ALL OF ITS OTHER FUNCTIONS?
ALWAYS LIKES TO TAKE THE CLOSEST SPOT.
THAT FATEFUL DAY...
POOPYHEAD, SHALL WE EAT SOME EGGS?
HECK YEAH!
THERE'S A WORLD OF A DIFFERENCE BETWEEN COOKED EGGS AND BOILED EGGS.
TASTES LIKE EGGS FROM THE OVEN.
THAT DAY, OUR ASSISTANT AND INTERN WAS SUPPOSED TO COME, SO WE WERE FULLY ENGROSSED IN OUR WORK...
CRACK
CRACK
...AND WE TOTALLY FORGOT ABOUT THE EGGS ON TOP OF THE HEATER.
BANG

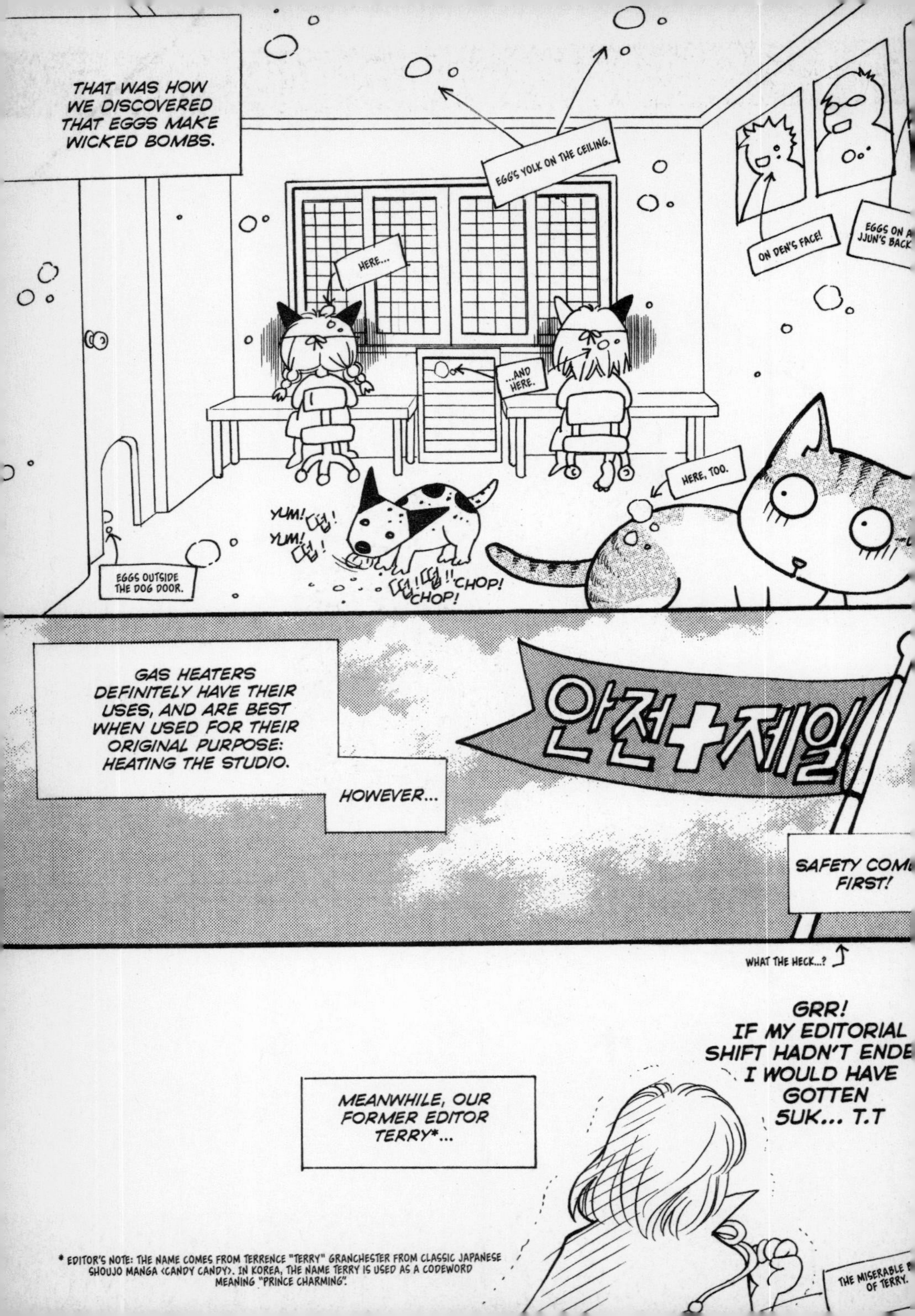
THAT WAS HOW WE DISCOVERED THAT EGGS MAKE WICKED BOMBS.
EGG'S YOLK ON THE CEILING.
ON DEN'S FACE!
EGGS ON A
JJUN'S BACK
HERE...
...AND HERE.
HERE, TOO.
YUM! 덥! YUM! 덥!
EGGS OUTSIDE THE DOG DOOR.
떱!떱!! CHOP! CHOP!
GAS HEATERS DEFINITELY HAVE THEIR USES, AND ARE BEST WHEN USED FOR THEIR ORIGINAL PURPOSE: HEATING THE STUDIO.
HOWEVER...
안전+제일
SAFETY COM
FIRST!
WHAT THE HECK...?
MEANWHILE, OUR FORMER EDITOR TERRY*...
GRR! IF MY EDITORIAL SHIFT HADN'T ENDE
I WOULD HAVE GOTTEN 5UK... T.T
THE MISERABLE
OF TERRY.

* EDITOR'S NOTE: THE NAME COMES FROM TERRENCE "TERRY" GRANCHESTER FROM CLASSIC JAPANESE SHOUJO MANGA <CANDY CANDY>. IN KOREA, THE NAME TERRY IS USED AS A CODEWORD MEANING "PRINCE CHARMING".

Preview

Legend

vol.1

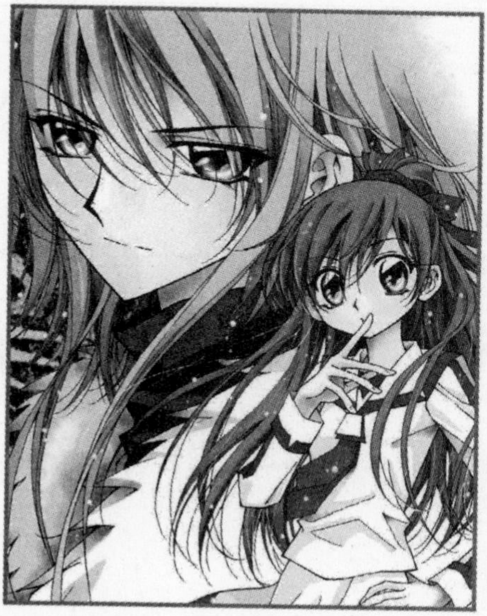

Kara ·Woo SooJung

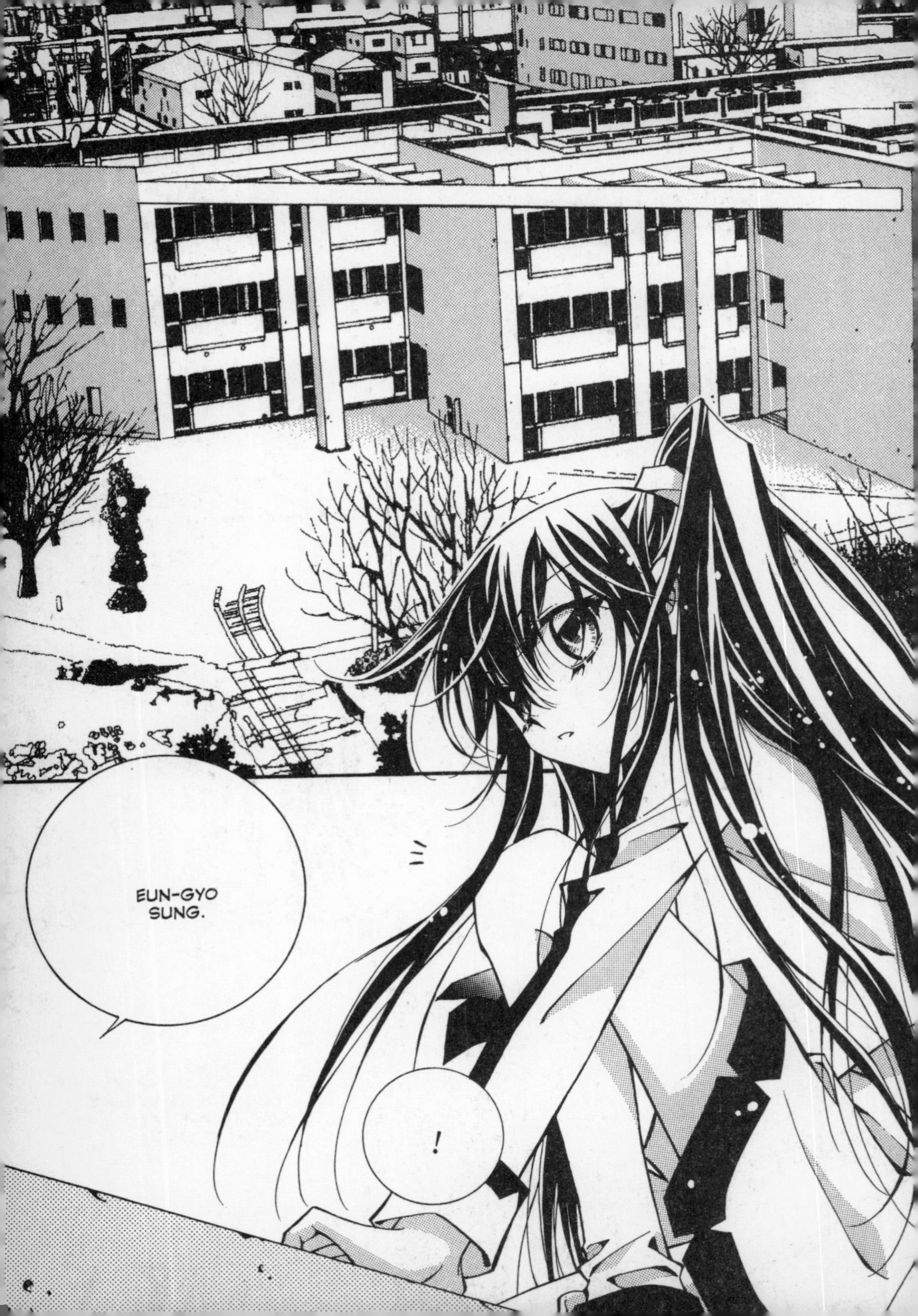
EUN-GYO SUNG.
!

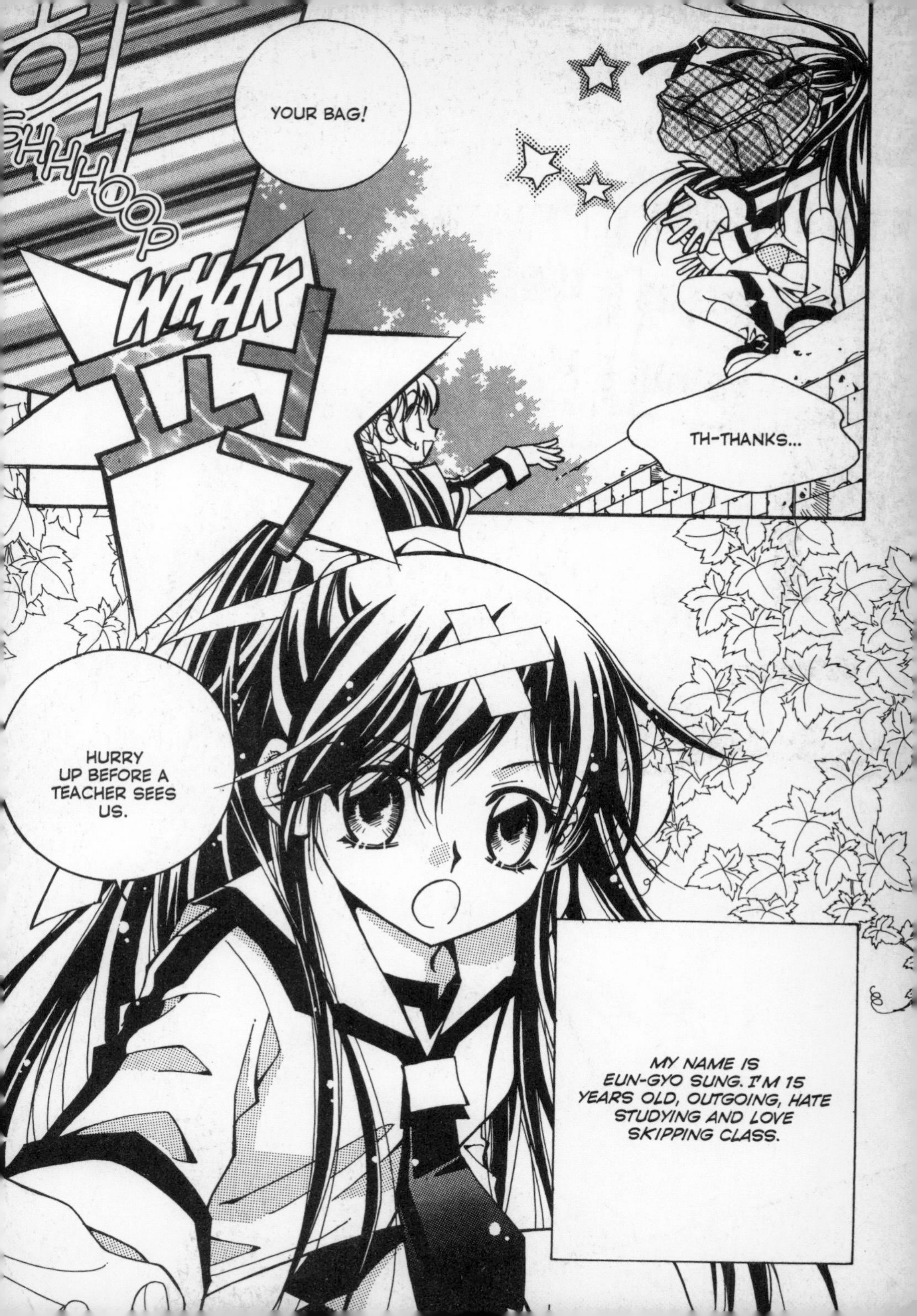
SHHHOOP
YOUR BAG!
WHAK
TH-THANKS...
HURRY UP BEFORE A TEACHER SEES US.
MY NAME IS EUN-GYO SUNG. I'M 15 YEARS OLD, OUTGOING, HATE STUDYING AND LOVE SKIPPING CLASS.

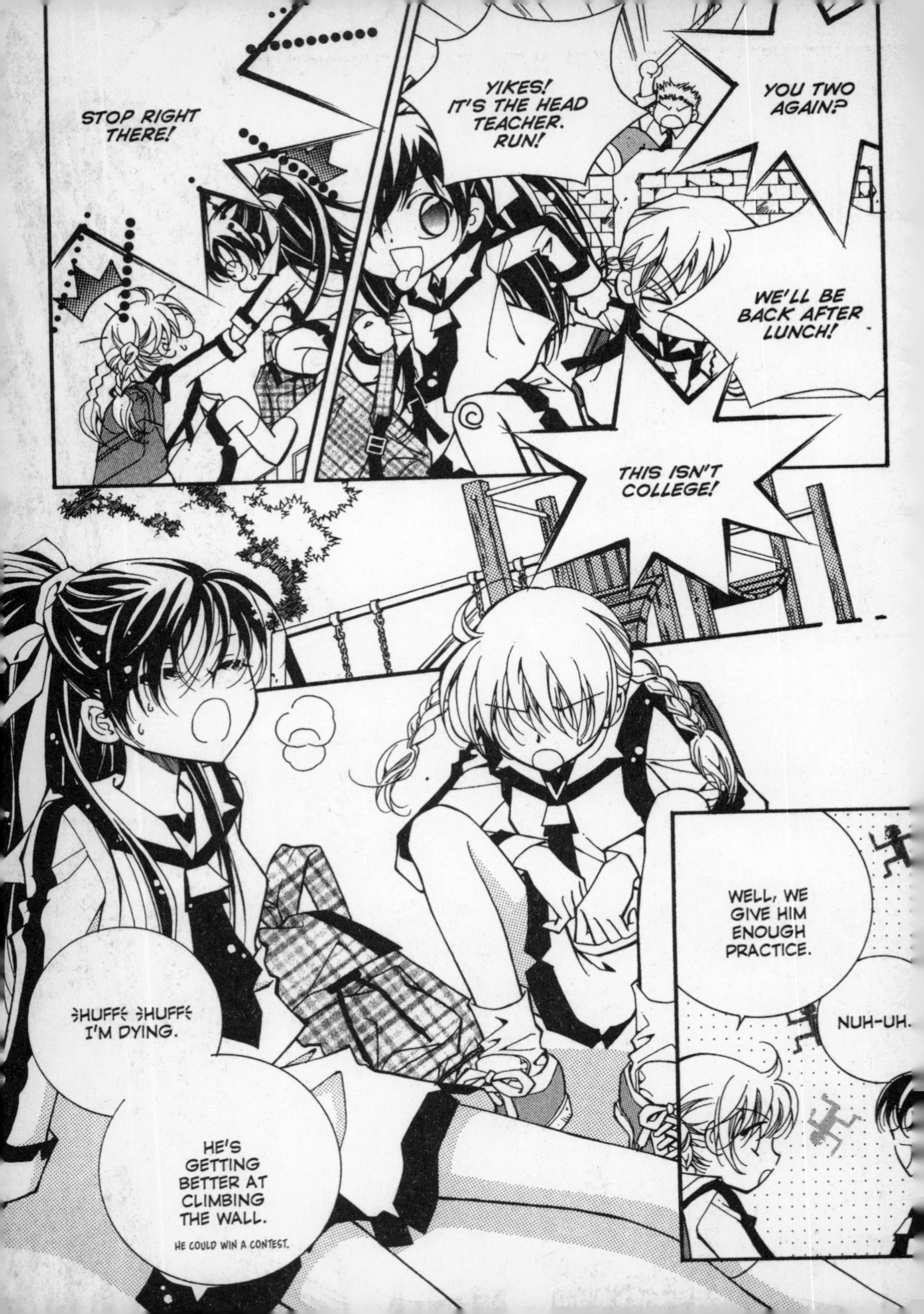
STOP RIGHT THERE!
YIKES! IT'S THE HEAD TEACHER. RUN!
YOU TWO AGAIN?
WE'LL BE BACK AFTER LUNCH!
THIS ISN'T COLLEGE!
HUFF *HUFF* I'M DYING.
HE'S GETTING BETTER AT CLIMBING THE WALL.
HE COULD WIN A CONTEST.
WELL, WE GIVE HIM ENOUGH PRACTICE.
NUH-UH.

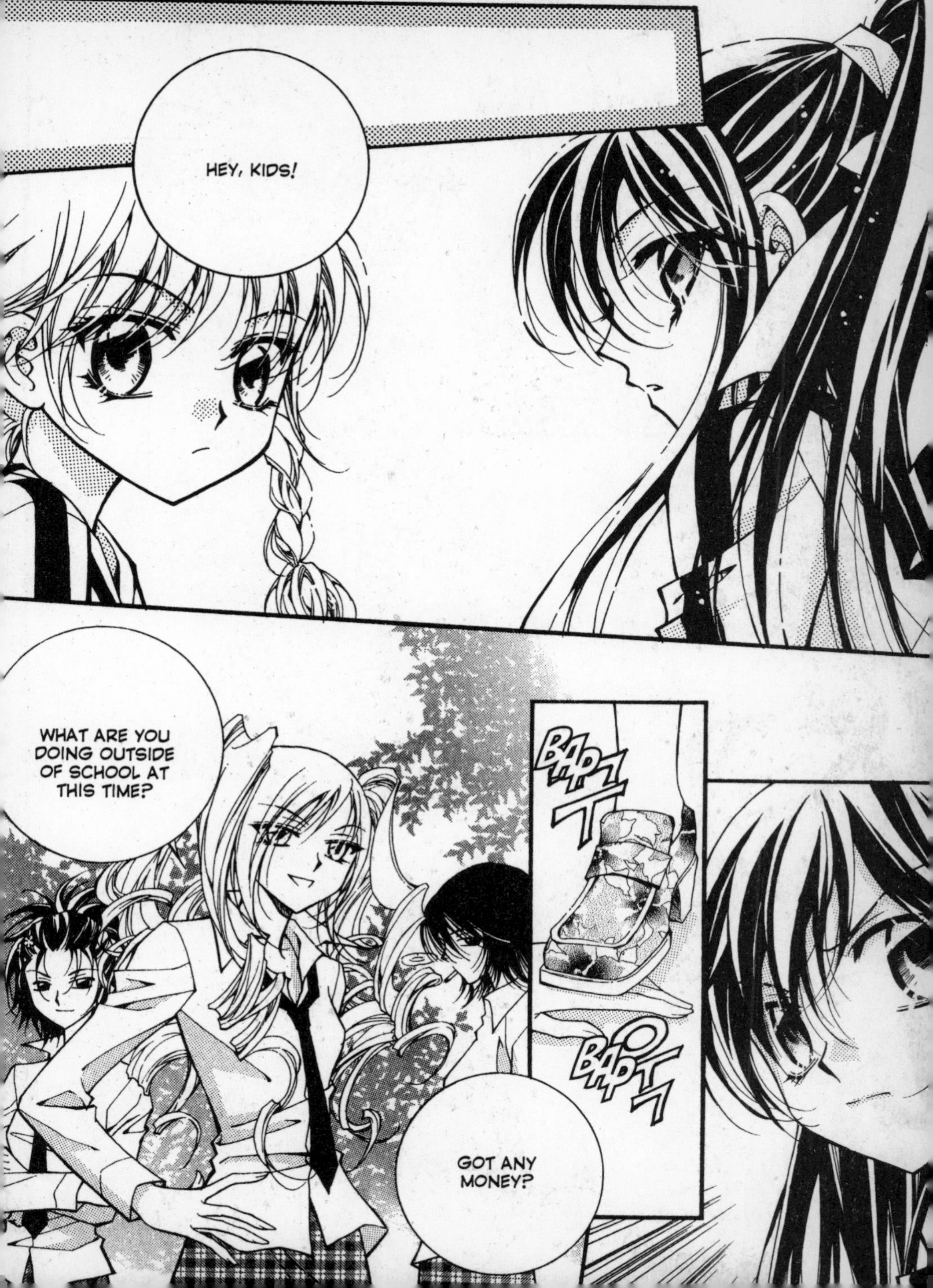
HEY, KIDS!
WHAT ARE YOU DOING OUTSIDE OF SCHOOL AT THIS TIME?
BAP
BAP
GOT ANY MONEY?

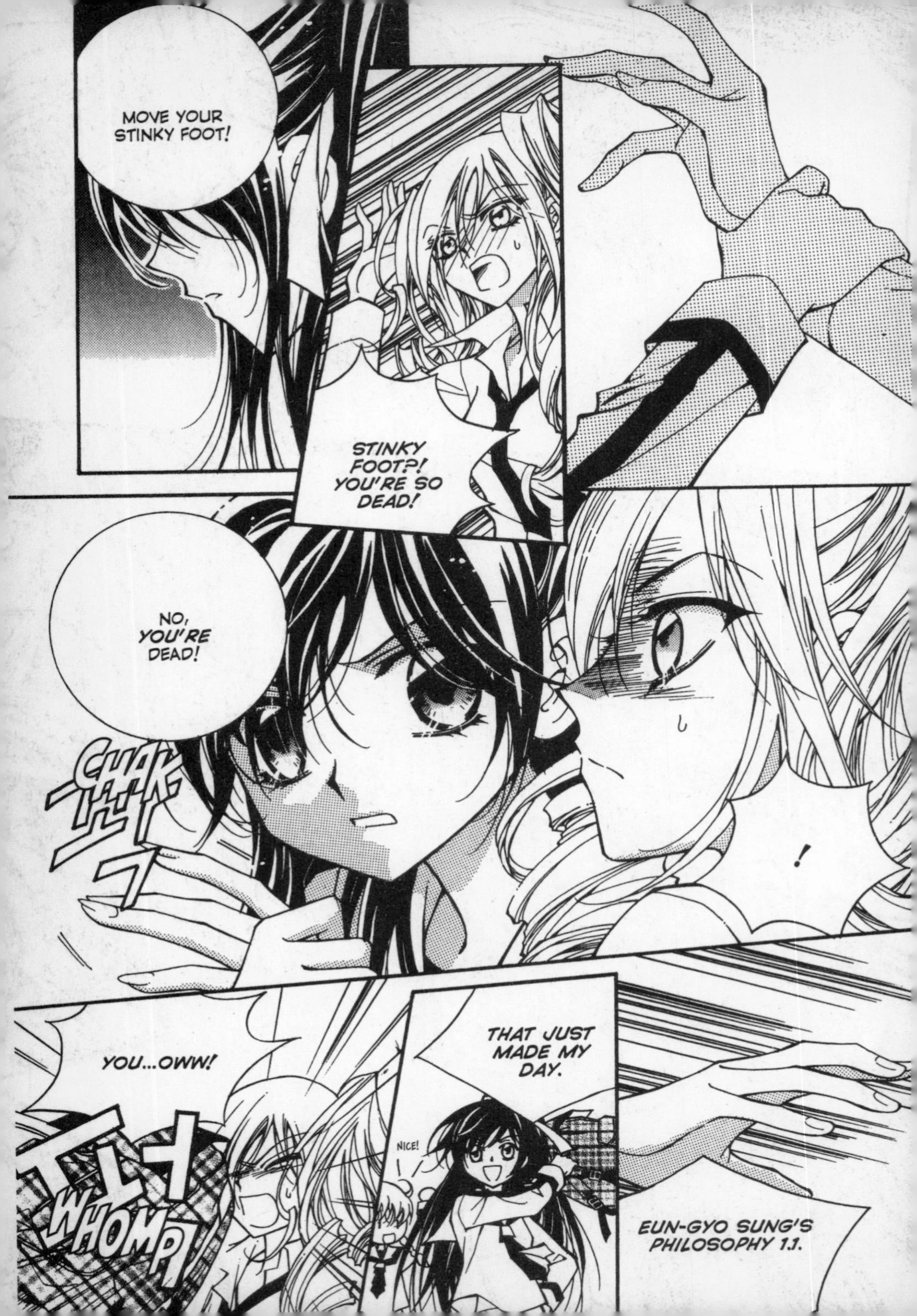
MOVE YOUR STINKY FOOT!
STINKY FOOT?! YOU'RE SO DEAD!
NO, YOU'RE DEAD!
CHAK
!
YOU...OWW!
WHOMP
THAT JUST MADE MY DAY.
NICE!
EUN-GYO SUNG'S PHILOSOPHY 1.1.

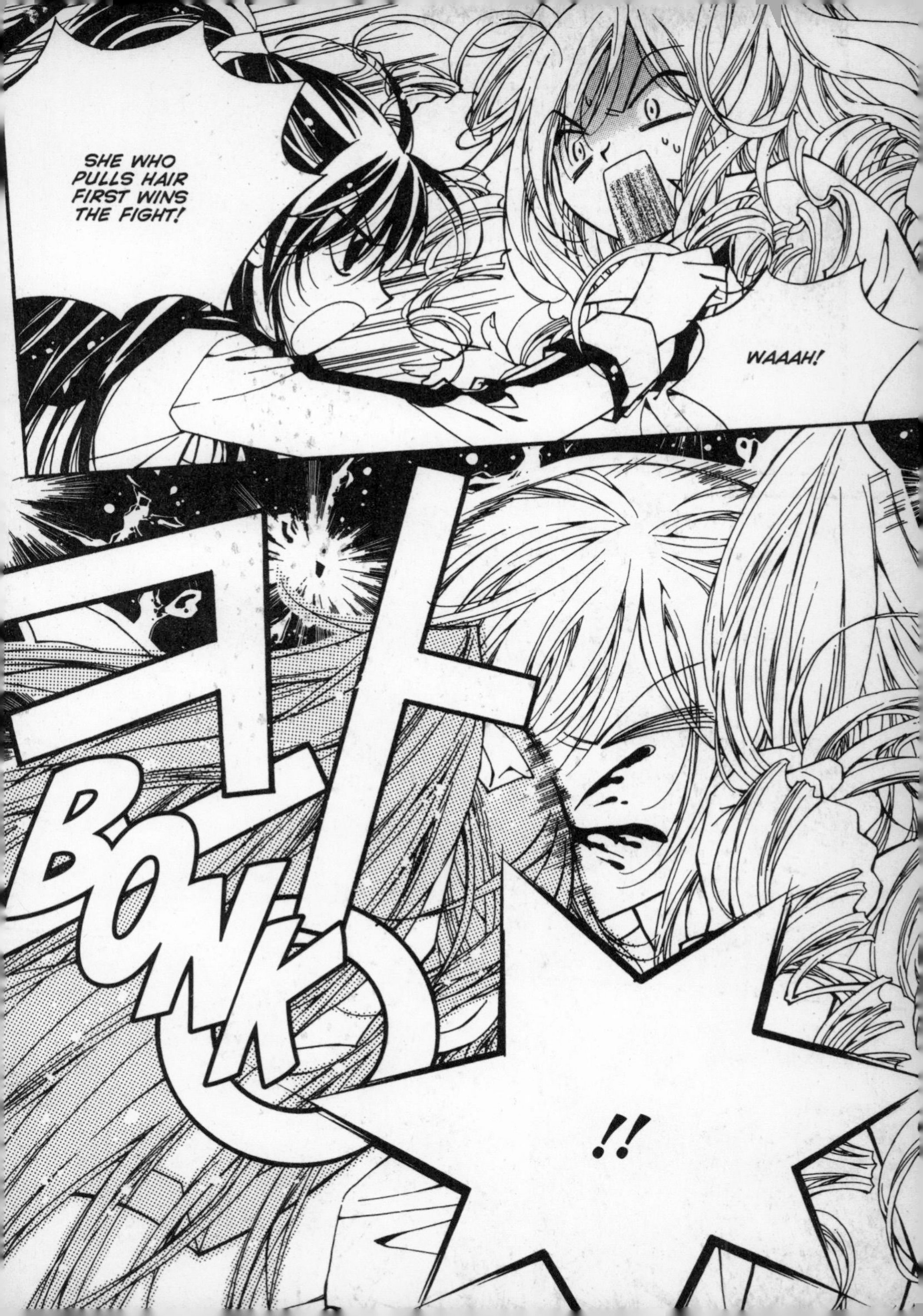
SHE WHO PULLS HAIR FIRST WINS THE FIGHT!
WAAAH!
BONK
!!

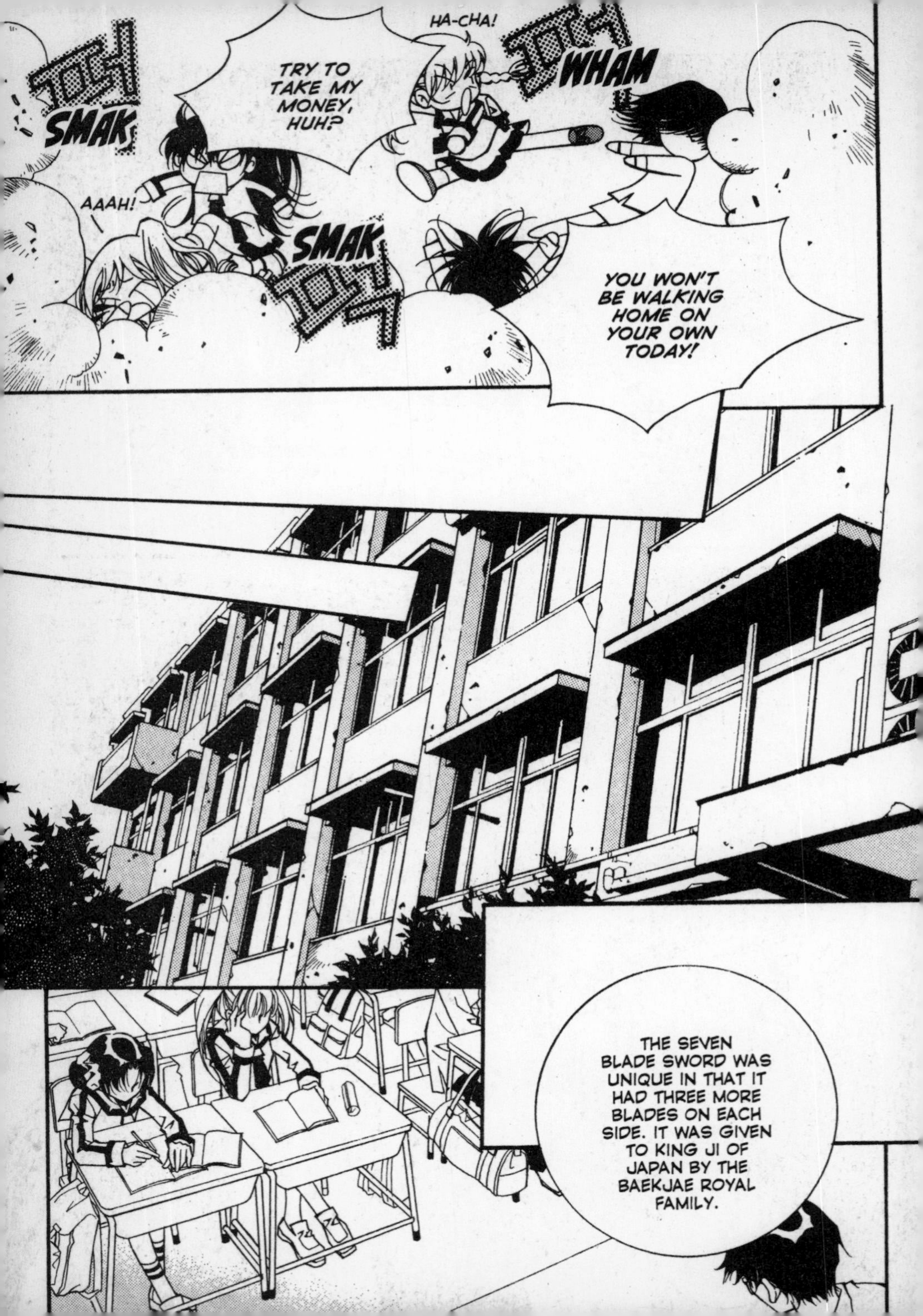
SMAK
TRY TO TAKE MY MONEY, HUH?
HA-CHA!
WHAM
AAAH!
SMAK
YOU WON'T BE WALKING HOME ON YOUR OWN TODAY!
THE SEVEN BLADE SWORD WAS UNIQUE IN THAT IT HAD THREE MORE BLADES ON EACH SIDE. IT WAS GIVEN TO KING JI OF JAPAN BY THE BAEKJAE ROYAL FAMILY.

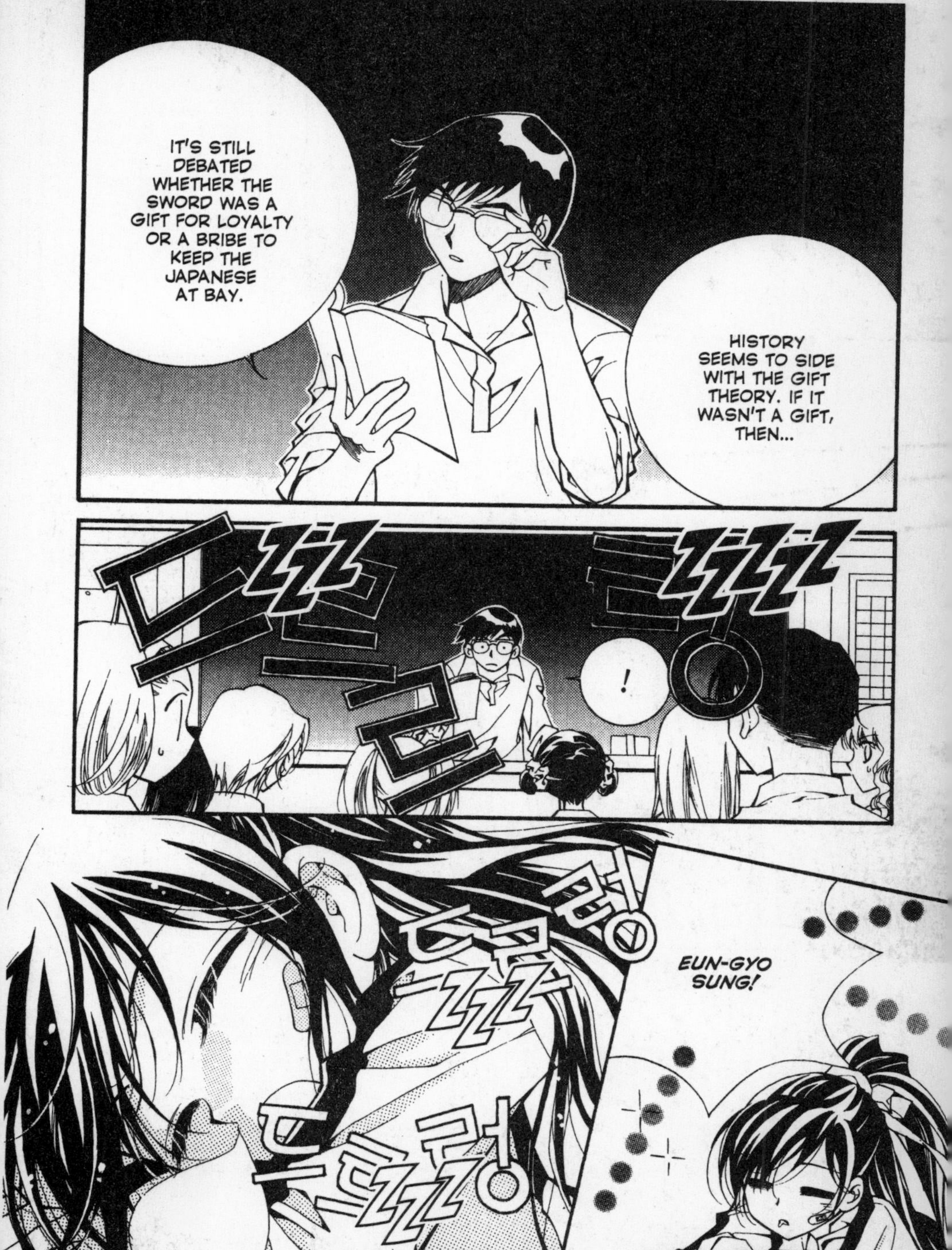

IT'S STILL DEBATED WHETHER THE SWORD WAS A GIFT FOR LOYALTY OR A BRIBE TO KEEP THE JAPANESE AT BAY.
HISTORY SEEMS TO SIDE WITH THE GIFT THEORY. IF IT WASN'T A GIFT, THEN...
!
EUN-GYO SUNG!

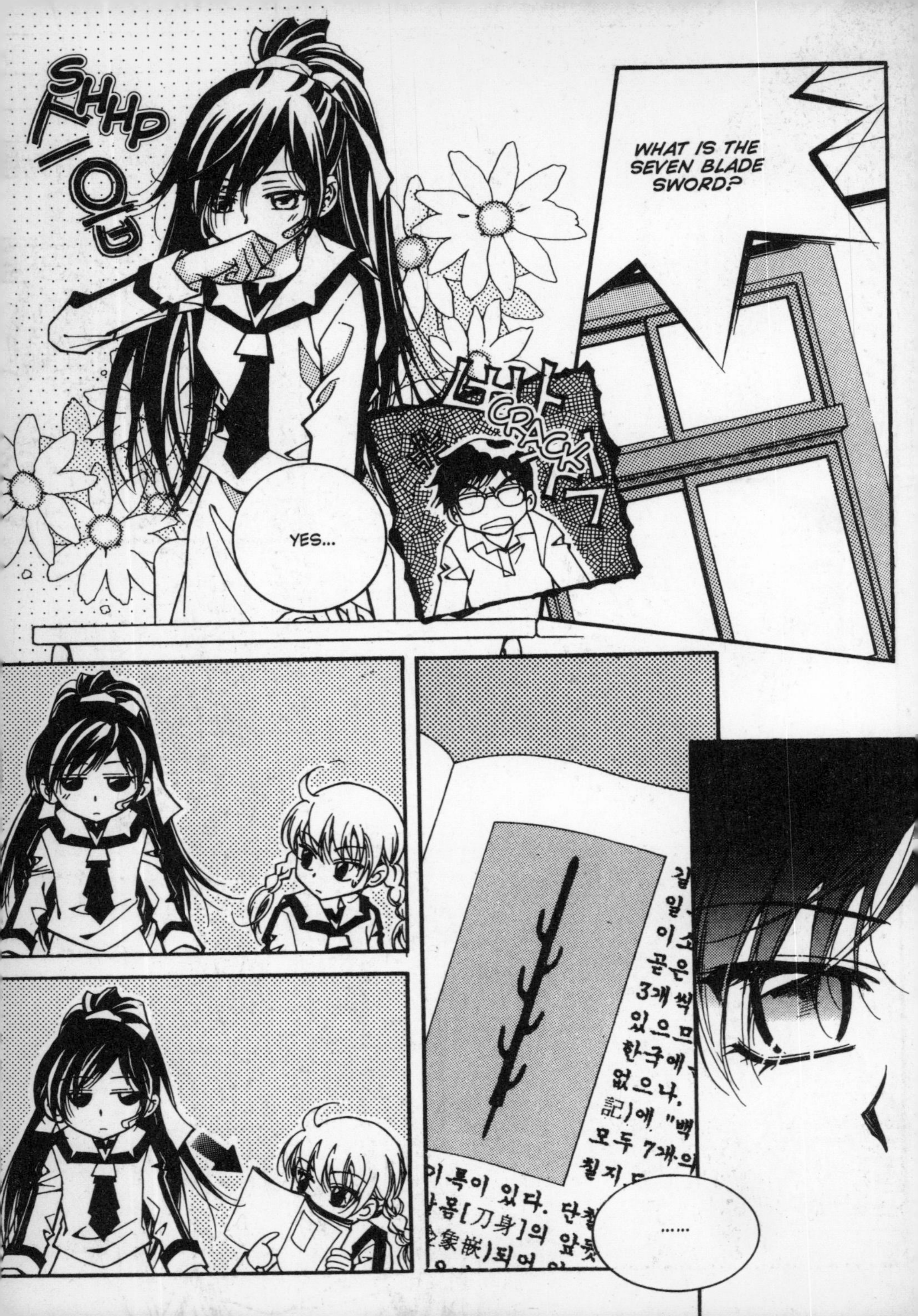
SHHP
YES...
CRACK
WHAT IS THE SEVEN BLADE SWORD?
......

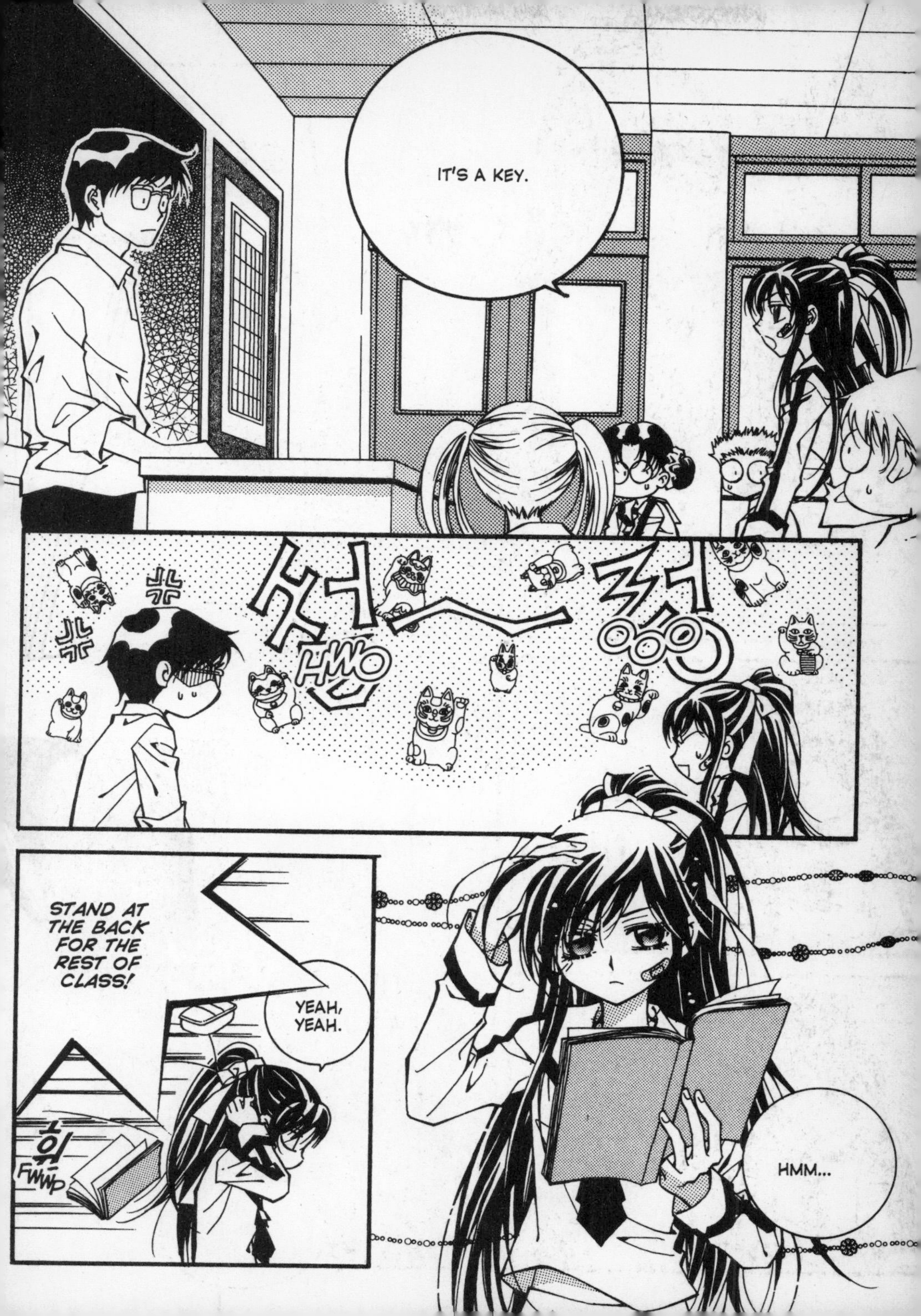
IT'S A KEY.
HWO
OOO
STAND AT THE BACK FOR THE REST OF CLASS!
YEAH, YEAH.
FWWP
HMM...

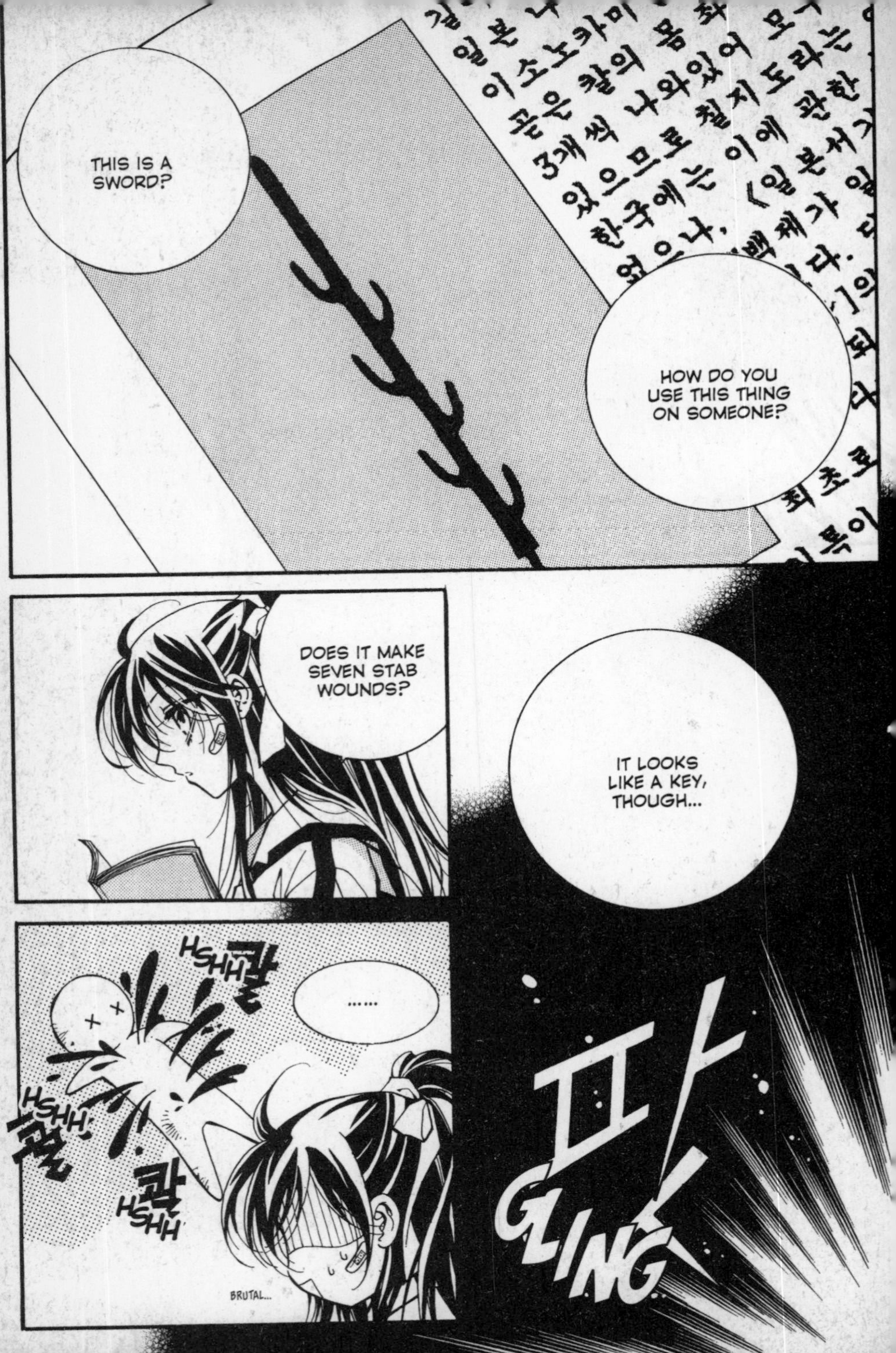

THIS IS A SWORD?
HOW DO YOU USE THIS THING ON SOMEONE?
DOES IT MAKE SEVEN STAB WOUNDS?
IT LOOKS LIKE A KEY, THOUGH...
HSHH 콱
......
HSHH 콱
콱 HSHH
BRUTAL...
GLING

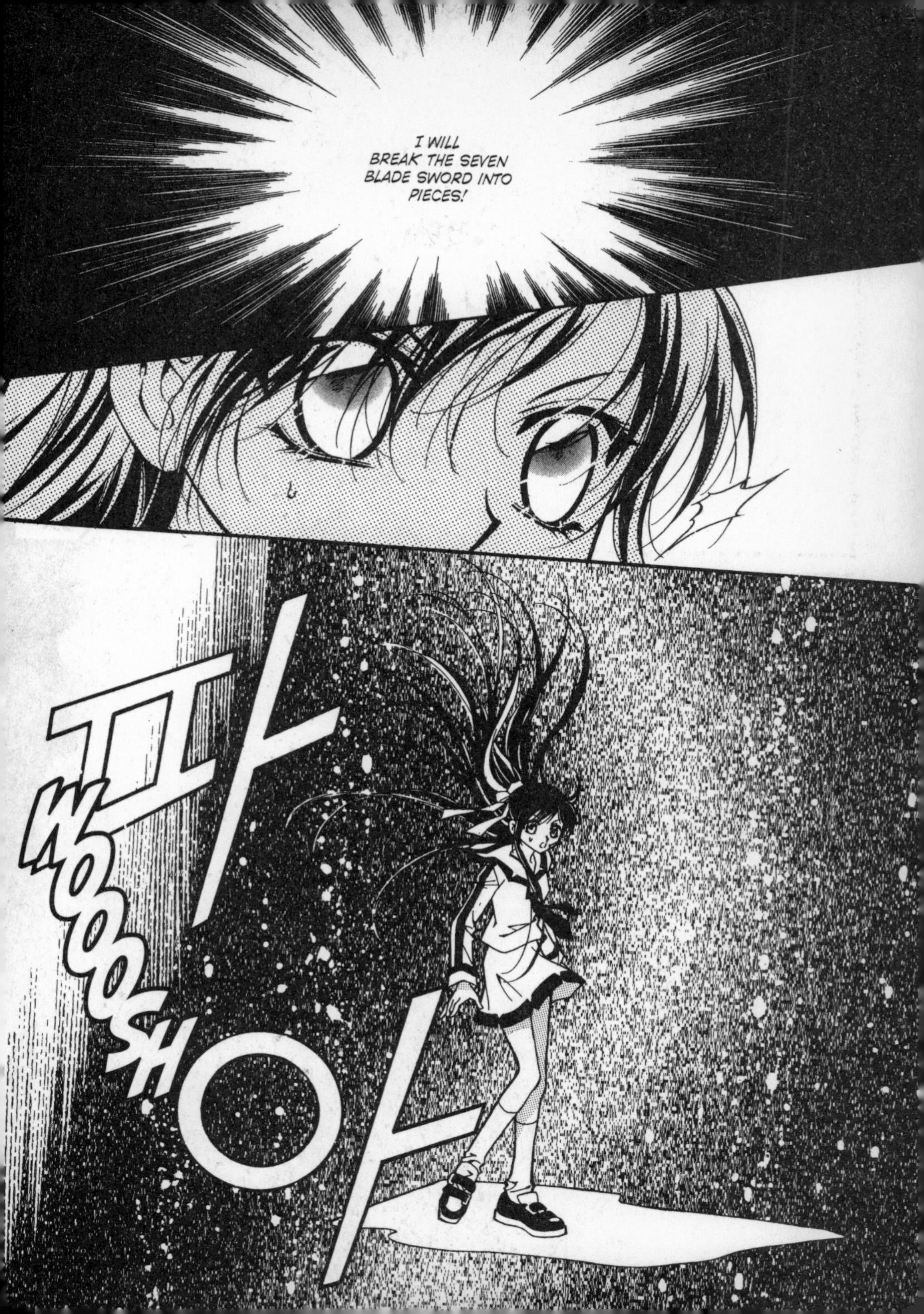
I WILL BREAK THE SEVEN BLADE SWORD INTO PIECES!
WHOOOSH

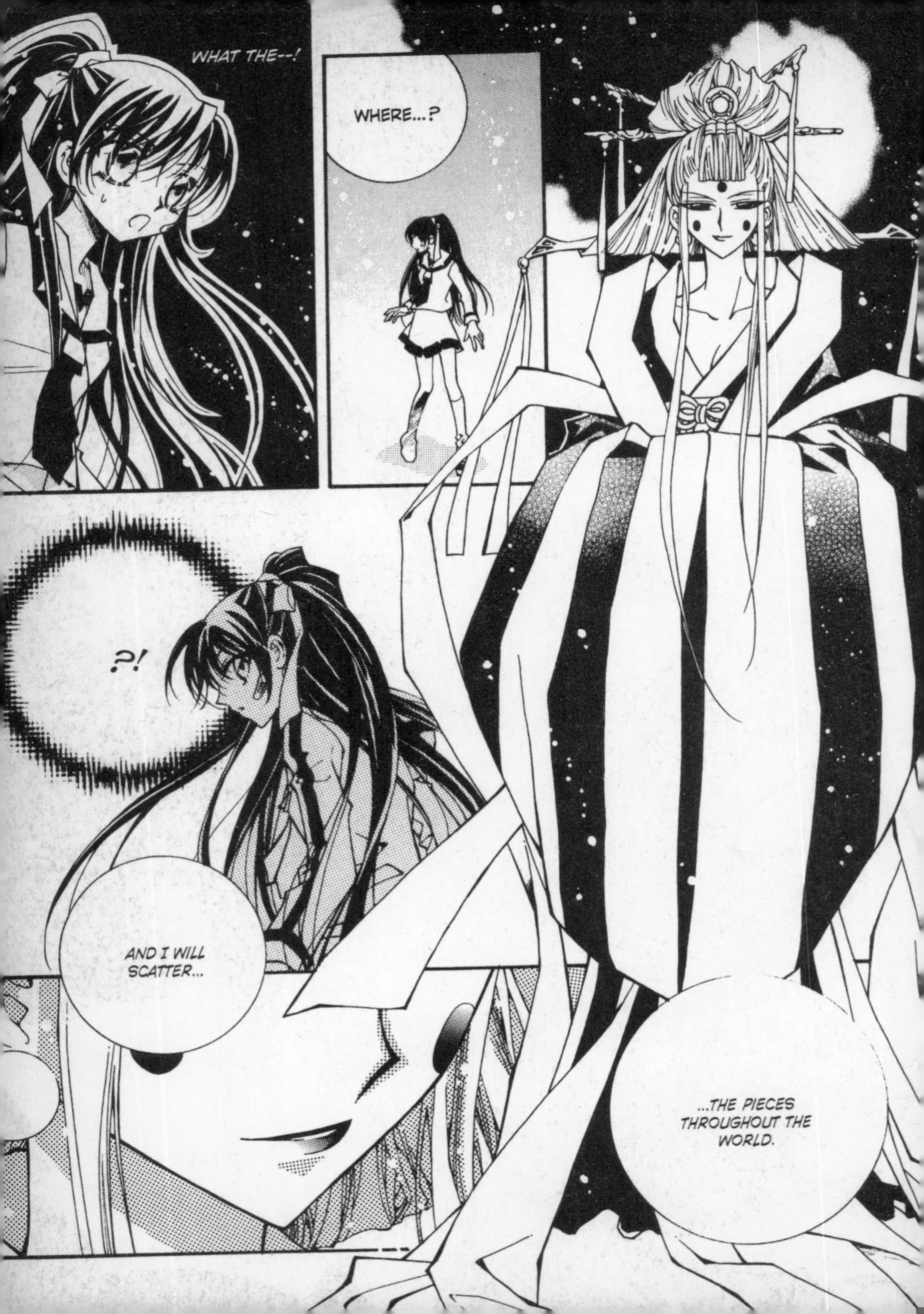
WHAT THE--!
WHERE...?
?!
AND I WILL SCATTER...
...THE PIECES THROUGHOUT THE WORLD.

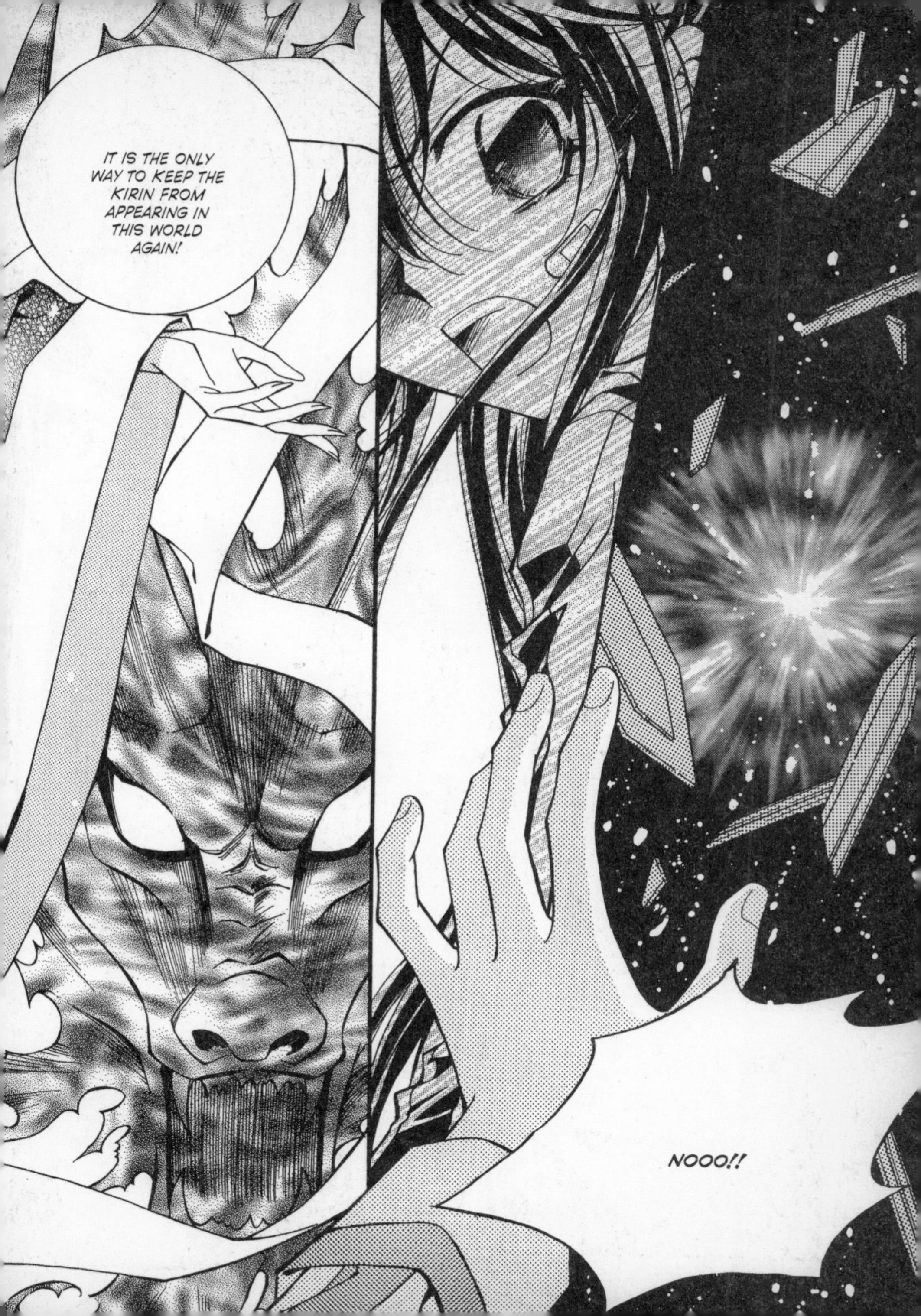
IT IS THE ONLY WAY TO KEEP THE KIRIN FROM APPEARING IN THIS WORLD AGAIN!
NOOO!!

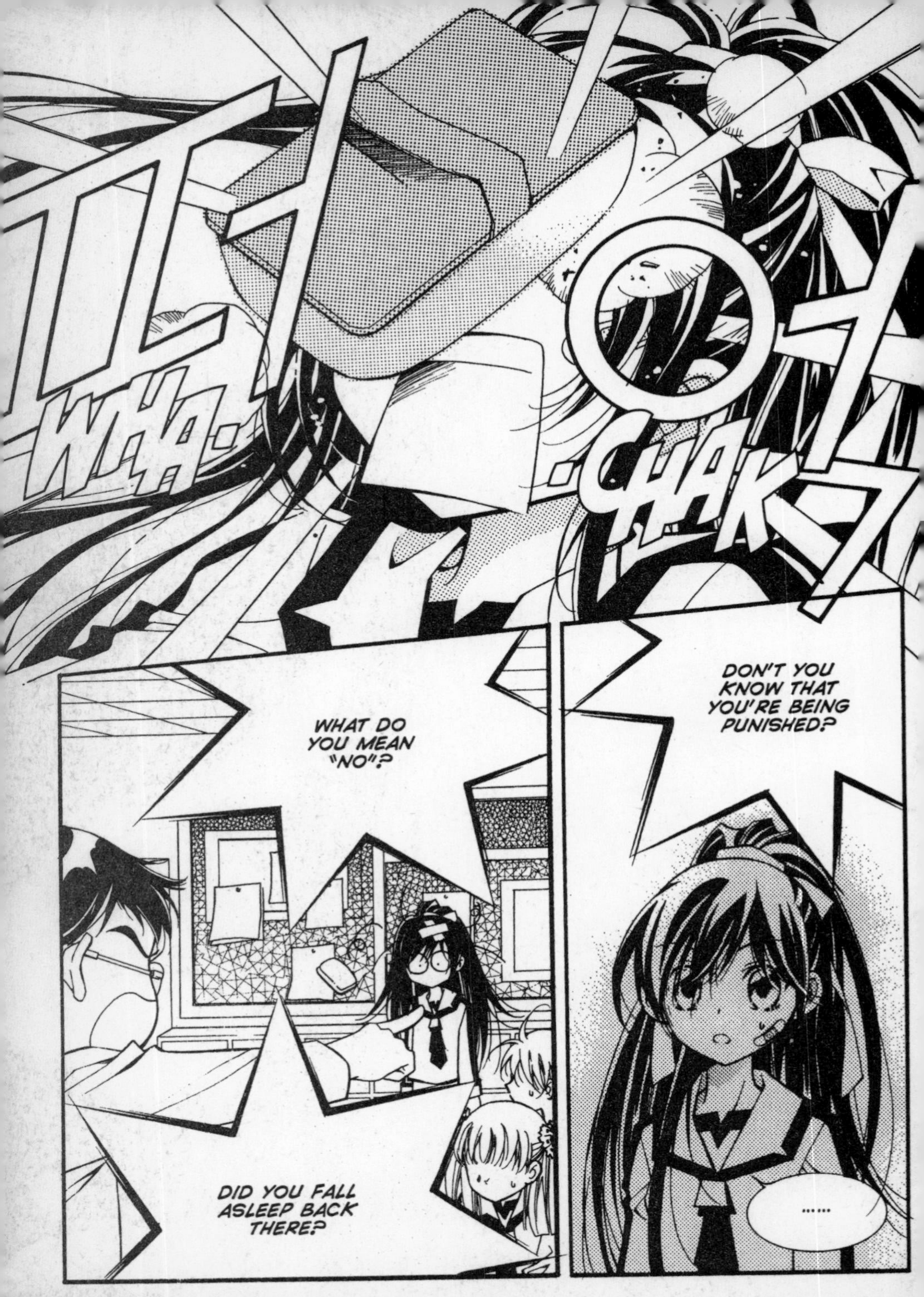
WHA-!
CHAK!
WHAT DO YOU MEAN "NO"?
DID YOU FALL ASLEEP BACK THERE?
DON'T YOU KNOW THAT YOU'RE BEING PUNISHED?
......

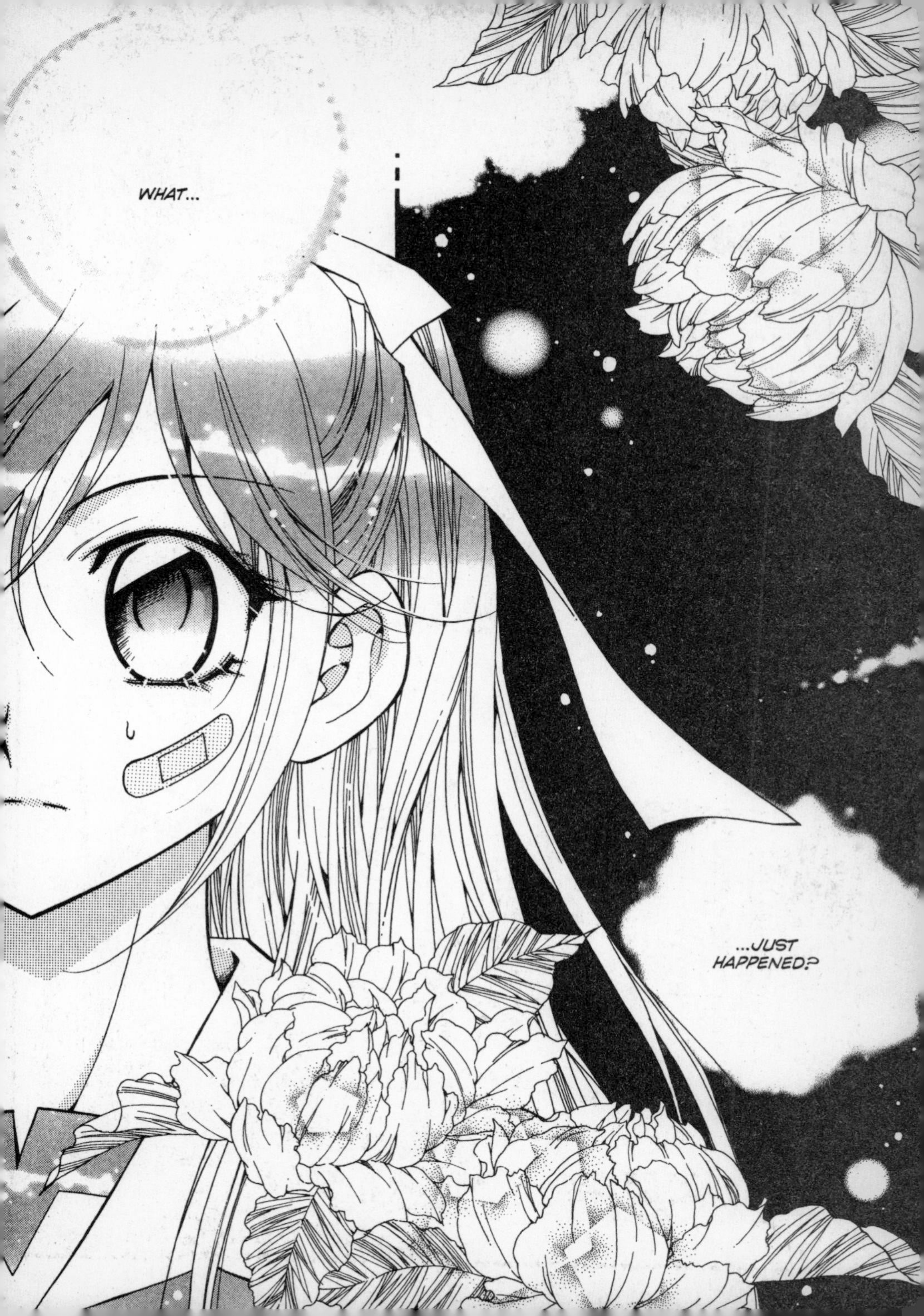
WHAT...
...JUST HAPPENED?

MINI INTERVIEW

NAME: EUN-GYO SUNG
AGE: 15
BLOOD TYPE: O
SIGN: SAGITTARIUS
HEIGHT: 152 CM
WEIGHT: WHY DO YOU WANT TO KNOW?

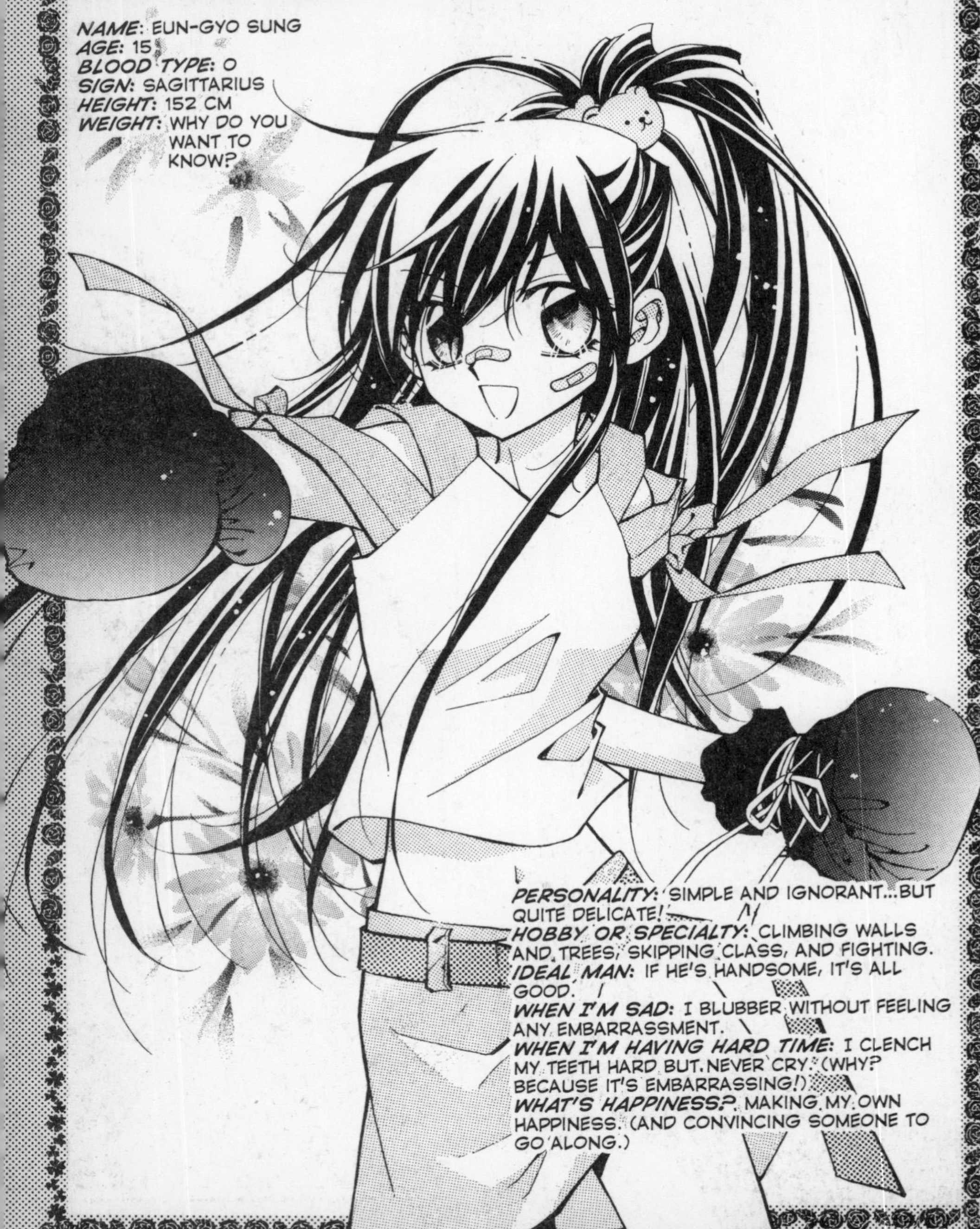

PERSONALITY: SIMPLE AND IGNORANT...BUT QUITE DELICATE!
HOBBY OR SPECIALTY: CLIMBING WALLS AND TREES, SKIPPING CLASS, AND FIGHTING.
IDEAL MAN: IF HE'S HANDSOME, IT'S ALL GOOD.
WHEN I'M SAD: I BLUBBER WITHOUT FEELING ANY EMBARRASSMENT.
WHEN I'M HAVING HARD TIME: I CLENCH MY TEETH HARD BUT NEVER CRY. (WHY? BECAUSE IT'S EMBARRASSING!)
WHAT'S HAPPINESS? MAKING MY OWN HAPPINESS. (AND CONVINCING SOMEONE TO GO ALONG.)

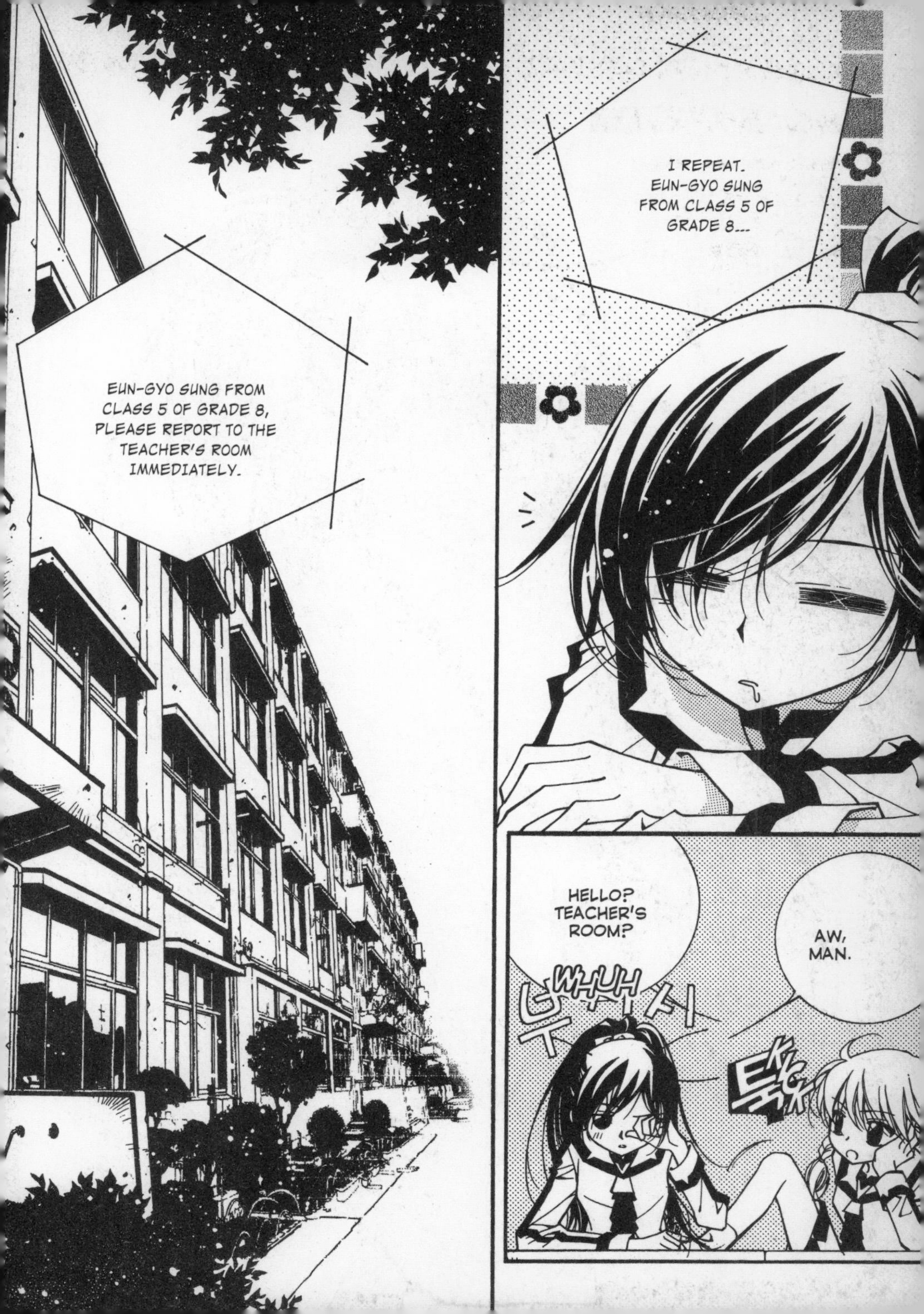
EUN-GYO SUNG FROM CLASS 5 OF GRADE 8, PLEASE REPORT TO THE TEACHER'S ROOM IMMEDIATELY.
I REPEAT. EUN-GYO SUNG FROM CLASS 5 OF GRADE 8...
HELLO? TEACHER'S ROOM?
WHUH
AW, MAN.
KICK

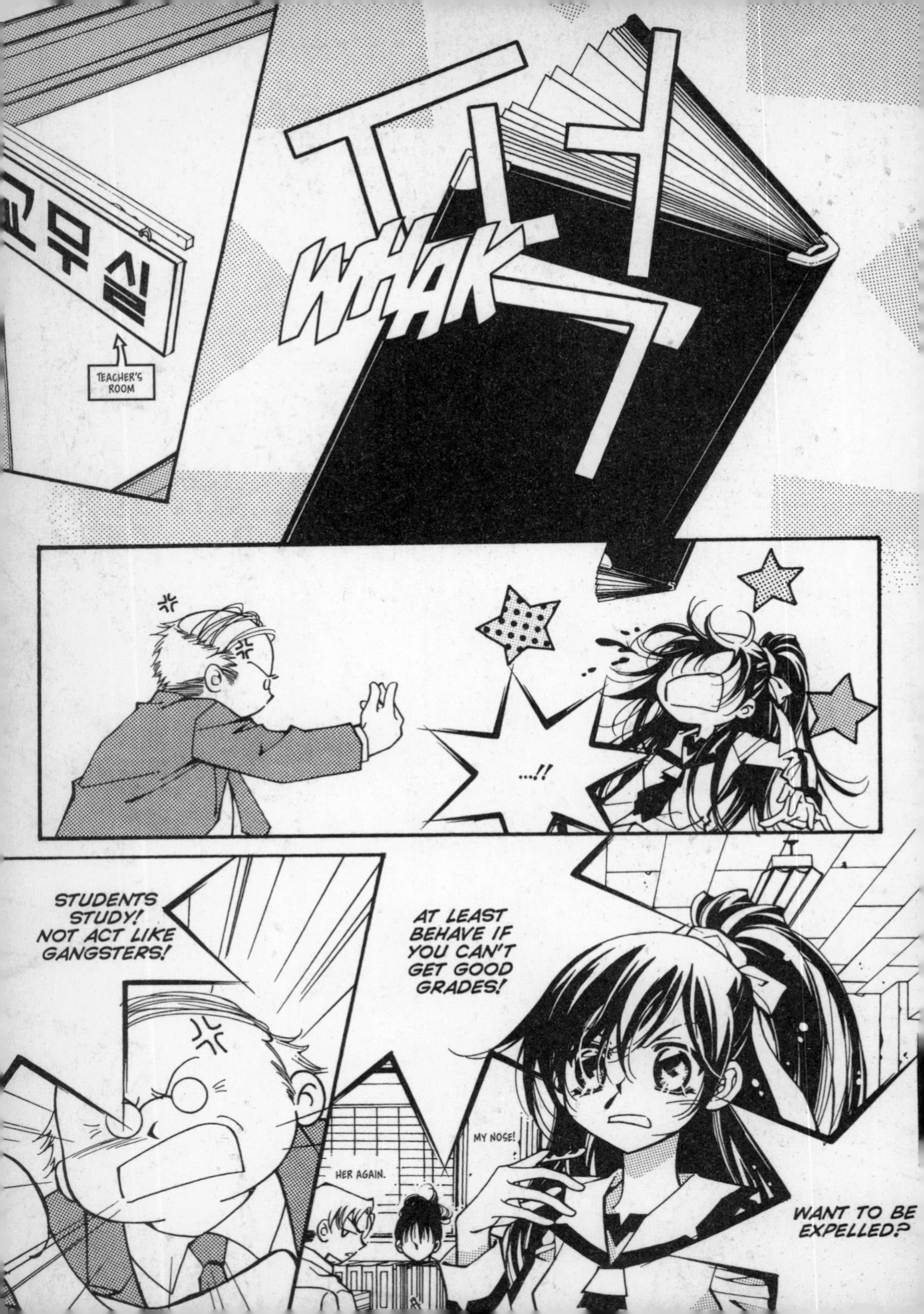
교무실
TEACHER'S ROOM
WHAK
...!!
STUDENTS STUDY! NOT ACT LIKE GANGSTERS!
AT LEAST BEHAVE IF YOU CAN'T GET GOOD GRADES!
HER AGAIN.
MY NOSE!
WANT TO BE EXPELLED?

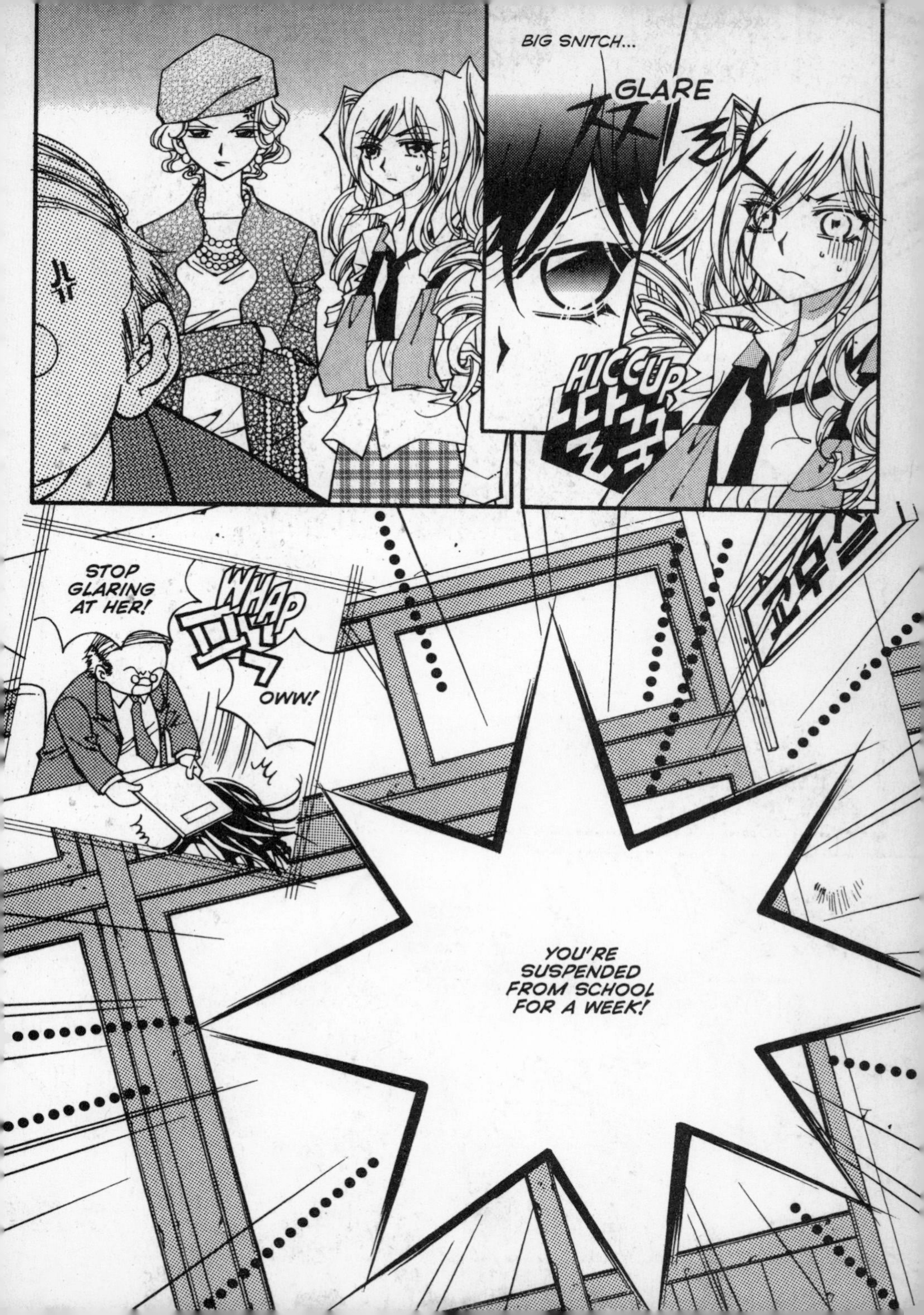
BIG SNITCH...
GLARE
HICCUP
STOP GLARING AT HER!
WHAP
OWW!
YOU'RE SUSPENDED FROM SCHOOL FOR A WEEK!

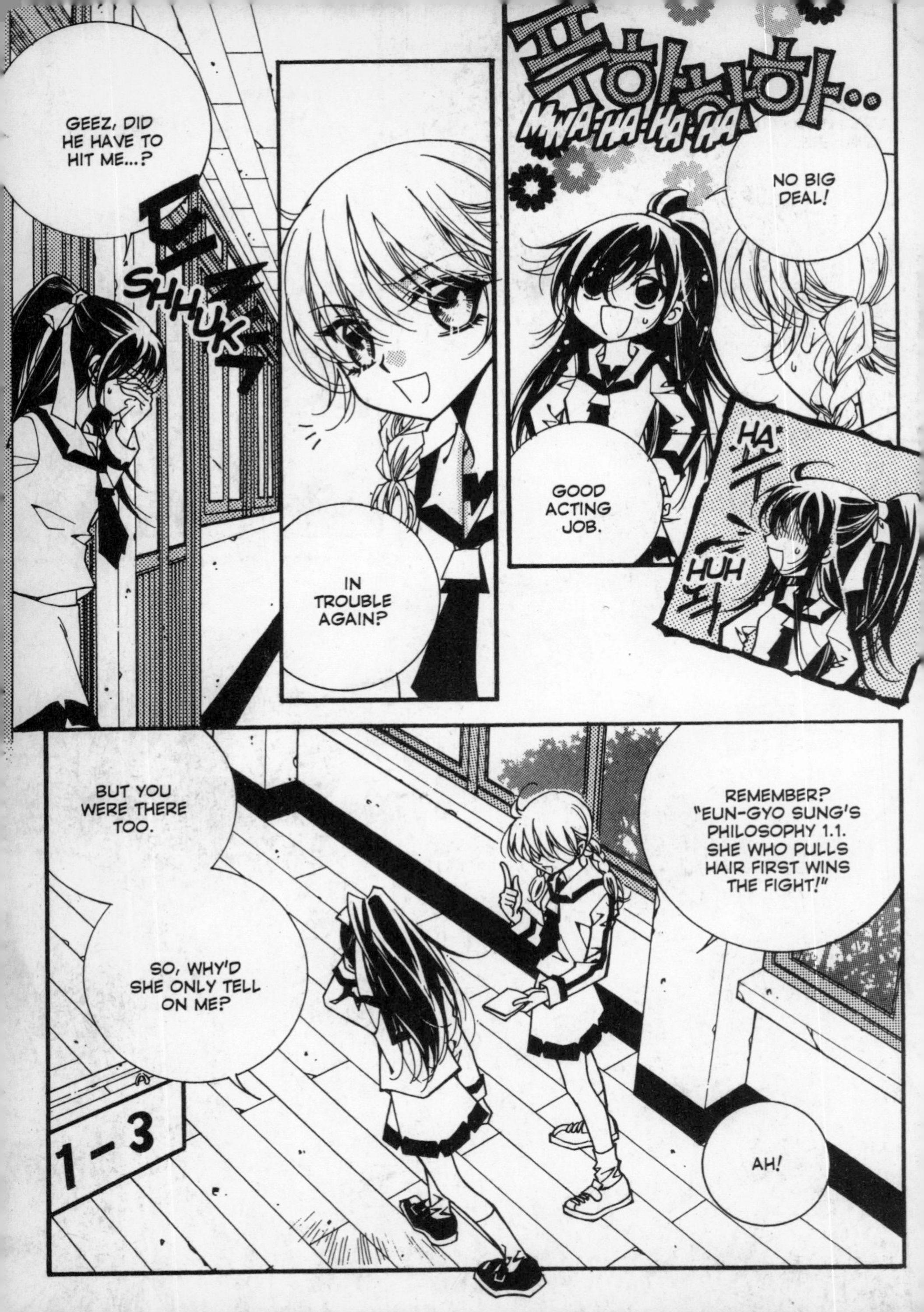
GEEZ, DID HE HAVE TO HIT ME...?
SHHUK
IN TROUBLE AGAIN?
푸하하하..
MWA-HA-HA-HA
NO BIG DEAL!
GOOD ACTING JOB.
HA
HUH
BUT YOU WERE THERE TOO.
SO, WHY'D SHE ONLY TELL ON ME?
1-3
REMEMBER? "EUN-GYO SUNG'S PHILOSOPHY 1.1. SHE WHO PULLS HAIR FIRST WINS THE FIGHT!"
AH!

Marshall —

thanks for your
friendship !

11/2001

Marshall -

Thanks for your friendship!

[illegible]

11/2001